IMPERIAL P

MCGILL-QUEEN'S STUDIES IN THE HISTORY OF IDEAS
Series Editor: Philip J. Cercone

1 Problems of Cartesianism
   Edited by Thomas M. Lennon,
   John M. Nicholas, and John
   W. Davis

2 The Development of the
   Idea of History in Antiquity
   Gerald A. Press

3 Claude Buffier and
   Thomas Reid:
   Two Common-Sense
   Philosophers
   Louise Marcil-Lacoste

4 Schiller, Hegel, and Marx:
   State, Society, and the Aesthetic
   Ideal of Ancient Greece
   Philip J. Kain

5 John Case and Aristotelianism
   in Renaissance England
   Charles B. Schmitt

6 Beyond Liberty and Property:
   The Process of Self-
   Recognition in Eighteenth-
   Century Political Thought
   J.A.W. Gunn

7 John Toland: His Methods,
   Manners, and Mind
   Stephen H. Daniel

8 Coleridge and the Inspired
   Word
   Anthony John Harding

9 The Jena System, 1804–5:
   Logic and Metaphysics
   G.W.F. Hegel
   Translation edited by
   John W. Burbidge and
   George di Giovanni
   Introduction and notes by
   H.S. Harris

10 Consent, Coercion, and Limit:
   The Medieval Origins of
   Parliamentary Democracy
   Arthur P. Monahan

11 Scottish Common Sense
   in Germany, 1768–1800:
   A Contribution to the
   History of Critical Philosophy
   Manfred Kuehn

12 Paine and Cobbett:
   The Transatlantic Connection
   David A. Wilson

13 Descartes and the
   Enlightenment
   Peter A. Schouls

14 Greek Scepticism:
   Anti-Realist Trends
   in Ancient Thought
   Leo Groarke

15 The Irony of Theology and the
   Nature of Religious Thought
   Donald Wiebe

16 Form and Transformation:
   A Study in the Philosophy
   of Plotinus
   Frederic M. Schroeder

17 From Personal Duties
   towards Personal Rights:
   Late Medieval and Early
   Modern Political Thought,
   c. 1300–c. 1650
   Arthur P. Monahan

18 The Main Philosophical
   Writings and the Novel *Allwill*
   Friedrich Heinrich Jacobi
   Translated and edited by
   George di Giovanni

19 Kierkegaard as Humanist:
Discovering My Self
Arnold B. Come

20 Durkheim, Morals,
and Modernity
W. Watts Miller

21 The Career of Toleration:
John Locke, Jonas Proast,
and After
Richard Vernon

22 Dialectic of Love:
Platonism in Schiller's
Aesthetics
David Pugh

23 History and Memory
in Ancient Greece
Gordon Shrimpton

24 Kierkegaard as Theologian:
Recovering My Self
Arnold B. Come

25 Enlightenment and
Conservatism in Victorian
Scotland:
The Career of
Sir Archibald Alison
Michael Michie

26 The Road to Egdon
Heath: The Aesthetics
of the Great in Nature
Richard Bevis

27 Jena Romanticism and Its
Appropriation of Jakob Böhme:
Theosophy – Hagiography –
Literature
Paola Mayer

28 Enlightenment and
Community:
Lessing, Abbt, Herder, and the
Quest for a German Public
Benjamin W. Redekop

29 Jacob Burckhardt and
the Crisis of Modernity
John R. Hinde

30 The Distant Relation:
Time and Identity in Spanish-
American Fiction
Eoin S. Thomson

31 Mr Simson's Knotty Case:
Divinity, Politics, and Due
Process in Early Eighteenth-
Century Scotland
Anne Skoczylas

32 Orthodoxy and
Enlightenment:
George Campbell in
the Eighteenth Century
Jeffrey M. Suderman

33 Contemplation
and Incarnation:
The Theology of Marie-
Dominique Chenu
Christophe F. Potworowski

34 Democratic Legitimacy:
Plural Values
and Political Power
F.M. Barnard

35 Herder on Nationality,
Humanity, and History
F.M. Barnard

36 Labeling People:
French Scholars on Society,
Race, and Empire, 1815–1849
Martin S. Staum

37 The Subaltern Appeal to Experience: Self-Identity, Late Modernity, and the Politics of Immediacy
Craig Ireland

38 The Invention of Journalism Ethics: The Path to Objectivity and Beyond, Second Edition
Stephen J.A. Ward

39 The Recovery of Wonder: The New Freedom and the Asceticism of Power
Kenneth L. Schmitz

40 Reason and Self-Enactment in History and Politics: Themes and Voices of Modernity
F.M. Barnard

41 The More Moderate Side of Joseph de Maistre: Views on Political Liberty and Political Economy
Cara Camcastle

42 Democratic Society and Human Needs
Jeff Noonan

43 The Circle of Rights Expands: Modern Political Thought after the Reformation, 1521 (Luther) to 1762 (Rousseau)
Arthur P. Monahan

44 The Canadian Founding: John Locke and Parliament
Janet Ajzenstat

45 Finding Freedom: Hegel's Philosophy and the Emancipation of Women
Sara MacDonald

46 When the French Tried to Be British: Party, Opposition, and the Quest for Civil Disagreement, 1814–1848
J.A.W. Gunn

47 Under Conrad's Eyes: The Novel as Criticism
Michael John DiSanto

48 Media, Memory, and the First World War
David Williams

49 An Aristotelian Account of Induction: Creating Something from Nothing
Louis Groarke

50 Social and Political Bonds: A Mosaic of Contrast and Convergence
F.M. Barnard

51 Archives and the Event of God: The Impact of Michel Foucault on Philosophical Theology
David Galston

52 Between the Queen and the Cabby: Olympe de Gouges's Rights of Women
John R. Cole

53 Nature and Nurture in French Social Sciences, 1859–1914 and Beyond
Martin S. Staum

54 Public Passion: Rethinking the Grounds for Political Justice
Rebecca Kingston

55 Rethinking the Political:
   The Sacred, Aesthetic Politics,
   and the Collège de Sociologie
   Simonetta Falasca-Zamponi

56 Materialist Ethics and
   Life-Value
   Jeff Noonan

57 Hegel's *Phenomenology*:
   The Dialectical Justification of
   Philosophy's First Principles
   Ardis B. Collins

58 The Social History of Ideas
   in Quebec, 1760–1896
   Yvan Lamonde
   Translated by Phyllis Aronoff and
   Howard Scott

59 Ideas, Concepts, and Reality
   John W. Burbidge

60 The Enigma of Perception
   D.L.C. Maclachlan

61 Nietzsche's Justice:
   Naturalism in Search of
   an Ethics
   Peter R. Sedgwick

62 The Idea of Liberty in Canada
   during the Age of Atlantic
   Revolutions, 1776–1838
   Michel Ducharme
   Translated by Peter Feldstein

63 From White to Yellow:
   The Japanese in European
   Racial Thought, 1300–1735
   Rotem Kowner

64 The Crisis of Modernity
   Augusto Del Noce
   Edited and translated by
   Carlo Lancellotti

65 Imprinting Britain:
   Newspapers, Sociability,
   and the Shaping of British
   North America
   Michael Eamon

66 The Form of Politics:
   Aristotle and Plato
   on Friendship
   John von Heyking

67 War as Paradox:
   Clausewitz and Hegel on
   Fighting Doctrines and Ethics
   Youri Cormier

68 Network Democracy:
   Conservative Politics and the
   Violence of the Liberal Age
   Jared Giesbrecht

69 A Singular Case:
   Debating China's Political
   Economy in the European
   Enlightenment
   Ashley Eva Millar

70 Not Even a God Can Save
   Us Now:
   Reading Machiavelli after
   Heidegger
   Brian Harding

71 Before Copernicus:
   The Cultures and Contexts
   of Scientific Learning in
   the Fifteenth Century
   Edited by Rivka Feldhay
   and F. Jamil Ragep

72 The Culturalist Challenge
   to Liberal Republicanism
   Michael Lusztig

73 God and Government:
   Martin Luther's Political
   Thought
   Jarrett A. Carty

74 The Age of Secularization
   Augusto Del Noce
   Edited and Translated
   by Carlo Lancellotti

75 Emancipatory Thinking:
   Simone de Beauvoir and
   Contemporary Political
   Thought
   Elaine Stavro

76 Life Embodied:
   The Promise of Vital Force
   in Spanish Modernity
   Nicolás Fernández-Medina

77 The Aesthetics of Fear in
   German Romanticism
   Paola Mayer

78 Objectively Engaged
   Journalism: An Ethic
   Stephen J.A. Ward

79 Progress, Pluralism, and
   Politics: Liberalism and
   Colonialism, Past and Present
   David Williams

80 Beyond Tragedy and Eternal
   Peace:
   Politics and International
   Relations in the Thought
   of Friedrich Nietzsche
   Jean-François Drolet

81 Inequality in Canada:
   The History and Politics
   of an Idea
   Eric W. Sager

82 Attending
   An Ethical Art
   Warren Heiti

83 Imperial Paradoxes:
   Training the Senses and Tasting
   the Eighteenth Century
   Robert James Merrett

Imperial Paradoxes

Training the Senses and Tasting the Eighteenth Century

Robert James Merrett

McGill-Queen's University Press
Montreal & Kingston • London • Chicago

© McGill-Queen's University Press 2021

ISBN 978-0-2280-0683-1 (cloth)
ISBN 978-0-2280-0684-8 (paper)
ISBN 978-0-2280-0796-8 (ePDF)
ISBN 978-0-2280-0797-5 (ePUB)

Legal deposit third quarter 2021
Bibliothèque nationale du Québec

Printed in Canada on acid-free paper that is 100% ancient forest free (100% post-consumer recycled), processed chlorine free

Funded by the Government of Canada | Financé par le gouvernement du Canada | Canada | Canada Council for the Arts | Conseil des arts du Canada

We acknowledge the support of the Canada Council for the Arts.

Nous remercions le Conseil des arts du Canada de son soutien.

Library and Archives Canada Cataloguing in Publication

Title: Imperial paradoxes: training the senses and tasting the eighteenth century / Robert James Merrett.

Names: Merrett, Robert James, author.

Series: McGill-Queen's studies in the history of ideas; 83.

Description: Series statement: McGill-Queen's studies in the history of ideas; 83 | Includes bibliographical references and index.

Identifiers: Canadiana (print) 20210167211 | Canadiana (ebook) 20210167483 | ISBN 9780228006831 (hardcover) | ISBN 9780228006848 (softcover) | ISBN 9780228007968 (PDF) | ISBN 9780228007975 (ePUB)

Subjects: LCSH: Aesthetics in literature. | LCSH: Food in literature. | LCSH: Fashion in literature. | LCSH: Travel in literature. | LCSH: English literature—18th century—History and criticism. | LCSH: French literature—18th century—History and criticism. | LCSH: Great Britain—Intellectual life—18th century. | LCSH: France—Intellectual life— 18th century.

Classification: LCC PR448.A37 M47 2021 | DDC 820.9/35709033—dc23

This book was typeset by Marquis Interscript in 10.5 / 13 New Baskerville.

In memoriam
James Chute Ede (1882–1965)
My first mentor and a kindly uncle

Contents

Acknowledgments xiii

Introduction 3

1 Aesthetic Empires: Symbolic and Psychological Learning 18

2 Literariness: Aesthetic and Cultural Dialectic 79

3 Spirits and Wine in Imperial Canada, 1630–1900 114

4 Cuisine, Eating, and Empires of Taste 157

5 Travel, Fashion, and Cultural Exchange 214

6 Comparative Imperial Aesthetics and Viticulture 283

Bibliography 343

Index 361

Acknowledgments

Imperial Paradoxes: Training the Senses and Tasting the Eighteenth Century originated in a lecture series honouring Edmund Kemper Broadus (1876–1936), the first professor of English appointed to the University of Alberta in 1908. His essay, "Addison as a Literary Critic," which appeared in *The University of Alberta Magazine* in February 1909, is a model of clear and incisive thinking, and expresses strong views about literary history. Professor Broadus alleges that the periodical journalism of Joseph Addison (1672–1719) embodies inadequate views of history, culture, and aesthetics, allegations *Imperial Paradoxes* tests by detailing those contexts. Broadus seems neither to examine eighteenth-century writing on its own terms nor to respect it as emanating from a unique historical moment; as discussed in chapter 2, he appears to treat the period's urban, commercial, and aesthetic modes as inimical to the transcendent aspirations of Romanticism.

This is not to imply that composing literary history is straightforward. The encyclopedic and dialectical expositions that inform *Imperial Paradoxes* arise from recent academic debates about learning, knowing, and literary pedagogy. In its attempts to renew literary history by drawing on cultural materialism and cognitive science, this study is obliged to acknowledge its dependence on the pioneering work of David Perkins. Besides probing whether literary history is possible, he asks, following Samuel Johnson (1709–1784), if it is necessary. To Johnson, literature is the source of both authorial misery and happiness. By analogy, Perkins avers that literary history has "an indispensable role in our experience of literature and a broader social or cultural function as well"; yet, while "we cannot write literary history with intellectual conviction ... we must read it. The irony and paradox of this argument are themselves typical of our present moment in history." If "the ideal cannot be achieved," he holds that "we must pursue it, for without it the otherness of the past would entirely deliquesce in endless subjective and ideological reappropriations. A function of literary history is, then, to set the literature of the past at a distance, to make its otherness felt."[1]

Having taught in the English Department at the University of Alberta for forty-five years courses ranging over the history of the language, the bible and myth, the sister arts, Shakespeare, modern Canadian and American literatures, as well as many in the eighteenth century, and having been involved for twelve years in senior administration on campus and in Ottawa, I have been exposed to paradigm shifts and epistemic revolutions affecting the curriculum, these alerting me to necessary tensions between change and continuity and between renewal and tradition. Hence, I trust the grounds of liberal arts education and forms of literary history upheld in *Imperial Paradoxes* are persuasively concerned with aesthetics, interdisciplinarity, cultural pluralism, philosophical relativism, and moral questions about colonial and imperial power.

In surveying ever-evolving debates about literary criticism, chapter 2 seeks to displace the remoteness of literary history by probing the following themes: how does the mind operate beyond rational awareness; how does embodied consciousness constitute identity; what signs are there that eighteenth-century authors sensed how the mind and imagination are embodied; how much are documentary references and material allusions in literary texts in harmony with aesthetic pleasure; and what are the educational and social benefits of aesthetic enjoyment?

I happily received the invitation to present the 2008 Broadus Lectures from Professor Garrett Epp, chair of the Department of English and Film Studies, later being encouraged to undertake this volume by the following colleagues: Ted Bishop, Dianne Chisholm, David Gay, Isobel Grundy, Ian MacLaren, David Miall, Jim Mulvihill, and Stephen Reimer. I have benefited from the mentorship of Michel Baridon, Thomas Cleary, Beatrice Fink, Evelyn Hinz, Samuel Macey, Haydn Mason, François Moureau, Tiffany Potter, and Annie Rivara, editors who advanced my work in comparative literary history and cultural exchange between England and France. The Social Sciences and Humanities Research Council of Canada awarded me a grant in 1992 to study in

---

1 Perkins 1992, 17 and 185.

the archives of sixteen French cities. My last trips took place in 2008, 2010, and 2013 when I lived in Bordeaux, Lyon, and Dijon for several months. I was aided by the directors and staffs of the municipal libraries of those cities, of the Archives départementales de la Gironde and of the Académie des sciences, arts et belles-lettres de Dijon, who always cheerfully helped me to access the rare newspapers, books, and manuscripts cited in this monograph. I thank Mr Mark Abley, acquisition editor for McGill-Queen's University Press, for so enthusiastically bringing my text to readers. In addition, I would like to thank Richard Ratzlaff, copy editor James Leahy, indexer Judy Dunlop, and Marcie Whitecotton-Carroll, who helped with file preparation.

R.J.M.
Edmonton, Alberta, 2020.

IMPERIAL PARADOXES

The face of the earth is continually changing, by the encrease of small kingdoms into great empires, by the dissolution of great empires into smaller kingdoms, by the planting of colonies, by the migration of tribes. Is there anything discoverable in all these events, but force and violence?
David Hume

The empires of the future are the empires of the mind.
Winston S. Churchill

Introduction

The Foundation of Empire is Art & Science. Remove them or Degrade them, & the Empire is No More. Empire follows Art & Not Vice Versa as Englishmen suppose.[1]

Distinct from the view of William Blake (1757–1827) above, the pyrrhonism of David Hume (1711–1776), evident in my first opening epigraph, conveys both the inevitability and impermanence of political empires as well as their exploitation of demographic shifts and brutal colonization.[2] In my second opening epigraph, Winston S. Churchill (1874–1965), in accepting an honorary doctorate for wartime opposition to imperialism, trusts it will be transformed into a realm of intellectual power.[3] To Blake, however, empire is not primarily a geographical or historical phenomenon. Nor is it an ultimate symbol of political power, military strength, or commercial expansion. It is a cultural ideal and mental state: secondary to the creative imagination, it exists only via a dialectic of art and science, of aesthetics and knowledge. In so expressing his love of paradox and contraries, Blake saw his unique inspirations opposing Baconian empiricism and pragmatism.[4] But Francis Bacon (1561–1626), as *The Advancement of Learning* (1605), *Novum Organum* (1620), and *New Atlantis* (1627) confirm, was a humanist familiar with Greek and Roman culture and a philosopher whose

---

1 Blake, *Annotations To Sir Joshua Reynolds's Discourses* (1966, 445).
2 Hume, "of The Original Contract" (1987, 471).
3 Churchill, "Anglo-American Unity: A Speech on Receiving an Honorary Degree at Harvard University September 6, 1943" (1945, 182).
4 "Penal codes and repressive laws cannot produce order: they are conceived as a desperate defense against chaos: order is not a matter of morality but of morale. Compulsion and obedience follow the anarchic will of tyranny: our imaginations, being one in God, achieve, when unrestricted, a spontaneous co-operation. That is part of what Blake means when he says that empire follows art and not art empire" (Frye 1969, 90).

insistence on the limits of knowledge made him reach passionately beyond those limits. Hence, his claim about setting up a college in *New Atlantis*: "The End of our Foundation is the Knowledge of Causes; the secret Motions of Things; and the Enlargement of the Empire of Man; by the effecting of all Things possible."[5] While that work discusses the military bases of empire, Bacon is more intent on promoting induction than deductive generalizations and on showing why a nexus of diverse kinds of knowledge represents an infinite range of human potential. Thus, Peter Shaw (1694–1763), his eighteenth-century editor, defends his use of fiction and metaphor in resisting the a priori philosophy of Aristotle: "*it must be carefully observed, that the only effectual way of conquering Prejudices, and delivering new Doctrines to advantage, is artfully to steal into the Mind under the Cover of Metaphor and Allusion.*"[6] Indeed, Bacon sustains rhetorical images for conceptual differentiation and mental ingestion, as in "of Studies," where he associates reading and various functions of the mouth:

Read not to contradict and confute; nor to believe and take for granted; nor to find talk and discourse; but to weigh and consider. Some books are to be tasted, others to be swallowed, and some few are to be chewed and digested; that is some books are to be read only in parts; others to be read, but not curiously; and some to be read wholly, and with diligence and attention.[7]

Admiring Bacon's revolutionary model of learning, Addison also applauded his dialectic and aesthetics. To him, Bacon was one of "the most extensive and improved Genius's we have had any Instance of in our own Nation, or in any other." By "an extraordinary Force of Nature, Compass of Thought, and indefatigable Study," he

amassed to himself such Stores of Knowledge as we cannot look upon without Amazement. His Capacity seems to have grasped All that was revealed in Books before his Time; and not satisfied with that, he began to strike out new Tracks of Science, too many to be travelled over by any one Man, in the Compass of the longest Life. These, therefore, he could only mark down,

---

5 Shaw 1733, 1:291.
6 Ibid., 1:lxx.
7 Bacon 1962, 50.

like imperfect Coastings in Maps, or supposed Points of Land, to be further discovered, and ascertained by the Industry of After-Ages, who should proceed upon his Notices or Conjectures.[8]

In treating natural philosophy as a transgenerational endeavour, Bacon recognized what Blake would not: society and individuals must concede that the senses are shaped and even distorted by customs and habits – the idols of the cave, herd, theatre, and marketplace. Those sensory distortions are remedied only by educational disciplines that move from fact to theory to practice and on to the production of discoveries and inventions beneficial to mankind. This formulation of collective knowledge through memory, reason, and imagination, far from being achieved in the course of a single era, requires an evolving fund of historical data.[9]

In this context, Bacon upheld the educational value of travel, a contentious topic *Imperial Paradoxes* scrutinizes. To Bacon, young men must be prepared for travel abroad and then guided by cultivated tutors. Only under guidance will they appreciate the world's diversity and plenitude. Relying on guidebooks, they should record their journeys in diaries. In hastening from place to place, they ought to change lodgings at every location to widen their acquaintance. Cultivating persons of influence more than popular events and entertainments, they should also visit architectural landmarks and public institutions, such as colleges, arsenals, and courts. Returning home, they should embody travel in discourse rather than in "apparel or gesture," answering interlocutors rather than boastfully telling stories. Not changing national manners for those of "foreign parts," a young traveller might well "prick in some flowers of that he hath learned abroad into the customs of his own country."[10]

If, in promoting travel and openness to the world, he celebrates conventional metaphors, Bacon voices the subtlest dialectic in his essay "of Empire." Its second paragraph describes imperialism's transitory, evanescent, and contrary aspects:

---

8 *Spectator*, no. 554, Friday, 5 December 1712 (Addison 1966, 4:245).
9 Porter 2001, 56–7.
10 "of Travel" (Bacon 1962, 54–6).

To speak now of the true temper of empire: it is a thing rare, and hard to keep: for both temper and distemper consist of contraries. But it is one thing to mingle contraries, another to interchange them. The answer of Apollonius to Vespasian is full of excellent instruction. Vespasian asked him, *What was Nero's overthrow?* He answered: *Nero could touch and tune the harp well; but in government, sometimes he used to wind the pins too high, sometimes to let them down too low.* And certain it is that nothing destroyeth authority so much as the unequal and untimely interchange of power pressed too far, and relaxed too much.[11]

Bacon's analogy between embodying emperorship and playing an instrument is brilliant yet doubly ironic: broad-minded and pluralistic, it could not be less dogmatic.[12] Another reason why he took Bacon as a model is that Addison aimed to help overcome the ideological factionalism in society following the Commonwealth and Restoration periods. He therefore appealed in *The Spectator* to citizens of many classes, representing their diverse interests and bringing them together as readers in the public sphere. Not only did he uphold Cicero's praise of Socrates for bringing philosophy down from the heavens, he wanted to make it "dwell in Clubs and Assemblies, at Tea-Tables and in Coffee Houses."[13] Conveying moral philosophy to Londoners, Addison addressed the man of letters and the man of the world in a style "palatable, practical and pleasing."[14]

Since Blake was not alone in treating political empires as secondary to empires of knowledge and imagination, *Imperial Paradoxes* focuses on issues in material culture that preoccupied British, Canadian, and French authors in the era when European empires were rising. Far from employing a chronological narrative delimited by national and geographical boundaries, it operates cyclical, encyclopedic, and cross-cultural methods. For it recognizes that, while, like Blake, his contemporaries opposed political imperialism, unlike him they valued the legacies of the Greek and Roman empires to an extent that led them to map imperialism as an extensive image of the interior world

---

11 Bacon 1962, 57–8.
12 To Porter, Enlightenment thinkers like Bacon were "broad-minded"; they "espoused pluralism" and "their register was ironic rather than dogmatic" (2001, xxi).
13 *Spectator*, no. 10, Monday, 12 March 1711 (Addison 1964, 1:31–2).
14 Porter 2001, 5 and 11.

of learning and of cognitive, psychological, and spiritual experience. In critiquing British imperialism for entailing consumerism, commerce, and capitalism, not a few authors realized it might be transmuted into a metaphor refining sense perception and aesthetic appreciation. Moreover, the imperialism embodied in new forms of finance, economic productivity, and global trade in consumer goods affected personal and social identity; it both defied and encouraged linguistic and literary nationalism. In probing tensions between consumerism and nationalism and between commercial progress and social conservation, *Imperial Paradoxes* unfolds the dialectic in material and intellectual culture that characterizes literature in the period of rising European empires. Crucial to this dialectic are the rivalries of Britain and France in arenas of eating, drinking, dressing, and travelling. That these imperial rivals scorned and imitated each other's food, drink, fashion, and tourism exposes inevitable contraries in societies, institutions, and individuals, such tensions serving as paradoxical signs illustrating the challenges in revising literary history.

The contrarian thinking that Blake evidences in his *Annotations to Sir Joshua Reynolds's Discourses* (1808?) defies orthodox aesthetic criteria by inverting the relations between abstract and concrete ideas upheld by followers of Bacon. Indeed, Blake's radical dissent led him to spurn the dialectic in humanist learning. In mocking the aesthetics of Reynolds (1723–1792) and Edmund Burke (1729–1797), Blake avers that the "Sublime" is not a matter of vague generality; it requires "Minute Neatness of Execution" since the "Grandeur of Ideas is founded on Precision of Ideas."[15] He early felt "Contempt & Abhorrence" for Burke's *A Philosophical Enquiry into the Origin of Our Ideas of the Sublime and Beautiful* (1757), a treatise that divided the beautiful from the sublime, attributing causes of the latter to emotional surprise and fear rather than to verbal precision.[16] While he exalted experiential acuity, Blake decried methodical gathering of empirical facts, given his defence of innate ideas and the higher faculties: "The Man who says that we have No Innate Ideas must be a Fool & Knave, Having No Con-Science or Innate Sense." Horticultural images attach to the inherited structure of the

---

15 On Reynolds and Burke as humanists, see Fussell 1965, 246 and 5. Blake scorns Reynolds and Burke as detractors of "Inspiration & Vision" (1966, 476–7).

16 Frye 1969, 91–2; Boulton 1968, lvi.

mind and the brain's perceptive capacities: experience does not generate cognition, for "Man is Born Like a Garden ready Planted & Sown. This World is too poor to produce one Seed." Thus Blake rejects Reynolds's view in "Discourse 7" of *Discourses on Art* (1797) that "Taste & Genius are not of Heavenly Origin."[17] Blake discards the tenet that aesthetic sense and compositional practices in communities of artists evolve and improve over the generations. In deriding Reynolds's rules of learning by practice and imitation, Blake belittles the materialism of "Epicurean or Newtonian Philosophy"; it is "Atheism" to disbelieve that "Mind & Imagination" are above our "Moral & Perishing Nature."[18] Perhaps his most polemical attack on the dualism that had long governed mind–body relations comes in the following: "Man has no Body distinct from his Soul; for that call'd Body is a portion of Soul discern'd by the five Senses, the chief inlets of Soul in this age."[19] This paradoxical assertion is an exhortation to elucidate how the literary imagination is transcendent because embodied. If Western philosophy has disparaged embodiment, literary history based on logical methods has evaded another of Blake's provocative views, namely, that there is no necessary difference between critical and creative writing. As chapter 1 outlines, the mixed modes of eighteenth-century texts support to some extent Blake's challenges to literal-mindedness.

17 "Discourse 7" states that "Genius and taste, in their common acceptation, appear to be very nearly related; the difference lies only in this, that genius has superadded to it a habit of power of execution: or, we may say, that taste, when this power is added, changes its name, and is called genius. They both, in popular opinion, pretend to an entire exemption from the restraint of rules. It is supposed that their powers are intuitive; that under the name of genius great works are produced, and under the name of taste an exact judgment is given, without our knowing why, and without our being under the least obligation to reason, precept, or experience ... One can scarce state these opinions without exposing their absurdity; yet they are constantly in the mouths of men, and particularly of artists. They who have thought seriously on this subject, do not carry the point so far; yet I am persuaded, that even among those few who may be called thinkers, the prevalent opinion allows less than it ought to the powers of reason; and considers the principles of taste, which give all their authority to the rules of art, as more fluctuating, and as having less solid foundations, than we shall find, upon examination, they really have" (Reynolds 1965, 96).

18 Blake 1966, 457, 459, 471, 473, and 475. See also "Singular & Particular Detail Is the Foundation of the Sublime" (Blake 1966, 459).

19 Blake, *The Marriage of Heaven and Hell* (1966, 149).

Embodiment was, in fact, a major concern of authors in eighteenth-century Britain and France. Many probed how the body and mind work and how closely they operate. Many questioned the dualistic philosophies which held that faculties operate hierarchically. While *Imperial Paradoxes* registers opposing views of mind–body relations, it shows how the senses were thought to function, how sensory images represented one another, and how synesthesia was related to consumerism. The period's aesthetic questioning is fascinating for exemplifying diverse views of politics emerging from the problematic triangular relations between Aboriginal, British, and French cultures before and after the Seven Years War (1756–1763), a conflict often seen as global. In 1794, Arthur Young (1741–1820), sympathetic to the French Revolution, viewed the long eighteenth century optimistically:

It is a question whether modern history has any thing more curious to offer to the attention of the politician, than the progress and rivalship of the French and English empires, from the ministry of Colbert to the revolution in France. In the course of those 130 years, both have figured with a degree of splendour that has attracted the admiration of mankind.[20]

But was the admiration universal?[21] Were the empires evolving in simply progressive ways? Were they not based on competing ideals of absolutism and liberal constitutionalism? Does literary history not reveal ambivalent and conflicting views about imperial development? Does it not expose the displacement of regional and ethnic identities? Such questions need to be confronted because they provoke answers that help renew liberal arts education without fixating either on the radical ideologies and utopian idealism or on the worldly materialism and corporatism of colleges and universities.[22] Such questions may advance the humanities' engagement with cultural complexities that relies on

20 Young 1970, 1:[iii].
21 To Postman, "all the knowledge we have is a result of our asking questions" and "question-asking is the most significant intellectual tool human beings have" (2000, 161).
22 Ginsberg (2011) says competition among elite universities for professors and students and for government, foundation, and alumni funds has led to the adoption of corporate models that increase the power of boards of trustees and reduce instructors' involvement in curricular planning. For more on these issues, see "Liberal Arts Tradition in Canada" (Merrett 2012).

"real-time" experience given the well-tested view that learning to read and comprehend is a lifelong process.[23] The distancing of the past by epistemic and paradigmatic cleavages needs to be balanced by evolutionary, gradualist thinking.[24] The past is neither easily avoided nor glibly simplified. Far from monolithic, eighteenth-century literary stances were as diverse as in all periods.

The tenets applied in this study grant that literary history is always to be rewritten, always to be revised, and always to serve pedagogical purposes. In guiding readers and students to experience literature, it raises questions without claiming categorical authority. *Imperial Paradoxes* seeks to balance extensive and intensive reading by employing comparative methods and exploring reciprocal relations between canonized works and popular culture. It recognizes that nationalism and internationalism in Britain, Canada, and France are mutually involved rather than distinct categories. A main point in Linda Colley's *Britons* is that Britishness was not fixed until after its imperialism was confirmed at the end of the century. Despite imperial aspirations, France, according to Peter Sahlins, remained regionally divided with distinct jurisdictions and tax laws, divisions arising from Louis XIV's absolutism, which, while it led to the diaspora of Huguenots, brought about in the Parlement of Paris a resistance that led to increased toleration of the rights of foreigners to own and inherit property.[25] Despite claiming to be the centre of the civilized world, France, like Britain, could not avoid developing a hybrid culture given its military, industrial, and commercial expansionism. The pan-European adoption of the classical languages by science and medicine was culturally powerful even as vernaculars saw the proliferation of translations, two-way dictionaries, loan words, and semantic exchanges. Increasing contentions about the international traffic in philosophical ideas as well as in products and processes related to eating, drinking, dressing, and travelling heightened debates about the

---

23 "We all read ourselves and the world around us in order to glimpse what and where we are. We read to understand, or to begin to understand. We cannot do but read. Reading, almost as much as breathing, is our essential function" (Manguel 1998, 7).

24 For two accounts, one popular and one academic, which challenge recent representations of the Enlightenment: Postman 1999, 34–5 and 74, and Ellis 1997, 22–32.

25 Colley 1992, 155–64, and Sahlins 2004, 171–2.

natural and learned experience of the senses and the psychology of taste in ways revealing that literary history has been cramped by geographical, linguistic, and national boundaries.

In efforts to reform the empire in America, Burke applied Baconian methods.[26] This is because he traced the Enlightenment back to the Renaissance: the progress of knowledge did not begin in the eighteenth century; the rebirth of letters had been cultivated by clergy, patronized by nobility, furthered by the Reformation, and confirmed by modern science.[27] Hence, *Reflections on the Revolution in France* (1790) vindicates the worth of monasteries to education.[28] It enthuses about their "accumulation of vast libraries, which are the history of the force and weakness of the human mind," their "great collections of antient records, medals, and coins, which attest and explain laws and customs," their "paintings and statues, that, by imitating nature, seem to extend the limits of creation," their "grand monuments of the dead, which continue the regards and connexions of life beyond the grave," their "collections of the specimens of nature, which become a representative assembly of all the classes and families of the world, that by disposition facilitate, and, by exciting curiosity, open the avenues to science."[29] To Isaiah Berlin, such pro-Catholic views make *Reflections* a "revolutionary text against the Revolution."[30] In 1773 Burke took son Richard to Auxerre to learn French, befriended senior clergy at the cathedral, and learned about the constitutional privileges of the monastic and secular clergy which he elaborated in *Reflections*. That visit to France deepened his sense of relations between aesthetics and politics that govern his book.[31] Richard billeted with the Parisots, a prominent Auxerrois family, later sustaining a

---

26 Bourke 2015, 454.
27 Ibid., 720–1.
28 Beales 2005, 436.

29 Burke 2009, 162. Burke's remarks echo Bacon's and Addison's appreciation of educational travel over luxurious consumerism. Many British travellers appreciated continental monasticism, including Horace Walpole (1717–1797), who made a point of visiting monasteries and enjoying their services (Beales 2005, 425).

30 Cited in Beales 2005, 416.

31 Burke was well informed about the socially and economically prominent classes in large French cities that provided the chief actors in the French Revolution (Hunt 1984, 160–1).

correspondence with Madame Parisot that conveyed to the Burkes the troubles of 1789: she told of her anxiety about food riots and peasants despoiling estates. Her moving accounts of mass hysteria aroused Burke's "aesthetic-affective" feelings which coloured his depiction of the humiliation of Marie Antoinette.[32]

Burke's figurative stance on imperialism, together with his gradualist, transgenerational, and dialectical view of artistic development, are major themes in *Reflections*. Thus, he defends the evolution of political sense against the utopian proponents of the French Revolution who "evade and slip aside from *difficulty*." To Burke as to Reynolds, it is "the glory of the great masters in all the arts to confront, and to overcome" difficulty; when they "overcome the first difficulty," they turn "it into an instrument for new conquests over new difficulties; thus to enable them to extend the empire of their science; and even to push forward beyond the reach of their original thoughts, the land marks of the human understanding itself."[33] Dialectic in political and artistic traditions is equivalent; each creates and refines rules as their achievements unfold. The "science of jurisprudence" is "the pride of the human intellect" since, "with all its defects, redundancies, and errors," it is "the collected reason of ages." The "union of minds" and "long succession of ages" vital to jurisprudence entail "an excellence in composition," art and politics needing "the aid of more minds than one age can furnish." Burke, no herald of "this enlightened age," defends "general prejudices," the "latent wisdom" of which is known by "our men of speculation."[34] To him, "just prejudice" lets an individual's duty become natural whereas enlightened men who think themselves superior lack respect for "the wisdom of others." Britons are no "converts" of Jean-Jacques Rousseau (1712–1788), François-Marie Arouet, that is, Voltaire (1694–1778), and Claude Adrien Helvetius (1715–1771), since "no discoveries are to be made, in morality; nor many in the great principles of government, nor in the ideas of liberty." The British embody political and cultural

---

32 White 2002, 5 and 64.
33 Burke 2009, 167.
34 "Some attention is surely due to what we can no more get rid of than we can go out of ourselves. We are creatures of prejudice; we neither can nor ought to eradicate it; we must only regulate it by reason; which kind of regulation is indeed little more than obliging the lesser, the local and temporary prejudices to give way to those which are more durable and lasting" (Reynolds 1965, 115).

tradition in a common sensibility: "We preserve the whole of our feelings still native and entire, unsophisticated by pedantry and infidelity. We have real hearts of flesh and blood beating in our bosoms."[35] His view of embodied sensibility appeals, given the imaginative power with which it decries systematic reason. To Burke the upholder of "pleasing illusions," sentiments incorporated over a stretch of time into political jurisprudence "beautify and soften private society," whereas in France the "new conquering empire of light and reason" would dissolve them. Imperious reason derives from a "barbarous" and "mechanic" philosophy "as void of solid wisdom, as it is destitute of all taste and elegance." This "sort of reason" which "banishes the affections" signals that "our institutions can never be embodied." No arrogant individualist, a legislator ought to have a "heart full of sensibility, ought to love and respect his own kind, and to fear himself."[36]

Burke's balancing of individual self-doubt about rational authority with a transgenerational evolution of political and aesthetic practice seems absent from today's pedagogical and curricular discussions, which, by contrast, are urgent and abstract. Still, one aim of the present study is to apply Burke's metaphorical and dialectical expressions of embodiment and empire to the revision of literary history by raising the following questions: is it possible to write literary history that coordinates intensive and extensive reading, that relates reading's existential aspects to embodied perceptions, and that trains us to enjoy the interrelations of the senses so that we may justify the metaphor of tasting eighteenth-century texts? Further, may literary history be written by facing up to how cognitive science displaces truisms about knowing and learning?

Unsurprisingly, on his deathbed Johnson asked for Burke, having always found his company delightful and relished his witty conversation.[37] Indeed, he shared Burke's profound understanding of ideological barriers to learning. Johnson's critique of political imperialism as it entangled Britain and France in diplomatic and cultural illusions that abused Aboriginal North Americans is treated later. For the moment it is proper to point out that, as a champion of moral imagination and social practice, he refused to belittle the import of fashion, being as concerned with aesthetics as Burke. In an essay in *The Adventurer* of

---

35 Burke 1999, 95, 170, 87, and 86.
36 Ibid., 77 and 169.
37 Damrosch 2019, 367.

1754, Johnson looks back to *The Guardian* – produced by Richard Steele (1672–1729) and Addison in 1713 – to consider its claim that "the world punishes with too great severity the error of those, who imagine that the ignorance of little things may be compensated by the knowledge of great." He holds that, since more people "detect petty failings than can distinguish or esteem great qualifications" and since "mankind is in general more easily disposed to censure than to admiration, contempt is often incurred by slight mistakes, which real virtue or usefulness cannot counterbalance." He finds "such mistakes and inadvertencies" unavoidable to "a man deeply immersed in study"; no scholar "can become qualified for the common intercourses of life by private meditation." The reason is that

the manners of the world are not a regular system, planned by philosophers upon settled principles, in which every cause has a congruous effect, and one part has a just reference to another. Of the fashions prevalent in every country, a few have arisen, perhaps, from particular temperatures of the climate; a few more from the constitution of the government; but the greater part have grown up by chance; been started by caprice, been contrived by affectation, or borrowed without any just motives of choice from other countries.

While moral and religious values transcend fashion because they are "constant and immutable, and depend not on the notions of men, but the commands of Heaven," their "external mode is to be in some measure regulated by the prevailing taste of the age in which we live; for he is certainly no friend to virtue, who neglects to give it any lawful attraction, or suffers it to deceive the eye or alienate the affections for want of innocent compliance with fashionable decorations."[38] Here Johnson's contingent worldliness and period taste are in equipoise with his ethical and religious conscience. To him, popular and customary modes are not overcome by abstract principle because they are plural

---

38 *The Adventurer*, no. 131, Tuesday, 5 February 1754 (Johnson 1824, 3:278–84). Johnson is alluding to No. 10 of *The Guardian* for Monday, 23 March 1713. The passage reads: "The Indiscretion of believing that great Qualities make up for want of things less considerable, is punished too severely in those who are guilty of it. Every Day's experience shows us, among variety of People with whom we are not acquainted, that we take Impressions too favourable and too disadvantageous of Men at first sight from their Habit" (Stephens 1982, 70).

in origin. Those who believe otherwise are self-deceived. Typically predisposed to censure rather than admire, they merit the discomfiture they meet. *Imperial Paradoxes* tries throughout to heed this salutary warning to scholars who almost necessarily privilege systematic ideas and private contemplation.

Chapter 1 of *Imperial Paradoxes* begins to amplify the topics outlined above. Explicating the aesthetic ideas of French and English thinkers, it compares their versions of metaphorical relations between material and psychological empires, sketching dialectical contexts for renewing liberal arts education in general and literary history in particular. It shows how eating, drinking, travelling, and dressing form body–mind transactions and establish comparative and cosmopolitan themes by applying sense transferences to political imperialism. It explains how the training of the senses led to theories of a sixth sense and created an inner rhetoric and self-educated civility that validates liberal arts education. This idealism is contrasted by prejudices opposing French absolutism and upholding the clerical foundation of English universities. Still, the aesthetic theories presented derogate from the dominance of the rational intellect, showing how the mutual operation of the senses validates the sister arts. There are no categorical boundaries between poetry, painting, and music just as there are no ultimate political boundaries between languages, regions, and nations. Nor can there be a single-minded development of tastes since there are no universal cultural habits given the diverse biologies of the brain. Environmental and evolutionary variations are explained by the dialectic of uniformity and difference in analogies applied to viticulture and cuisine. Treating natural and acquired tastes, the chapter shows how the senses evolve in the face of customs that derive from consumption of food, drink, fashion, and travel. Poets and novelists employ imperial metaphors in texts promoting the idea that the senses are not cognitively static and showing that, in their embodiment, they are not subject to reason. By contrast, the reactionary English theatre spurned the drama of the classical empires and derided the city of London's imperial aspirations. Its licence and libertines degraded beneficiaries of the restored political order and the new capitalism. Stereotypes of the professional and mercantile classes and the nouveaux riches early dominated characterization, yet by 1800 the theatre had reversed its reflexive procedures to rely on tropes of social hierarchy and imperial wealth gained from India and the Caribbean. This reversal is paralleled by architectural criticism, which, in describing Paris and London, employs classical imperial models to indicate the failure to create grand public spaces. Finally, the chapter examines consciousness-altering stimulants as an aspect of trade and commerce. Whereas anthropology upholds ancient values in the communal sharing of entoptic imagery, these self-generated percepts are subject to debate in modern secular societies, the pleasures and harms effected by mind-altering substances dividing communities and individuals. If Menippean texts celebrate festivity and bacchic indulgence, the corruption of the wine trade by adulteration and capitalism led to medical views that subordinate bodily intelligence and aesthetic taste to insanity and that ignore the human desire to extend perception into the mind itself.

Notes on special terms in *Imperial Paradoxes* taken from the OED:

aesthetic
: Its etymological and philosophical meaning derives from the Greek for "things perceptible by the senses," things material rather than thinkable or immaterial. It also means "perceptive, sharp in the senses." To Immanuel Kant (1724–1804), the term applies to "the science which treats of the conditions of sensuous perception." The word first appeared in English circa 1800 (1970, 1:147–8).

dialectic
: A term in philosophy applied by Kant to criticism that shows the mutually contradictory character of the principles of science when employed to determine objects beyond the limits of experience such as the soul, the world, God. Georg Wilhelm Friedrich Hegel (1770–1831), who denied that such contradictions are ultimately irreconcilable, applies the term "(a) to the process of thought by which such contradictions are seen to merge themselves into a higher truth that comprehends them; and (b) to the world-process, which, being in his view but the thought-process on its objective side, develops similarly by a continuous unification of opposites" (1970, 3:310).

synesthesia "a. A sensation in one part of the body produced by a stimulus applied to another part. b. Agreement of the feelings or emotions of different individuals, as a stage in the development of sympathy. c. Production from a sense-impression of one kind, of an associated mental image of a sense-impression of another kind." One cited example: F.W.H. Myers (1903), *Human Personality*, I, xl: "Vestiges of the primitive undifferentiated sensitivity persist in the form of *synaesthesia*, e.g. when the hearing of an external sound carries with it, by some arbitrary association of ideas, the seeing of some form or colour" (1970, 10:373).

1

Aesthetic Empires:

Symbolic and Psychological Learning

Gastronomy governs the whole life of man; for the tears of the new-born child are for its nurse's breast, and the dying man derives pleasure from the final potion, which, alas, he will never digest ... Its influence is felt by all classes of society; for while it is gastronomy which rules the banquets of kings, it is also gastronomy which stipulates how many minutes a humble egg should be boiled ... The material subject of gastronomy is everything which can be eaten; its immediate object, the preservation of the individual; and its methods of attaining that object, cultivation which produces foodstuffs, commerce which exchanges them, industry which prepares them, and experience which devises the means of turning them to the best possible account ... Gastronomy examines taste as an organ of both pleasure and pain; it has discovered the gradual increase of excitement to which taste is liable, regulated the rate of that increase, and fixed upon a limit beyond which no self-respecting person should go.[1]

BODILY SENSING, AESTHETICS, AND IMPERIAL METAPHORS

In defining gastronomy, Jean-Anthelme Brillat-Savarin (1755–1826) relates ingestion and digestion to personal survival, economic productivity, aesthetic culture, and imperial authority. With acute interdisciplinarity, he associates eating and drinking with imperialism in the world of experience and cognition: above contempt of the body, he attributes psychological import to corporeal functions and endows physiology with cultural and political purpose. That gastronomy may help renew literary history is clear when we realize that Blake, Burke, Johnson, Brillat-Savarin,

---

1 Brillat-Savarin 1994, 52–3.

and other authors apply experimental psychology to question dualisms of reason and imagination against literary criticism's tendency to value intellect more than the dialectic of art and science. The interdisciplinary focus of *Imperial Paradoxes* is sharpened by the reciprocity of body and mind, the collaboration of reason and imagination, the cognitive function of metaphor, and the double vision inherent in the semiotics of taste, topics germane to the revision of aesthetic theory.

In my epigraph, a writer, born in 1755, defends the culture of gastronomy, his view of taste slighting seventeenth-century empiricism and exploring mind–body relations made familiar today by cognitive science. *The Physiology of Taste*, published anonymously before its author died in January 1826, reflects a life of legal and political activism on behalf of tradition in an age of revolution. Defying common notions of the bodily senses, it applies evolutionary stances to their functional reciprocity. It argues that, since the purpose of taste is "the preservation of the individual," the "organs" that preserve the "species" are "senses." Elevating their cognitive worth, Brillat-Savarin treats the person as a "*sensitive ego*" whose soul is the "common centre" of "sensations." Synesthesia reveals that, since the senses are imperfect – no single inlet conveying a full impression of external reality to the brain – cognition evolves because the senses are complementary:

Thus touch corrected the errors of sight; sound, by means of the spoken word, became the interpreter of every feeling; sight and smell gave added powers to taste; hearing compared sounds and judged distances; and physical desire influenced the organs of all the other senses.

A corollary of synesthesia is artistic evolution. After "many centuries," the senses still "extend their dominion"; musical harmony was recently invented, "the sphere of taste" having grown in the "last few centuries" because sugar, alcohol, ices, vanilla, tea, and coffee provide "our palate with hitherto unknown sensations." This aesthetic gain is positive given the "universal truth, that man is far better equipped for suffering than for pleasure." So, a "guest at a sumptuous banquet, in a hall adorned with mirrors, statues, and flowers, a hall balmy with scents, beautified by the presence of pretty women, and filled with the strains of sweet music" needs "no great effort of the imagination to be convinced that all the sciences have been pressed into service to enhance and set off the pleasures of taste."[2] For Brillat-Savarin, both science and imagination explain the aesthetics of gastronomy; physiology, the "faculty of appreciation," and culture affect embodied taste. Central to pleasure and pain, the apparatus of taste registers qualities in things and sensations. The tongue with its papillae (tastebuds) is not the sole organ of taste: cheeks, palate, and "nasal fossae, to which physiologists have perhaps not paid sufficient attention," are such organs. Even gums are organs of taste. While the tongue does not exclusively savour, the number of papillae so varies in individuals that "the empire of taste also has its blind and deaf subjects." In refining physiology, he stresses the complexity of savours: their number is "infinite, for every soluble body has a special savour which is not quite like any other." They are "differentiated by simple, double, and multiple combinations, so that it is impossible to classify them, from the attractive to the most intolerable." Linguistic limits to discrimination prove that gastronomy is a field of inquiry fit for scientific experimentation,

for if it is granted that there exists an indefinite number of series of basic savours, all capable of being modified by an infinite number of combinations, it follows that a new language would be needed to express all the resultant effects, mountains of folio volumes to define them, and undreamed-of numerical characters to label them.

Since taste sensations arise from a "chemical process operating through the medium of humidity," he tests the five senses. Because experiments show that without the "cooperation of smell there can be no complete degustation," he is "tempted to believe that smell and taste are in fact a single sense." Hence, "sapid bodies are necessarily odorous, and thus have a place in the empire of smell no less than in the empire of taste."[3] Imperial metaphors apply to more than single senses; his apology for gastronomy as a "new science" dependent on "the combined power of time and experience" avers that it serves nations: it "arose to nourish, restore, preserve, persuade, and console us" and, "not content with strewing flowers in the path of the individual," it "contributes in no small measure to the strength and prosperity of empires." If scientists debate

2 Ibid., 29–34 and 44.
3 Ibid., 37–41.

how diet influences "the faculty of thought" and "whether the mind [is] affected by the senses, or respond[s] itself without the cooperation of organs," the reciprocity of body and mind is clear in cuisine since a "well-ordained banquet seems like an epitome of the world, every part of which is duly represented," and, since meals are "a means of government," the "fate of nations" is often "sealed at a banquet."[4]

Brillat-Savarin's imperial imagery raises issues to which literary history has paid scant attention: it prepares the application of food history, consumerism, and synesthesia to criticism. His focus on the physiology of taste and the politics of culture, on aesthetics and imperialism, helps us to reconceive pedagogy, to consider how the liberal arts might newly embrace science, and to see that literary learning may advance activism, despite Stanley Fish's tenet that literariness must remain in academic enclaves that cannot expect to wield influence in the world.[5] One effect of Brillat-Savarin's book is that literary history, by abandoning compartmentalized practices, gains procedures that cross disciplines. Another is that cultural knowledge is dialectical: embodied in particularities, it promotes generalities since, while it must register the changing worlds of science, technology and globalism, it must accept that evolution continues in and through human cognition. Brillat-Savarin reminds us to renew aesthetic principles and, given their constant unfolding, to probe how the senses operate despite their limits. This entails rejecting simplistic notions of cultural progress and epistemic revolution as well as discarding elitist ideas of scholarly expertise that will not engage common readers. To defenders of the humanities like Martha Nussbaum and Mark Kingwell, students are citizens of the

---

4 Ibid., 49, 51, and 54–5.

5 To Stanley Fish, literature is never propositional since it remains open to questions and further interpretations; it is never "totalizing" because its impulse is "to probe ever deeper the incorrigible duplicity of assertion." Insisting on "the boundaries between the literary and the 'extra-literary'" and relying on a "strong sense of a discipline or a profession with its well-developed credentialling procedures and ways of distinguishing sharply between insiders and outsiders," Fish defends "the very special precincts of the academic world." But, if "the larger society has no interest" in literary critics, how can it be said that they do "a job the society wants done" (1995, 34, 42, 52, 64, and 20)? In criticizing new historicism and cultural studies, Fish says the "public justification of academic practices is too important a task to be left to academics" (1995, 126), surely a curious conclusion?

world for whom theories of pedagogy and reading should look beyond ethnic and national identities to universals enabling their creative imagination to grow out of material and historical embodiment. Since students aspire to bring imaginary worlds into being, literary history should recognize this desire by revising its procedures and admitting what Harold Fromm says is necessary for it to remain relevant to communities of readers: aesthetic experience is concretely experienced as an overwhelming, unifying emotion that is absolute, unambiguous, and so prepossessing that it overcomes volition and the intellect's resistance to remove us from our customary selves. It is also the motivating reason for subsequent literary analysis.[6]

---

6 "Radical changes are occurring in what democratic societies teach the young, and these changes have not been well thought through. Thirsty for national profit, nations, and their systems of education, are heedlessly discarding skills that are needed to keep democracies alive ... The humanities and the arts are being cut away, in both primary/secondary and college/university education, in virtually every nation of the world. Seen by policy-makers as useless frills, at a time when nations must cut away all useless things in order to stay competitive in the global market, they are rapidly losing their place in curricula, and also in the hearts and minds of parents and children. Indeed, what we might call the humanistic aspects of science and social science – the imaginative, creative aspect, and the aspect of rigorous critical thought – are losing ground as nations prefer to pursue short-term profit by the cultivation of the useful and highly applied skills suited to profit-making ... In the absence of a good grounding for international cooperation in the schools and universities of the world ... our human interactions are likely to be mediated by the thin norms of market exchange in which human lives are seen primarily as instruments for gain. The world's schools, colleges, and universities therefore have an important and urgent task: to cultivate in students the ability to see themselves as members of a heterogeneous nation (for all modern nations are heterogeneous) and a still more heterogeneous world, and to understand something of the history and character of the diverse groups that inhabit it" (Nussbaum 2010, 2 and 80). "Corporations and firms ... have equally usurped our private selves and our public spaces. They have created bonds of belonging far stronger than any fractured, tentative nation could now hope to offer, providing structures of identity, ways of making sense of one's place in a complex world ... The idea of citizenship is not the only way we can pursue our commonalities and needs, not the only way to entertain our longings and dreams. But it is a crucial one; and, when linked to the deep insight that we owe a duty of justice to our fellow citizens, the concept of citizenship sheds its dark origins on the project of *keeping people out* and, reversing the field, becomes a matter of *bringing people in* – not loving them or liking them or even agreeing with them, much of the time, but making room for them to be at home too" (Kingwell 2001, 2 and 22; cf. Fromm 1991, 8–9).

TRAINING THE SENSES
AND EXPLORING THE INNER REALM

Characteristics of Men, Manners, Opinions, Times (1711) by Anthony Ashley Cooper, the third Earl of Shaftesbury (1671–1713), promotes sensibility like Brillat-Savarin. A Neoplatonist defender of the liberal arts, Shaftesbury makes metaphor an instrument of humane thinking, fine breeding, and fashionable manners. A patrician elitist, he depreciated empiricism, preferring embodied learning and self-discourse as models of civility. Disgust with imperialism's bureaucracy makes him stress how politics debases sociability. In upholding the latter, he is hostile to both systematic secularism and religious dogma. So, he charges empires with impeding democratic participation: they distance magistrates from the populace, hindering political processes from being perceptible and experiential.

Vast empires are in many respects unnatural; but particularly in this, that be they ever so well constituted, the affairs of many must, in such governments, turn upon a very few, and the relation be less sensible, and in a manner lost, between the magistrate and people, in a body so unwieldy in its limbs, and whose members lie so remote from one another and distant from the head.

Since "strong factions" proliferate in empires, "associating spirits, for want of exercise, form new movements, and seek a narrower sphere of activity." The result: "wheels within wheels" and "one empire within another." Since nothing so delights men "as to incorporate," factions choose a "wrong social spirit," producing "members of separate societies." Ironically, the "associating genius of man is never better proved than in those very societies, which are formed in opposition to the general one of mankind, and to the real interest of the State." Imperial factionalism abuses "that social love and common affection which is natural to mankind" as well as sapping political order.[7]

Shaftesbury parallels imperialism and artistic vanity: while genteel men are self-correcting, vain authors demean common readers. The integration of gentility and aesthetic acuity defines true sociability:

---

7 Cooper, "*Sensus Communis*; An Essay on the Freedom of Wit and Humour in a Letter to a Friend" (1964, 1:76–7). Subsequent references employ Cooper's title, as by convention.

"gentlemen of fashion" are those to whom "a natural good genius, or the force of good education, has given a sense of what is naturally graceful and becoming." As "masters of an ear in music, an eye in painting, a fancy in the ordinary things of ornament and grace, a judgment in proportions of all kinds, and a general good taste in most of those subjects which make the amusement and delight of the ingenious people of the world," gentlemen, if they misbehave, feel their "inconsistency," knowing they "live at variance with themselves, and in contradiction to that principle on which they ground their highest pleasure and entertainment."[8] But literati avoid self-knowledge in the forms supposed to transcribe and enhance it. Memoirists are self-important; far from unifying external and inner discourse, they write histrionically, their words a "frothy distemper" that proves publication no sure route to sensibility. While they "entertain the world so lavishly," they have "no opportunity of privately conversing with themselves." They neither exercise "their own genius" nor know its strength; rushing into print, they "exhibit on the stage of the world that practice which they should have kept to themselves, if they designed that either they or the world should be the better for their moralities." This scorn for publication stems from theorizing cognitive refinement, tendance of the soul, or, in Plato's terms, the sixth sense. Shaftesbury's objection to cultural relativism reflects his view that sensibility should transmute mundane self-expression, personal confession, and narrative realism, such modes displacing aristocratic reserve. So, he derides garrulity: "Who indeed can endure to hear an empiric talk of his own constitution, how he governs and manages it, what diet agrees best with it, and what his practice is with himself?" It is "indecent" to publish "meditations, occasional reflections, solitary thoughts, or other such exercises" that pretend to "self-discoursing practice." Such writers "conceive suddenly, but without being able to go out their full time, [so] that after many miscarriages and abortions, they can bring nothing well-shapen or perfect into the world. They are not, however, the less fond of their offspring, which in a manner they beget in public. For so public-spirited they are, that they can never afford themselves the least time to think in private for their own particular benefit and use."[9]

---

8 Shaftesbury 1964, 1:89.
9 Shaftesbury, "Soliloquy or Advice to an Author" (1964, 1:108–9).

After wittily applying unfruitful birthing imagery to compulsive secular authors, he treats religious enthusiasts as cuttingly. Pseudo-ascetics, they are indecorous pedants. They "have no real converse either with themselves, or with heaven, whilst they look thus asquint upon the world, and carry titles and editions along with them in their meditations." They ignore the "rules of criticism and profane learning." A cleric will not "play the critic on himself" nor "regulate his style or language by the standard of good company, and people of the better sort." Spurning this indecorum, Shaftesbury recommends "exercise of self-converse" to all who "write after the manner of holy advisers." A "good thinker" should be "a strong self-examiner and thorough-paced dialogist." Trite secular or religious authors through the "grand artifice of villainy and lewdness, as well as of superstition and bigotry" discomfit readers, putting us at a "greater distance and formality with ourselves" by evading the "improving practice of soliloquy." But good authors have the "sovereign remedy and gymnastic method of soliloquy" that holds "when by a certain powerful figure of inward rhetoric the mind apostrophises its own fancies, raises them in their proper shapes and personages, and addresses them familiarly, without the least ceremony or respect." Self-searching is the end of "liberal education"; it leads to "the perfection of grace and comeliness in action and behaviour." Truly literate authors will have "formed their motions under the best masters" at an early age.[10]

Shaftesbury did not appeal to readers by equating political and cultural imperialism. Rather he inverted their relation, seeing artistic gain arising from Rome's political regress and holding that its imperialism led to self-inflicted barbarity. Not blaming gothic invaders, he thinks internal tyrants rendered civility fragile and parallels literary with political schisms. Thus, he advances pan-European sensibility by complicating the history of imperialism and humanist aesthetics. He asserts that the "rise of arts and fall of liberty" coincided in Rome:

No sooner had that nation begun to lose the roughness and barbarity of their manners, and learn of Greece to form their heroes, their orators and poets on a right model, than by their unjust attempt upon the liberty of the world they justly lost their own. With their liberty they lost not only their force of eloquence, but even their style and language itself.

10 Shaftesbury 1964, 1:110, 112, 115, 123, and 125.

Imperialism, a "fatal form of government," made the world "slavish and dependent," Rome's hope lying in the "merciless hands of the barbarians, and a total dissolution of that enormous empire and despotic power, which the best hands could not preserve from being destructive to human nature." The "genuine tyrants who succeeded to this specious machine of arbitrary and universal power" ignored creativity; "barbarity and Gothicism were already entered into arts ere the savages had made any impression on the empire." Illiteracy grew with Rome's "persuasive arts," the "rise of true and philosophical critics" turning the public against "false wit or jingling eloquence." Sound critics were lauded but poor ones debased the "provinces" of learning. Schisms hurt scholarship: "Etymologists, philologists, grammarians, rhetoricians, and others of considerable note and eminent in their degree" flourished, "revealing the hidden beauties which lay in the works of just performers" and "exposing the weak sides, false ornaments, and affected graces of mere pretenders."[11]

Shaftesbury stresses aesthetic training, Rome's fall sharpening his sense of the lack of "right taste in life and manners." If "civility and humanity be a taste; if brutality, insolence, riot, be in the same manner a taste, who, if he could reflect, would not choose to form himself on the amiable and agreeable rather than the odious and perverse model?" If "a natural good taste be not ready formed in us, why should not we endeavour to form it, and cultivate it till it become natural?" Such training calls for principled self-discourse and a "right sort" of reading that mediates "correction of humour and formation of a taste" since the fine manners of companions may be undone by authors "of another kind" to whom "we shall find our palate strangely turned." He whose studies are "ill chosen" is culpable; he is not "well-read" who consumes too many authors; he must "of necessity have more ill models than good, and be more stuffed with bombast, ill fancy, and wry thought than filled with solid sense and just imagination."[12] This gustatory view of barbarism in the British empire damns exotic literature. People are not "scrupulous" about reading; youths take whatever is at hand. "What was first put into our hand when we were young, serves us afterwards for serious study and wise research when we are old." This "exercise of youth" deters

---

11 Ibid., 1:143–5 and 1:156–7.
12 Ibid., 1:218 and 220–1.

taste; it is "so solemn and profound, that we dare not so much as thoroughly examine the subject on which we are bid to meditate." Its "diet" fills "our grave humour," quelling "the appetite towards further research and solid contemplation." New topics are seen as "holiday, diversion, play, and fancy" so that we think "it an injury to our diversions to have regard to truth or nature, without which, however, nothing can be truly agreeable or entertaining much less instructive or improving." We surfeit on "a wrong kind of serious reading" – the ridiculous and exotic. The "more remote" its "pattern" is "from anything moral or profitable, the more freedom and satisfaction we find in it."

We care not how Gothic or barbarous our models are, what ill-designed or monstrous figures we view, or what false proportions we trace or see described in history, romance, or fiction. And thus our eye and ear is lost. Our relish or taste must of necessity grow barbarous, whilst barbarian customs, savage manners, Indian wars, and wonders of the terra incognita, employ our leisure hours and are the chief materials to furnish out a library.

Bodily images apply to the erosion of taste by popular reading. He is angry that gentlemen's reading makes them "philosophise after a newer manner than any known." Curious about foreign cultures, they are "more credulous, though after another manner, than the mere vulgar." To his disgust, they accept as "authentic" and "canonical" tales of "Incas or Iroquois, written by friars and missionaries, pirates and renegades, sea-captains and trusty travellers." Infidels to Christianity, they "dwell with the highest contentment on the prodigies of Moorish and Pagan countries. They have far more pleasure in hearing the monstrous accounts of monstrous men and manners than the politest and best narrations of the affairs, the governments, and lives of the wisest and most polished people."

Championing the Grand Tour, Shaftesbury would detach gentlemen from exotic, escapist travelogues that impede the training of aristocratic sensibility. While denigrating the Roman empire, he defends its classical texts against adventure stories that present non-European cultures. To him, corrupt modern taste prefers a "Turkish history to a Grecian or a Roman, an Ariosto to a Virgil, and a romance or novel to an Iliad." Readers with such tastes do not question the genius of modish authors, the validity of their observations, or "the texture" of their lies. They are so "enchanted" by "the travelling memoirs of any casual adventurer" they lose themselves in his affairs.

No sooner has he taken shipping at the mouth of the Thames, or sent his baggage before him to Gravesend or Buoy in the Nore, than straight our attention is earnestly taken up. If in order to his more distant travels, he takes some part of Europe in his way, we can with patience hear of inns and ordinaries, passage-boats and ferries, foul and fair weather, with all the particulars of the author's diet, habit of body, his personal dangers and mischances on land and sea. And thus, full of desire and hope, we accompany him till he enters on his great scene of action, and begins by the description of some enormous fish or beast. From monstrous brutes he proceeds to yet more monstrous men. For in this race of authors he is ever the completest and of the first rank who is able to speak of things the most unnatural and monstrous.

Such narratives stunting self-discourse, they should be met by "that simplicity of manners and innocence of behaviour which has been often known among mere savages, ere they were corrupted by our commerce, and, by sad example, instructed in all kinds of treachery and inhumanity." True sensibility honours the myth of the noble savage, now perverted by modernism. Philosophers should probe "this strange corruption in ourselves" that parts us from "nature" and "that just purity of manners which might be expected, especially from a people so assisted and enlightened by religion." But this probing is unlikely, for "modern moralists" are so far "from condemning any unnatural vices or corrupt manners, whether in our own or foreign climates, that they would have vice itself appear as natural as virtue."[13] So he lessons authors: since harmony, symmetry, and proportion are naturally grounded, they must accept that they are copyists after nature and that principles that apply to life and manners apply to writing. The standards of virtue being universal, the principles "discoverable in the characters and affections of mankind" and best "human practice and comprehension" constitute "the just foundations of an art and science." Authors must grant this conceptual analogy since "things are stubborn and will not be as we fancy them, or as the fashion varies." No doubt their style will conform to their period and nation but, if their works do not embody natural ideals, they will be judged incorrect when critically examined.

---

13 Ibid., 1:221–3 and 227.

For nature will not be mocked. The prepossession against her can never be very lasting. Her decrees and instinct are powerful and her sentiments inbred. She has a strong party abroad, and as strong a one within ourselves; and when any slight is put upon her, she can soon turn the reproach and make large reprisals on the taste and judgment of her antagonists.

Writers who grant "this prerogative" train their taste "by the just standard of nature." They search their minds since "custom and fashion are powerful seducers"; if they detect no resistance, they are "very little different from the vulgar." Then they must follow "the wholesome practice" of readying their strongest faculties and "best forces" of wit and judgment to descend into "the territories of the heart" and to "decline no combat, nor hearken to any terms" until they have "pierced into its inmost provinces and reached the seat of empire." They will form no treaties with themselves until "this necessary campaign" has led them to all "inward conflicts" by which they will gain "some tolerable insight" into themselves and their "own natural principles." This call for self-exploration in military and imperial metaphors rejects "sacred writ" as a model. Biblical heroism is irrelevant to sensibility, as are divines who are not "commissioned for all instruction and advice relating to manners or conversation." Self-knowledge and revelation are distinct provinces with settled boundaries.[14]

Richard Hurd (1729–1808), renowned churchman and literary historian, defied Shaftesbury's scorn for empiricism and the clergy's educative role. This scorn is clear when Shaftesbury praises the addressee of *Sensus Communis* for not being corrupted by education. In defence of literary humanism, he urges that a gentleman in his "diversions" may learn from a good poet or historian what will give him "a truer relish of their sense ... better than a pedant with all his labours and the assistance of his volumes of commentators." He recalls classical times when youths lived with philosophers in schools where they were inured to discipline, exercised in the severest courses of temperance and self-denial, and trained in embodied precepts to "maintain their country's honour in war, rule wisely in the State, and fight against luxury and corruption in times of prosperity and peace." Some of "these arts"

14 Ibid., 1:228–32.

may be "comprehended in university learning," but "as some universities in the world are now modelled, they seem not so very effectual to these purposes, nor so fortunate in preparing for a right practice of the world, or a just knowledge of men and things."[15]

ORTHODOXY AND INSULARITY OPPOSING SENSIBILITY

After the Seven Years War (1756–1763) when travel to Europe boomed, Hurd published *Dialogues on the Uses of Foreign Travel* (1764) featuring Shaftesbury and John Locke (1632–1704) in dispute with one another. Secretary to the first Earl of Shaftesbury, who urged Charles II to found the Board of Trade to promote colonization, and adviser to the second earl, Locke supervised the third earl's education, aiding him after 1689 in managing the family estates.[16] Hurd knew of Locke's ties to Shaftesbury. Locke spent three years in France between 1675 and 1679 – a year in Paris as tutor to Caleb Banks to whom he showed the sights, and fifteen months in Montpellier, where he studied agriculture, viticulture, and Roman antiquities. On this visit, Locke noted the weakness of provincial governors, the desuetude of the Estates, the draining of money from regions by corrupt aristocrats, and disparities in the tax system. He worshipped with Protestants whose temples were destroyed before the Edict of Nantes was revoked in 1685.[17]

At age sixteen, Shaftesbury began his Grand Tour, stopping to see Locke in Holland for some months, then spending time in Paris before going to Italy, where he studied art and architecture. He returned there to die. Sickness stopped him following his grandfather into the House of Lords and turned him to philosophy. Friends with Locke up until the latter's death, Shaftesbury, besides opposing his mentor's empiricism, contract theory, and egoism, honoured the stoics and synthesized ethics and aesthetics, as we have seen.

---

15 Ibid., 1:81–82.
16 The full title is *Dialogues on the Uses of Foreign Travel; Considered as a Part of an English Gentleman's Education: Between Lord Shaftesbury and Mr. Locke*. My points on Shaftesbury's philosophy are indebted to John McAteer, "The Third Earl of Shaftesbury (1671–1713)," *Internet Encyclopedia of Philosophy*. www.iep.utm.edu/shaftes/ (accessed 5 December 2013).
17 See Lough's introduction to Locke (1953, xxxiii, xxxvi, and xxxix).

Shaftesbury's didactic stance is defied by Hurd's Locke. The earl holds that "Foreign Travel is, of all others, the most important and essential part of Education." He scorns British insularity; the island's youth embody "rustic and licentious habits." Lacking "civility," they merit charges of "inhospitality," so "the benefits of *foreign travel* ... cannot be obtained too soon." Their education forms "low Habits and sordid practices," the "Saxon or Norman character" turning them to hunting, horse-racing, and diversions that bind their conversation to "the stable or kennel" and that "plunge" them "into the brutalities of the Bottle and Table" where they "disable themselves" with beef and liquor, "sottish debauch" trapping them in "low intrigues and vulgar amours."[18]

Since education should "form the Understanding, and regulate the Heart," Hurd's Locke spurns the notion of "*Citizen of the world*," favouring that of "a worthy citizen of England" and giving "this small Island ... the pompous appellation of the world" since it is that "in which our adventurer is to play his part." Hurd constrains Britain's sphere of influence to spite its imperial aspirations. Moreover, while Locke concedes his nation's bad manners, he denies that "ill qualities" will "drop off" in travel. A boy's development should be "slow and gradual." Unless he gains a sense of human nature before touring, his "enterprize" will be "untimely"; "knowledge of the world" is less "a knowledge of [its] external modes and customs" than "of a higher kind; such as respects the creature *Man*, considered in his essential parts, his *Reason* and his *Passions*." Before travelling, a youth must be able "to penetrate" men's "interior frame" and "inspect their proper dispositions and characters." He must have "a well-informed and well-disciplined understanding." Deriding the "fashionable mode of Education," Locke urges that a youth should first study himself and "the great and good men of his own country." While "weak and fantastic people" claim to know the world, no text "composed by any capable man ... instructs us in the proper way of getting into this great secret." Far from pushing a youth into the world, one should "keep him out of that world, as long as you can." Then only "the ablest friend or tutor" should lead him "gradually, cautiously, imperceptibly into an acquaintance" with it by training him in "moral Duty." Otherwise, on entering the world he will meet vice

---

18 Hurd 1764, 35–6 and 41–2. Hurd's sense of grace is completely ascetic and anti-bodily and he totally ignores Shaftesbury's internal discipline of self-discourse (1764, 109, 112, and 115).

"assured, prosperous, and triumphant in the first croud he encounters"; he will be duped by a "better dressed, better manner'd ... plausible society" whose "negligent sarcasms ... follies of wit, and polite raillery" will defy all he holds sacred. Those who seem decorous are "deformed by every impotent and selfish passion; wasted in sloth and luxury; in ruinous play; criminal intrigues; or, at best, unprofitable amusements." Unless youth are tutored, exposure to the world will lead to misanthropy and "sceptical and prophane impiety." Since Locke's disciples, John Toland (1670–1722) and Anthony Collins (1676–1729), turned him into a prophet of deism, his image as defender of orthodoxy shows that Hurd would keep youth "at a distance from the world" and have tutors stress "the certain inevitable misery of conforming to it."[19]

Demeaning Shaftesbury's humanism in Locke's denial of his pupil's philosophy, Hurd rests more on truisms than insights in his insular pedagogy. If the "civility, that prevails on the Continent, may be more studied and exquisite than our's," it is "not therefore to be preferred" since those "refinements" are to be explained by "correspondent policies."

In the more absolute monarchies of *Europe*, all are Courtiers. In our freer monarchy all should be Citizens. Let then the arts of address and insinuation flourish in *France*. Without them, what merit can pretend to success, what talents, open the way to favour and distinction. But let a manlier character prevail here. We have a Prince to serve, not to flatter: We have a country to embrace, not a court to adore: We have, in a word, objects to pursue, and interests to promote, from the cares of which our finer neighbours are happily disburthen'd.

Granting continental views of Englishmen's "roughness," Hurd offsets their defects "by their useful sense, their superior knowledge, their public spirit, and, above all, by their unpolished integrity." Seeing a "reasonable sense" of "Politeness" as "the duty of humanity," Locke elevates it above "no culture of the human mind, no instruction in Letters and Business, no discipline of the passions, no improvement of the head and heart." Denying Shaftesbury's view of the servility bred by university education, Locke thinks clerical tutors are better equipped than classically minded philosophers to direct the education of

---

19 Ibid., 73–4, 100, 122–3, 128–35 and 139–40.

upper-class youth likely to undertake the Grand Tour. Thus, Hurd's depiction of Shaftesbury and Locke reveals an insular nationalism and conservative orthodoxy that resist imperial aspirations in as much as these are symbolized by the Grand Tour.[20]

Locke was a fit vehicle for Hurd's insularity, the empiricist despising the market forces that drove fashionable consumption of French viticultural and culinary modes, as we shall see. The issue here concerns how Locke's resistance to French culture narrowed English aesthetic sense. His French travels show him to have been a severe critic. At Poix, a village between Abbeville and Amiens, supper heightened his discomfort at its inn. Noting the loquaciousness by which men in the stocks outside minimized their pain, he finds similarities indoors; the hollow rhetoric of the meal offers no consolation for the "ill meat & worse cookery." His companions and he do not fill their bellies since the "Soup & ragoo & such other words of good savour lost here their relish quite, & out of 5 or 6 dishes were served up to us, we patched up a very untoward supper." The meal is mean, if in French terms "the most material part" is that it is "fashionable." Its form – first and second courses plus dessert – is a "ceremony" if the "whole bill of fare [was] noe thing but some cabbage & a frog that was caught in it, & some haws of the last season." The "formalitys" lend Locke's remarks irony: of the haws, he says "so fine a sweetmeat" is "disguised under the fine name of Pomet de Paradise."[21]

His contempt for French dining formality makes it unsurprising that he transcribed recipes into his travel journals. He understood nutrition and, being familiar with kitchen practices, culinary processes, and cookbook writing, knew how to provide traditional English dishes for his companions and himself. On 27 July 1676 when at Celleneuve, he wrote out the following:

To make herb potage, cut the herbs and put them in a pipkin and there boyl them in sufficient quantity butter, and then after put water to them and so boyl them yet longer, and when it is enough, beat some egg in verjuice and

---

20 Ibid., 159–61. Note Hume's praise of French culture and rejection of the analogy of absolutism and cultural backwardness in "of Civil Liberty" (Hume 1953, 103–4).

21 Draft of a letter written at Montpellier and dated 1 March 1675/6 (Locke 1953, 279).

mix with it, and you will have good soup. If you boyl hearbs in water first and after add butter, soup not so good.

In April the following year when at Bordeaux, he records three traditional English recipes: one for a pudding, one for a fricassee, and one for a soup:

Take 2 eggs, the raw livers of any poultry or, for want of that, some liver of veal or mutton, mince the livers very small with some good suet or, for want of suet, with the fat of bacon, mixing crumbs of bread with it. Make up this with the eggs beaten into a past & in the flap of a breast of mutton or the belly of a boild hen it makes a very good puding.
Cut chickens in peices, par boile them in as little water as may be with onion or chalot. In the same liquor frie them in a friing pan. A litle nutmeg with some time & other sweet herbs cut small & mixd adde a relish. An egge or 2 beaten with this liquor it is fried in compleates the sauce & makes a good fricacy.
Take Spinage q. v., boile it in water s. q. When it hath boiled a while, put to it a good peice of butter. When it is sufficiently boild, take the yolkes of 2 or 3 eggs, beat them well with a little vinegar, & when they are well beaten, take a litle of the liquor where in the spinage is boild & mix with the egs, continually stiring them that they curdle not, & when you have thus mixed a pretty good quantity of the liquor with the eggs, then pour the egs into the bullion, & soe pour the bouilon, eggs & all, forwards & backward in two vessells till they are well mixd & then put all into a dish where slices of bread are, & this is noe ill soope. This may be donne with other hearbs, as lettuce, purslane & divers others which, put togeather before the water be put to them, they will eat tenderer & better.

His most complicated recipe, one for crepes, was transcribed at Lyons on 10 November 1678. A salient point in the recipe is his familiarity with culinary manuscript circulation:

Take fine wheat flower 1/4 lb., water q.s. to make a liquid batter, the whites of 4 egs, sugar & rose water or any thing else to season it q.s. Take butter q.s., melt it in a skillet & be soe hot that it smoakes, & into this butter over the fire let some of this batter, about 2 or 3 spoonfulls, run out of a tunnell with 3 holes or litle pipes set at a distance one from an other, whose hollow is almost as big as that of a small goose quill. The tunnell must be let in to the end of a stick soe that when the batter is in & let run into the butter, it may be shaked up & downe soe that the streames of butter, falling crosse one an other, may make a kind of lace or net. When it is a litle boild in the butter, with an iron hooke turne it & soe let it boile on the other side, & then draw it out on a rolling pin & it will be something like a wafer, but it is presently boiled & has a very pleasant tast. My Lady Chichley has one of the tunnells to make them.[22]

Locke's journals show he extended his culinary habits in order to survive in the villages and cities of France; he not only transported his Englishness but also shunned experimental cuisine evident in French-inspired cookbooks of the 1670s. We return to culinary politics in later chapters. The topic to continue exploring here is the relation between aesthetics and empire.

THE EMPIRE OF SENSATION AND AESTHETIC ANTI-THEORY

Jean-Baptiste Dubos (1670–1742), a contemporary of Shaftesbury, embodied a sensibility open to cross-cultural exchanges between England and France. Like Shaftesbury, he defended idealist norms against state elitism and, as a humanist, he gave a classical turn to art on behalf of civility: since nobility is his norm, only grand actions may inspire citizen readers.[23] Luc Ferry calls Dubos the best eighteenth-century aesthetic theorist since his classicism affirms the "incontestable primacy of emotion over intelligence." To Ferry, *Critical Reflections on Poetry, Painting and Music* "present themselves as a theory of the effects of art on the human heart"; they reject "the domain of law or rules and find themselves placed within the sphere of fact, of psychology and anthropology." Dubos values embodied knowledge more than cerebration; he thought philosophers more self-deceived about aesthetic experience than citizens. His outlook is limited; as Ferry notes, he "does not envision, as Kant will, the possibility of a critique of dogmatic rationalism which does not prohibit all references to indeterminate criteria." But,

---

22 Locke 1953, 107, 141, 246–7. I have removed italics from citations in Lough's edition of Locke's manuscript and corrected misspellings that would otherwise be confusing.
23 Bate 1961, 3 and 9.

in coming to aesthetics through cuisine, he makes theorizing about taste far from "tiresome for the writer and disgusting for the reader."[24]

Initially he expounds taste in reflections on imperial eminence; since political dissimulation exploits false embodiment, he privileges psychological ideas of empire. Politicians are histrionic; they move the public by acting as if moved themselves. Emperors are deceitful, not sensitive: "of all the talents proper for raising man to a state of *empire* and command, a superiority of wit and knowledge is not the most effectual." An emperor moves men as he pleases; his art is "acquired principally" by "seeming to be moved, and penetrated with those very sentiments he intends to inspire." He is "a complete actor." Oliver Cromwell (1599–1658) won a reputation for virtues he lacked by speaking "in so pathetic a manner, as to bring" enemies "over to his party." Europe saw "him convert to his benefit an event, which, it was thought, would have terminated in his ruin": it complimented him on "this success, with several virtues which he was a real stranger to; and, by this means, his reputation was established." Since reason cannot inhibit such dissimulation, Dubos spurns Plato's view that yielding to the "passions, even those artificial ones produced by poetry, weakens the spiritual *empire* of the soul, and disposes us to let ourselves be swayed by the irregular motions of our appetites." Plato confuses "order in the actions of man" by holding that conduct should be "directed by the understanding, and not governed by the appetites of the sensitive soul."[25]

Keen to explore aesthetics, Dubos relates pictorial rhetoric to the empire of the sensitive soul. Painting is paradoxical: powerful and delicate, its style, not content, addresses the sight and the soul. Pleasing effortlessly, the painter may not grasp how he represents things. If a good designer and fine colourist, he makes us take two-dimensional paint for real fruit: painting "has so great an *empire* over our soul, that a picture may be rendered agreeable by the very charms of the execution, independent of the objects which it represents." Facing the "art of the imitator," we admire his counterfeiting yet wonder how it works on us. He who colours skilfully may be a "great artist" even if he does not "know how to make use of his talents in the representation of

---

24 Ferry 1993, 42–4.
25 Dubos 1748, 1:33–4 and 37.

affecting objects, or to give his pictures that spirit and resemblance to life" so clear in Raphael (1483–1520) and Poussin (1594–1665).[26]

It is a necessary paradox that artistic creations exert negative and positive cognitive effects. Poetry rouses pleasure in the moment of reading that blanks out memory of former readings and critical rules. It absorbs by erasing psychological awareness and social recall. The attentiveness required by reading is all-demanding. Whereas critical analysis needs rereading with intellectual effort, the actual reading process is *sui generis* even if readers are aware of textual faults:

Actual pleasure, which has so great an *empire* over man, as to make him forget past misfortunes, and render him blind to future calamities, may cancel the memory of the most shocking blunders of a poem, when they are once out of sight. With respect to those relative faults which are discovered only by going back and reflecting upon what we have seen, they cause but a very small abatement in the pleasure of the reader or the spectator, even when he reads or sees the piece, after having been previously instructed of its defects.

Suspension of the critical faculty also occurs in the theatre; a tragedian may offer "a coarse preparation" of plot that will yet prove moving if well managed since the mind forgets the known outcome "in order to have a more perfect enjoyment of the pleasure" from the enactment. With memory suspended "at the spectacle," we have "no desire of coming at the knowledge of the events before they are made public. We avoid anticipating our intelligence; and, as what we have seen at other representations escapes our memories, so we may likewise forget what a poet's indiscretion has made him prematurely reveal." Desire for pleasure makes the mind "stifle the voice of reason." The most engaging poems bewitch us by concealing their faults, and we willingly forget the faults that have been pointed out. A charming poem is therefore more moving than a rule-bound piece.[27]

Dubos admits the distinct roles of eye and ear given the semiotic mediation of the sister arts. Painting affects the sight through natural signs but poetry exploits artificial conventions of speech communities.

---

26 Ibid., 1:58.
27 Ibid., 1:241–2. In *The Preface to Shakespeare*, Johnson sets aside neoclassical unities since audiences know where they are and join in the creation of illusion (1824, 2:85, 95, and 97).

Painting's effects are stronger because the "sight has a much greater *empire* over the soul than any of the other senses": the soul's experiential instinct has "the greatest confidence" in sight, for "metaphorically speaking ... the eye is nearer the soul than the ear." Painters, unlike poets, do not use institutional signs. Their "natural signs" do "not depend on education"; their force comes "from the relation which nature herself has fixed between our organs and the external objects" for our preservation. Exhibiting "nature herself," painting deludes our senses but not our minds. Yet, if painting has "a greater *empire* over us than poetry," we are more moved by poets than by painters.[28] This paradox rests on the cognitive appeal of oral and print culture: eye-reading of texts is less sensitive than auditory response to acoustic delivery. Recitation enhances the harmony of verse and flatters the ear by increasing the pleasure subjects yield, while solitary reading is "in some measure a pain," for the eye reads without "any agreeable sensation" unlike its "application" to "objects exhibited by pictures." A community's linguistic history stops eye-reading from being immediately pleasurable. The exercise of solitary reading involves complex mental translations:

As words are arbitrary signs of our ideas, so the different characters of which writing is composed, are arbitrary signs of the sounds whereof the words are composed. 'Tis therefore necessary, when we read verse, that the characters should immediately excite the idea of those sounds, of which they are arbitrary signs; and 'tis necessary likewise that the sounds of words, which are also no more than arbitrary signs, should excite the ideas affixed to these words. With whatever expedition and facility these operations are performed, they cannot be gone through so readily.

Recitation when "the word we hear raises immediately the idea connected with it" enriches reading by acoustic mediation. A beautifully printed book with "characters" that are "extremely regular and black, and are ranged in an elegant proportion on a clear white paper, affords a very pleasing sensation to the eye." But "the taste a person has for the art of printing, is a distinct thing, that has nothing in common with the emotion caused by reading a poem." For when we attend to the poetic

---

[28] Burke reverses Dubos's view of the superiority of painting over poetry (Burke 1968, 60).

subject, "the beauty of the impression" is lost because of the "ease" which it gives "the eye in distinguishing the characters and assembling the words." This visual experience, no intrinsic pleasure, so reduces feeling for the "harmony of the verse" that by instinct we "pronounce aloud those verses which we read only for ourselves, when we think they should be numerous and harmonious." This "unpremeditated operation" of the mind is understood "only by reflection."

To Dubos, the sister arts, whether they privilege seeing or hearing, displace the faculty of evaluation. If recitation saves auditors from "the trouble of reading," it lets them sense "cadence and harmony." More indulgent than readers, auditors are more flattered by acoustic mediation than by print. Of course, recitation suspends judgment only until readers analyze in private the verses heard in public. Experience confirms that "the eye is a much severer critic, a much subtler examiner of a poem than the ear" since it is less "seduced by pleasure." While works please differently enjoyed in public or in private and while the more a work engages a given sense, the "less we are capable of detecting and computing its faults," Dubos complicates the visual and oral divide by analyzing how we re-experience a painting or stage play. In these cases, suspended judgment is more deliberate because viewers and audiences heighten pleasure by depreciating novelty and relishing familiarity. "The pleasure we receive from pictures and excellent dramatic poems is greater even upon our seeing them a second time" when there is "no further danger of being deluded." First-time experience is dazzling, even confusing, making the mind "too restless and volatile to fix itself upon one particular thing." It takes in little. But, when next we see "an excellent tragedy, or a beautiful picture," the mind fixes itself on "parts of the object" of which it already has "a cursory view."[29]

Besides detailing body–mind interactions to guide criticism, Dubos treats biological changes that affect perceptual capacity along with cultural modes that limit national manners: our senses alter over time; members of a nation have distinct perceptual and cultural habits; and acculturation grounds aesthetics. Consequently, he proscribes efforts to transform tastes. Since men "have not an equal delicacy in the same sense," some with "the sense of seeing better in proportion than the other sensitive faculties," critics should not aim to amend sentiments

29 Dubos 1748, 1:321–32, 330, and 332–5.

because they cannot change human organs. Thus, he recommends "the best way is for everyone to continue in their own opinion, without censuring that of others." For aesthetic sense is as bodily and contingent as cerebral and universal: a person is no more responsible for his tastes than a "man whose palate is so formed, as to receive a greater pleasure from Champagne than Spanish wine." Preference in painting "depends no more on our reason, than the passion we have for one kind of poetry in preference to another." Taste rests on the "organization, present inclinations, and the situation of our minds." It is changed not by argument but by "some physical alteration in our bodies," such as aging. But this change we cannot detect unless "by the help of reflection" since "it is made gradually and imperceptibly."[30]

Like Shaftesbury holding that professional critics degrade sense experience, Dubos urges that the brain's complex anatomy be explored so that we might understand the physiology of taste:

The organs of the brain, or the parts of the human body, which, physically speaking, decide the spirit and inclinations of men, are without comparison more compounded and more delicate, than the bones and other parts which determine their stature and force: They are more compounded than those which decide the sound of the voice and the agility of the body. Wherefore two men who happen to have their blood of a quality different enough to occasion an external dissimilitude, will be much more unlike one another in mind; and will have a greater difference of inclinations than of shape and complexion.

Since biology and social practices modify our organs and aesthetic sense, Dubos trusts in the humanist tradition, claiming that we discover a sixth sense when, after being moved by works of art, our familiarity with them deepens our sensibility beyond the reach of logical analysis. Yet, he ponders if we can be assured that this sixth sense is universal, for nations differ more in mental inclination than in physiology. How can ecology apply to aesthetics if the "conformation of the organs and the temperament of body give an inclination to particular virtues and vices" in "the generality of every nation" with their diverse luxuries? "According to the different taste of countries, people are ruined by sumptuous

30 Ibid., 1:394–6.

buildings, or magnificent equipages, or by keeping nice and delicate tables, or in fine by downright excess of eating and drinking." So do different mental habits in nations mean their citizens are "of the same species?" Do peasants from North Holland and Andalusia "think in the same manner" and have "the same passions? ... Are they actuated alike by those passions they feel in common? Are they willing to be governed in the same manner?" Surely, while their external differences are great, their mental habits differ more widely.

Dubos approaches issues of human evolution and cultural difference through analogies to viticulture, climate, and environment. Transplanted vines afford a recurrent metaphor. The "vine transplanted from Champagne to Brie, produces very soon a wine, which has none of the qualities of the liquor it afforded in its primitive soil." As "qualities of the earth decide the particular taste of fruits in different countries, so they determine the nature of the air." Hence, "the different taste of wines, which grow in neighbouring provinces."[31] Viticulture lets us probe the influence of the material world on our physiology: environmental changes create "a vast number of vicissitudes and alterations" that apply to nations and vines. Manners of people "of two different ages" have altered along with changed "qualities of the French air." As "the quality of our air varies in some respects, and continues unvaried in others, it ensues that the French in all ages will have a general character which will distinguish them from other nations; tho' this will not prevent a difference between the French of different ages. 'Tis thus that wines have a particular taste in each soil, which they always preserve, tho' they are not always of equal goodness."[32]

Ecological imagery helps emphasize the redundancy of critical rules. If "the chief end of poetry and painting is to move us, the productions of these arts can be valuable only in proportion as they touch and engage us." So an "exquisitely moving" work is excellent but one that "does not move and engage us, is good for nothing," even if not "obnoxious to criticism for trespassing against rules." While one work may be bad "without any violation of rules," another that ignores rules "may be an excellent performance." Hence, Dubos reiterates that we know art through our senses:

31 Ibid., 2:189–90, 192, and 199.
32 Ibid., 2:219 and 224–5.

Now our senses inform us whether a work touches or makes a proper impression upon us, much better than all the dissertations composed by critics, to explain its merit, and calculate its perfections and defects. The way of discussion and analysis, which those gentlemen employ, is indeed very proper, when the point is to find out the causes why a work pleases or not; but this method is inferior to that of the sense, when we are to decide the following question: Does the work please, or does it not? Is the piece good or bad in general? For these are both the same thing. Reason therefore ought not to intervene in a judgement which we pass on a poem or picture in general, except it be to account for the decision of our senses and to explain what faults hinder it from pleasing, and what charms are capable of rendering it engaging. Reason will not permit us (if I may say so) to reason on a question of this nature, unless it be designed to justify the judgement which the sense has passed. The decision of the question does not belong to the jurisdiction of reason: This ought to submit to the judgement pronounced by sense, which is the competent judge of the question.

A culinary analogy upholds these strictures and heralds the sixth sense: on deciding "whether a ragoo be good or bad," we do not consult reason. We do not define "the qualities of each ingredient that enters into the composition of those messes" before saying whether the stew is good or bad. For we "have a sense given us by nature to distinguish whether the cook acted according to the rules of his art." We "taste the ragoo, and tho' unacquainted with those rules" can tell "whether it be good or no. The same may be said in some respect of the productions of the mind, and of pictures made to please and move us." Alluding to Plato, Cicero, and Quintilian, Dubos expands sensuous capacity beyond tongue, skin, eye, ear, and nose. The "sixth sense" tastes the creative works of painters, poets, and musicians. While the eye judges a painter's colouring and the ear the moving accents of a recitative, the sixth sense is "a portion of ourselves, which judges from what it feels, and which, to express myself in Plato's words, determines, without consulting either rule or compass." It is "called sense or sensitive perception." Its seat is the heart. "Our heart is made and organized" to feel and judge; its operation precedes reasoning, just as "the action of the eye and ear precedes it in their sensations." We weep at a tragedy before noting whether its plot is moving or well imitated since our "sense tells us its nature" before inquiring into it. We as readily know whether a poet has chosen a moving object or a painter a beautiful figure. Painters admit "they have a sudden sense which goes before all examen, and that an excellent picture which they never saw before, makes so quick an impression upon them, as enables them, before any discussion, to judge in general of its merit." To Dubos, anybody with understanding can appreciate everything, for "by understanding we mean a justness and delicacy of sense." When we decide on "the merit of a work that was made to move us, 'tis not the rules that are our watch, 'tis the impression we receive from the work. Our watch goes right, in proportion as our sense is delicate." So, logicians are not the best at "knowing when a man speaks good sense, and reasons justly." Dubos again deflates critical discourse since analysis is irrelevant to aesthetic excellence; in conforming to rules, poets and painters aim to please. "One may say indeed, that a work, in which the essential rules are violated, cannot be pleasing. But this is better known, by judging from the impression made by that work, than by forming a judgement of it from the dissertations of critics, who very seldom agree with respect to the importance of each rule." Here Dubos follows Cicero: "*All men are capable of judging by the help of an inward sense, tho' unacquainted with rules, whether the productions of arts are good or bad, and whether the reasons they bear, be conclusive.*" He also cites Quintilian: "'tis not by reasoning we judge of works made to move and please. We judge by an inward motion, which we know not how to explain."[33]

Dubos believes artists betray the sixth sense when rules justify their works and decry those of others. Detractors of new works repeat the prejudices of self-justifying artists. Lacking "an essential interest" in "the right side of the question," the public may "be imposed upon" by assuming that artists are authorities. But "most painters and poets do not judge by their senses, nor by paying a deference to their natural taste improved by comparisons and experience; but by way of analysis. They do not judge like men endowed with the sixth sense ... but as speculative philosophers." Vanity leads the public to "espouse the opinion of artists" and to prefer it "to that of men of taste and sense." Critics who defer to artists' technical terms do so "to gain the admiration and attention of others in repeating them." They let professional artists stifle their natural sentiments.[34] The sixth sense is vital to Dubos's defence of the appeal of the arts against those who ignore the empire of aesthetic

33 Ibid., 2:237–41 and 243.
34 Ibid., 2:277–8.

cognition. Realizing how little we know about the operation of creative and responsive minds, he will not offer a single criterion of aesthetic sense. Rather his scientific impulse approaches taste in the face of our ignorance about cognitive processes. For him, taste operates in the realm of ineffable subjectivity. His experiential analogies put physiological and cognitive experience on a continuum. What struck English readers is his relative freedom from national prejudices apparent when he contrasts French and Italian taste. To him, Italians' "inward sense" is more "lively" than that of the French, who do not cultivate "the common sensibility of man for painting," since they lack the "comparative taste" available to Italians at Rome. This taste, "formed within us, even without thinking of it," allows viewers "to judge of a present by an absent picture." Such is the lot of those bred in the centre of painterly production: Rome, not Paris. Again, he reverts to analogies of oral and auditory experience to explain how comparative taste develops: "We cannot give our opinion of the goodness of a liquor 'till after we have tasted it, nor of the excellence of a tune, 'till we have heard it." The task of the sixth sense is "to know whether the object presented to us, be moving and capable of engaging us; as it belongs to the ear to judge whether the sounds are pleasing, and to the palate, whether the taste is agreeable." As no discourse persuades one without Latin to appreciate Horace's odes, so no description of a wine "which we had never tasted, would be able to give us a right notion of the taste of that liquor." If linguistic or gustatory experiences never provide absolute judgments of taste, they remain necessary. Those who know no Latin cannot rank a poet who uses it but should heed those who know Latin rather than critics not moved by his poems. Here a drinking analogy applies: we scorn a sophist who says those who find pleasure in wine have a "depraved taste" and builds his case on "the example of five or six abstemious persons" who hate liquor. By this analogy, those who read "the ancients, without relishing them, are in as small a number with respect to their admirers, as men who have a natural aversion to wine are in comparison to such as love it."[35]

An admirer of the classics, Dubos is deferential in his cultural comparisons, as in his respect for Addison when he stops himself comparing the merits of French and Italian music. To do so would mean criticizing

---

35 Ibid., 2:293, 370–2.

the Englishman. To Dubos, Addison is "a man of wit and abilities, who reproaching his countrymen with the taste which several of them seem to have for the Italian operas, maintains that there is a music suitable to each language, and particularly adapted to each nation." Rather than disagree with Addison that "French music is good in its kind, and so is the Italian," Dubos chooses not to challenge the Englishman's cultural relativism.[36]

IMPERIAL MYTHS, LITERARY PROPAGANDA, AND SATIRE

Born seventy years before Brillat-Savarin, an English poet turned empire into an anti-myth in *The Dunciad* (1742–1743). Alexander Pope (1688–1744) presents Dullness as an empress and regressive divinity destructive of civilization: "Still her old Empire to restore she tries" on British institutions.[37] The previous line mockingly elevates primitive ignorance by asserting that Dullness originally "rul'd, in native anarchy, the mind." "Daughter of Chaos and eternal Night," she stands for un-creation, miscegenation, anti-humanism, and pre-literacy.[38] In Book III, Elkanah Settle (1648–1724) guides Colley Cibber (1671–1757) to acknowledge Dullness's "boundless empire," Pope implying that popular, commercially successful poets sponsor a decline in enlightenment which her "imperial sway" speeds.[39] Book IV celebrates the advent of Dullness envisioned earlier: the "Empress" receives petitions to expel the remnants of high culture. When senseless Italian opera warns of the musical genius of George Frederick Handel (1685–1759), the "great Empress" banishes him. Next, an orator who debases court rituals asks her to receive a young aristocrat corrupted by fashion, begging her to accept the aristocrat's whore to ensure the longevity of her posterity. In the end, Dullness obeys her parents by restoring the "dread Empire" of "CHAOS" whose "uncreating word" extinguishes the light of the world, the "great Anarch" burying all in "Universal Darkness."[40]

---

36   Dubos refers to *Spectator*, no. 29 for 3 April 1711 (1748, 1:378).
37   Pope 1963: *Dunciad* Bk. 1, l. 17.
38   Ibid.: *Dunciad* Bk. 1, l. 12.
39   Ibid.: *Dunciad* Bk. 3, ll. 68 and 124.
40   Ibid.: *Dunciad* Bk. 4, ll. 69, 282, 333, and 653–6. On Pope's ironical defence of Christian humanism in the *Dunciad*, see Merrett 2004: 58–76.

Indebted to John Dryden (1631–1700) for his inventiveness with the heroic couplet, Pope no doubt admired his predecessor's imagery in *Absalom and Achitophel* (1681), which associates empire with illicit royal aspiration. Opponents of Charles II and monarchy hide their disloyalty behind imperialism. The illegitimate Duke of Monmouth blasphemously pretends to divinity in stating that his "soul disclaims the kindred of her earth / And, made for empire, whispers me within: / 'Desire of greatness is a godlike sin.'" His seducer, the first Earl of Shaftesbury, asserts the people's "right supreme / To make their kings, for kings are made for them," adding hypocritically that "All empire is no more than pow'r in trust." When a banished rebel, Monmouth dramatizes himself as "a prey to arbitrary laws!" and "Cut off from empire, and no more a son." In resolving the Exclusion Crisis, the king pities Monmouth. Having raised him "to all the height his frame could bare," Charles is sure God did not ordain "his fate for empire born." In the end, the king legitimates his successor.[41]

In mid-century, James Thomson (1700–1748) and Mark Akenside (1721–1770) treat imperialism with nationalistic and heroic rhetoric. Thomson's *Britannia* (1729) laments the nation's refusal to seize Spain's commerce. Britannia regrets that "the British lion" no longer roars. Having lost her "liquid reign" because her "feeble sons" retreat from her "empire o'er the conquered seas," she urges them to "be terrible, untamed, / Unconquerable still" since, while empires on land collapse "Self-crushed," sea power best upholds "lavish nature" whose resources are meant for "huge empires."[42] In *The Pleasures of the Imagination* (1744), Akenside emphasizes patriotism and the spiritual decline that accompanies its abeyance: "If no bright forms of excellence" colour a man's "image of his country," if neither "the pomp / of sacred senates, nor the guardian voice / of Justice on her throne, nor aught that wakes / The conscious bosom with a patriot's flame," he will betray his country rather than sacrifice himself. The result: ambition seizes the "empire of the soul" and growing vice stunts the imagination. Then, "oft adorn'd / With solemn pageants, folly mounts the throne, / And plays

---

41 Dryden 2001, 124, ll. 370–2; 125, 409–11; 132, ll. 700–2 and 704; 139, ll. 961–3.

42 Thomson 1908: 472, l. 52; 474, ll. 90 and 103; 476, ll. 178–9; and 477, ll. 207–10. Note the caustic remarks about Thomson's political naivety by Johnson (1952, 2:351).

her idiot antics, like a queen. / A thousand garbs she wears; a thousand ways / She wheels her giddy empire." Like Shaftesbury, Akenside insists "the Muse's Empire" be regulated by the stoical concept of nature.[43]

Henry Fielding (1707–1754) and Laurence Sterne (1713–1768) also illustrate how imperial metaphors serve diverse imaginings that subordinate reason to distinct theologies. *The Life of Mr Jonathan Wild the Great* (1743) offers the following self-discourse in the mouth of the imprisoned Heartfree, who thus confronts his wife's alleged infidelity:

But are my Passions then voluntary? Am I so absolutely their Master, that I can resolve with myself, *so far only will I grieve?* Certainly, no. Reason, however, we flatter ourselves, hath not such despotic Empire in our Minds, that it can, with imperial Voice, hush all our Sorrow in a Moment. Where then is its Use? For either it is an empty Sound, and we are deceived in thinking we have Reason, or it is given us to some End, and hath a Part assigned it by the All-wise Creator. Why, what can its Office be, other than justly to weigh the Worth of all Things, and to direct us to that Perfection of human Wisdom, which proportions our Esteem of every Object by its real Merit, and prevents us from over or undervaluing whatever we hope for, we enjoy, or we lose. It doth not foolishly say to us, *Be not glad*, or *Be not sorry*, which would be as vain and idle, as to bid the purling River cease to run, or the raging Wind to blow. It prevents us only from exulting, like Children, when we receive a Toy, or lamenting when we are deprived of it.[44]

Heartfree opposes notions of all-powerful rationalism. An extensive realm, his mind registers sorrow yet tempers emotional pain in the process of denying reason imperial power. His reasonableness serves divine teleology, and a balanced moral judgment sustains his equanimity in the face of the rumour that his wife has abandoned him. Sterne, the wittily irreverent clergyman, deploys empire in *A Sentimental Journey* (1768) in a spirit of facetious individualism that mocks authority figures. When Yorick sups with his frisky spaniel and French valet, he is satisfied to his "heart's content" with his "empire," and, "if monarchs knew what they would be at," they would imitate him. In saying Yorick constantly falls in love with women, Sterne borrows a fragment from *The Anatomy*

---

43 Akenside 1857: 46, ll. 37–41; 47, ll. 53–4 and 66–70; and 51, l. 191.
44 Fielding 2003, 87–8.

of Melancholy (1621) by Robert Burton (1577–1640) that ends with the comment that Cupid's "empire extendeth from heaven to earth, and even to the depths of the sea." Sterne similarly humanizes imperialism when fortifying his claim that "states and empires have their periods of declension, and feel in their turns what distress and poverty is" by telling the story of the Marquis who surrenders his sword and recovers this noble symbol after taking up commerce. A final example humanizing imperialism occurs in an ironical image of female consistency. There are "three epochas in the empire of a French-woman": she is first a coquette, next a deist, and finally a *"devôte."* These phases sustain her empire: "when thirty-five years and more have unpeopled her dominions of the slaves of love, she re-peoples it with the slaves of infidelity – and then with the slaves of the Church."[45]

Political debate about empire lies behind its diverse metaphorical functions. Burke and Johnson in their views of the American colonies testify to this diversity. To Burke, the British empire will survive only by making concessions. His Whig view concedes the American appeal to liberty and empire's geographical limits: imperial policy must be tempered by cultural history and the role of social manners. In contrast, Johnson upholds the crown's authority. His belief in hierarchy and subordination restricts liberty: individuals are subjects born in systems of government, not states of nature. His anti-utopianism argues that forms of representation are never totally inclusive. A strict monarchist, he holds that authority is more basic than representation. What alleviates his Toryism is disgust with the imperial rivalry of England and France that displaces North American Aboriginals.

In a "Speech on Conciliation with America," made in Parliament on 22 March 1775, Burke, in self-dramatizing style, would "restore order and repose to an empire so great and so distracted as ours." He proposes peace. "Not peace through the medium of war; not peace to be hunted through the labyrinth of intricate and endless negotiations; not peace to arise out of universal discord, fomented from principle, in all parts of the empire," but "simple peace sought in the spirit of peace, and laid in principles purely pacific." The "disobedient spirit in the colonies" is natural: the colonists took English liberty to America; three thousand

---

45 Sterne 2003, 27, 30, 67–9, and 92. On Burton see the editorial note (2003, 230). For the female appropriation of empire, see my analysis of *The History of Emily Montague* in chapter 3 of this volume.

miles of ocean weaken government; "extensive empires" have less power "at the extremities." Burke trusts to conciliation since, as "we must give away some natural liberty, to enjoy civil advantages, so we must sacrifice some civil liberties, for the advantage to be derived from the communion and fellowship of a great empire."[46]

In denouncing the French Revolution for instituting regicide, jacobinism, and atheism, Burke subordinates political theory to sensibility. He spurns the revolution's "*correspondent system of manners*" which represents a "determined hostility to the human race" in rejecting tradition and custom. Its systematic prescriptions elicit the core of Burke's humanism:

Manners are more important than laws. Upon them, in a great measure, the laws depend. The law touches us but here and there, and now and then. Manners are what vex or sooth, corrupt or purify, exalt or debase, barbarize or refine us, by a constant, steady uniform, insensible operation, like that of the air we breathe in. They give their whole form and colour to our lives. According to their quality, they aid morals, they supply them, or they totally destroy them. Of this the new French Legislators were aware; therefore, with the same method, and under the same authority, they settled a system of manners, the most licentious, prostitute, and abandoned that ever has been known, and at the same time the most coarse, rude, savage, and ferocious. Nothing in the Revolution, no, not to a phrase or gesture, not the fashion of a hat or a show, was left to accident.

Legislating linguistic and dress codes is the worst abuse of authority Burke can imagine.[47]

In *An Introduction to the Political State of Great-Britain* (1756), Johnson thinks trade with the American colonies unproblematic; it is "in reality, only an intercourse between distant provinces of the same empire." No supporter of British policy letting trade between France and Spain flourish, he is wary of French forts constraining the colonies' westward expansion and of French cultivation of Natives. But his antipathy to money-grubbing British traders is fierce: "Our factors and traders having no other purpose in view than immediate profit, use all the arts of

---

46 Burke 1968, 55–6, 61, and 64.
47 Burke 1796, 38–9.

an *European* counting-house, to defraud the simple hunter of his furs." They "hourly alienate the Indians by their tricks and oppressions."[48] *Observations on the Present State of Affairs* (1756) reiterates disgust with abuse of Natives. The fairest-minded colonists "have no other merit than that of the scrivener who ruins in silence over a plunderer that seizes by force; all have taken what had other owners, and all have had recourse to arms rather than quit the prey on which they had fastened." His hostility to military and commercial propaganda in the Seven Years War informs *Observations* (August–September 1758) when he states that boasting about the "petty conquest" of Louisbourg is absurd since that fortress was not the seat of the French empire in North America. The riots provoked by John Wilkes (1725–1797) led Johnson to emphasize the lack of constitutional sense in the British populace. He asserts in *The False Alarm* (1770) that, "with all its renown for speculation and for learning," the country "has yet made little proficiency in civil wisdom." He advises Wilkes's supporters that the House of Commons's legal power over its members takes precedence over voters' rights. Like Burke, Johnson upholds gradual political evolution: governments are "formed by chance, and gradually improved by such expedients, as the successive discovery of their defects happened to suggest, are never to be tried by a regular theory. They are fabricks of dissimilar materials, raised by different architects, upon different plans. We must be content with them as they are."[49]

Johnson's reactions against radical political and military action in *Thoughts on the Late Transactions respecting Falkland's Islands* (1771) stem from his view that empire depends on international compacts. Thus, he warns that "the whole system of European empire" is endangered by petty disputes over a "few spots of earth," like the Falklands. While George Anson (1697–1762) thought the islands vital to "future expeditions against the coast of Chili," Johnson contends that they function in peace only as "a station for contraband traders, a nursery of fraud, and a receptacle of theft." Securing them would merely open "a port in which all pirates shall be safe," thereby increasing international tension. A stronger reason why the government should resist the

---

48 Johnson 1968, 10 and 15–17.
49 Ibid., 25, 36–7, 39, 41, and 47.

propaganda of adventurers about natural resources on distant islands is the cost in human lives.

The life of a modern soldier is ill represented by heroick fiction. War has means of destruction more formidable than the cannon and the sword. Of the thousands and ten thousands that perished in our late contest with France and Spain, a very small part ever felt the stroke of an enemy; the rest languished in tents and ships, amidst damps and putrefaction; pale, torpid, spiritless, and helpless, grasping and groaning, unpitied among men, made obdurate by long continuance of hopeless misery; and were at last whelmed in pits, or heaved into the ocean, without notice and without remembrance. By incommodious encampments and unwholesome stations, where courage is useless, and enterprise impracticable, fleets are silently dispeopled, and armies sluggishly melted away.

Johnson's sympathy for the common soldier and sailor is matched by feelings for the British people, their families devastated by war. Imperial aspirations do not move them to hope:

The wars of civilized nations make very slow changes in the system of empire. The public perceives scarcely any alteration but an increase in debt; and the few individuals who are benefited, are not supposed to have the clearest right to their advantages. If he that shared the danger enjoyed the profit, and after bleeding in the battle grew rich by the victory, he might shew his gains without envy. But at the conclusion of a ten years war, how are we recompensed for the deaths of multitudes and the expence of millions, but by contemplating the sudden glories of paymasters and agents, contractors and commissaries, whose equipages shine like meteors, and whose palaces rise like exhalations.[50]

Opportunistic speculation in military procurement and capitalistic greed sponsored by officialdom deepen Johnson's sense of class rivalry and passion for common humanity.

Taxation No Tyranny (1775) confirms why he blasts American populism, exceptionalism, and individualism: colonial governments derive authority from charters; by "royal grant" they wield "the solemnities of

---

50 Ibid., 60, 62–4, and 77–8.

legislation, the administration of justice, the security of property." The colonies, "however distant," are "constituent parts of the British Empire," with Parliament having the right to bind colonists by statute for the good of the empire. As regards the franchise in Britain, one-person-one-vote is not a basic principle since representation involves several kinds of delegation: the entire population does not qualify to vote, many being "wholly unconcerned in the government of themselves." Since in the realm of liberty electors are never unanimous, their consent to be governed is often passive: "As all are born the subjects of some state or other, we may be said to have been all born consenting to some system of Government." The Americans, these "lords of themselves, these kings of *Me*, these demigods of independence," are inconsistent; governed by charters, they forget that representation in states is diverse: "formed by chance, and settled by custom." Since many British "towns neither enjoy nor desire particular representatives" and "are included in the general system of publick administration" that entails they suffer "with the rest of the Empire," the "use of the Empire" means Britain retains "the sole right of taxing" the colonies.[51]

LONDON: THEATRICAL IMAGES OF THE SEAT OF EMPIRE

Were our English Stage but half so virtuous as that of the Greeks or Romans, we should quickly see the Influence of it in the Behaviour of all the Politer Part of Mankind. It would not be fashionable to ridicule Religion, or its Professors; the Man of Pleasure would be out of Countenance, and every Quality which is Ornamental to Human Nature, would meet with that Esteem which is due to it ... It is one of the most unaccountable Things in our Age, that the Lewdness of our Theatre should be so much complained of, so well exposed, and so little redeemed ... The *Athenian* and *Roman* Plays were written with such a regard to Morality, that *Socrates* used to frequent the one, and *Cicero* the other ... Cuckoldom is the Basis of most of our Modern Plays. If an Alderman appears upon the Stage, you may be sure it is in order to be Cuckolded. A Husband that is a little grave or elderly, generally meets with the same Fate. Knights and Baronets, Country Squires, and Justices of the Quorum, come up to Town for no other Purpose.[52]

51 Ibid., 109–13 and 116–18.
52 Addison, *The Spectator*, no. 446, Thursday, 31 July 1712 (1963, 3:375–7).

The most eminent instance of the flourishing of learning in absolute governments is that of France, which scarcely ever enjoyed any established liberty and yet has carried the arts and sciences as near perfection as any other nation ... With regard to the stage, they have excelled even the Greeks, who far excelled the English. And, in common life, they have in great measure, perfected that art, the most useful and agreeable of any, *l'art de vivre*, the art of society and conversation.[53]

The level manners of a polished country like this, do not supply much matter for the comic muse, which delights in variety and extravagance; wherever, therefore, I have made any attempt at novelty, I have found myself obliged either to dive into the lower class of men, or betake myself to the outskirts of the empire: the centre is too equal and refined for such purposes.[54]

The passages above make strong claims about eighteenth-century theatre. In the first, Addison laments the contrast between the philosophical drama of ancient Greece and Rome and the morally lax plays of fashionable London stages. The latter, he claims, degrade audiences with stereotypes coarsened by seduction and cuckoldry: not socially constructive, its plays fail to promote refinement of manners. In the second passage, Hume, an admirer of Addison's style and moral outlook, rejects the conservative view, voiced by Hurd and others, that England's constitution guarantees its refined culture.[55] Instead, Hume praises the French stage for surpassing the quality of Greek plays and leaving English ones far behind. Resident there for some years, Hume supports France's claim to have perfected the art of living.[56] However, Richard Cumberland (1732–1811), the

---

53 Hume, "Of Civil Liberty" (1953, 103–4).

54 Cumberland, "Advertisement to *The Fashionable Lover* (1772)" in Bell 1977c, 6:iv.

55 "Fine writing, according to Mr. Addison, consists of sentiments which are natural, without being obvious. There cannot be a juster and more concise definition of fine writing" (Hume, "of Simplicity and Refinement in Writing," 1965, 42). He also admired "Mr. Addison's elegant discourses on religion" (Hume, "Of Essay Writing," 1965, 41).

56 Hume lived for three years in France at Rheims and La Flèche, Anjou, when composing his *Treatise of Human Nature* and twenty-six months in Paris when serving as secretary of the British embassy from 1763 on. He found Parisian company "sensible, knowing, and polite ... above all places in the universe" (Hume, "My Own Life," 1987, xxxiv and xxxix).

sentimental playwright, found English society of the 1770s so refined that his sole resource for comedic novelty was to hunt out lower-class characters and types from the margins of empire.

Despite his aspirations for social and political harmony, the spatial and demographic growth of London during the eighteenth century effected largely by the rising empire did not answer Addison's vision for a city modelled on Athens and Rome. As London's conurbation spread, it divided itself into districts and quarters that mirrored the fashions, habits, and means of a society that increasingly adopted forms of hierarchy.[57] Class rivalries aggravated by inequitable distribution of property, titles, and court favours in the Restoration inspired satire, invective, and retaliation in the minds of writers and artists.[58] The city's growing imperial status magnified topographical allusions in plays to such an extent that their reflexive dramatic powers declined in the presence of ideological stereotypes. If fashionable consumerism was compellingly mocked along with characters who demean the theatre as an institution, the constant allusions to streets, squares, and off-stage physical environs tended to restrict the aesthetic appeal of dialogue and plot. By 1800, London was reflected back to playgoers conventionally as the cynosure of fashion and empire.[59]

Like Addison, Daniel Defoe (1660–1731) wanted London to be a coherent symbol of the nation, as his *A Tour through the Whole Island of Great Britain* (1724–1726) makes plain. Hence, he praises it for having spread beyond its ancient walls and liberties from Blackwall in the east to Tothill Fields in the west, from the river in the south to Islington in the north, from Peterborough House in Westminster to Cavendish and Hanover Squares reaching past Hyde Park. However, unlike the

---

[57] A source of information about streets and districts is *Trivia; Or, The Art of Walking the Streets of London* (1716) by John Gay (1685–1732). See Gay 1926, 57–87. On audience behaviour affected by indoor theatre architecture, see Brown 1995, 206.

[58] For a survey of lascivious decadence in the city, see Gatrell, chapter 1, "London and the Pleasure Principle" (2006, 23–50).

[59] "All the best-known comedies are set culturally and topographically in London *town*: not in the court nor in the city, often portrayed as a nest of Cromwellian vipers, and certainly not in the country (a remote place somewhere in Hampshire where there is nothing for a gentleman to do). Rambling (perambulating the town in search of sex) is an accepted pastime, and its conclusion in marriage is predictable only in terms of comic convention" (Thomson 1995, 213).

"city of Rome" that had "very few irregularities" in shape, London's sprawling conurbation lacks design: "New squares, and new streets rising up every day to such a prodigy of buildings" it is a "disaster ... as to the beauty of its figure." Haphazard growth stretches it out to "the pleasure of every builder, or undertaker of buildings, and as the convenience of the people directs." London lacks symmetry: three miles divide St George's in Southwark from Shoreditch in Middlesex, but only two divide Peterborough and Montague houses. Not half a mile wide at Wapping, the city is less at Redriff. Disorder abounds in unfettered growth: Redriff reaches to Deptford, Islington to Mile-End; St George's joins Southwark to Newington, Lambeth, and the Borough; Westminster stretches to Chelsea, St Giles's to "Marybone," and Great Russell Street via Montague House to Tottenham Court.[60] Defoe's view of London's modernization is conflicted. While he denies urban sprawl erodes municipal authority, he laments that 17,000 houses replaced the 13,000 burned in Cheapside's square mile. Happy that new building materials and broader streets will retard fires, he regrets lots being rebuilt to a higher density; one merchant's house in Swithen's Alley was replaced by twenty. Knowing density increased before the Great Fire, he spurns the removal of the Earl of Bedford's garden to open up Covent Garden and that of Hatton House to develop Holborn. He condemns nobles for razing palaces on the Strand to redevelop the riverside, troubled that 200,000 persons inhabit Spitalfield's 320 acres where no one lived before 1666. To him, development in Holborn, Bloomsbury, and Soho is motivated only by profit and fashion: aristocrats increase population density in the old city and aggravate class distinctions between districts.[61]

On Defoe's map, London is the hub of commerce and finance, Westminster the centre of gallantry and splendour, and the "outparts" where most people reside house industry. Yet he stresses the reciprocity of City and Court – their "constant communication of business": the Custom House is the source of public revenue with the Bank of England, the Navy Office, the South Sea, East India and African Companies instrumental to the creation of paper money, funds, and stocks. He accepts that the "constant daily intercourse" between Court and City

---

60 Defoe 1974, 1:314–15.
61 Ibid., 1:321–2, 325, and 329. As the lower-class population increased, the "well-to-do started living away from their businesses, and aldermen were opting for country seats or sophisticated squares" (Porter 1994, 97).

causes a "prodigious conflux of the nobility and gentry from all parts of England" since the rich depend on capital markets, and fees from stock trading yield revenue to government. Yet he grieves such interests fragment society: "new cities" spring up within the city because of stockjobbers, Defoe thereby induced to warn landlords and builders that the boom cannot last since peace plans and more stringent public management will end the national debt and make financing it unnecessary. Such wishful thinking, doubtless affected by the South Sea Bubble, trusts that those drawn by millions invested in joint-stock companies will fall away, well-to-do families returning to country seats to reduce their costs. Still, ties between Court and City being tight, he trusts the former dare not spurn the latter as formerly: the Court needs City wealth, for institutions like the law courts are shared, operating out of the Guildhall and Westminster, and the Bank of England must help government to fund the army and navy.[62]

Defoe's strained efforts to create an orderly map of London and integrate its courtly and business realms help explicate comic dramaturgy. So, one may ask how the liberties of Whitefriars, Blackfriars, and Aldgate are presented; how, since Bedford House was torn down in 1703, Covent Garden is figured, given its decline before and after the opening of the playhouse there in 1732; and how the aristocratic fashioning of West End squares is depicted. More generally, one may question how much comedic typology reflects urban geography and what characters are most stereotyped.[63]

William Wycherley (1640–1715) belittles courtly titles, landed property, and monied wealth, using the capital's public spaces on stage to dupe vicious characters. In *Love in a Wood* (1671), Lady Flippant, widowed sister of Gripe, a usurer, exposes herself in the marts of St Paul's Church in Covent Garden and St Martin's in the Fields and in playhouses, Hyde Park, and Mulberry Gardens. Lust to live at the court end of town makes her hate her puritanical brother. Wycherley's retaliation against characters stresses London's dark side: Flippant is only fit to be a prostitute in Whetstone's Park, a lane between Holborn and Lincoln's

---

62 Ibid., 1:335–6 and 339.
63 On the "propertied patricians" who developed "Bloomsbury, Bedford and Russell Squares in west-central London, and, above all, Hanover, Berkeley and Grosvenor Squares in Mayfair and Cavendish, Portman and Manchester Squares in Marylebone," see Porter 1994, 96–113.

Inn Fields, and Gripe, a customer of Mrs Joiner the bawd who hates wits and bishops, shuns Drury Lane Theatre, preferring assignations in the West End.[64] While Ranger hunts sexual prey in St James's Park, Dapperwit keeps Lucy Crossbite up an obscure alley. Ranger spurns her since she visits Lamb's Conduit in Holborn and wants a contract that will send wealthy neighbours back to country seats jealous of her. Such a contract is beyond Dapperwit, although he treats her at New Spring Garden, the Neat House in Chelsea, and Colby's Mulberry Gardens near St James's Park. This false wit is punished by marriage to Gripe's daughter and a future running a coffee house in Covent Garden.[65] Wycherley's *The Gentleman Dancing Master* (1672) ridicules a city family. Servant Prue is kept from low entertainments at Hatton Garden, Tottenham Court, Islington, and Moorfields, while her mistress, Hyppolyta, an heiress locked up by her father, is barred from upper-class resorts at the theatre, the park, and Mulberry and New Spring Gardens. Schooled at Hackney, she would betray her education by visiting the West End. If £12,000 inherited from her mother lets her resist her father, she takes a lover from unfashionable Ludgate. Her father, who trades to Spain and claims his forebears are buried in the church of Great St Ellen's in Bishopsgate, hails from a pin maker, felt maker, and wine cooper buried only in the churchyard. His patriarchalism involves absurd self-misrepresentation, like his daughter.[66]

When, in *The Country Wife* (1675), Horner moves to fashionable Russell Street, this locale broadcasts his pretended sterility, letting him exploit male impotence and female lust. A true wit, he knows how modish sites are sexualized, but his gull Sparkish, a false wit, sees no difference between eating houses in Covent Garden, Bow Street, and Fleet Street nor, in hatred of the theatre, is he aware of his slavish homoerotic courtliness. Pinchwife, a retired businessman who claims to "know the town" is universally deceived. He is a Cheapside husband and Lombard Street alderman, according to Horner. In Wycherley's world, women consort with potent wits rather than rich or courtly men. Thus, Mistress Alethea provides Margery Pinchwife, her sister, with "town documents" that list favoured resorts: Mulberry Gardens, St James's Park, the New Exchange, and Whitehall. The freedom women enjoy comes from

---

64 Wycherley 1996, 6, 18, 10, and 63.
65 Ibid., 44, 42, and 94.
66 Ibid., 100–1, 123, and 180.

making such spaces theatrical. To Lucy, Alethea's maid, modern women marry not for rural seats but for pretty houses in Lincoln's Inn, St James's Fields, or Pall Mall with access to public spaces.[67] Similarly, George Etherege (1636–1692) upholds women's need for urban space in *The Man of Mode* (1676). Harriet cares less that Dorimant toys with shopwomen in the New Exchange and stalks women in the Park and Mall so long as she enjoys "this dear town." Ignoring his philandering, she directs his role as Courtage, a time server who enacts truisms in St James's Park, the setting in her mind for harmless discourse as distinct from Hyde Park's corrupt modish formality. While Mrs Loveit retreats to Pall Mall lodgings, uninventive with the double standard, Harriet enjoys street cries. Forced to move to the country with its "hateful noise of rooks," she finds "music in the worst cry in London," recalling "My dill and cowcumbers to pickle!"[68]

William Congreve (1670–1729) smuttily maps sites for social retaliation. Settings in *The Old Batchelor* (1693) include the piazza of Covent Garden, the Exchange, and St James's Park, where landed and monied wealth is debased by sexual posturing: Bellmour, the libertine, would finish Fondlewife's education by cuckolding him and reducing him to an "equal Dignity with the rest of his Brethren," and Heartwell, the old bachelor who degrades "great Families in Town," says that to marry a "Wife of Birth" is to be cuckolded by an "illustrious Whore."[69] *The Double Dealer* (1694) accents Sir Paul Plyant's inability to control his wife. With a fortune, a country seat, houses in town, and a personal estate, he has no son to inherit his wealth since his wife feigns abstinence while whoring in town. Lady Wishfort in *The Way of the World* (1700) renews stereotypes: an old woman bent on rivalling young ones, vanity saps her puritanical upbringing. Her sense of locale accents her duplicity: goaded by Foible's lies about Mirabell, Lady Wishfort's vengefulness covers a slumming mentality. She would see him in tatters in a Long-Lane

---

67 Ibid., 201–2, 205, 255, 206–7, and 240.
68 Salgado 1968, 74, 80, 102, 136, and 144. Steele, *The Spectator*, No. 65, Tuesday, 15 May 1711, calls this "whole celebrated Piece ... a perfect Contradiction to good Manners, good Sense. And common Honesty." He continues: "I allow it to be Nature, but it is Nature in its utmost Corruption and Degeneracy" (1:202–3). See Addison *Spectator*, No. 251, on street cries.
69 Congreve 1925, 30 and 34.

penthouse or as a Gibbet-Thief. Yet she is vulnerable to male power from parading in Hyde Park and harbouring fantasies of pastoral retreat.[70]

Topography in Steele's *The Tender Husband* (1705) is doctrinaire in mocking cits. Samuel Pounce, marriage broker and vicious lawyer, knows the "different nations of Cheapside, Covent Garden and St. James," his class sense matched by Hezekiah Tipkin, a miserly Lombard Street banker with £50,000 in stocks and a retreat at Hackney. While the Gubbins, country bumpkins, are degraded, genteel fortune hunters win out. Tipkin's "very good credit" and "very bad conscience" underscore the chasm between his wife's coarse pretensions and his niece's obsession with romances.[71] In *The Relapse* (1696), John Vanbrugh (1664–1726) mocks bumpkins seeking status. Lord Foppington, who attends St James's Church in Piccadilly, which draws wealthy residents from St James's Square, is willing to marry Miss Hoyden for her money. Grotesquely she behaves as if born and bred in St James's Parish.[72] Although *The Beaux' Stratagem* (1706) is set by George Farquhar (1677–1707) in Litchfield, he no more seriously elaborates relations between setting and demography. London allusions abound in the rural scene since the fortune hunters, Aimwell and Archer, must repair their urban hedonism and the heroines, Dorinda and Mrs Sullen, embody the truism that the city liberates women from male tyranny. With their French tastes and culinary jealousy of those who "live only in their Palates," the fortune hunters have abandoned Hyde Park, the Mall, and "White's, Tom's, or Will's" coffee houses. But the women cherish urbanity: Dorinda thinks marriage to Aimwell will provide "Title, Place and Precedence, the Park, the Play, and the drawing-Room, Splendour, Equipage, Noise and Flambeaux," and Mrs Sullen trusts that "London, dear London, is the Place for managing and breaking" her brutish husband. Far from sustaining this motif, the play employs coincidence: his brother dying, Aimwell becomes the lord he pretends to be, and the women are saved from thieves and smugglers by the adventurers. The ending accentuates female dependence, the gap between their talk about power and its enactment being unbridgeable.[73]

70 Ibid., 381 and 415.
71 Bell 1977a, 8:10–13 and 24.
72 Vanbrugh 1989, 74 and 128. On the farce as "the dominant dramatic form of the period," see Holland and Patterson 1995, 266.
73 Moore 1933, 507, 550, 549, and 514.

Topography is incidental in Steele's *The Conscious Lovers* (1722) because his ideological wish to fuse mercantilism and sentiment assigns allusions to minor characters. Since Bevil father and son avoid dialogue with each other, the dramaturgy is burdened with narrative recall while servants mimic their betters in going about the city. Tom, Bevil Jr's servant, visits Westminster chocolate houses, lackeys being "the men of pleasure of the age," while Phillis, Lucinda Sealand's maid, dresses like "a woman of condition," taking in plays, operas, and ridottos in the winter and Bellsize and other parks for "summer diversions." Urban spaces, no help to the genteel, mock affected servants and let Sealand, "the great India merchant," resort to St James's Park as Sir John Bevil's equal. Stressing mercantile gentility, the denouement upholds Sealand's entry into the beau monde:

Sir, as much a cit as you take me for – I know the town and the world – and give me leave to say that we merchants are a species of gentry that have grown into the world this last century, and are as honourable, and almost as useful, as you landed folks that have always thought yourselves so much above us, for your trading, forsooth! is extended no farther than a load of hay or a fat ox.[74]

Ironically integrating genteel and mercantile worlds, John Gay (1685–1732) in *The Beggar's Opera* (1728) relates all city classes to the criminal underworld. The beggar-poet frequents St Giles-in-the-Fields, a crime-ridden slum east of Charing Cross Road. Anti-hero Macheath patronizes chocolate houses in Marylebone (the centre of gambling where he games with lawyers and lords) and coffee houses in the Temple (one of the Inns of Court). His gang hangs out in Newgate prison and headquarters in Moorfields. His whores hail from Hockley-in-the-Hole and brothels in Vinegar Yard and Lewkner's Lane near the Theatre Royal in Drury Lane. The Peachums, a crooked business couple, live in the city but have a warehouse at Redriff in Rotherhithe, the hub of London's dockland. They train thieves at Hockley-in-the-Hole, the site of bull- and bear-baiting and blood sports near Clerkenwell. Polyvalent allusions link courtly, commercial, and political modes. Peachum feels equal to lawyers, judges, surgeons, sporting gentlemen, and lords, while Polly,

---

[74] Bell 1977a, 4:14–15, 17, 9, and 81.

his abused daughter, sees herself in operatic mode as a flower crushed at Covent Garden market.[75]

Samuel Foote (1720–1777) also attributes vice in the West End to city affectation. In *Taste* (1752), a forger sells works at the court end of town to citizens: Carmine's rise from sign painting for a brothel in "Goodman's-fields," the "Cat and Fiddle in Petticoat-lane," the "Goose and Gridiron in Paul's church yard" and for "Prim Stiff," a Ludgate Hill mercer, exploits citizens' pretensions. Lady Pentweazel of "Blow-bladder-street" thinks Carmine paints as well as Peter Lely (1618–1680) and Godfrey Kneller (1646–1723), being so flattered by him that she helps dupe aldermen, her daughter's husband being "Mr. Deputy Dripping of Candelwick-ward."[76] The city infects the West End in Foote's *The Commissary* (1765); Mrs Mechlin, a bawd peddling smuggled goods, is so welcome in "the liberty of Westminster" that she wins the custom of an "old liquorish dowager from Devonshire Square" with £40,000 in the four per cents and "two houses at Hackney."[77] In Foote's *The Lyar* (1762), Miss Grantam of "Grosvenor-square" finances sexual lust. She has money "in India bonds, some in the bank, some on this loan, some on the other; so that if one fund fails," she has "a sure resource in the rest." She parades in the parks since decency is a "mere bourgeois, plebian quality."[78] Rivalry between brothers William and Robert Wealthy in *The Minor* (1760) conveys Foote's disgust with the effect of commerce on family life. William thinks city wealth must be transmuted by fashion and manners gained on the Grand Tour, while Robert holds that trade offers the best way to know the world. While William exposes his son to urban corruption in preparation for his patrimony, Robert leaves his daughter to the protection of a piously hypocritical bawd, Mrs Cole. Foote's fiercest lines are spoken by William and son, Sir George. William loads his brother with the "civic vices" of "hypocrisy, couzenage, and avarice" manifest in church going to "St. Bride's," outings to "Islington, or Mile End" and a country seat that is a "boarded box at Clapham." Sir George despises Robert's "mercantile mud," agreeing to marry his daughter only if he gives up his country seat and quits his house in

---

75 Gay 1926, 487, 491, 501, 503–4, and 492–3.
76 Bell 1977b, 1:165–6, 164, and 167. Lely and Kneller were leading court painters in Restoration and early eighteenth-century England.
77 Ibid., 4:50 and 55–6.
78 Ibid., 2:163 and 151.

"St. Mary Ax for Grosvenor-Square." While Sir George's patrimony derives from soap boiling, his insults of Robert Wealthy are upheld by the plot: his spendthrift habits are offset by protecting Robert's outcast daughter.[79] The demeaning of city place names shows that Foote wants audiences to scorn lifestyles outside the West End, as we see once more in *The Mayor of Garratt* (1763), which depicts an election in a horticultural town south of Wandsworth, Fulham, and Putney. Mrs Sneak, the daughter of Sir Jacob, the lord of the manor supervising the vote, laments being "join'd to a sneaking slovenly cit; a paltry, prying, pitiful pin-maker." Marriage to a citizen means she is "jostled and cramm'd with the crowd," given "no respect, no place, no precedence," "choak'd with the smoke of the city" and offered "no country jaunts but to Islington" and taken to "no balls but at Pewter's-hall." Her husband drinks contentedly with his club members – packers, grocers, and midwives – at "the Nagg's-Head in the Poultry."[80]

Scorn of citizens successful in imperial commerce tends to dominate comedies as the century unfolds. In *The Clandestine Marriage* (1766) by George Colman (1732–1794) and David Garrick (1717–1779), Sterling is laughably tasteless in applying fashion to his country house and gardens. Preoccupied by his warehouse and the stock exchange, he uses luxury with aggressive respectability. But he is heedless of his daughters' sensibilities. The elder, snobbish about the proud wives of "city-knights," lusts for "the dear regions of Grosvenor-Square" far from "the dull districts of Aldersgate, Cheap, Candlewick, and Farringdon Without and Within." She feels remote from the "sphere of the great world" and the court. Fanny the younger, distraught in her secret marriage, is happy at the prospect of visiting Tunbridge with her husband and other citizens. To Sir John Melvil, Miss Sterling, his betrothed, is "a medley of Cheapside pertness, and Whitechapel pride." To Lord Ogle, an impotent lecher yet benevolent critic of Sterling's dynastic aims, the capitalist proud to be able to provide a dowry in cash or India bonds will never leave "Blackfriars" behind. To Ogle, Sterling's landscape improvements epitomize his cramped house in "Gracechurch Street."[81]

Aesthetic pretensions and would-be prestige are also frustrated in Colman's *The Musical Lady* (1762), a farce that decries female taste for

[79] Bell 1977c, 15:16–17 and 51–2.
[80] Bell 1977b, 2:22, 11, and 13.
[81] Wood 2007, 89–90, 106, 97, and 103.

Italian opera. Young Mask, a gambler indebted to tradesmen in "Broad-court" and "Temple-gate," deceives his father into thinking he studies law and tricks a city heiress into marriage. Leaving chambers in "King's-Bench Walks" supplied by his father for a stinking garret overlooking "White Friars," he marries the heiress whose musical taste he pretends to share only after exposing it as illusory. Then he boasts his British power to give legacies to his children.[82] *The Old Maid* (1761) by Arthur Murphy (1727–1805) also punishes female vanity. Miss Harlow, a "Faded Toast," wants to be courted by Clerimont because he lives in "Hill-street" off Berkeley Square and has a country house. But sour manners stop her securing him and Captain Cape, the military man whose voyages to India have earned a fortune but who displeases her with his middling lifestyle in a "charming box of a house upon Hackney-Marsh."[83] Murphy's *The Citizen* (1761) more bitterly links demographic fashion and class crudity in the city. The Philpots, canting father and crooked son, unknown to each other keep the same girl at the court end of town, this incest accenting capitalistic perversity. Young Philpot, scorning citizens whose commissions in the customs afford them country seats with modish gardens "at Hogsdon, and at Kentish-Town, and at Newington-butts, and at Islington," scams them with insurance plots. When Old Philpot is unmasked, he returns to "Mincing Lane," vowing never to travel west of "Temple-bar," displacement the farce's chief action. Both Philpots are displaced from the West End for illiteracy.[84]

Comedies in the 1770s try without much success to balance satire and sentiment.[85] While sharp business practices, gambling, and disloyalty are exposed, moral issues are resolved by coincidence: unmotivated reform is quick and forgiveness sudden. Cumberland's *The Fashionable Lover* (1772) is an example. Its critical voice belongs to Colin Macleod, a Scottish servant to Lord Abberville, a libertine who indulges in French cuisine yet starves tradesmen. The lord agrees to take a wife from "Fish-street-hill." To effect his marriage he employs Bridgemore, a corrupt moneylender whose wife blames him for behaving in the mode of "Leatherseller's-hall." To Abberville, the Bridgemores are fit for "the

---

82 Bell 1977b, 2:319 and 332.
83 Ibid., 2:234 and 211.
84 Ibid., 3:11, 37, and 34.
85 On the "uneasy alliance" of satire and sentimentality, see Holland and Patterson 1995, 266.

company of Cordwainers." He visits them to seduce their lodger, Augusta Aubrey, "the last surviving orphan of a noble house." Dr Druid, a Welsh antiquary retained by Abberville, upholds his master's snobbery by mocking street names: "your Poultry, your Pye-Corner, and Pudding-Lane, your Bacon-Alley, and Fish-street hill" prove "the map of London would furnish an admirable bill of fare for a Lord Mayor's dinner." A developer, Bridgemore would raise buildings from London Bridge to Westminster to stock shops and warehouses "with good profitable commodities." Druid scorns this mentality that would "turn the Tower of London into a Pantheon" and "make a new Adelphi of the Savoy." Abberville is unmasked, and Bridgemore, who stole from Augusta's father, his partner, is exposed as without ethics or dignity to transmit to his posterity.[86]

Urbanity and rusticity are topics by which Oliver Goldsmith (1730–1774) and Richard Brinsley Sheridan (1751–1816) match London topography to debates about fashion and taste. In Goldsmith's *She Stoops to Conquer* (1773), Marlowe, the university-educated son of a knight, is mocked less for going with "the duchesses of Drury Lane" than for sartorial and sexual posturing exposed wittily by Kate Hardcastle. Yet Goldsmith's urban allusions also deflate rural folk. Marlow so dislikes Mr Hardcastle's rural bill of fare that he finds his supper fit for "the whole Joiner's Company, or the Corporation of Bedford." His scorn for trade guilds and local government is matched by his friend Hastings's snobbery in flattering Mrs Hardcastle. On saying she epitomizes the breeding of "Ranelagh, St James's, or Tower Wharf," he smirks at her urban inexperience. This is reinforced when she admits to never having visited such noble resorts as "the Pantheon, the Grotto Gardens, [and] the Borough." That fashions reach her by way of the "Miss Rickets of Crooked-Lane" (where no one ranked higher than a cheese-monger lives) reveals the class system belittling her. Yet, that Marlow fears being laughed at in town and caricatured in print shops as a result of Kate's stage power shows that he is as risible as Mrs Hardcastle.[87]

In *The School for Scandal* (1777), London seduces Lady Teazle, a country girl who "plays her part in all the extravagant fopperies of fashion and the town, with as ready a grace as if she had never seen a bush or

---

86 Bell 1977c, 6:iv, 15, 17, 26, 33–4.
87 Wood 2007, 177, 180, 186, and 205.

a grass-plot out of Grosvenor Square." Playing fast and loose with her uxorious husband, Sir Peter, she fills her dressing room with as many "flowers in winter as would suffice to turn the Pantheon into a greenhouse." She must have her coach and "a pair of white cats" to draw her to "Kensington Gardens."[88] After making herself vulnerable to Joseph Surface, the avaricious, hypocritical lecher, she confesses her admiration of her husband's tenderness, showing that Sheridan, like Goldsmith, relies on aristocratic patriarchy rather than assailing the double standard. Sir Oliver controls the denouement through his imperial wealth gained in India and through his paternalistic role playing which unmasks Joseph and celebrates Charles Surface's fidelity.

URBAN GEOGRAPHY AND IMPERIAL ARCHITECTURE IN LONDON AND PARIS

James Stuart (1713–1788), a student of Greek architecture and friend to Whig patricians, claims the following in his *Critical Observations on the Buildings and Improvements of London* (1771):

Nothing seems more capable of affording satisfaction to a liberal mind, than the many public improvements of elegance and convenience which have been lately made in this metropolis. Every inhabitant participates of their advantages, and every man of generous feelings shares in the reputation which his country acquires from them. Perhaps then it is the right of every individual to discuss with decent freedom the merits and demerits of public works, and even of private undertakings as far as they relate to public ornament. A discussion of this sort may serve to turn men's attention to these subjects, and be the means of introducing a greater correctness of taste for the future.

To Stuart, architecture is a liberal art based on classical models accessible through travel and cross-cultural comparisons. Hence, his remarks on Louis XIV's effort to give France "universal dominion in the arts and sciences, as well as in arms." This monarch sped public works: he "cut canals, extended public roads, and established regular posts throughout his kingdom. He regulated the police of his capital, and he added to

---

88 Moore 1933, 890 and 893.

its commodiousness and its decoration, by lighting and a better manner of paving its streets." When he stopped, France stopped: "at this day" she is no more "advanced in those articles as she was a century ago."

Hence, its post-chaises, which were then so justly admired, now appear, after the improvements of England, as clumsy and incommodious as the boots of their postillions. Even the lamps of Paris, which the poets of those days, compared to the planets themselves, 'pendent from the vault of heaven,' are now discovered, by travellers who have seen the illuminations of London, to be no more than a few scattered tin lanthorns hung by packthread in the middle of narrow and dirty streets.

In his nationalism, Stuart finds little to praise in London's architecture; he sees no distinctions of taste in Westminster and the city: "though we claim a right, from prescription, to laugh at the bad taste of our neighbours in the city, I am afraid our pretensions to superiority in the west end of the town are founded more upon presumption than truth."[89] He seeks model developments. St James's Square comes close. Not perfect in style, it "strikes the mind ... with something of more ease and propriety than any square in London. You are not confined in your space; your eye takes in the whole compass at one glance, and the water in the middle seems placed there for ornament and use." But other squares lack a uniform plan: "they are gardens, they are parks, they are sheep-walks, in short they are every thing but what they should be." If they have a governing concept, it is the absurd one of "*rus in urbe.*" He decries Grosvenor Square with a commercial image: it is "filled up with bushes and dwarf trees, through which a statue peeps, like a piece of gilt gingerbread in a green-grocer's stall." Cavendish, Hanover, and Red Lion squares are "all, more or less, tinctured with the same absurdity, an awkward imitation of the country, amid the smoke and bustle of the town." By contrast, spacious royal parks on the outskirts, "all within reach, and open to the health and amusement of the inhabitants," render "mock-parks in the middle of the town still more unnecessary and absurd." Stuart wants London's fifteen major squares improved in order to best "Paris, her proud rival."[90] His imperial vision foresees

89 Stuart 1771, 1–6.
90 Ibid., 8–10, 14–15, and 21.

Oxford Road becoming "the noblest street in Europe," should palaces and temples be built along it. A start is being made by the Pantheon and by the new church planned for Marylebone. Still, houses of men of rank do not serve public display; they should be more than roomy and convenient, "the meer requisites of a packer, or a sugar baker." The "insipid" front of St James's Square does not befit "the residence of the first duke of England." Hopefully, individuals who have studied abroad will enrich "our island with models of the most perfect kind." Italy has "become, in a manner, our own; and even Greece, Syria, and Asia Minor, hitherto unexplored, were made, for our use, to open their hidden treasures of the sublime and graceful *Antique*." Such models should make "two capital subjects" more easily built in London, namely, a senate-house and a palace for the monarch of "this mighty empire."[91]

Stuart's hopes for urban geography and imperial architecture based on Greek and Roman styles illustrate how his period linked national identity to design of public spaces. Enhancing the grandeur of capitals met the civic need to make planning symbolize more than personal taste. Classical forms enabled cultural critics to look past local eccentricity and historical contingency. In this regard, *An Essay on the Study and Practice of Architecture* by Marc-Antoine Laugier (1713–1769), a Jesuit abbé, is noteworthy since its publication in 1756 anticipates Stuart by putting the science of building as a liberal art on a par with poetry and painting and by arguing that aesthetic response to material culture should cultivate public experience and cognition:

The sight of an edifice, built with all the perfection of art, creates a pleasure and enchantment, which becomes irresistible. This view raises in the soul noble and most affecting ideas. We experience therein that sweet emotion, and that agreeable transport that such works excite, which bear the impression of true superiority of genius. A fine building speaks most eloquently for its architect.

Like Stuart, Laugier promotes the tradition of Greek building so well copied by Rome, lamenting that the "barbarity" that "buried the liberal arts under the ruins of that empire" affects "modern architecture." Although French architects in "the past age" tried to re-establish

---

91 Ibid., 28, 36, and 38.

classical models and to abandon "the ridiculous geugaws of the Goths and Arabians," barbarity threatens to return. No professional, Laugier contends that the "knowledge of rules is not prohibited to any body, altho' the execution is given but to some." So, like Stuart, he says architecture should embellish "entire cities." not just "particular houses." But French cities remain "in a state of negligence, of confusion and disorder, wherein the ignorance and rusticity of our forefathers have put them." Houses were built without changing "the bad disposition of the streets" or the deformed "decorations made by chance, and according to the caprice of every one." Cities are merely "houses, heaped together confusedly, without œconomy, without design." This disorder is most shocking in Paris, its centre hardly having changed "for three hundred years." In some ways "a fine city," Paris is "inferior to many, by all the advantages which render a city commodious, agreeable and magnificent": its "avenues" are "miserable," its "streets ill contrived and too strait, the houses simply and trivially built, the squares few in number and inconsiderable in themselves; the palaces almost all ill disposed."

Like London, Paris is inferior to its environs from the stance of landscape design patronized by Louis XIV. The Sun King introduced to gardening the taste for natural graces in "the imagination of the poets." To Laugier, this landscape movement eschewed the "slavery of fashion, a slavery so common and often so dangerous in France." It arose from the "empire of the fine, an empire always so invincible." This imperial aesthetic renders "the neighbourhood of Paris superiour to Paris itself": suburban gardens "gain every day a more smiling appearance, more true, more natural." From a stance opposing Stuart's, Laugier insists "we should furnish new allurements to inclination, which makes us look for all the refreshments the country affords." Still, as a cultural critic Laugier shares with Stuart the belief that not one of the arts has "arrived to the last degree of perfection." Much may be improved even in "masterpieces" such as the gardens of Versailles; if their formality causes immediate "astonishment and admiration," it soon causes "sadness [and] weariness." They lack "a smiling aspect" which "carries with it a landskip adorned with a thousand country graces, the contemplation of which produce moments of sweet meditation, which retains the soul in a delicious repose." The gardens have too much artificial symmetry: "Art far from being concealed proclaims itself, in every part and in every manner, it is like one of those discourses full of affectation, all the turns of which are studied, all the periods elaborated, where every thing is measured by rule."[92]

INTOXICANTS AND THE INWARD TURN OF EMPIRE

In exploring the built environment and the design of urban spaces meant to satisfy leisure and luxury, this chapter implicates economic and social imperialism into consumerism that aimed to extend bodily experience. It also illustrates the paradox that, while societies articulate rules for constructing space and play, they look beyond rational awareness to show that imperialism is an unsatisfactory political ideology. This state of affairs leads us to ask why daily life strikes humans as limited. Why do humans desire more than mundane reality? Why do we seek to transform our outlook on ourselves and the world? Will we better understand mind–body relations if we probe how we use stimulants such as drugs, alcohol, and art to expand cognition? A further question: might not anthropology explain how and why our senses co-operate in aesthetic experience?

In *Essential Substances* (1994), a study of intoxicants, Richard Rudgley argues that the "universal human need for liberation from the restrictions of mundane existence is satisfied by experiencing altered states of consciousness." To Rudgley, all substances that "alter the state of consciousness" are intoxicants. Since "political, legal, economic, religious and ceremonial life all shape the way in which intoxicants are used," he probes attitudes to intoxicants by recalling ancient societies: imagining their otherness reveals ourselves.[93] He first rejects cognitive dualism: "abstract representation (and thinking) did not evolve out of naturalistic depiction and practical thinking, but rather coexisted with it." At Lascaux near Montignac, France, the "dark, wet and inhospitable caves were, we know, not generally used as dwellings"; their voluminous art "suggests that they were sacred sites, perhaps used for rituals, initiations and visionary quests by prehistoric shamans."[94] While images of predators (lions, bears, wolves) and prey (deer and bison) are

---

92 Laugier 1756, 3–6, 8, 234–45, and 258–63.
93 Rudgley 1994, 3–5.
94 Ibid., 14 and 16.

recognizable, they are depicted symbolically, overlaid on one another and even upside-down. To Rudgley, the images are communally generated cerebral projections. Anyone who has "seen" the spidery web of the retina in the days when angiogram photography decided the state of its tissue and the physiology of the optic nerve and who experiences manganese light fluxing from surgical scars will grant what Rudgley reports when he cites David Lewis-Williams and Thomas Dowson to the effect that in "certain circumstances the visual system generates a range of luminous percepts that are independent of light from an external source." Since these "derive from the human nervous system, all people who enter certain altered states of consciousness (ASC), no matter what their cultural background, are liable to perceive them." These "visual percepts are sometimes called phosphenes or form constants," the generic term "entoptic phenomena." They are experienced in three stages: the first is when entoptic images are *sui generis*; the second when they are embellished with iconic significance; the third when they assume "more hallucinatory iconic imagery."[95]

To Rudgley, the "fundamental role" of intoxicants is to stimulate communal experience by the inter-subjective sharing of entoptic imagery. "The offering of tea, cigarettes, cola or betel to friends and strangers alike is a common form of extending hospitality, and qat parties provide a forum for social and business transactions." Tasting and chewing leaves signals hierarchy: "Both the pretensions of the British middle class, embodied in porcelain tea sets, and the elaborate equipment of betel chewers hint at the vying for social status that goes on just below the surface of these apparently innocuous customs." In "the modern West" intoxication is "arbitrary and hedonistic"; the secular taking of tea and tobacco, "first used in other cultures in sacred and ceremonial settings," robs them of "spiritual significance." The secularization of intoxicants means "that altered states of consciousness are not perceived as culturally valuable." Debates about the legitimacy of alcoholic beverages, opium, and tobacco show that stimulants have no steady legal status, even if seekers "after scientific or poetic truth" were "among the first to experiment with new or little-known psychoactive substances" and have "acted as catalysts for social change." Thus, we distinguish between "normal" and "altered states of consciousness": some states of intoxication are valid

---

[95] Ibid., 16–17.

forms of pleasure and spiritual searching, others are held to harm individuals and society. That intoxicants are regarded so differently shows that secular society is conflicted "over the nature of consciousness" and over how its altered states are allowed to shape culture.[96]

A text confirming Rudgley's thesis is *Ebrietatis Encomium: Or, The Praise of Drunkenness by Boniface Oinophilus* (1743).[97] It upholds the necessity of getting drunk, claiming it is an ancient, primitive, and catholic practice, universal in cultures and among religious and learned men. Since one must be merry, one must grant that wine dispels sorrow and excites mirth. Sometimes getting drunk is good for the health, and occasionally good for old people. Wine creates wit, eloquence, and sociability while ending animosities. Drunkenness is promoted by poets and philosophers. With many references to classical authors, the text rebuts objections to drunkenness, denying that it causes evil, effects "chimerical" mirth, destroys reason, makes men untrustworthy, and distracts them from civic duty. It offers six rules for getting drunk: don't do it too often; only do it in good company; with good wine; at convenient times; never force others to get drunk and, paradoxically, be moderately drunk. After recalling that Erasmus saved himself from the plague by taking "a Glass of *Burgundy* at a proper Season," the author defines perfect wine as having "four Properties" that please "these four Senses; the Taste by its Savour, the Smell by its Flavour, the Sight by its clean and bright Colour, and the Ear by the Fame of the Country where it grows." Two other admonitions are offered: "artificial Wines, and a many other Liquors, containing a great deal of gross viscous Matter, excite a Drunkenness more long and dangerous than that which is produced by ordinary Wines. Another Thing is, Never to get drunk with Brandy, Spirits, and Strong waters."[98]

Ebrietatis Encomium is a Menippean satire that imitates *The Praise of Folly* (1511–21) by Desiderius Erasmus (1467?–1536), a conduit of Renaissance humanism to the Augustans. With brilliant irony, the

---

96 Ibid., 137 and 172–5. Walvin shares Rudgley's views in "Questions of Taste, Addiction, and Empire" (1997, 193–8).

97 *Ebrietatis Encomium: Or, The Praise of Drunkenness by Boniface Oinophilus*, 2nd ed. London: E. Curll, 1743. The text first published in French in 1722 was written by Albert-Henri de Sallengre. It was translated by Robert Samber.

98 Sallengre 1743, 165–6, and 169. The table of contents methodically and nicely lays out the topics of the thirty-two short chapters.

goddess Folly, like Pope's Dullness, turns herself into an anti-myth; she boasts she is the daughter of Plutus, the god of riches, and of Youth. She was suckled, she says, by Drunkenness, the daughter of Bacchus, and by Ignorance the daughter of Pan. Her servants were Self-love, Flattery, Oblivion, Laziness, Pleasure, Madness, Wantonness, Intemperance and Dead Sleep whose "faithful counsels" let her subject "all things" to her "dominion" and erect "an empire over emperors themselves." In her myth, Bacchus is a bushy-haired stripling who spends his life in drinking, dancing, revels, and May games. Happy to be mad rather than wise, "he delights to be worshipped with sports and gambols; nor is he displeased with the proverb that gave him the surname of fool, 'A greater fool than Bacchus.'" Folly is allowed by nature to dominate reason with her passions; while reason is found only in a "narrow corner of the brain," Folly's passions have the rest of the body to themselves. Anger and lust are "two masterless tyrants," the one possessing the heart, the "fountain of life itself," the other stretching "its empire everywhere." Folly deifies these tyrants as heroes celebrated in rites that founded cities and preserved "empire, authority, religion, policy and public actions." To her, nothing in human life is not one of her pastimes.[99]

WINE AND MEDICINE

Taking literally what *Ebrietatis Encomium* suggests, William Younger finds the "contrast between extreme elegance and excessive intoxication" a paradoxical mark of eighteenth-century culture. Since heavy drinking was common, his assertion of the paradox is tested in this book. On one hand, Brillat-Savarin seems moderate in claiming a man can enjoy a long life by drinking two bottles of wine a day.[100] On the other, drinking songs corroborate Shaftesbury's disgust with male imbibing.[101] Excessive wine drinking was thought to cause gout, the period's fashionable disease according to Roy Porter. That its name comes from French *goût*, which conveys several senses of taste, reflects ignorance

---

99   Erasmus 1958, 14–15, 23, 26, 41. *The Praise of Folly* was written in 1509, first published in 1511, and then revised until 1521.

100   Younger 1966, 336, 339, and 337.

101   See, for example, *The Buck's Bottle Companion: Being a Complete Collection of Humourous, Bottle, and Hunting Songs* (London: R. Bladon, T. Lawes, T. Crowder, C. Ware, and T. Payne, 1775).

about the medical condition. For centuries gout had been linked to issues of heredity, gender, and blood circulation.[102] Scores of texts analyzed the disease, proposed cures, or facetiously dismissed the possibility of a cure given its inevitability. Uncertainty about arthritis partly explains the proliferation of such texts. The following titles are illustrative: *The Honour of the Gout* (1727) sees the condition as "one of the greatest Blessings which can befal Mortal Man." Despite a person's lifestyle, it is unavoidable and "preferable to a Crown imperial"; *The Dishonour of the Gout* contests this "Ludicrous" view; and *A Full and Plain Account of the Gout* (1767) offers relief but denies the possibility of curing it, its author having suffered with it for thirty years.[103]

By century's end, doctors confronting gout and diseases allegedly caused by alcohol turned their attention to social habits and cultural trends arising from the wine trade. John Wright in his preface to *An Essay on Wines, Especially on Port Wine* (1795) says that port "formerly looked on as a luxury" is now "regarded as a necessary part of food." He clarifies "on evident principles" the "difference betwixt good and bad Port Wine" so that everyone "may distinguish easily what is useful or genuine, and detect adulteration, by his senses." He treats the "component parts of wine" to "evince, that corporeal as well as mental taste, may be acquired on true principles of judgment or distinction, without producing fastidiosity, or giving rise to affected delicacy." He teaches readers to train their bodily and mental senses "to increase the satisfaction of enjoyment" by giving "cursory hints of how Port may be hurried into a taste of seeming maturity." What is served in "inns and other public houses" and "in families where one might expect a glass of good wine" shows the English have no sense of "pure Port"; what the trade supplies is "very often in such a state as not to please the palate, and half a pint will frequently hurt both the head and the stomach."[104] Wright offers rules for detecting false port and the forced fining of vintners:

---

102 Porter 1999, 258, 586, 77, and 345.

103 Philander Misiatrus, *The Honour of the Gout* (London and Dublin: George Faulkner, 1727), especially page 59; John Marten, *The Dishonour of the Gout: Or, A Serious Answer to a Ludicrous Pamphlet, Lately Publish'd Entitled The Honour of the Gout*, 4th ed. (London: J. Isted, 1737); Ferdinando Warner, *A Full and Plain Account of the Gout*, 2nd ed. (London: T. Cadell, 1767).

104 Wright 1795, [v], vi–vii, and ix.

To judge properly of Port, draw a cork or two every six months, after it hath been in bottle. ☞ When wine is very transparent, its taste pleasant, and its flavour fragrant, wait no longer, whatever its real or nominal age ... Port, like all other wines, ripens or remains crude, in a short or a long time, according to its lightness or thinness, or firmness, strength or consistence, according to the fermentation it hath undergone, the quality of the grapes, the quantity of water added to their juice, or the portion of brandy put to it.

But rules for determining "the proper age of any wine" are not "unconditional" since "one cellar will forward wine, or other fermented liquors, as much in a few months, as another will in three or four years." Forcing wines to appear "ripe" early "never fails to injure every thing that is valuable in them." A rich wine dealer he knows has iron stoves in his cellar that issue a "universal warmth." This "may suit the economical tasteless man, who takes in his wine by the dozen, and will have it cheap, but he can never expect to have a glass of tolerable wine after such treatment." Those who buy "such wine by the pipe, may find it extravagantly dear in the end"; it may "bring on disorders of the bowels, nervous complaints, and sometimes rheumatic indispositions." Fining wine with arsenic and corrosive minerals to make it transparent and mellow is yet more dangerous; when "the finest particles" are "daily taken into the body in small quantities, they gradually produce diseases which have a tendency to putridity, to scurvy, dropsy, dysentery, stinking breath, cutaneous eruptions, rheumatism, rottenness and blackness of the teeth, and a train of nervous disorders, that make even strong men valetudinarians." But such complaints remain "obscure to their physicians."[105]

Wright, unlike other doctors, holds that some disorders benefit from treatment with "a proper allowance of light fragrant small sound wine," if not with a strong one diluted with water. He cites a "light pleasant Port, somewhat of the nature of Burgundy" made experimentally in Portugal without brandy: it is "to my palate the pleasantest wine I ever tasted, even superior to the Creme de Noyeau, a pint was a delightful pittance, a bottle gives brilliancy to wit, and three pints even to a milksop never conjures up blue devils, nor leaves nausea, heat, fever or headach behind." He orders "some pipes." In favour of traditional "Red Port Wine" which when aged is pleasant and elegant, he knows it is "on the

---

105 Ibid., 44–5.

decline" since merchants are so eager for a "ready return" that they sell it as soon as they get it from the vats of vignerons, even before it is one year old.[106]

Imperial Paradoxes probes whether writers cultivate eating and drinking; if resistance to embodied taste is confirmed, aesthetic sense is limited. A major instance is *An Essay Medical, Philosophical, and Chemical on Drunkenness and Its Effects on the Human Body* (1804) by Thomas Trotter (1760–1832), who finds humans "ever in pursuit of pleasure" and adding to "the catalogue of their diseases" evils that are the "immediate offspring of their luxuries." He glimpses mind–body relations even as he voices truisms about faculty psychology and natural depravity: it is "natural to the human mind" to quit "the paths of duty" and yield "pretensions to the character of rational beings" to "inordinate use of spirituous liquors." The "habit of inebriation," being "so common in society" it affects "all ranks and stations of life," he thinks "the source of inexpressible affliction to friends and relatives" since it has "seldom been the object of medical admonition and practice." Still he faults priests and moralists for simply calling it "a vice degrading to our nature"; they ignore "the physical influence of custom, confirmed into habit, interwoven with the actions of our sentient system, and reacting on our mental part."[107]

While Trotter's medical observations on inebriation are vague, his contextual sense of motives is acute: these are as "diversified as the varieties of corporeal structure"; pleasure seekers take the "poisonous bowl"; the depressed "call for the cheering draught"; "duties of office" cause "frequent hard drinking." Soldiers and sailors imbibe "while narrating the dangers of the battle and the storm," as do "the huntsman and the jockey" in telling "the joys of the chace and course." Men of genius forget in wine "the outrages of fortune, and the ingratitude of the world," while gloomy men who seek in the bottle "the feelings and sentiments of exalted beings" merely "gravitate to their original clay, or sink deeper into their parent mud." These topers are not categorized in their social and psychological conditions; Trotter's moralism is too dominant. When closest to a medical view, he admits the mixed settings in which inebriation occurs render clinical analysis problematic. He is

---

106 Ibid., 46 and 43.
107 Trotter 1988, 1 and 3.

truer to his profession when granting that the stages of inebriation complicate diagnosis. The talents of William Hogarth (1697–1764), he says, would be necessary to depict "the shades and gradations of feature" of those passing "from perfect sobriety to the last stage of intoxication."[108]

Aesthetic experience enters Trotter's mind only obliquely; mistrusting that one may train the senses and learn to see, smell, and taste qualities in wine, he posits that bodily pleasures not only sap mental awareness but are dulled by wine which cannot yield cultivated enjoyment via the gustatory organs. It stimulates deceptively and depressingly: the "soul, as if unconscious of its danger, looks with bodily organs that bespeak rapture to the deceitful bowl." Desire for transcendence ends in brutality; men forget the bowl mediates "every degree of sensation, from pleasure to pain, from the purest perceptions of intellect, to the last confusion of thought"; it "raises man above the sphere of mortals, and ends, by bringing him to a level with the brutes." There is a stage before that descent: the acme of "pleasurable feeling" reached, the mind enters a "*reverie*," the "boundary, between the agreeable sensations of sobriety, and the delirious tumults of thought, which usher in complete inebriation." The reverie is defensive; the "system has been enough excited to bring forth pleasurable sensation, to subdue pain, and sufficient judgment remains to analize the reflections which arise from condition of life, so as to fortify the present moment against all the intrusive approaches of care or sorrow." Were Bacchus's votaries to stop here, one could grant their wish to "forget those ills which flesh is heir to." But "*drunken reverie*" rejects self-regulation; the "grave philosopher himself becomes convivial … and applauds the jest and the song."[109]

For Trotter, gustatory pleasures are ineducable because transient and efforts to train them are debasing. Bibulous conviviality is paradoxical since unsustainable: "like all human enjoyments, the exhilarating powers of wine lose their fine zest and high relish, by being too frequently indulged." Sots extending pleasures ignore that, in trying to amend the dullness caused by habitual drinking, they become more vulnerable to inebriation. So they take wine "on an empty stomach; or after very long fasting." Having served in the British navy, Trotter knew Captain Bligh's account of his passage to Timor after the mutiny on *The Bounty*.

---

108 Ibid., 4.
109 Ibid., 15–16.

Allowances of water and provisions being "so exceedingly small," his crew was brought to inebriation by "a tea spoon" of rum, their bodies "so susceptible of stimulus" they suffered "accumulated excitability." Evading "the connection between body and mind," Trotter accepts that "our intellectual part can be disturbed, and so completely deranged, by bodily diseases, as to be incapable of using its reasoning powers"; this is "a fact sufficiently established to be universally admitted." Shunning "opinions on the nature of a soul, of a nervous power, or of a sentient principle," he avers that, while drunkenness is a "temporary madness," it is long-lasting in those with a "predisposition to insanity and idiotism." Apparently, cold weather leads to alcoholism: heat "bestows on the mental faculties cheerfulness and vivacity" so "inhabitants of hot countries are observed to be more gay and volatile than those of the northern regions." While the former need "less excitement from diet," the "shivering native of Lapland or Labrador" facing year-long freezing takes "an unusual glow and animation from spiritous potation." Climate "conspires to make him a drunkard: because, when he first tastes a beverage that imparts chearfulness and strength; he is not aware that it is the first step to a course of indulgence, that must ultimately impair his health, and abridge his understanding." However, Trotter admits that treating drunkenness is a challenge because doctors themselves are susceptible. He does not "debar the profession from the festive board" since they "stand most in need of relaxation" given attendance at "scenes of pain, sorrow, and death." He who lingers "in the gloom of a sick chamber" deserves social and domestic comforts. So, Trotter permits colleagues to enjoy elegant amusements.[110] As with doctors, he makes concessions about other causes of inebriation. Its "seeds" are "often sown in infancy," modernity severing humans from nature and habituating them to "*fashion.*" Nursing infants should receive "a mild bland nourishment, that is suited to the delicate excitability of a tender subject." Yet they are "deprived of the breast, long before the growth of the body has fitted the stomach for the reception of more stimulant food. Instead of its mother's milk, the infant is fed on hot broth, spiced pudding, and, perhaps also, that enervating beverage tea." Afflicted with dyspepsia, children take medicines in which wine is a menstruum. To Trotter, wine, if a remedy for typhus fever, cures no

110 Ibid., 28–30, 41–2, 127, 138–9.

other disease nor helps with misfortunes of life, which must be "opposed with religious and moral sentiments."[111]

Despite disparaging priests and moralists, Trotter resembles them in saying wine is "no friend to vigour or activity of mind: it whirls the fancy beyond the judgment, and leaves body and soul in a state of listless indolence and sloth." Thus, he bewails drinking wine at dinner because it "vitiates taste and healthful appetite." The modish beverages of tea and noyau he also charges with causing bodily harm. "Souchong tea" is a "harmless and agreeable beverage," if made weak and taken once a day with cream and sugar, but "hyson, and all the greens, are powerful narcotics, that destroy the stomach" and cause illnesses unrelieved by "spiritous potation"; the "permanent effects" of addiction to tea are "disease, pain, derangement of intellect, a miserable existence, or premature death." His moralizing about beverages underscores Trotter's restricted notions of mind and consciousness, his disregard for aesthetic taste, his devaluation of communal festivity, and his refusal to acknowledge the human desire to extend perception into the mind itself. The ritual at "feasts and entertainments" of "handing cordials round in the time of dinner" he dismisses as "against all rules of temperance." Those are brandy "impregnated with narcotic substances, which add to the noxious qualities of the spirit." People who "blush to taste brandy" do not realize "these *liqueurs*" contain ingredients such as laurel-berries and bitter almonds along with "burnt wine." His prejudices scorn the "taste of the mouth" as useless to patients who crave brandied medicines which cause "a *vacuum* in sensation." That void in sensory perception is filled only by "vinous stimulus," while the habit of inebriation remains and the mind does "not earnestly" pursue "something that can engage it."[112] Thus Trotter generates and aggravates habits of thought that create aesthetic problems for readers. His pretensions to be a medical scientist confirm how taste was often simply hypostasized as the faculty of judgment, while being ambivalently viewed as innate and cultivated by breeding. Typically he does not probe his operating metaphors, seeing them as expository devices rather than cognitive instruments. Yet he helps us appreciate that Brillat-Savarin re-motivated metaphors of embodied taste and rightly questioned his era's understanding of cognition and imagination.

111 Ibid., 148 and 150. On nursing, see chapter 4, section iv, which discusses Dr John Arbuthnot as a satirist.
112 Ibid., 164–6, 168–9, and 183–4.

2

Literariness:

Aesthetic and Cultural Dialectic

Man has no Body distinct from his Soul; for that call'd Body is a portion of Soul discern'd by the five Senses, the chief inlets of Soul in this age.[1]

ADDISON AND CULTURAL HISTORY

A striking aspect of "Addison as a Literary Critic" is that Broadus is so sure about literariness that he feels no need to renew its definition; he is certain it has finished developing into a uniquely self-sufficient mode of discourse. From a categorical sense that would preclude cultural evolution, he decries Addison's critical reputation, alleging that, since the Augustan author views the pleasures of the imagination as either primary or secondary, the "inadequate psychology" of his "scheme of imagination is almost too obvious to need pointing out." When he adds that his "'reproductive imagination' is fatally limited by being restricted to the sense of sight," he avoids seeing that Addison linked imagination to a broader view of sensory perception, ignoring his advanced grasp of synesthesia detailed below.[2] Nor, on the other hand, does Broadus treat the imagination from the standpoint of the fusion of perception and spirituality by which Blake decried the dualism of body and mind. In spurning Augustan authors, Blake's revolutionary notion of the organic unity of body and soul that refused to see them as dialectical contraries also opposed the inward turn of imperial metaphors which

---

1 Blake, *The Marriage of Heaven and Hell*, plate 4 (1966, 149).
2 Edmund Kemper Broadus, "Addison as a Literary Critic," *University of Alberta Magazine* (February 1909): 4.

Imperial Paradoxes presents in chapter 1. Still, Broadus's attack on Addison's imagination – one anticipated and rebutted by Johnson – resembles Blake's assault on the neoclassical humanism of Reynolds and on the empiricism running from Thomas Hobbes (1588–1679) to Locke that limited imagination to mental impressions of visible objects and the memory of absent ones.[3] Alleging that Addison "cannot free himself from the shackles of his sense-impressions," Broadus also charges that the "creative imagination, which compounds a world of thought and action, wherein we see ourselves, and something yet other than ourselves reflected, is apprehended very meagerly if at all" by Addison.[4] This claim about literary representation being both human and more than human assumes that creative imagination transcends the senses to effect an ineffable world to which it transports readers. No doubt, Locke's positivistic objections to rhetoric aroused post-Restoration resistance to metaphor as a mode of cognition which the studies of George Lakoff and others have recently contested.[5] Still, an issue lurks in Broadus's hint that Addison drew on Locke: does the periodical journalist treat sensation as merely preliminary to reflection?

Allied questions stem from Broadus's denigration of the *Spectator* papers on Milton when he declares that, far from enhancing the poet's reputation, Addison was "more contributive than fundamental" since he did not detect "the informing spirit" of *Paradise Lost*. To Broadus, Addison's criticism is neither creative nor original because it lacks a spiritual sense of literary unity. External causes explain this lack; he catered to an "audience of fairly cultivated Londoners, who liked to have their minds titillated with a quotation from the classics, or a half-humorous, half deprecating opinion on current literature." Hence, Addison's critique of Milton is simply "a curious combination of dry formalism in the manner, and light discursive comment in the matter." Having to "ingratiate" himself with readers, he made "no pretence of

---

3 See the Preface xi.
4 Broadus 1909, 5.
5 On the distinction between conceptual and image metaphors, see Lakoff and Turner 1989, 1–139. Their application of cognitive science is examined below. Pinker, while accepting Lakoff's "metaphor metaphor" and its challenges to traditional rationalism, questions his species of relativism (2002, 209ff.; 2007, 246–7). Pinker challenges empiricist and rationalist thinking of the seventeenth and eighteenth centuries through the medium of cognitive science.

weighing the poem in the balances"; he had no "real conception of the marvellous architectonic power of Paradise Lost," blind to its "human" unity. Without defining the relation between the transcendent and human features of Milton's poetic appeal, Broadus avers that social prejudice and a formulaic aesthetic stopped Addison from seeing *Paradise Lost* as more than a sermon and recognizing its "inner artistic necessity." The essayist's outlook "fails utterly when brought into contact with the fact that Milton, the Puritan, became Milton the genius, and his masterpiece was transfigured from a sermon to a work of art." Assumptions here entail a secularized sacramentality upon a view of aesthetic unity that not only applies to primary works of creation but also equates them to works of criticism. Since artist and critic should be equally creative, Broadus states that Addison's critique, far from being "a work of art," remains "a mass of admirable but unrelated comments." His thinking is as circular when giving extrinsic reasons for Addison's failed vision: he ultimately challenges the essayist's status by decrying the period in which he wrote and urging further studies to explore why he embodies an age "that had hardly found itself before it began to feel within it the stirrings of a new mood."[6]

Broadus would advance literariness and literary thinking by belittling eighteenth-century society. Besides a progressivist bias, we may note a graver fault: he overlooks Johnson's account of Addison in *Lives of the English Poets* which stresses that *The Tatler* and *The Spectator*, far from addressing literary scholars, respected the general public in order to establish the role of the common reader when there was a need to counter political strife and social fragmentation. Those periodicals, Johnson says, "were published at a time when two parties, loud, restless, and violent, each with plausible declarations, and each perhaps without any distinct termination of its views, were agitating the nation; to minds heated with political contest, they supplied cooler and more inoffensive reflections." Johnson defends Addison's inclusive sensibility. His "various pictures of the world" show that he "had conversed with many distinct classes of men, had surveyed their ways with very diligent observation, and marked with great acuteness the effects of different modes of life." Aware that Addison's criticism had been "condemned as tentative or experimental, rather than scientifick" and that he was blamed for

6 Broadus 1909, 7–10, 12–13, and 20.

"deciding by taste rather than by principle," Johnson agilely counters that critics "who have grown wise by the labour of others" often "overlook their masters: Addison is now despised by some who perhaps would never have seen his defects, but by the lights which he afforded them." Critics do not see that his "instructions were such as the characters of his readers made proper." Johnson then explicates those instructions:

That general knowledge which now circulates in common talk, was in his time rarely to be found. Men not professing learning were not ashamed of ignorance; and in the female world, any acquaintance with books was distinguished only to be censured. His purpose was to infuse literary curiosity, by gentle and unsuspected conveyance, into the gay, the idle, and the wealthy; he therefore presented knowledge in the most alluring form, not lofty and austere, but accessible and familiar. When he shewed them their defects, he shewed them likewise that they might be easily supplied. His attempt succeeded; enquiry was awakened, and comprehension expanded. An emulation of intellectual elegance was excited, and from his time to our own, life has been gradually exalted, and conversation purified and enlarged.

To Johnson, Addison advanced Milton's reputation by speaking to contemporaries in "remarks" that may have been "superficial" but "might be easily understood, and being just, might prepare the mind for more attainments. Had he presented Paradise Lost to the publick with all the pomp of system and severity of science, the criticism would perhaps have been admired, and the poem still have been neglected; but by the blandishments of gentleness and facility, he has made Milton an universal favourite, with whom readers of every class think it necessary to be pleased." Keen observations and sympathetic imagination make him a literary and social critic: "As a describer of life and manners, he must be allowed to stand perhaps the first of the rank ... He copies life with so much fidelity, that he can be hardly said to invent; yet his exhibitions have an air so much original, that it is difficult to suppose them not merely the product of imagination."[7]

In praising Addison, Johnson joins cultural history to textual criticism since artistic vision should serve the community that must be moved at

---

[7] Johnson 1952, 1:408, 427, and 446–8.

the same time to practise the uses of literature.[8] This double vision heightens deficiencies in a professionalism that would reduce literary study to an esoteric pursuit. Johnson is upheld by Kingwell, who lauds Addison's constructive politeness for perpetuating Montaigne's style of frank informality that is vital to civic duties.[9] By contrast, Broadus, in dispraising Addison's society, embodies biases of Western intellectual history and European romanticism, notably when he says sense impressions are "shackles" to the imagination and spirit. If the eighteenth century upheld one theory, it was a belief in taste as a faculty that transcends physiology and empiricism, a belief Shaftesbury and Dubos, along with others, tried to displace. By criticizing Addison as an Augustan, Broadus reinscribed into literary history notions of disembodied taste that were being revised and reformed. Still, one truism linking the Augustan and Romantic periods is the superiority of spirit over body, a dualism voiced by Broadus in an over-intellectualized stance on aesthetics that evades Blake's challenges to epistemology, as illustrated in the Preface.

In the epigraph above, he rejects the distinctness of body and soul; our senses and spirit are inseparable. As Northrop Frye says, Blake was a "spiritual utilitarian" for whom literary criticism had to accept the "identity of content and form." Against Lockean reflection that was no more than a "memory" and less than inevitably multiple sensations, Blake held that images of the form of perception are the content of knowledge. In opposing empiricism, he denied the imagination is a transcendent faculty. For him, it denotes life in perceptive individuals in society; there "is not only infinite variety of imaginations, but differences of degree as well."[10] Broadus shares neither Blake's imaginative diversity nor his metacritical dialectic of the material and immaterial; he will not see literariness as an aesthetic domain in which economic, political, and social mores operate.

Hence, Peter Briggs's study of Addison's acoustic imagination helpfully resists aesthetic purity to reveal how a psychology of sound informs the essayist's cultural criticism. Briggs shows that Addison

---

8 See notes 23, 24, and 25 with respect to the works of John Ellis.

9 Kingwell 2001, 114–17. Michel de Montaigne (1533–1592) was a remarkable French essayist who combined philosophy, anecdote, and autobiography in his writing.

10 Frye 1969, 8, 10, 15, 19, and 21.

appreciated London street criers, diverse registers of the human voice, and classical music. Mocking social fantasies, Addison says that a "Citizen who is waked by one of these Criers, may regard him as a kind of Remembrancer, come to admonish him that it is time to return to the Circumstances he has overlooked all the Night-time, to leave off fancying himself what he is not, and prepare to act suitably to the Condition he is really placed in." Cries of watchmen, coal men, and carmen on "their early Rounds about the City in a Morning" deflate those whose "Moon-shine in the Brain" views such men as "noisy Slaves" who work "strange Confusion" in their affairs.[11] Clearly, Addison had an expansive sense of sound and music – "its various tonalities, its social place or places, its affective powers, and finally the affinities and tensions between formal music and ordinary spoken language." His "keen ear" had learned that sounds endure unlike the "dramatic immediacies of sight." So, he recorded a range of conversational styles and demonstrated how they modulate into one another: he presents "talk of the town, genial moralizing, light satire and occasional censure, various crotchets and personal enthusiasms, even mild self-congratulation, all without breaking stride or losing forward momentum." His acuity about the "audible environment" ensured he was no snob. His belief that the Hebrew Bible had "introduced a measured harmony" and social solidarity into the English language led him to hold that a person of ordinary sharpness who is alert to rural and urban sounds is well able to enjoy the linguistic and chromatic clashes in opera, his auditory sensibility no lesser than that of professional musicians. Citing *Spectator*, No. 29, Briggs stresses Addison's contention that "A Man of an ordinary Ear is a Judge whether a Passion is express'd in proper Sounds, and whether the Melody of those Sounds be more or less pleasing" since this claim subordinates "the Art to the Taste" and gives primacy to "the Delicacy of Hearing and Taste of Harmony."[12] In esteeming Addison's acoustic synesthesia and musical sensibility, Briggs rejects biases in literary history that ignore the cultural value of sense transference to cognition. In the process he treats the problems that inhere in the specializations of literary criticism:

11 *The Spectator*, no. 597, Wednesday, 22 September 1714 (Addison 1966, 4:365–7).
12 *The Spectator*, no. 29, Tuesday, 3 April 1711 (Addison 1964, 1: 89).

Professional training has made criticism ... correspondingly less likely to admire the directness, the spontaneity and cultivated ease, the assumption of shared and dependable values that so long made Addison available and helpful to common readers. Addison asserted a shared sensibility, which he was forging even as he assumed its existence ... As we have changed the strategies and functions of literary criticism, we also changed its expected audience: professionals now write to and for their fellow professionals, and we are beholden to our peers for whatever standing we enjoy as critics.[13]

Addison is an antidote to professionalism. Take his inclusivity when he refers to "Modern celebrated Clubs," those "little Institutions and Establishments" that are "founded upon Eating and Drinking." Since most men agree about food and drink, "the Learned and Illiterate, the Dull and the Airy, the Philosopher and the Buffoon," all may join the Kit-Cat, a club taking its name from mutton-pie, or the Beef-Steak and October, clubs whose designations allude to meat and beer.[14] Despite his casual stances to readers of all types, Addison's appreciation of psychology and embodiment is well informed and exploratory, as evident in his papers on the pleasures of the imagination.

While traditionally calling sight the most perfect and delightful of the senses since it fills "the Mind with the largest Variety of Ideas," he treats this distal sense paradoxically, saying it "converses with its Objects at the greatest Distance." He applies other metaphors to sight when comparing it to the "Sense of Feeling," which, if giving us "a Notion of Extension, Shape, and all the other Ideas that enter at the Eye, except Colours," is "confined in its Operations, to the Number, Bulk, and Distance of its particular Objects." Still, sight "may be considered as a more delicate and diffusive kind of Touch, that spreads itself over an infinite Multitude of Bodies, comprehends the largest Figures, and brings into our reach some of the most remote Parts of the Universe." Metaphors of spreading, covering, fetching, and carrying qualify his

---

13 Briggs 2005, 158–63 and 171. Relevant here is the work of Fish. See note 22 below.

14 *The Spectator*, no. 9, Saturday, 10 March 1711 (Addison 1964, 1:30). *The Spectator*, no. 508, Monday, 13 October 1712 (Addison 1966, 4:102–4), jokes about a club member who takes all dining decisions on himself. A despot and tyrant, he runs an "odd Sort of Empire" and alone selects the tavern, "the Seat of Empire," along with the menus.

allusion to Locke's distinction between primary ideas of sensation and secondary ideas of reflection since they illustrate how visual images may be retained, altered, and compounded "into all the Varieties of Picture and Vision that are most agreeable to the Imagination."[15] Thus, a man in prison may create "Scenes and Landskips more beautiful than any that can be found in the whole Compass of Nature." This aestheticism goes beyond representational imagery: since he may derive "a greater Satisfaction in the Prospect of Fields and Meadows, than another does in the Possession," he enjoys "a kind of Property in every thing he sees," this producing a "kindly Influence on the Body, as well as the Mind," according to Bacon's "Essay on Health."[16] As his exposition of imaginative pleasures unfolds, Addison's sense of the dialectic of pleasure and pain and intuitions about synesthesia grow keener. Seeing great, uncommon, and beautiful things may involve a mixture of delight and disgust, and in meeting astonishing and loathsome things the eye can lose itself. If tired of looking at static hills and valleys, relief comes when motion makes them slide away "from beneath the Eye of the Beholder." In the following passage, Addison may be seen anticipating Brillat-Savarin's subtle approach to synesthesia:

As the Fancy delights in every thing that is Great, Strange, or Beautiful, and is still more pleased the more it finds of these Perfections in the same Object, so it is capable of receiving a new Satisfaction by the Assistance of another Sense. Thus, any continued Sound, as the Musick of Birds, or a Fall of Water, awakens every moment the Mind of the Beholder, and makes him more attentive to the several Beauties of the Place that lye before him. Thus if there arises a Fragrancy of Smells or Perfumes, they heighten the Pleasures of the Imagination and make even the Colours and Verdure of the Landskip appear more agreeable for the Ideas of both Senses recommend each other, and are

---

15 An analysis of *Spectator*, no. 411, by Hugh Blair (1718–1800) shows how Addison's metaphors personify taste (Corbett 1971, 541). Blair praises Addison for "the most delicate and refined luxury" in "Figurative Language" and for an imagination "at once, remarkably rich, and remarkably correct and chaste." He lauds Addison's sense of "imaginary glories" and visionary beauty" in *Spectator*, no. 413. To Blair, Addison is "the safest model to imitate," his style being "commonly very musical" and "splendid without being gaudy"; it has "great elegance joined with great ease and simplicity" and is "distinguished by a character of modesty, and of politeness." (1783, 1:343–4; 2:40–1).

16 *The Spectator*, no. 411, Saturday, 21 June 1712 (Addison 1963, 3:276–8).

pleasanter together, than when they enter the Mind separately: As the different Colours of a Picture, when they are well disposed, set off one another, and receive an additional Beauty from the Advantage of their Situation.[17]

In his continuing exposition, Addison sets experience above rational analysis, refusing to assign a "necessary Cause" to the mixed pleasures of the imagination since "we know neither the Nature of an Idea, nor the Substance of a Human Soul, which might help us to discover the Conformity or Disagreeableness of the one to the other." As Hume limits knowledge to contingency and habitual association, so Addison holds that one can only speculate about how the senses operate and merely classify "under their proper Heads" what in experience pleases or displeases the imagination.[18]

To Hume and Burke, Addison's aestheticism made him a member of a mindful community worth joining. Basing taste on experience not reason, Hume, unlike Broadus, thought Milton and Addison shared "an equality of genius and elegance."[19] In advancing what J.T. Boulton calls his sensationalist synesthesia and his dialectic of the positive and negative feelings aroused by the sublime, Burke reveals affinities with Addison.[20] Indeed, Addison inspired followers. Consider his definition of taste. He cited the Roman Emperor Gratian, who ruled from A.D. 367 to 383 and sympathized with Christianity, for his claim that "fine Taste" is "the utmost Perfection of an accomplished Man," defining it as "that Faculty of the Mind, which distinguishes all the most concealed Faults and nicest Perfections in Writing." In all languages, this metaphor proves the "very great Conformity" between mental taste and the "Sensitive Taste which gives us a Relish of every different Flavour that affects the Palate." Hence, "there are as many Degrees of Refinement in the intellectual Faculty, as in the Sense." He next offers a supportive anecdote: he knew a person with so fine a taste that "after having tasted ten different Kinds of Tea, he would distinguish, without seeing the Colour of it, the particular Sort." He even discriminated between two or three sorts of tea mixed in equal proportions and told where

17 *The Spectator*, no. 412, Monday, 23 June 1712 (Addison 1963, 3:279–82).
18 *The Spectator*, no. 413, Tuesday, 24 June 1712 (Addison 1963, 3:282).
19 Hume, "of The Standard of Taste" (1965, 7).
20 Burke 1968, lxxiii, 121–4 and 153–6. According to Roston, Addison and Burke appreciated divine aspects of the sublime (1990, 229–33).

they came from. Tasting tea is an analogy for one with a "fine Taste in Writing": he will discern "not only the general Beauties and Imperfections of an Author, but discover the several Ways of thinking and expressing himself which diversify him from all other Authors, with the several Foreign Infusions of Thought and Language, and the particular Authors from whom they were borrowed." Addison then concludes that taste is "*that Faculty of the Soul, which discerns the Beauties of an Author with Pleasure, and the Imperfections with Dislike.*" Partly innate, this facility arises from reading "the celebrated Works of Antiquity" and modern works "which have the Sanction of the Politer Part of our Contemporaries" and from conversation with men of a "Polite Genius."[21] In "of the Standard of Taste," Hume follows Addison:

A good palate is not tried by strong flavor, but by a mixture of small ingredients, where we are still sensible of each part, notwithstanding its minuteness and its confusion with the rest. In like manner, a quick and acute perception of beauty and deformity must be the perfection of our mental taste; nor can a man be satisfied with himself while he suspects that any excellence or blemish in a discourse has passed him unobserved. In this case, the perfection of the man, and the perfection of the sense of feeling, are found to be united.[22]

Later in this essay, Hume presents the discipline in which readers must exercise taste to overcome national biasses, a stance Addison shared with Shaftesbury. To Hume, a sensitive man imposes "a proper violence on his imagination" to forget himself and his circumstances as he reads. Otherwise prejudices will pervert comprehension. He must place himself in the same situation as that of the original audience. A reader who resists selflessness makes no allowances for readers of different ages and countries, rashly condemns those peculiar views that addressed the first audience, and misses seeing the original beauties and blemishes of given works.[23]

The Spectator confirms Addison's dialectical practices as literary historian and literary critic, showing that he had a keen knowledge of classical literature, appreciated the *zeitgeist* and cultural climates that inspired

---

21 *The Spectator*, no. 409, Thursday, 19 June 1712 (Addison 1963, 3:271).
22 Hume, "of The Standard of Taste" (1965, 12).
23 Ibid., 15.

groups of authors, and held strong views about contrary relations between empire and artistic achievements. In the same paper that defines taste, he reports that

Men of great Genius in the same way of Writing, seldom rise up singly, but at certain Periods of Time appear together, and in a Body; as they did at Rome in the Reign of Augustus, and in Greece about the Age of Socrates. I cannot think that Corneille, Racine, Moliere, Boileau, la Fontaine, Bruyere, Bossu, or the Daciers, would have written so well as they have done, had they not been Friends and Contemporaries.[24]

Earlier he made a similar point about writers in the "Reign" of Augustus Caesar, sensibly adding a dark shade to his picture. At first, he claims that the "greatest Wits that ever were produced in one Age, lived together in so good an Understanding, and celebrated one another with so much Generosity, that each of them receives an additional Lustre from his Contemporaries, and is more famous for having lived with Men of so extraordinary a Genius than if he had himself been the sole Wonder of the Age." The fame of Vergil and Horace grew from their being "Friends and Admirers of each other." Yet, if most authors celebrated Vergil, "Bavius and Maevius were his declared Foes and Calumniators."[25] Familiar with personal conflicts in the Roman empire – for instance, that Horace and Vergil hated Mark Antony – Addison knows that a disinterested perspective is needed by biographers. Since biographies written when subjects are alive are either too praising or too critical, writers at a distance from subjects and not drawn in by partisanship do a better job:

It is therefore the Privilege of Posterity to adjust the Characters of Illustrious Persons, and to set matters right between those Antagonists who by their Rivalry for Greatness divided a whole Age into Factions. We can now allow Caesar to be a great Man, without derogating from Pompey; and celebrate the Virtues of Cato, without detracting from those of Caesar. Every one that has been long dead has a due proportion of Praise allotted him, in which whilst he lived his Friends were too profuse and his Enemies too sparing.[26]

---

24 *The Spectator*, no. 409, Thursday, 19 June 1712 (Addison 1963, 3:272).
25 *The Spectator*, no. 253, Thursday, 20 December 1711 (Addison 1963, 2:252).
26 *The Spectator*, no. 101, Tuesday, 26 June 1711 (Addison 1964, 1:311).

Addison so respected the ancients that he held the moderns had nothing to discover about critical principles. He thought theoretical refinement ended with Aristotle and that Horace, having had nothing new to convey, was to be praised only for expressing and applying the philosopher's rules. In his mind, critical originality was unobtainable, a sentiment that must have appalled Blake.[27]

Addison's familiarity with Roman imperialism deepened his cultural criticism and wish to promote civil society. Thus, he extended Shaftesbury's view of liberty with a more inclusive outlook. The best form of government, he says, grants liberty to all individuals and stops men from subjecting one another. Yet despotism still arises if legislation is not created by persons of different ranks. In other words, a government of "publick Peace and Tranquility" must conform to "the Equality that we find in humane Nature." Every person deserves liberty since we "all share one common Nature." If limited to sections of society, it had better not exist, for then "such a Liberty only aggravates the Misfortune of those who are deprived of it, by setting before them a disagreeable Subject of Comparison." If "Legislative Power" is not lodged "in several Persons ... of different Ranks and Interests" but in persons of the "same Rank" who "have an Interest to manage peculiar to that Rank," what results is no different from "a despotical Government in a single Person." The "Division of the three Powers in the *Roman* Constitution" in which "the Consul represented the King, the senate the Nobles, and the Tribunes the People" was no natural "Form of Government" since the "consular Power" had "Ornaments without the Force of the regal Authority." Such a power imbalance did not stop "many hopeful Heirs apparent to great Empires" from becoming "such Monsters of Lust and Cruelty as are a Reproach to Humane Nature." Absolute princes in Europe are restrained from tyranny by wealthy subjects who would form new constitutions if so abused. But "in all despotick Governments," led by a prince who supports "Arts and Letters," there falls out "a natural Degeneracy of Mankind," as in "Augustus's Reign" when the "Romans lost themselves by Degrees, till they fell to an Equality with the most barbarous Nations that surrounded them."[28]

Preparing the way for Adam Smith (1723–1790), Addison lauds the evolution of trade and commerce, his cultural criticism employing

---

27 *The Spectator*, no. 253, Thursday, December 20, 1711 (Addison 1963, 2:253).
28 *The Spectator*, no. 287, Tuesday, 29 January 1712 (Addison 1963, 2:355–59). Addison's political remarks draw on Polybius, Cicero, and Suetonius.

imperial metaphors of possession and consumption when describing visits to London's Royal Exchange. His pride as an Englishman comes from observing the "Assembly of Country-men and Foreigners" doing business there and making "this Metropolis a kind of *Emporium* for the whole Earth." Likening merchants to diplomats, he fancies the Exchange "a great Council, in which all considerable Nations have their Representatives": factors "in the Trading World are what Ambassadors are in the Politick World; they negotiate Affairs, conclude Treaties," and maintain a correspondence with "wealthy Societies" that are "divided from one another by Seas and Oceans." In his global fancy, he adopts different identities. At times, he is a "Dane, Swede, or Frenchman," at others "a Citizen of the World." The "mutual Intercourse and Traffick among Mankind" means "Food often grows in one Country, and the Sauce in another." Thus, the "Fruits of *Portugal* are corrected by the Products of Barbadoes." In the realm of fashion, the "single Dress of a Woman of Quality is often the Product of an Hundred Climates." Without commerce, England is barren: "no Fruit grows originally among us, besides Hips and Haws, Acorns and Pig-nutts." Climate hinders horticulture and fruit production: "our Melons, our Peaches, our Figs, our Apricots, and Cherries, are Strangers among us, imported in different Ages, and naturalized in our English Gardens." These fruits would "degenerate and fall away into the Trash of our own Country, if they were wholly neglected by the Planter, and left to the Mercy of our Sun and Soil." International trade enriches "the whole Face of Nature among us. Our Ships are laden with the Harvest of every Climate: Our Tables are stored with Spices, and Oils, and Wines: Our Rooms are filled with Pyramids of China, and adorned with the Workmanship of Japan: Our Morning's-Draught comes to us from the remotest Corners of the Earth: We repair our Bodies by the Drugs of *America*, and repose our selves under *Indian* Canopies ... the Vineyards of *France* [are] our Gardens: the Spice-Islands our Hot-Beds; the *Persians* our Silk-Weavers, and the *Chinese* our Potters." Without "enlarging the *British* Territories," trade "has given us a kind of additional Empire" and "multiplied the Number of the Rich, made our Landed Estates infinitely more Valuable than they were formerly, and added to them an Accession of other estates as valuable as the Lands themselves."[29]

29 *The Spectator*, no. 69, Saturday, 19 May 1711 (Addison 1964, 1: 214–15).

EDUCATION AND LITERARINESS

A Statue lies hid in a Block of Marble ... the Art of the Statuary only clears away the superfluous Matter, and removes the Rubbish. The Figure is in the Stone, the Sculptor only finds it. What Sculpture is to a Block of Marble, Education is to an Human Soul.[30]

Addison takes this aesthetic imagery from Aristotle's "Doctrine of Substantial Forms," because he admires the philosopher's tenet that education, when improving a noble mind, "draws out to View every latent Virtue and Perfection." This image of immanent education gains force from its context: it appears in a number of *The Spectator* that attacks slavery and upholds sympathy for savage nations by denying there can be any excuse for the contempt with which the English "treat this part of our species." Given this progressive attitude and Johnson's view of Addison as one of the "benefactors of mankind," one asks why he did not retain pedagogical authority beyond the 1880s in England and America. He not only fell into disfavour but was personally abused.[31] The desuetude of the teaching of Latin, classical rhetoric, philology, and oratory may partially explain this decline. Besides Broadus, critics and scholars such as T.S. Eliot and Walter Jackson Bate derided his bourgeois values, calling him priggish and arrogant and charging him with having a negative effect on English culture. Yet, to many contemporaries he possessed charming personal manners and was lauded for effective public administration. At this point, one must grant that Broadus, a graduate of Chicago and Harvard, was a devoted, if austere, teacher and a pioneer with his wife in establishing Canadian letters in the curriculum of schools and universities. He taught in the early days of English studies when, a new field, it aimed at being an academic discipline with legitimate fields of research. Emerging from the dominance of classical literature and philology, English studies did not easily find a coherent way forward; it suffered from competing goals held by rival universities. In attempting to create an inclusive middle class and deflect readers' aristocratic pretensions, and in thinking trade and commerce beneficial to all classes and trying to instill a desire for civility and political

---

30 *The Spectator*, no. 215, Tuesday, 6 November 1711 (Addison 1963, 2:139–40).
31 Miller 2014, 654.

stability in the public, Addison, one would think, might have retained his pedagogical appeal. A man of parts who embodied different forms of professionalism as a journalist, politician, and dramatist, he was a syncretist, a pluralist and anti-utopian thinker who respected imperial cultural ideals while challenging imperial political goals. He was a pragmatist who valued literary and political compromise. Since social constructivism coexisted with his intuitions about the collaboration of our senses and the reciprocity of perception and cognition, *Imperial Paradoxes* tests how much this is true of other eighteenth-century writers and explores how eighteenth-century texts may be made more accessible to readers through its contexts of food, drink, fashion, and travel.

While *Imperial Paradoxes* seeks to re-motivate the teaching of eighteenth-century literature, it adopts contemporary principles, as will become clear in this chapter. Cultural and social changes beyond the control of English studies have caused universities and colleges to admit, often reluctantly, pedagogical and curricular innovations hastened by technology and mass media that have broadened notions of literacy and questioned the relevance of English literature to the business world. Another way of putting this is that literature may have been subsumed by literariness and that curricular reforms in the humanities are changing relations between rhetoric and literature: the ideological nature of texts, textuality, and representation has dominated these reforms. One result is that literary works are seen as having local political rather than universal interest. Canonical works are not "repositories of truth and beauty" but ambiguous discourses that resist appropriation by "practical or dogmatic" ends. Robert Scholes describes these changes when, saying "literariness" is an arena of "paradox and interminable analysis," he severs it from "literature" by denying the latter's "special mystical privileges." But changes bring problems: professors are "unwilling to give up [their] claims to special status as interpreters of quasi-sacred texts"; unable to replace their "pragmatic need to justify departmental structures founded on the historical narrative of the Story of English," they must admit the gap between their pedagogical practices and the needs of students.[32]

---

32 Scholes 1998, 1–2, 9, 12, 18–20, 25, 27, 36, 47, and 83–4.

Enthusiastic about social and curricular change, Lawrence Levine spurns Eurocentric history, glad the American university is "no longer the site of homogeneity in class, gender, ethnicity, and race." To him, cultural change demands pedagogical revolution. Criticism of contemporary higher education he relates to conservative fear of the lapse of institutional hierarchy and encroachment of democratic society. He is sure "the American academic world is doing a more thorough job of educating a greater diversity of students in a broader and sounder array of courses covering the past and present of the worlds they inhabit than ever before in its history." As a student, he learned "nothing about how people acted in their families, their churches, their homes, their places of work, what they did with their leisure time, how they felt about their lives and the lives of those about them." What he celebrates is the incorporation into academic history of actuality, which gives it an unmatched "depth and range and diversity and sophistication." His premise is that American culture was "forged" not from European nations but from a "larger and more diverse complex of peoples and societies." The problem with initial university teaching was that Western ideas and culture were equated with superior civilization. Of course, there is still room for improvement:

We need to integrate learning more fully and to have more sequential courses that build on one another. We need to minimize the use of inaccessible jargon wherever possible, particularly in those fields where jargon has become a way of life. We need to make a greater effort to communicate with colleagues in other disciplines, with students, and with the general public. We need to ensure that teaching ability is considered seriously in all faculty personnel decisions. We need to learn how to respond to the considerable challenge of teaching the most wide-ranging and heterogeneous body of students in the history of American higher education.

In analyzing the cognitive values of mundane imagery, *Imperial Paradoxes* grants Levine's emphasis on actuality but not his dismissal of rhetoric and claims about the cultural narrowness of European literariness.[33] His saying that America's culture has been "forged" into a total inclusivity seems like wish fulfillment. Moreover, he ignores that professionalism

---

33 Levine 1996, xvii, 11–12, 15, 17–18, 20, 27, 29, 31, 33, 39, and 64.

might dilute university education since corporatism harms the liberal arts according to Benjamin Ginsberg in *The Fall of the Faculty: The Rise of the All-Administrative University and Why It Matters*.

To Ginsberg, academic administration has become such an end in itself that it discourages new ways of thinking, degrades program design, and diverts resources from teaching and research. He claims that administrations that control curricular developments and diversity policies form alliances with activist groups that wrest decision making from faculty. He argues that the "shadow curriculum" of race and gender institutes erodes program integrity, humanities' enrolment, and the professoriate's morale.[34] He sees disadvantages to students emanating from systemic changes: economic contingency leads to the merging of departments, the discontinuation of programs, and the rotation of courses that makes it difficult to finish a four-year degree in four years. Professional and business schools that embrace corporate and consumerist culture drive professors to justify curricular goals against societal pressures, leading to distracting internal debates. While literary and non-literary writers have always been conflicted, unanimity about literary pedagogy is harder to attain. Ginsberg recalls issues that Addison roused in Broadus, such as immanent impulses, transcendent elitism, and aesthetic refinement. In aiming to get as close to readers as possible, Addison set their aesthetic gains above his pretensions to artistic uniqueness. Indeed, his persona comes across as one who would transfigure neither himself nor his writings with the literariness Broadus championed.

According to Gerald Graff, today's humanities professors adopt avant-garde stances against middle-class aspirations: defending textual autonomy and rejecting the correspondence theory of truth, they sever life from writing. Marked by a psychology of "alienation" and belief in the "autonomy" of the imagination, they deny rational ways of understanding experience to degrade literature's referentiality.[35] Unlike Levine, Graff thinks capitalism is the force external to universities that weakens forms of reality to "stimulate higher levels of consumption." Anti-bourgeois academics hold that "sign and meaning, meaning and referent, do not correspond" but do not want them to. Trapped in linguistic dysfunction, they accept entrapment so as not to "compromise the

---

34 Ginsberg 2011, 1–7, 36, 97, and 102.
35 Graff 1979, 1, 3, and 5–6.

autonomy of human consciousness."[36] Far from teaching how literature treats experience, they would free it from "social complicity." Such humanists decry the classical reasoning of the Renaissance and Enlightenment, which was "moral and evaluative *and* objective," preferring a mode that is "value-free, instrumental, [and] purely calculative." This mode rejects all authority as a "caricature" of realism. Further, some humanists "suggest that the entire artistic tradition of the West has been exposed as a kind of hyperrational imperialism akin to the aggression and lust for conquest of bourgeois capitalism." Yet, says Graff, there is no difference between the old myth of the poet soaring above common sense to create "a new cosmos ex nihilo" – the one upheld by Broadus – and the "alternate stereotype of the poet as marginal person" living in "autistic fancy." Romanticism and postmodernism hold the same view of artists as special people who shun "ordinary objective judgment." To Graff, this fusion of imaginative autonomy and artistic alienation is self-destructive: it conforms to the "crisis of modern thought, which pursues a desperate quest for meaning in experience while refusing to accept the validity of any meaning proposed." Paradoxically, the modern mind is "unable to believe in the objective validity of meanings yet is unable to do without meanings." Thus, a destructive contradiction in aesthetics: "the significance which must be ascribed to art in order to justify its importance has had to be eliminated from art in order to guarantee its innocence and authenticity." Some humanists think this loss a gain since the spirit is not thereby enslaved by nature and reason, and literature is freed into autonomy from the objective world. Claiming to accept what was forced on them, they divide the artist from the community.[37]

Graff confronts this professional dogma with dialectic. Promoting its cognitive functions, he asserts that literature is propositional and presentational. Surveying unresolved intellectual conflicts in universities, he avers they impede students' learning. Besides asserting that academics no more uphold tradition than "the contemporary corporation," he claims the decorum of common rooms and faculty clubs does not inform the economy that prizes quantity of production more than "proof, evidence, logical consistency, and clarity of expression." His point is that, if literary works mean through parable or implication, they still

---

36 Ibid., 7–8 and 22.
37 Ibid., 25, 26, 28, 31, 36–7, 44–5, 46–7, and 48.

make truth claims. A text that says truth is "totally problematic, unknowable, relative" or a "function of multiple perspectives masks the same kind of truth-claims as do such assertions outside literature." Even if generalizations are undercut by ironies, they may be controlled by the generalizations in a dialectical fashion constituting "a kind of thematic proposition." In Graff's dialectic, that language refers to itself does not mean that is all it refers to. While meanings arise from systems of semantic and syntactic rules, that does not mean they are formed only by those rules and "not answerable to anything external."[38]

Graff further explains the harm done to teaching by dogma in *Beyond the Culture Wars: How Teaching the Conflicts Can Revitalize American Education*. If conflict and dialectic always motivate creative artists and literary historians, as Postman says, Graff thinks the public views post-secondary education as a "conflict-free ivory tower" that universities try to symbolize.[39] They welcome "diversity and innovation" but keep "warring parties in noncommunicating courses and departments," basing the curriculum on a rule of "live and let live." Exposed to professors' conflicts, students are kept from debates they need to hear in order to become more than passive spectators in their education. To Graff, universities organize themselves to hide links between fields of knowledge and disciplines, discouraging interdisciplinary learning by the structure of departments and programs. Since the curriculum is delivered by courses not in dialogue with one another, academic inquiry is not modelled to students. Instructors may connect teaching and research, but, since universities do not, they rob undergraduates of occasions to validate the applicability of research. For Graff, the important challenge is how to enrich undergraduate experience.[40]

Graff's call for pedagogical reform is not shared by Stanley Fish, who upholds the tradition of Broadus's transcendent literariness. A Milton scholar, Fish despises Addison. To Fish, the "poetic we have inherited

---

38 Ibid., 49, 89, 90, 96–7, 162–3, 189, and 196.

39 "The problem of making meaning from a text involves as much withholding meanings as adding them, and knowing the rules that govern when it is appropriate to do either is at the core of reasonable interpretations." To Postman, information solves no human problems. One needs to know how to avoid foolish opinions: education involves determining what body of knowledge is relevant to solving real problems (1999, 79, 90, 93, and 95).

40 Graff 1992, 5–6, 12, 31, 35, 52, 58, 106, and 122–3.

from Coleridge and Poe (the poetic of Romanticism) imagines literary productions as objects of a very particular kind – self-contained, densely layered, and saturated with a kind of meaning that can only be teased out by interpreters with special skills." Addison lacks them: his laudatory judgments say nothing more than the obvious; he is engaged "not in criticism, but in cheer-leading of a kind we now associate with the journalistic reviewers of the popular press." This sentence admits a refusal to read critical texts of the past with sympathy. In saying aesthetics did not concern Addison, Fish is mistaken: he further limits the historical and social functions of literary criticism by declaring it generates no insight into daily affairs and cannot justify activism. Content that in "our time the relationship between art and the production of civic virtue is thin to the point of vanishing," he sees professors as "gatekeepers of an academic guild" whose "purposes are exactly the opposite of those informing the intelligibility of literary activity before the Enlightenment." Literature avoids propositions; something "must be left over, unaccounted for, open to still another turn of the interpretive screw; were this not so, the work could be said to have engaged in totalizing ... and thereby forfeited its right to be called 'literary.'"[41]

While Addison embraced classical rhetoric's sense of probability and indeterminacy, John Ellis, a formalist, applies abstract stances to literariness. Like Fish, Ellis posits a chasm between criticism and activism, denying the reference theory of truth's relevance to literature. He sets aside aesthetic responsiveness: criticism should not "delight the sensibilities of the literary mind." He insists theory be removed from "practical reformatory zeal," which makes criticism "intolerably polemical": the field is simply "a matter of logical analysis." Linguistic history with its conflicted views of evaluative words, rhetorical features, and vague intuitions about literariness is no help. Since literary texts do not necessarily deviate from grammar, since metaphors occur in daily speech, and since verbal density is not only the property of literary texts, literariness is to be found only in "those pieces of language used in a certain kind of way by the community." Moreover, we "no longer respond" to literature "as part of the immediate context we live in and as something to use in our normal way as a means of controlling that context; nor do we concern ourselves with the immediate context from which it emerged,

---

41 Fish 1995, 27–30 and 32–4.

and so are not taking it up to learn, in our normal way, something about that actual everyday context." Hence he reiterates that texts "are made into literature by the community, not by their authors."[42] He adds that "a literary framework of investigation" does not arise from individual texts but from comparative and contrastive groupings. Since literary evaluation based on aesthetics or content is circular, the critic must discover non-evaluative criteria. Hence, the need for a systematic and performative definition:

Just as a work of literature must be seen primarily as a text that performs a certain task and is treated in a certain kind of way, rather than a text having certain qualities, so a good work of literature is primarily one that performs that task well and is eminently suitable for its characteristic use as a piece of literature.

Since textual performance matters above all, "descriptive analysis is an investigation of the value of a text purely as that," and that is "the only possible kind of investigation of value." Critics who will not see that "general summary aesthetic statements" are "crude and vague" abandon "a productive, analytic role to become part of the scene (the consuming public and its literary texts) which it was their job to analyze." To Ellis, critics are not common readers, nor do they study texts in the contexts of their origins, for that is "to annihilate exactly the thing that makes them literary texts." In saying that to explain texts by their contexts destroys their literariness Ellis could not be further from Addison's stance or that of *Imperial Paradoxes*. That a text may exist in several states does not claim Ellis's attention. To him, knowing its development adds nothing to its meaning, which is only a matter of how it functions in community. Genetic questions depend on first appreciating its structure, and there is "is no valid inference from the genesis of a thing to its structure"[43]

In *Literature Lost: Social Agendas and the Corruption of the Humanities*, Ellis argues that literary criticism prizes activism against the oppression of race, gender, and class too homogeneously. Replaying the myth of the noble savage – featured in Shaftesbury's philosophy as we have

---

42 Ellis 1974, x. 1, 7, 9, 11–13, 27, 31, 39, 41–3, and 47.
43 Ibid., 56, 64, 70, 72, 79, 84, 88, 92–3, 98, 103, 105, 112–15, and 119–20.

seen – this activist outlook forgets that the Western intellectual tradition has been marked by "a high degree of self-criticism." There is little new, says Ellis, in this outlook. The "view that the Western canon of great books reflects ruling class values" that exert "social control of the lower classes" simply repeats Rousseau's "crude and unrealistic conspiracy theory." Ellis further charges that racial and tribal strife is more dominant in the Third World than in the West so that political correctness based on cultural relativism foretelling an egalitarian future is mere utopianism. Our "Western cultural inheritance," if not perfect, raised "us from the barbarism of a state of nature." Its "record of human thought" is deep, complex, and diverse, enhancing human dignity "in a thousand different ways." Its literature is neither homogeneous nor ideologically uniform. It voices "the diversity of life itself" unlike "race-gender-class criticism." This defence allows Ellis to maintain his formal definition of literature as transcending its original historical and geographical contexts. That literature has no common properties does not entail that it is no category. Indeed, Western literature may be called universal to the extent it interests anyone who wishes to contemplate its diversity: since classic authors clash, they present more questions than answers. But race-gender-class critics misread the canon's "aesthetic pleasure"; far from entailing "a self-absorbed withdrawal from serious matters," the canon enables humans to support "activities that are useful through the pleasure experienced in performing them." Ellis insists that the canon results from "the activities of all kinds of writers, many of them loners and oddballs who irritated their ruling classes." No "propagandists for the social order, they were often viewed in their own times as dangerous subversives." Still, the canon neither transcends politics nor is inevitably political, these stances of Graff's constituting an impossible binary. For politics is part of universal experience but not central to it. Ellis's corrective to the view that literature has nothing to do with politics is that it has something to do with politics, not that it has everything to do with politics. To Ellis, Graff's notion of teaching the culture wars forgets that liberal education examines multiple sides of a question. He charges Graff with urging the marketplace of ideas upon us in defence of those who would close it down and make the classroom a place to initiate social change but not to encourage intellectual curiosity.[44]

---

44 Ibid., 4–5, 8–9, 18–19, 25, 31–2, 36–7, 42–7, 49–50, 54, 62, 71, and 223.

Imperial Paradoxes follows David Perkins's *Is Literary History Possible?* since scholars differ over literary history as much as over literariness. While Fish says this history is professionally undesirable, Perkins claims it is practically necessary but theoretically unjustifiable. For him, the definition of literature is indeterminate given the multiplicity of potential genres and because contexts cannot explain aesthetic purposes. Since literary changes do not match events outside literature, persuasive immanent explanations are hard to find; we "cannot write literary history with intellectual conviction, but we must read it." Social science cannot advance literary history since historical representations are rhetorical. Again, literary history's form is problematic whether it be narrative or encyclopedic, the latter the preferred type. If the latter sacrifices coherence, the former "cannot exhibit the simultaneity of diverse durations, levels of reality, sequences of events, and multiple points of view." A narrative historian commits to "causality, continuity, coherence, and teleology in events," suppressing what does not match his plot. He tends to identify with one age and devalue others, like Broadus. Literary history employs "metaphors of origins, emergence from obscurity, neglect and recognition, hegemony, succession, displacement, decline, and so forth," which express "archetypal emotions." A historian of the Romantic period sees the eighteenth century "as a synthesis." If he studies the Enlightenment, he must present the later Renaissance as homogeneous. Narrative literary history must deal in plots limited by logic and form, there being three: rise, decline, and rise and decline. Whether the topics are a "genre, a style, the reputation of an author," plots are limited to what actions or transitions can be predicated of such "heroes." Narrative literary history simplifies the past's complexity. Periods, genres, and other categories are necessary because they organize perceptions of literature and serve "rhetorical and narrative purposes" but are unrelated to historical realities. No literary history is credible because it cannot employ modern historiography, which reveals it to be an institution the processes of which must be "dialectical and open-ended." Furthermore, text and context are problematic, not being categorically distinct. Texts are "a nexus of meanings," readers uncertain of which are in the text and which in the context. Interpretation relies on the convention that text and context may be differentiated. But those terms refer to unique moments of interpretation. Dissimilar works with the same context cannot have their differences explained by context but by "some other explanatory principle." When literary historians select certain authors or texts rather than others, they depend on qualitative judgments unsupported by criteria: they operate without logically supported methods. Their interpretations by context make context itself an interpretation. Theories of the eighteenth century's declining imagination caused by "increasingly refined manners, civilized rationality, the growth of literary criticism, and the greater abstraction of language as it matures, that is, to causes external to literature itself" seem contextual rather than immanent. But since literature partially creates conditions that cause its decline, the relation between external and immanent causes is dialectical.[45]

MODERNIZING THE HUMANITIES

The scholars surveyed above, apart from illustrating conflicted aspects of literary history, make explicit and implicit references to paradox and dialectic which suggest that the role of the senses in literary study and the impact of mind–body relations on the imagination deserve more attention. The survey also indicates that fresh insights into verbal, situational, and dramatic ironies and into rhetorical figures of speech may help to renew literary history. It suggests that pedagogy may also be refreshed through the history of the language and linguistic science, namely, loan words that stem from economic expansion and cultural invasions, etymology that arises from multicultural polysemy, and semantic theories that explain the structure of the lexicon and sense development. Since literary insights are gained from performative meaning in daily speech, philology may enrich liberal arts education for undergraduates. To encourage interdisciplinarity and cross-cultural studies, *Imperial Paradoxes* shows that Europe learned from and was a model for other civilizations. It indicates how rivalries between France and England obliged them to encounter natural history and world geography when words for new things entered their lexicons. Hence, literary pedagogy may usefully explore how imperial aspirations were met and frustrated and nationalisms promoted and superseded.

To modernize liberal arts education also entails testing traditional Western philosophy with evolutionary ideas of mind–body relations that place cognition beyond the reach of abstract reason. By reconceiving

---

45 Perkins 1992, 5, 7–8, 17, 19–20, 32–3, 37, 39, 43, 48, 67, 72, 106, 114, 122, 126, 129, 136, 159, 170, 178–9, and 185.

the relevance of cognitive science to literary imagination, we may gain a fuller appreciation of how the embodied mind gives rise to unconscious cognition and informs aesthetic experience. Advances in theorizing how individuals learn confirm that evolution may change our understanding of cultural transmission and provide insights into deep history: we may grasp how categories are made in the bodily senses and how metaphors function in cognition. As we have seen, eighteenth-century authors applied the metaphor of empire to the workings of the mind from sensing that the interior world can be mapped. Yet the reciprocity of their cognitive and aesthetic effects evolved in tandem with faculty psychology and moral philosophy. Hence, one cannot simply base the principles of reading and interpretation for today's students on experiential rules that insist on new ideas of physiology changing our understanding of how the brain, mind, and senses operate. Such changes invite teachers of literature to review how the senses have been treated by Western philosophy and how aesthetic theory needs revision. Evidently, cognitive science is modifying our understanding of how the senses work and of how this working, far from having been integrated into literary scholarship, has been treated as a common-sense phenomenon. The lack of critical attention to synesthesia and the interaction of the senses in the brain has restricted hermeneutics. Oddly, taste has for centuries been treated simply as a mental abstraction while distaste has been realized concretely. The opposing histories of taste and distaste require study since the social sciences have been challenging cultural practices with regard to personal, social, political, and national identities since Broadus published his essay. This makes it untenable to set aside the ongoing evolution of human nature in favour of a singular model of interpretation. Literary criticism must face claims that there may be no universal human nature, that we may have plural identities, and that our brains have a plasticity unrecognized until recently.

Literary criticism must renew itself given challenges to the humanities within universities and colleges, challenges from inside and outside the teaching profession. The liberal arts tradition is in decline because of professional and vocational training and the commercialization of research promoted by universities and granting councils. As Briggs and others point out, humanities professors are, if not sharing Broadus's certitudes, intent on reproducing themselves with clones and by emphasizing "presentism." The humanities are seemingly offering fewer courses on the literature of the past, certainly of pre-1880 texts. Broadus's attitude to literary progress has proved astute yet retrograde. Still, the case made by defenders of the liberal arts that emphasizes creativity, personal initiative, and critical thinking in the production of self-directing citizens is less persuasive than might be since the defence may be repeated without acknowledging that intellectual disputes have always informed the arts. Nor does it help their cause to emphasize, given testimony by first-year university students, that high-school teaching of grammar, rhetoric, and poetry has been overtaken by the apparently more relevant "social studies." Students nowadays have not usually been exposed to the methods of précis, explication, and intensive study of texts from etymological, semantic, and grammatical viewpoints. Along with this lack of formal studies, another major educational gap is unawareness of the branches of philosophy. The challenge for instructors at all levels in the education system is to resist doctrinaire sloganeering about such topics as imperialism while at the same time testing the paradoxical notion that literary discourse is distinctive and unique while explicable by the ordinary rules of linguistic science. The following study of imperialism as it emerged in eighteenth-century rivalries between England and France presents cultural paradoxes that question national boundaries and uphold cross-cultural studies and embodied aesthetic values.

In *What's Happened to the Humanities?*, Alvin Kernan argues that ethnocentricity in higher education has been displaced by multicultural, pluralistic, and politicized standards, and that the humanities have grown less significant as the "demoversity" has been forming. While those trained in this new education system read extensively with "an odd sense of language as transparent," older critic-readers study "intensively" with a sense of the ambiguity of language and with a feeling for irony and paradox that celebrates, not reduces, the "fullness of the world."[46] *Imperial Paradoxes* denies charges of the ethnocentricity of Addison and English literature, aided by Frank Kermode's essay "Changing Epochs" in Kernan's volume. Kermode rejects calls for revolutionary and epistemic change in the intellectual world: if cultures suffer historical breaks, he thinks claims for such change exaggerated. He rebuts the "rhetoric of proclamation" and its revolutionary calls that the past can be rejected: such claims are made impatiently and

---

46 Kernan 1997, 4, 6, and 9.

arrogantly. As imperfect slogans of art movements, they should be defied. They are less "a reaction against something known, studied, and then declared obsolete than an attempt at total rejection of literature and certain ideas because they are past; an attack that is supported not by detailed dismissive study of documents but by grand theoretical efforts to occlude completely any consideration of them, for such consideration would be in danger of falling under the influence of paradigms already rejected in principle." Today's "association of older modes of thinking with imperialism" is merely assumed, texts once thought of as "primary" being no longer "involved in the argument" since they are denied their former status. Kermode's preference for "intense reading" may seem "very inadequate" in the face of apocalyptic calls for "epistemic coupures" that would dismiss the humanities rather than have them decline gradually. He concludes that, while the humanities were once threatened from outside the university, opponents now seek to abolish them from within.[47] Sharing Kermode's sense of the displacement of the humanities, Christopher Ricks in "The Pursuit of Metaphor" holds that resistance to "theory's empire (an empire zealously inquisitorial about every form of empire but its own) may take many forms." He feels obliged, despite the difficulties involved, to define the "least compromising form of the question emanating from the opposition" to theory. Debating with himself the propriety of limiting philosophizing about theory, he says that "pursuit of theoretical elaborations may be intrinsically misguided" and "though onerous, idle." He argues that "no one has ever been able to arrive at satisfactory terms for the constituents, the elements of a metaphor," and that abstractions about them are hopeless: the "constitutive terms, the antitheses, with which we have to make do, will not do. They are indispensable, inadequate, misleading, and unimprovable. Extraordinary efforts have been made: all have failed. The rudiments are immediately the impassable impediments." To Ricks, metaphor, far from simple- or single-minded, is "often myriad-minded."[48]

Imperial Paradoxes draws for support on Paul Fussell and Postman. To Fussell, the mind "must work by means of metaphors and symbols," since "imagery is the live constituent in that transmission of shaped

---

47 Ibid., 166–7, 171, and 175–6.
48 Ibid., 181–4.

illumination from one intelligence to another which is literature." He traces a habitual reliance on "image-systems" in eighteenth-century writers since preference for certain images "seems almost to shape the mind itself or at least to predispose it towards certain equally habitual objects of concern." He concentrates on explicating the writings of Burke, Johnson, Pope, Reynolds, and Swift as they opposed economic, industrial, and scientific innovation from traditionally philosophical and moral viewpoints. Fussell's contention is that "the shape of literary history" is better revealed by the contrast between orthodox humanists and their opponents than by "the customary chronological opposition of one 'period' to another." In saying Swift and Burke battle "a simple-minded Puritan utopianism which has seized the arguments of the seventeenth-century party of the Moderns and applied them, with a superficially persuasive admixture of the new sentimentalism, to the same old reality," Fussell shows that humanists understood that "reality" was "as complex and unmanageable as ever." In this context, Johnson is the ideal critic: looking "always first at 'the mind of man' rather than at literature," he gives responses which are for that reason eminently humanistic. To him, no "work of literature exists by itself, for only in being experienced by an imagination does it come into being." What the imagination does in this experience determines the work's value, and "the way the mind actually behaves – rather than the way it ought to behave – is often more important for criticism than merely technical merits of the faults in the work itself."[49] To Postman, the "famous prose writers of the Enlightenment" saw themselves less as professional authors than as "intellectuals who had something to say to the public – not merely to one another – and who had found a form to say it." They grasp the "relationship of language to thought and reality"; they did not doubt "language was capable of mapping reality. Many were sceptical – were aware of a multitude of linguistic traps – but that the world of non-words could be represented with approximate verisimilitude by words was implicit in almost everything they wrote." They knew "that certain ways of seeing and categorizing are products of language habits," but still thought language capable of expressing transcendent truths. They appreciated kinds of public discourse as instruments of democracy and valued the art and science of forming and sustaining questions,

---

[49] Fussell 1965, viii, 21, 25, and 61–2.

skills that have given way to technological information hunting in modern school systems. Logic and rhetoric mattered to Enlightenment thinkers, alerting them to the nature of propaganda as well as to legitimate ways of searching for truth and disciplining their use of language. With all the boosterism about the information revolution, educational training in logic seems more necessary. Postman adds the need for locating history in all subjects, it being a "meta-subject"; not only do school subjects have histories but they have multiple histories that need to be told by different peoples with different points of view.[50]

Recent philosophical and psychological commentaries on how the mind and the imagination work together have brought synesthesia forward as an arena of inquiry that offers potential for renewing humanist values. George Lakoff and Mark Turner have probed the concept of the cognitive unconscious, a concept not remote from the "deep structure" of transformational grammar in the 1970s. For them, metaphor resides in mental categories, not just in words, since we know unconsciously and automatically many basic metaphors for understanding life. Far from having numerous ways of grasping such issues as life and death, we have very few. "Where one might expect hundreds of ways of making sense of our most fundamental mysteries, the number of metaphorical conceptions of life and death turns out to be very small. Though these can be combined and elaborated in novel ways and expressed poetically in an infinity of ways, that infinity is fashioned from the same small set of basic metaphors." The power of poetry comes from giving "noticeable and memorable" form to conceptual patterns of "ordinary, automatic modes of thought."[51] This argument rests on the claim that reason cannot transcend the body and that imaginative aspects of reason evident in metaphor, metonymy, and mental imagery are integral to it and not merely a "peripheral and inconsequential adjunct to the literal." This experientialist view of the mind holds that thought grows fundamentally out of embodiment. Thus, cognitive science studies reason and its categories empirically. From this stance, metaphor is a conceptual phenomenon, a property of both poetry and daily language, and a matter of social discourse. As the following chapters show, talk about consumer products is metaphorical.[52]

50 Postman 1999, 65, 74, 147, 161, 163, and 173.
51 Lakoff and Turner 1989, 2, 5, 26, and 72.
52 Lakoff 1987, xi and xv.

Lakoff and Turner conclude from reports on many psychological and cognitive experiments that our "most important abstract concepts, from love to causation to morality, are conceptualized via multiple complex metaphors" that are "an essential part of those concepts, and without them the concepts are skeletal and bereft of nearly all conceptual and inferential structure." Every complex metaphor arises from "primary metaphors" embodied in three ways. The first is through "bodily experience in the world" linking "sensorimotor experience with subjective experience." The second concerns "source-domain logic" arising from "the inferential structure of the sensorimotor system." The third evolves from instantiation "neurally in the synaptic weights associated with neural connections." This system of primary and complex metaphors belongs to the cognitive unconscious to which "most of the time we have no direct access" and which we cannot control. Thus, "abstract concepts" are "structured by multiple complex metaphors" that confirm "the cognitive unconscious, the embodiment of mind," and the metaphorical basis of thought.[53]

Similarly, Carolyn Korsmeyer probes Western philosophy while discussing aesthetics and embodied taste. She starts from the position that the "literal sense of taste has rarely caught the attention of philosophers except insofar as it provides the metaphor for aesthetic sensitivity." Philosophy, identifying gustatory experience with our animal nature, has excluded taste rather than vision from explorations of rationality and epistemology. Upholding a hierarchy of the senses, philosophy has viewed "taste preferences as idiosyncratic, private, and resistant to standards." While it has treated sight and hearing as cognitive, intellectual, or higher senses, it has tended to think of "taste, touch and smell" as bodily or lower senses. But since eating, if felt as "sensations in the body," is significant beyond the pleasure and nutrition it affords, we realize that "all five senses contribute to some particularly rich eating experiences." Since foods figure in "symbolic systems that extend from ritual ceremonies of religion to the everyday choice of breakfast," we see that "tastes convey meaning and have a cognitive dimension" overlooked by philosophers. Despite "the parallels between literal and aesthetic taste" behind the metaphor for perceiving beauty, "gustatory taste" is usually excluded from aesthetic theories. It is also "excluded from among the

---

53 Lakoff and Johnson 1999, 73.

senses that have art as their objects." For Korsmeyer, there is a dubious tension in aesthetic theory "between the idea of taste as a sense pleasure and taste as a discriminative capability" since "fine discernment is accomplished by means of the pleasure, yet the pleasure itself is too sensuous to count as aesthetic." Still, cross-cultural studies reveal that diverse food and taste preferences around the globe raise "interesting theoretical questions about the relativity and objectivity of perception." Such studies show that foods generate symbolic meaning in various ways that are both "representational and expressive." The epistemological issue seems to be that philosophical tradition is governed by notions about the relative distance between the organs and objects of perception, notions that ignore embodiment of the senses in favour of the separation of mind and body. Since Aristotle, the distal senses of sight and hearing have been treated as turned outwards upon the world while the proximal senses of smell, taste, and touch have been regarded as dependent on the state of the perceiver's body. The arts of the eyes and ears which justify mimesis and portrayal of human life and moral character are apparently not matched by perfumery and cooking. Cartesian rationalism and British empiricism reinforced sense hierarchy by making visual perception the instrument of intellectual generalization. They further restricted philosophical investigation by introducing a gendered binary: reason, equated to male physical and rational power, was regarded as superior to feelings and emotions linked to female bodily sensitivity. This value structure embedded in the sense hierarchy leads Korsmeyer to see that the ancient science of the senses is even more limited. It ignores how the senses work together in their embodiment. The case of Braille, which substitutes touch for sight, is a case in point. She objects to the domestic–public binary which degrades meals cooked at home by women, servants, and slaves since it neglects the sense of taste and its complicated objects in meals, feasts, and ritual that Brillat-Savarin outlined. This neglect she remedies by appraising the sister arts.[54]

Gabrielle Starr advances this remedy by testing interacting senses in the sister arts through neuroscience, since beauty matters in the architecture of the brain. Hence, the applicability of the "neuroscience of aesthetics." Since aesthetic experience changes, change gives insight into more than aesthetics; it probes "the dynamic interrelations of neural

---

[54] Korsmeyer 1999, 1, 3–7, 17, 21, 24–5, 27, 29, 30, 33, and 35–7.

processes," confirming the "cross-disciplinary principles that have been at the heart of aesthetic inquiry from its beginnings." Starr further says: "Aesthetic experience relies on a distributed neural architecture, a set of brain areas involved in emotion, perception, imagery, memory, and language. But more than this, aesthetic experience emerges from *networked* interactions, the workings of intricately connected and coordinated brain systems that, together, form a flexible architecture enabling us to develop new arts and to see the world around us differently." Aesthetic experience is coherent in all artistic domains: "the arts mediate our knowledge of the world around us by directing attention, shaping perception, and creating dissonance or harmony where none had been before." Aesthetic experience gives us "a restructuring of value." It does this since it is "both thought and felt"; it is something "cognitive," "sensory," and "emotional." It combines kinds of mental life that are subjective, contingent, experiential, and computational at a neural level. It concerns "ways of not only assigning perceptions a value but revealing a hierarchy and interrelation of values" that surpass "what we first perceive." Starr holds that her "model of aesthetic experience" reveals "why and how the Sister Arts might function as they do, in complement as well as competition, always open to new kin." Her study then passes on to probe aesthetic dialectic: "how we both differentiate among and integrate the kinds of pleasure that come by way of different senses and from the different Sister Arts."[55]

DEEP HISTORY AND LITERARY HISTORY

Rudgley's study of the importance to civilization of intoxicants and mind-altering substances digested in chapter 1 may help – when supplemented by Daniel Lord Smail's *On Deep History and the Brain* – to renew literary history. Challenging historiography, deep history complicates the issues of when history may be said to begin. Far from starting with official public records and printed documents, deep history, as far as Smail is concerned, views paleolithic humanity through the evolution of the brain, cognition, and neurophysiology. Related to the philosophy of embodiment, deep history extends the concept of textuality. Through its sense of semiosis, it sets aside the conventional binaries of nature

---

55 Starr 2013, xi, xiii–xv, 3, 14, 16, and 31.

and nurture, conservation and progress, holding that, since culture predates writing on paper and printing, it operates in speech, rituals, and practices gleaned from geological and anthropological records. To Smail, professional prejudices limited history as an academic subject by the end of the nineteenth century when documents were the *sine qua non* of historians who shared "the same disciplinary impulses" that affected "other fields of inquiry." This "documentary ideology" sought to detach history from the preoccupation of archeology and anthropology with prehistory. But, as Smail says, while brain studies prove that nature and nurture are reciprocally creative, they also show that the process of integration is never complete or static; it evolves constantly, allowing new and changing cultural practices to come into being. Cellular and genetic structures are shared by body and brain, the environment shaping genetic development and differentiation and these shaping the environment. However, he argues, the "short chronology of the standard historical narrative of the twentieth century was built on a rigid Cartesian distinction between body and mind." This stance belittled the brain's history, reducing its development to the use of tools. But recent work in neuropsychology and neurophysiology shows that body states are physiological entities, "characteristically located in specific parts of the brain and put there by natural selection." Again, "the plasticity of such emotions as disgust" means that "the interaction between universal cognitive or physiological traits and particular cultural histories is never simple." Deep history heightens "a genetic and behavioural legacy from the past," the result being that it shows that "organisms are built by the interaction of genes, environment, and random developmental noise, to the point where there can be no nature without nurture and vice versa."

Smail bolsters his viewpoint by citing Antonio Damasio, the neurophysiologist who challenges the overemphasis on cognition in evolutionary psychology. Damasio claims "that a great deal of 'thinking' actually gets done by means of brain–body chemistry interacting with the nervous system, not neural activity alone." This means that "experiences are constantly being mediated through brain–body chemistry" and that "there is no thinking that is independent of the feedback mechanism linking sensory input, body chemistry, the body map, and neural activity." To Smail, this claim leads to the conclusion that culture is fundamentally "a biological phenomenon" realized "by the plasticity of human neurophysiology." This claim prompts him to consider the "mood-altering practices, behaviors, and institutions generated by human culture" that he labels "*psychotropic mechanisms.*" "Psychotropy," he says, "is one of the fundamental conditions of modernity, and explaining its historical trajectory is one of the most valuable results of a deep historical perspective." The "mildly addictive" and "mood-altering" properties of coffee, sugar, chocolate, tobacco, and even fortified wines and spirits imported from Africa, Arabia, and the New World which circulated in seventeenth- and eighteenth-century Europe show that that imperial continent depended on the foreign for increasing the control of states over citizens and intensifying social stratification through consumerism. Imports, then, rendered the economy psychotropic. Further, the cultivation of leisure activities and "autotropic commodities" such as "reading, travel, food" and "pornography" made the "long eighteenth century ... the century of addiction." Smail suspects "the act of buying things helps stimulate the parasympathetic nervous system, cleansing the body of epinephrine and norepinephrine and inducing the production of neurotransmitters, like dopamine, that ease stress." Thus, "the desire to alter one's body chemistry, lies at the very heart of the modern consumer economy." A further conclusion seems to be that a "neurohistorical approach" to history offers "a new interpretive framework, where human neurophysiology is one of the environmental factors in macrohistorical change." His fifth chapter, "Civilization and Psychotropy," shows that in eighteenth-century Europe "imperial cultural appropriation led to a dependency on stimulants," which sheds new light on "the network of international rivalries and dependencies."[56]

CODA

Imperial Paradoxes aims to rehabilitate literary history in higher education through intensive and extensive readings that acknowledge the theoretical challenges that have confronted historiography recently. It upholds the pedagogical exposure of students from multicultural societies in North America and Europe to the historical imagination exercised by humanist rhetoric articulated in diverse genres of the long eighteenth century. This rhetoric defies ideological systematization and doctrinaire

---

56 Smail 2008, 44–5, 112–13, 115, 118–19, 136, 144–5, 154, 161–2, 179, 183, and 185.

thinking. It supports David Bromwich's contention that "higher education is the learning of certain habits, above all a habit of sustained attention to things outside one's familiar circuit of interests; and it is the beginning of a work of self-knowledge that will decompose many of one's given habits and given identities ... the aims of education are deeply at odds with the aims of any coherent and socializing culture. The former is critical and ironic, the latter purposeful and supervisory."[57] Hence, humanist rhetoric mocks simplistic ideas of progress and the golden age. Eighteenth-century literariness is dialectical: it operates competing notions of reason, rationalism, and reasonableness; it opposes and champions rational opposition to tradition, superstition, and imagination. The functional terms by which the period's writing have been defined, such as imperialism and enlightenment, were contested and creatively adapted, as my first two chapters have begun to demonstrate. The feasibility of literary history based on historical, geographical, and national categories is rendered questionable by pluralism and globalism. But *Imperial Paradoxes* broadens literariness to include writing well beyond canonically approved texts and to appeal to the common reader, who has been ignored by the elitist, professional academic specialization of literary criticism and theory. In this situation, I hope that cognitive science may help to rehabilitate literary history and that deep history, with its commitment to anthropology and neurobiology, may also contribute to its renewal. The material aspects of mind–body relations featured in the following chapters attempt to move beyond the antimony of nature and nurture, tradition and progress, to concentrate on literary history's curiously and fascinatingly dialectical functions.

57 Bromwich 1992, 50.

3

Spirits and Wine in Imperial Canada, 1630–1900

A central aspect of the fate of being a Canadian is that our very existing has at all times been bound up with the interplay of various world empires ... To most Canadians, as public beings, the central cause of motion in their souls is the belief in progress through technique, and that faith is identified with the power and leadership of the English-speaking empire in the world ... Not only in our present but in our origins, Canada was made by western empires. We were a product of two north-western empires as they moved out in that strange expansion of Europe around the world.[1]

IMPERIAL ORIGINS OF WINE SYMBOLISM

For George Grant writing during the Vietnam War, Canada's identity is bound up with that of the United States and its imperialistic foundation in progress by technology. Yet Canada's history has been marked by several European empires. Touching on Canada's early relations with the United States, the present chapter's main concern is the imperial rivalry of England and France along with their political modes and cultural traditions. It details this concern by surveying the symbolic history of spirits and wine, a process that exposes important motifs, such as conflicting attitudes towards mind-altering substances and settlement and towards consumption and temperance as well as reliance on and mistreatment of Aboriginal peoples.

Spirits and wine are produced in distillation and vinification processes with diverse cultural histories: their provenance and production have been subject to legal and sumptuary regulations as well as commercial

---

1 Grant 1969, 63–5.

proscriptions and trade embargoes even as they have symbolized political ideals and social rituals. As commodities serving physiological and medicinal functions, they have aided Canada in several ways: as water purifiers, beverages, painkillers, palliative drugs, and in customary festivities. Spirits and wine constitute sets of communal signs. Encoded in writing, these sets wield textual and historical meanings. Treating spirits and wine in semiotic terms, this chapter analyzes them for historical signs of the physiology and philosophy of taste, while suggesting how the codes embedded in spirits and wine betoken Canada's aspirations and confirm the curious interdependence of cultural and literary history. By 1800, spirits and wine in Britain had become contentious signs; in the previous hundred and fifty years they were at the centre of economic debates and partisan conflicts. Parliament's use of excise duties to block and to foster trade with European nations led to claret and port signifying consumption that divided Tories from Whigs, Jacobites from Hanoverians, and country squires from city merchants. Differentiations between French and non-French wines served as metonyms for factions holding divergent views on imperial rivalry with France and on colonial expansion. That it was no producer may partly explain the political energy and cultural imagination exerted by Britain on the systematic consumption of wine. Eighteenth- and nineteenth-century Canadian texts, published mainly in London, inscribe various systems of consumption since, in Britain's rise to empire, internal disputes about foreign policy, the economy, and lifestyles, together with its financial and technical investments in the vineyards of France and Portugal, caused all spirits and wines – especially French wines that had long served the rituals of crown, court, and military life – to become the focus of philosophical debates.[2] Such debates involved physiology and aesthetics because, as Terence Hawkes reminds us, all

five senses, smell, touch, taste, hearing, sight, can function in the process of *semiosis*: that is, as sign-producers or sign-receivers. The uses of perfume, of the texture of a fabric in clothing, the ways in which the tastes produced by cooking signal status, location, "identity," "foreignness" are manifold.

---

2 For a fuller discussion of political symbolism that compares the Whig ideology of port to the Tory ideology of claret, see Merrett 1991.

Moreover, each of these senses responds in concert with the others to sign-systems designed to exploit them in differing hierarchies.[3]

The drinking codes and consumer hierarchies developed in Britain were resisted in Canada. In *The Facts of the Case*, F.S. Spence upheld the minority report of the 1896 Royal Commission on the Liquor Traffic, calling for the prohibition of spirits and wine on the grounds liquor undermined the nation's economic and social health. Claiming support from clerical and medical groups, Spence argued that the "liquor habit" brought disease and insanity upon the "dependent classes," leading them to pauperism and crime. Half the public expenditure on hospitals and prisons, he said, was attributable to drink. He added that the loss of "one-tenth the producing power of this country is destroyed by intemperance" and by drunken workers, and that a member of Parliament in 1874 estimated "the annual loss of life in Canada through the liquor traffic" to be four thousand. Certain that liquor destroys "family affections" and "domestic peace," Spence denied that wine and beer might be "temperance drinks." Praising the rise of temperance societies from their origin in Nova Scotia in 1827, he berated the "mischievous alliance" of parliamentarians and liquor vendors. A government could alone be judged good which protects citizens from the disorders of drunkenness and the unruliness of Indians. While the majority report thought "overindulgence in liquor" caused by "the love of sociable society," the minority report ascribed it to addiction. Spence's zeal is irreproachable, but spirits and wine figured, if ambivalently, in Canada's nation building from the early days.[4]

EXPLORATION, ABSTEMIOUSNESS, AND ABORIGINAL CULTURE

When in 1631, Thomas James (1593–1635) sailed into Hudson's Bay, he had to admit, as he does in *The Dangerous Voyage of Capt. Thomas James in His Intended Discovery of a North West Passage into the South Sea*, that the passage was not the commercially viable mission he had set out to fulfill and that his embodiment of England's hope to displace New France from Canada was premature. However, by following Henry Hudson and

---

3 Hawkes 1977, 134–5.
4 Spence 1973, 29–30, 34, 57, 83, 134, 197, and 296.

charting "desart Parts" in the name of King Charles I, James realized the worth of spirits and wine to hazardous exploration. From seeing how difficult it was to preserve wine in the northern cold, he learned to ration it scrupulously and to value its utility in the long, frigid winter. He came to view wine as less a beverage than a water purifier; his sack in sweetening melted snow was seven times diluted. Wine served his medical need for a tonic and a palliative. Although winter ruined most, he offered his weakest men a "Pint of Alicant a Day," having planned for springtime recuperation by guarding a tun – along with brandy – for that necessity. When his gunner was injured, James gave him "Sack altogether," the undiluted wine easing his death pangs. Loyalty to the Crown explains why James, in the face of physical danger, kept his "best Liquor" for celebrating the King's birthday, thus perpetuating associations between fine wine, court culture, commercial exploration, and imperial expansion.[5]

Later explorers, who lived among Aboriginal peoples and developed a sense of the natural history and ethnography of the north, grew less sure about these associations when working for fur-trading companies. Samuel Hearne (1745–1792), charged with discovering a North West Passage near the Coppermine River after the Seven Years War, encountered hardships and cultural horrors that unsettled his European mores and tastes. His travelogue, *A Journey from Prince of Wales's Fort in Hudson's Bay to the Northern Ocean 1769·1770·1771·1772* (1795), expresses admiration for, and disgust with, European decadence, Aboriginal tribal warfare and sexual licence, as well as Native eating and drinking. Facing up to inevitable hunger since that eating entailed "either all feasting, or all famine," Hearne reports his struggles with pains of digestion and evacuation, this aspect of survival quelling his sense of taste. Finding Native indolence in securing food "so void of common understanding," he often cites a passage on sleep from *Night Thoughts* (1744) by Edward Young (1683–1765) to steel himself to hunger. Appalled that deer are killed "merely for the tongues, marrow, and fat," he objects to such waste but makes himself try to countenance cultural difference:

---

5 James 1740, 119, 83, 51, and 25. Fine accounts of the importance of the wine trade to the history of civilization are given by Younger (1966) and Johnson (1989). On the association of the English Crown with Bordeaux, see Younger 1966, 263–4. Johnson's analysis of Magellan's stocks of wine on his expedition round the world is apropos (1989, 170).

As national customs, however, are not easily overcome, my remonstrances proved ineffectual; and I was always answered, that it was certainly right to kill plenty, and live on the best, when and where it was to be got, for that it would be impossible to do it where every thing was scarce: and they insisted on it, that killing plenty of deer and other game in one part of the country, could never make them scarcer in another.

Happy to eat raw fish and venison, he balked at raw muskox; "the flesh of the musk-ox is not only coarse and tough, but smells and tastes so strong of musk as to make it very disagreeable when raw, though it is tolerable eating when properly cooked." On treks from Prince of Wales's Fort for the Hudson's Bay Company, he longed for yet decried Christendom's luxuries given Natives' irregularity, "want of food" causing them sometimes to eat "the whole day." He admits he "never spent so dull a Christmas" as when he "reflected on the immense quantities, and great variety of delicacies which were then expending in every part of Christendom, and that with a profusion bordering on waste." He cannot stop wishing to be "again in Europe, if it had been only to have had an opportunity of alleviating the extreme hunger" he suffered "with the refuse of the table of any one of [his] acquaintance." Striving to curb the disgust Esquimaux dishes visit on his "European palate," he ponders cultural rapprochement through food: whereas Indians of the north would not at first eat

any of our provisions, sugar, raisins, figs or even bread ... so that they had no greater relish for our food than we had for theirs. At present, however, they will eat any part of our provisions, either fresh or salted; and some of them will drink a draft of porter, or a little brandy and water; and they are now so far civilized, and attached to the English, that I am persuaded any of the Company's servants who could habituate themselves to their diet and manner of life, might now live as secure under their protection, as under that of any of the tribes of Indians who border on Hudson's Bay.

Further, life on the margins of civilization and a wish to grow closer to Aboriginal culture changed his outlook on spirits and wine. He abstained from drinking brandy since he had lost the taste for it: "Having been so long without tasting spiritous liquors," he turns abstention into a means of charting Indian society and defying stereotypes that Spence upheld. He reports that, while northern natives remote from the fort do not like brandy, only taking it as a reward for hunting geese, southern natives are so addicted from having been exposed to Europeans that they buy it improvidently. This distinction, in modifying truisms about Native drunkenness, implies that the Hudson's Bay Company has scope for moral trade in the north. Still, when he distinguishes between brandy and wine on the basis of alcoholic strength, he not only equates Native refinement with European good taste but also hints that the former is superior to the latter: Matonabbee, his Indian guide, epitomizes cultural refinement; he relishes "Spanish wines, though he never drank to excess; and as he would not partake of spiritous liquors, however fine in quality or plainly mixed, he was always master of himself." Matonabbee's elegant manners add "to the vivacity of a Frenchman, and the sincerity of an Englishman ... the gravity and nobleness of a Turk." Yet Hearne complicates his typology of drinking habits and cross-cultural contacts in reporting that northern Indians do not remain far from the fort: for each hawk's head they bring in, they are rewarded with "a quart of brandy." By thus ensuring a sufficiency of partridge and rabbit, the company inures them to brandy, which, in Hearne's view, endangers Native culture and debases its trade. His contrast between the drinking habits of northern and southern natives fails. That he applies brandy, the "spirits of wine," as a salve for swollen legs and stiff ankles confirms that single-minded evaluations of spirits and wine give way to the paradoxes of living in the north and render doubtful the integrity of imperial commerce.[6]

The meaning of spirits and wine in *Travels through the Interior Parts of North America* (1778) by Jonathan Carver (1710–1780) is confused by its bibliography. Unable to find a publisher in America, Carver moved to London and enlisted the aid of the journeyman writer Alexander Bicknell (d. 1796). In editing and compiling Carver's journals, Bicknell assured the text's commercial success by catering to British, not American, readers and by persuading Sir Joseph Banks, his own patron, to be its dedicatee. Stressing the search for the Northwest Passage, Bicknell added accounts of Indians being civilized by Europeans. To inflate Carver's agency, he interpolated passages from French missionaries and travel writers – Louis Hennepin (1626–1706), Louis Armand, Baron de Lahontan (1666–1716), and Pierre François Xavier de

6 Hearne 1958, 21, 28, 25, 76, 20, 89, 43, 104–5, 175, 225, 257, and 121.

Charlevoix (1682–1761) – thereby rendering the book's style "ornate, involved, and often flowery."[7] Carver's reliance on Bicknell aggravated inconsistencies between American and European propaganda in the *Travels* and deepened the text's ambivalence about spirits and wine. Despite blaming Europeans for ruining Natives with alcohol, Carver himself gave "spirituous liquors" to tribal chiefs in the 1760s. Granting that drink renders Indians more aggressive, Carver rejects as prejudice European claims that spirits make them ferocious. His stance is no more steady when he avers that the "baneful juices" imported by Europeans alter the character of Indians for the worse. Confusion mounts when he claims the Indians whom he describes are remote from European settlements and unaffected by English and French vice. Only rarely are his cultural observations measured. His account of how Indians' abstinence induces dreams that yield psychic insight into hunting trails is credible since his scorn for the redundancy of European fasting is subtle and frank:

The Indians do not fast as some other nations do, on the richest and most luxurious food, but they totally abstain from every kind either of victuals or drink; and such is their patience and resolution, that the most extreme thirst could not oblige them to taste a drop of water; yet amidst this severe abstinence they appear cheerful and happy.

But his claims for Aboriginal uniqueness are one side of a rhetorical coin that depicts French Canada on the other with a coarse invective about Jesuits' failure to eliminate the influence of liquor on Indigenous peoples. If, sneers Carver, the Jesuits encouraged Indian tribes to trade captives back and forth in the hope this trade would reduce the overall killing of Natives, the "pious fathers" failed to foresee that exchanging prisoners would establish a "mode" of slavery that perpetuates tribal

---

7 Parker 1976, 31. In an "Anecdote of the late Captain Carver" by "A.B." in the *European Magazine* of November 1783 (vol 4: 346–7), Bicknell records a dream Carver had before leaving America in 1769, a dream that, predicting the independence of the colonies, confirms spiritual foresight: an arm, descending from a cloud, holds England's royal standard, which the winds shred. Carver told this dream several times to Bicknell in 1778 when he was working on Carver's book. Bicknell was susceptible to Carver's dream since he was for years incensed by Joseph Priestley's materialism, which he attacked in several of his own works (Merrett 2002a: 37 and 46–7).

strife and institutionalizes liquor. To emphasize the futility of Catholic missions and to exaggerate conflicts in French culture, Carver says that Jesuits' calls to ban liquor were countered by *coureurs de bois*, whose fur collecting led them to live amid the Natives whom they "clandestinely" habituated to spirits. His cultural remarks are made more inconsistent by his habit of seeing natural history in terms of European sumptuary customs: he upholds the French tradition of brandying fruits when he recommends that of all berries sand cherries are the best for "steeping in spirits" and that, if black cherries are inedible, they give brandy an agreeable flavour and the attractive "colour of claret."[8] Such remarks show that his taste in spirits and wine had little connection to his rhetorical posturing.[9]

In *Letters from Canada* published in 1809 at London, Hugh Gray treats the wine trade as an index of national development, but his remarks on the consumption of alcohol, to the extent they implicate imperialism, no more avoid inconsistency than did Hearne or Carver. Gray's data, collected from records of legal imports between 1802 and 1805 are impressive: 550,000 gallons of brandy and rum along with 170,000 gallons of Madeira, port, and Spanish and French reds, the quantities of each being fairly equal. To Gray, data about the consumption of spirits and wine signal Canada's growing participation in international trade and its capacity to furnish Europe with producer goods. Staves for barrel making "form a leading article of exportation" and are "becoming daily better known, and better liked in Britain, as well as in the wine countries, particularly in Portugal and Madeira." Canada's lumber industry is happily playing a larger role in the global wine trade. But opportunities for capital growth are unhappily limited by British ambivalence towards the conquest of Canada. This ambivalence effecting uncertainty in law and jurisprudence is the greatest evil of the conquest since it harms "the conquerors and conquered" equally. That ancient laws have been destroyed and new ones not understood or enforced hinders cultural assimilation and economic development. The Quebec Act of 1774 is Gray's target. Accepting that the habitants' property and religious rights were upheld in the capitulation agreements of Quebec and Montreal, he dislikes the "British legislature's" giving "way

---

8 For a revealing account of brandy's role in creating tensions between missionaries and traders in New France, see Morton 1963, 54–72.

9 Carver 1974, 24–5, 221, 285, 347–8, 30, and 503.

to the importunities of the Canadians" for the renewal of their civil and criminal codes. Wishing to forge Canada's identity in the image of British imperialism, he avers that national economic development will advance only if policies opposing cultural diversity are enacted: the economic role of Natives must be restricted; the habitants of Upper Canada made to surrender their cultural traditions; and the 1774 Quebec Act rescinded.[10]

From the time his arriving ship buys fish from Indians with brandy and he is shocked to see this "exchange" gladdening their hearts, he grants little to their communal and economic sense. His belief that Canada's future lies in imperialism subjects the myth of the noble savage to the truism that Aboriginals are "extremely fond of strong spirits" and given to "the most dreadful cruelties" on account of European influence. So, he urges that Natives be limited to hunting territories and denied traditional presents of brandy at "our military posts." He also wants to displace habitant culture: opposing the French Civil Code since it contains "no bankrupt laws" and precludes imprisonment for debt, he argues for the withdrawal of Canadians' rights under the British constitution. Although he speaks French, he spurns the bilingualism of the English community, preferring to harbour myths about the commercial and agricultural backwardness of the habitants, who do little more in winter, he claims, than cut firewood and replenish "their rum bottle" in Quebec or Montreal. When he professes surprise that French "courtesy and urbanity" survive in the Canadian wilds, he exposes his condescending appropriation of the French culture he likes to scorn. His manners – when he picnics at Chaudière with friends posing as river gods and claims the group's appetite transcends class since outdoors a cottager's potatoes and milk are as "noble" as "ragouts and burgundy" – betray snobbery and a false egalitarianism that enact the social hierarchy he pretends to degrade.[11] Gray's classical allusions

10 Gray 1971, 174, 209, and 104–12.
11 Characters in *The History of Emily Montague* import classical mythology into Canada to validate their patriotism. Deities reside in Canada mainly because of Emily. Her presence is the habitation of the Graces; she is Venus attended by the Graces. In England Rivers sees her as led by them. There too, Temple pictures his wife Lucy as Venus attended by the Graces, and, since England is supposedly alone among nations in permitting marital choice to women, the country is personified as Venus tended by the Graces. Arabella projects nereids, naiads, and other "tutelary deities" onto the Canadian scene. In esteeming his "native Dryads" more highly than an "imperial

and affected consumerism cannot mask the aggressive colonizer: the mercantilist prospects Gray paints for Canada are blurred by tints of political and cultural nostalgia.[12]

During and after the Napoleonic Wars, the wine trade in Canada served increasingly complex political and moral signs; the function of spirits and wine in nation building promoted conflicting views of social and institutional life. Equally a necessity and a luxury to soldiers in the British army, wine precluded abstract ethical debate. In *Richardson's War of 1812*, the author, John Richardson (1796–1852), shows that port was instrumental to British military strategy, re-invigorating the army after heroic exhaustion. Having been a prisoner in America where he grew sicker when treated with "raw whisky," Richardson contrasts cultures as well as military and medical regimens. Finding "a few bottles of port wine" in his "provision-basket" when "thoroughly exhausted" by "hunger, thirst and fatigue" after his escape, he drinks one bottle "at a draught," a luxury not to be "exchanged for a throne" given its "instantaneous" production of "the most delicious moments of repose" ever.[13]

After Waterloo, accounts of trading companies and colonial enterprises intensified issues of mercantilism and free trade. In *Narrative of a Voyage to Hudson's Bay* (1817), Edward Chappell (1792–1861) attacks the Hudson's Bay Company's seeming promotion of free trade; its charts of the bay are deliberately false so as to guard trade secrets. This "illiberal concealment" aims to stop its "trading concern" from being a "topic of general conversation in the mother-country." Also alleging that Lord Selkirk's efforts to establish the Red River Settlement as a "colony" involve "mighty speculations," he decries competition between the North West and Hudson's Bay Companies for unnecessarily letting Indians "profit." To prove the Hudson's Bay Company's dullness to Aboriginal society and trading opportunities, Chappell praises Esquimaux productivity with seals: he likens their production of fluid containers from seal skins to the making of wine casks from "the skins of animals" by mountaineers in Portugal and Spain. His analogy values trading with Esquimaux. Still, he reveals limited sympathy with Native

---

palace," Rivers shows that this nexus of classical allusions proclaims a universal enlightenment in the name of a beleaguered, Anglican rural gentry (Brooke 1985, 139, 23, 355, 373, 56, 30, 301, 303, and 407).

12 Gray 1971, 35, 160–1, 178, 121, 101, 266, 128, and 96.
13 Richardson 1974, 289 and 246.

culture when, repeating the observation that Indians become intoxicated when given "a quart of rum, mixed with three quarts of water," he ignores their communal sensibility and self-induced spiritual visions. While prizing the exportation of Aboriginals' raw materials that lets British manufacturing sustain "a lucrative trade with many nations of Europe" and appreciating that Britain thereby exports goods to Indians that "no civilized people" would "take off our hands," he says that abolishing the Hudson's Bay Company's monopoly would spur Esquimaux industry and give Indians "an adequate return for their commodities." He condescends to Aboriginal drinking because he both opposes royal charters and strenuously promotes imperial free trade.[14]

Defenders of the Hudson's Bay Company and Selkirk's Settlement confirm that wine and spirits, while involved in the rivalry between fur-trading companies, aggravated stereotypical views of Aboriginal peoples. Defenders in the anonymous *Statement Respecting the Earl of Selkirk's Settlement upon the Red River*, published in London in 1817, ascribe the destruction of the settlement in 1815 and 1816 to Montreal's North West Company, which, they contend, kept Indians intoxicated to induce them to destroy the colony. If relations between fur traders and settlers were at first good, the defenders maintain that as soon as "it was decided that the anathema pronounced in this country against colonization, as being 'at all time unfavourable to the fur trade,' was to be carried into effect; and that the settlement was no longer to be allowed to exist, the services of the Half-breeds to the colonists were prevented." These Natives were directed to harass the settlers "by every means in their power": this involved reducing their provisions and driving "the buffaloe from the plains." Apparently, the North West Company's manipulation of the Cree was less successful. While these Indians were brought down from the interior and "kept in a state of intoxication" with "the express purpose of assisting in driving away the settlers," they proved to be a "more civilised race than their employers." Not "pleased with their errand," they went home after sending "the pipe of peace to the colony, as an assurance of their friendship." That the defenders of the Hudson's Bay Company felt obliged to counter charges that Selkirk imprisoned men and kept them in a "state of inebriety" to get them to sign and execute deeds reveals how much drunkenness informed the

---

14 Chappell 1970, 174–5, 167–8, 163, 100, 213, 219, 228, and 232.

mercantile policies of the major trading companies in Montreal and London. Such propaganda shows that the image of the drunken Indian was founded on commercial and colonial rivalry.[15]

By 1820 when Joseph Sansom (1765/6–1826), an American Republican taking after Carver, published *Travels in Lower Canada* in London, it had become usual for travel writers to decry Quebec's national aspirations in propaganda about wine and food. When Sansom says that he finds "tolerable wine" in a "squalid inn" and that "liquor" is unavailable at "post-houses" since "police regulations" ban "unnecessary tippling houses," he berates public hospitality in Lower Canada. At the best inn in Yamachiche, he finds the "ragout de mouton, et de veau" inedible, having been "deteriorated in the cooking." When "disappointed" by "comforts" of a French hotel in the summer heat of Montreal, he vaunts his refinement and spurns European influences. He will countenance French views hostile to Britain since they permit him to assert that the production and consumption of wine are matters of national and imperial significance. So, he reports that a French confectioner who served at Pondicherry prefers Lisbon wine to Madeira because the latter reflects English taste for fortified wines. To the confectioner, Madeira is the poorer since it cannot travel without a "powerful admixture" of brandy and since the "pernicious intermixture of Cogniac" is effected in London, the fermentation and fining also performed there. The confectioner drinks "nothing but port, claret, and the Spanish wines" in the belief they lengthen life rather than shorten it, as Madeira does to Englishmen in India. However, Sansom sees the habitants of Lower Canada as severed from their roots: he insists that Canadians are "no longer enlivened by the exhilarating wines of the mother-country," by which he means France, and that they lack the sense of "military glory" and "thoughtless gaiety" of the European French. In claiming habitants lack national pride, he holds that subjection to the British government denies them the ability to put down their roots. Far from urging military appropriation of Lower Canada by the United States, he thinks such an appropriation is evolving naturally. To him, "so little profitable is the sovereignty of Canada to the kingdom of Great Britain" since she so "fattens on the wealth of Britain" that this "unprofitable possession" will burn "a hole in the pockets of

---

15 Anon. 1970, 18, 23, and 144–5.

the possessor." Since Upper Canada is already "an American settlement" that will "sooner or later fall into our hands by the operation of natural causes," the States need not extend its territory by force. Canada will lose its British and French ties since "a powerful colony of American blood must in time become an independent nation, and will naturally be to us an amicable neighbour." Sansom is facile about lack of cultural identity in Lower Canada:

A Canadian is ready to admit the superiority of the American character, and shews nothing of French partialities, save the display of the Gallic cock, which is perched upon the spire of every steeple, and upon the top of every cross, together with the sun, the flower-de-luce, and other degraded emblems of French monarchy, which British policy has wisely permitted these harmless people to retain as long as they were content to let go the substance of national independence, and grasp a shadow.

The "operation of imperious circumstances" blocks Quebec's resistance to the American empire because its commitment to the language, customs, and symbols of France is tenuous.[16]

Sansom's propaganda is otherwise questionable. Disregarding the Hudson's Bay Company's westward search for natural resources, he forgets that the British empire relied on trading companies to extend its administrative and political influence, commerce being one means by which it amassed territory. Reaching into Rupert's Land, under governor George Simpson (1787–1860), the company and its apologists perpetuated English codes. *Peace River*, the journal of Simpson's 1828 passage from Hudson's Bay to the Pacific, reveals his quest for trading routes and fur- and mineral-yielding locales on which, in his capacity as company chief officer, he deployed wine and spirits in the tradition of Thomas James to uphold hierarchical order in his band of explorers and to consolidate group motivation. Port, Madeira, and spirits were as available at inland forts like Cumberland House as at York Factory, Simpson knowing the regulated importation of wine and spirits was vital to transportation in the northwest. On this canoe voyage he rationed alcohol with a discrimination that implemented a system of incentives and rewards confirming social order: he gave his oarsmen

---

16 Sansom 1972, 32, 45, 54, 58–9, 63–4, and 75.

"drams four times a day," while reserving "a glass of wine" for guests and himself. Each time the voyageurs pick up spirits and wine at inland forts, the social distinction between the kinds of alcohol is reinforced. That the more numerous kegs of port and Madeira had to be shouldered on long portages must have weightily impressed this distinction on the oarsmen. While Simpson did reward his men with "a bumper of Port Wine" for exceptional effort, their "rum" supply was occasionally exhausted, no doubt reinforcing that, if it rewarded heroic labour, it also marked their lesser standing. Moreover, they could not enjoy "two or three extra glasses of spirits" in the company of Indians since the governor then upheld "the propriety of discontinuing the use of spiritous liquors." While Indians are given glasses of "weak rum," they are invited to take tobacco when trading furs. Simpson, aware that liquor had been the "most profitable of trade with the Indians" in the context of company rivalry and convinced of his Company's long-term, monopolistic future in the country, stood for reducing thousands of gallons of spirits into the fort system to curtail Native intoxication.[17]

THE REFINED SENSIBILITIES OF FEMALE SETTLERS

The settlement accounts of women pioneers in Upper Canada published in England between 1836 and 1853, the years when the Hudson's Bay Company faced losing its trading monopoly and seeing its imperial influence diminish, show the relation between wine and spirits and the importation of English cultural values attenuating; it was becoming less subject to traditional codes. Hailing from similar backgrounds in England, Catharine Parr Traill (1802–1899), Anna Jameson (1794–1860), and Susanna Moodie (1803–1885) concentrated on domestic self-sufficiency and intensely questioned the codes associated with wine and spirits. Yet, while they raised different questions about these codes, they did not simply or uniformly endorse the temperance movement.

In *The Backwoods of Canada* (1836), Traill sympathizes with "the poorer sort of emigrants" who, "debilitated by the privations and fatigue" of transatlantic voyages, "indulged in every sort of excess, especially the dangerous one of intoxication," which made them susceptible to death

17 Simpson 1970, 2, 23, 13, 10, and 62–3.

from cholera. Her "fellow-feeling" extends to eight disconcerting Irish rowers whose scow, on meeting a stranded steamboat bearing a group of demanding, well-provisioned settlers, conveys them to Peterborough with "marvellous ill-grace." Having to row four miles more than usual given the river's low flow, the Irishmen labour "under the exciting influence of whiskey" that sees them rudely resist the imperious demands of the settlers with "their enormous load of furniture" until the rowers have "satisfied their hunger." Far from treating intoxication as a lower-class phenomenon, Traill thinks it a vice most common "among the better class of emigrants." Despite her high standing as a member of a transplanted military community, she has no wish to replicate English social structure in the new land. Prizing settlers' independence from both necessities and luxuries, she values "good conduct" rather than rank as the "distinguishing mark between the classes." One sign of her trust in Canada as "the land of hope" is admiration for the work "bee," the institution that, in harmoniously crossing class boundaries, employs "Canadian nectar (whiskey)" as a rite that ensures communal solidarity through "work and entertainment." Another such ritual sign is her admiration of "those well skilled in the manufacture of home-made wines and beer."[18]

Jameson, in *Winter Studies and Summer Rambles in Canada* (1838), announces her enjoyment of wine, which the care she takes bringing it on outings confirms. Voyaging in a "birch-bark canoe" on Lake Huron, the lone woman among twenty-one hunters and fishermen, she relishes a glass of "good madeira"; it goes well with a feast of newly caught "fish and pigeons." She also appreciates wine as medicine, taking port as a stomachic and Madeira as a soporific. When "too sick to eat" after a twenty-mile rough lake crossing, she puts into "some port wine and water" broken biscuit since this is all she can ingest and keep down. On a wet, stormy night when feeling she will get no rest, "some hot madeira" helps her have a "deep, sound sleep." Mindful of the picturesque scenery of the grape harvest in Italy, she is not averse to imposing European wine images upon the "somewhat different" Canadian scene of agricultural labour. Hence, she lauds Colonel Talbot, the colonist who founded Port Talbot on Lake Erie and, in "aristocratic pride," built a "chateau" with "cellars for storing wine, milk, and provisions." Contrariwise, she

---

18 Traill 1971, 26, 37–8, 99, 94, 58, and 119.

faults average Anglo-Saxon settlers, seeing in their alcohol consumption gross pretensions to civility, stupid indifference to public policy, and barbarity to Aboriginal people. Thus, Erindale is a "half-civilised community" for, when its risible militia affects refinement by drinking imported wines, its festive banquets subside into drunken bouts, violent riots, and "even fatal accidents." The double standards by which such drunkenness is hypocritically tolerated lead her to decry prohibition and reject calls for legislation that would raise duties on licences issued to liquor vendors:

An Act, for a limited time, to impose an additional duty on licenses to vend spiritous liquors can do but little good in the present state of society here. You might as well think to dam up a torrent with a bundle of reeds, or put out a conflagration with a cup of water, as attempt to put down drunkenness and vice by such trifling measures.

But, while stressing that it "should be one of the first objects of the government to put down, by all and every means, a vice which is rotting at the core of this infant society – poisoning the very sources of existence," she insists that "all their taxes, and prohibitions, and excise laws, will do little good, unless they facilitate the means of education." She sees "ignorance, recklessness, despondency, and inebriety" prevailing in the Canadian population, rating its morality as "frightfully low." Immigrants who arrive "with sober habits quickly fall into the vice of the country; and those who have the least propensity to drinking find the means of gratification comparatively cheap, and little check from public opinion." The basis for these remarks is that taverns in Upper Canada outnumber bookshops and that imported whisky is untaxed while excise duties raise book prices by a third. Since popular culture remains dull to relative economic and social costs, she urges that it be educated to the evils aggravated by legislative complacency. Since "the people have work and wealth" but not "education [and] amusements," they turn grocery stores into "drinking-houses," which easily elude the law that "forbids the sale of spiritous liquors in small quantities by any but licensed publicans"; when customers ask for cakes or nuts, they are served large glasses of whisky without the shopkeeper risking penalties. In the same breath, she expresses outrage that "the severe law against selling intoxicating liquors to the poor Indians, is continually eluded or violated, and [that] there is no redress for the injured, no punishment to reach the guilty." Angry that Christians in Upper Canada more cruelly destroy the Indians than military conquerors, she attributes her community's hypocrisy about the Bible and fire water to racism: the "refuse of the white population along the back settlements have no perception of the genuine virtues of the Indian character." While her satire contrasts abstemious "French peasants" with addicted Britons and Americans, its most effective strategy is a refusal to condemn Aboriginals' drunkenness. Appreciating their festivity, she says that, regardless of their intoxication, "wild yelling and whooping," she had "a feeling of perfect security" at an Indian revel. Having observed no "mischief" or unruliness, she adds a paradox to her claim that an Englishman who lowers Indians to his level with whisky is a "ruffian of civilised life."[19]

Unlike Traill and Jameson, Moodie struggled to adapt to pioneer life, unable to compromise her English propriety. *Roughing It in the Bush* (1852) tells that on her arrival she was repelled by poor immigrants who took brandy for consolation against physical hardship and social displacement. Critical of their "extravagant expectations" and "absurd anticipations" about Canada, "the land of Goshen," she was herself bitterly disappointed that the new land lacked a familiar hierarchy. Her disgust with its disorder – reflected in the alienation conveyed by her title – led her to harp on the drawbacks of pioneer life and to recoil from the mores evident in the public consumption of spirits and wine. While her husband took spirits into the bush in his awareness that rum was the payment "workmen" demanded and whisky was the currency in which to pay for hired help, she remained aloof: she neither trusted her "wine-glasses and tumblers" to local servants nor participated in the system in which neighbours cadged "whiskey" from one another. If she ideally hoped immigrants would become economically and socially independent, her anecdotes emphasize the desperate fates of pioneers who rely on the consolations of whisky. Matching her stories of obsessive, suicidal drinkers is her disgust with the institution of bees for clearing land: the logging parties on her farm she views as destructive revels. Not against serving "whiskey-punch" to house guests, she despised the "logging-band," most of whom made the house ring "with the sound of unhallowed revelry, profane songs, and blasphemous swearing." Their

---

19 Jameson 1970, 3:314, 322, 252, 337; 1:23; 2:195–98; 1:303, 166; 2:39, 80–1, 146–7, 251, 313; 3:56 and 290.

"delirium of drink" turns the bees into "hateful" feasts and "tumultuous, disorderly meetings."[20]

Moodie's hostility to pioneer consumerism finds expression in satirizing the drinking habits of the professions and gentry in *Life in the Clearings* (1853). Like Jameson, she is appalled that drinking rather than literature is the resort of the polite classes. Hence, she favours educating the young to the ills of drunkenness rather than inducing them to take temperance pledges. After saying facetiously that the "sin of authorship meets with little toleration in a new country," she declares that "persons of this class," by whom she means potential authors, "finding few minds that could sympathize with them, and enter into their literary pursuits," yield to "despondency" and fall "victims to that insidious enemy of souls, *Canadian whisky*." To her, "this frightful vice of drinking prevails throughout the colony," so much so that professional "gentlemen are not ashamed of being seen issuing from the bar-room of a tavern early in the morning, or being caught reeling home from the same sink of iniquity late at night." She has heard that "some of these regular topers place brandy beside their beds that, should they wake during the night, they may have within their reach the fiery potion for which they are bartering body and soul." Signing a temperance pledge is no "permanent remedy for this great moral evil. If an appeal to the heart and conscience, and the fear of incurring the displeasure of an offended God, are not sufficient to deter a man from becoming an active instrument in the ruin of himself and family, no forcible restraint upon his animal desires will be likely to effect a real reformation." Thus, "the temperance people begin at the wrong end of the matter, by restraining the animal propensities before they have convinced the mind. If a man abstain from drink only as long as the accursed thing is placed beyond his reach, it is after all but a negative virtue, to be overcome by the first strong temptation." A better remedy for "incurable drunkards" is to threaten them with incarceration in lunatic asylums. Being obliged to surrender the "management of their affairs" to "their wives or adult children" would "operate more forcibly upon them" than the signing of a pledge which they "can break or resume according to the caprice of the moment."[21]

---

20 Moodie 1970, 31, 73, 66, 71, 182, and 162.
21 Moodie 1976, 44–6.

Despite her ascetic reaction to sumptuary refinement and scorn of conventional expectations of wifely hospitality, Moodie is open to signs in drinking and eating. The charges in the bill of fare at the Clifton Hotel in Niagara that she confronts along with American tourists shock her; she complains that the cost of bed and board excludes wine, noting that "every little extra is an additional charge" raised by the hotel's "grand view of the Falls." Sharing a gentleman's dislike of "kickshaws" and ignorance of "French names for dishes," she will not say so directly. Rather she tells a story that conveys how Canadians are unfamiliar with "the great world." Theirs are "bread and butter doings when compared with" the "grand fixings" of New York, such as champagne. Staring at tourists seated at a table opposite, she feels "guilty of violating Lord Chesterfield's rules of politeness." The tourists take their eating seriously, contriving "to taste everything in the bill of fare" and never lifting "their eyes from their plates" which are piled up to get their money's worth. By contrast, her sympathy for young brides whom custom makes receive guests and undergo public scrutiny a week after their weddings is heartfelt: it is a "trying piece of ceremonial" that their "cake and wine" should be judged on these visits. Still, she enjoys the cordiality that New Year's parties uniquely restore in Canada and the United States. With the service of "rich cakes, fruit, wine, coffee, and tea," the day is happy and cheerful: "all faces wear a smile, old quarrels are forgotten, and every one seems anxious to let ill-will and heart-burnings die with the old year."[22]

Clearest in Moodie's attitudes to spirits and wine, although also found in Traill and Jameson to a degree, is a distaste for the social codes and institutional aspects of drinking. By the end of the nineteenth century, female commentators consistently presented a chasm between permissible domestic and objectionable public drinking. Hariot Dufferin (1843–1936), the governor general's wife, who recorded her observations in *My Canadian Journal* between 1872 and 1878, pertinently describes this chasm. From her social pinnacle, Lady Dufferin's remarks on wine rituals resist male drinking codes that involve English domestic values. As a vice-regal guest, she enjoys "cake and sweet wine" at a convent in Sillery and takes with pleasure "tea and mulled claret" at a skating party. Upon organizing a New Year's levée and dutifully laying on "tea"

---

22 Ibid., 252–5 and 273–4.

as well as "champagne," she is disappointed that the guests who are all "gentlemen" mostly drink the wine. Since champagne is so commonly served at receptions and public banquets where the Queen is toasted, its savour palls on her because it is associated with the overindulgence of formal rites. Although her husband transports his own wine on his tours of Canada, she becomes tired of the drinks she has to consume on their grand tour of the United States. She needs "neither meat nor wine," being content with "tumblers full of iced milk, good bread, butter, eggs, fish and iced cream." A tea drinker, she is increasingly unhappy that public functions offer only the male refreshments of "punch, brandy, gin, and champagne." Yet, on less formal occasions, Lady Dufferin appreciates the service of alcohol for its domestic associations. She is happy when serving "tea and claret-cup" to American dignitaries visiting Quebec City and environs and when tasting "Rhine wine and German cake" in a Mennonite community on the Red River. At home she asks the household, "upstairs and down," to toast a newly christened baby and she gladly perpetuates the tradition of a "'Yorkshire wassail-bowl.'" Her account reveals that traditional drinking values entered the domestic sphere even if royal and imperial rituals lost symbolic power from routinized public consumption.[23]

EXPLORATION IN THE NORTHWEST

On frontiers, where exploration remained a primary activity, drinking codes retained their efficacy by precluding overindulgence, as the 1872 expedition by Sandford Fleming (1827–1915), recorded by George Munro Grant (1835–1902) in *Ocean to Ocean* (1873), reveals. In this text, spirits and wine function as instruments of geographical charting and the measured ordering of land in accord with tenets of the British empire. Fleming rewarded his men with small amounts of brandy for heroic effort on long portages, especially when they had been exposed to bad weather. In his mind, brandy was "the right kind of sauce" for voyageurs. When their bottle was "exhausted," they were content to pass "round the cork for each to have a 'smell' at, in lieu of a 'drain.'" Like James long before, Fleming guarded spirits for the sweetening and purifying of drinking water: he gave "a little whiskey" to his men to "take

---

23 Dufferin and Ava 1971, 30, 53, 126, 108, 181, 240, 288, 401, 335, 77, and 301.

the bad taste" from water and "kill the animalculae." The amount they drank may have been small, but its ritual imaginary was large. After one fortnight's work when his thirteen companions had been "abstemious," he gave them a "kettle of whiskey-toddy" into which "three half-pints" of spirits had been poured. This tiny quantity not only produces hilarity but also draws the company together in formalizing pledges to the Queen, the Dominion, sweethearts, wives, and their chief. The company took alcohol once a week; in celebration of that period's voyages, the "whole party" would gather "round the camp-fire after supper to offer the Saturday night toasts of 'wives and sweethearts' and 'the Dominion and the Railroad,' immediately after 'the Queen.'"[24]

Grant does not shun the problem of Indians and alcoholism. Frank about serving "a glass of the mildest toddy" to Valad, a Native guide, he notes how the toddy relaxes the Indian's "gravity and taciturnity" for the better but then excuses the spirits taken by Fleming's men and served to Natives. Admitting that "a little did us good and we were thankful for the good," he insists that it "would have been mean to have left Valad out"; the group wanted "to show an Indian that it was possible to be temperate in all things" and "to use a stimulant without abusing it." They thought it "on the whole a better lesson to enforce practically, than to have preached an abstinence" that would have been misunderstood. This promotion of moderate indulgence defines itself over against criticism of imperial history and Yankee "'free-traders'" who, on the loss of "the Hudson's Bay monopoly," arrive from the south "plentifully supplied with a poisonous stuff, rum in name, but in reality a compound of tobacco, vitriol, bluestone and water." These traders finish "the work that scrofula and epidemics were already doing" since "an Indian will part with horse and gun, blanket and wife for rum." Grant earlier stresses the cultural loss and potential for internecine strife caused by free trade when he argues that "when the Indians have no horses they cannot hunt. When they cannot hunt, they are not ashamed to steal, and stealing leads to wars." He thinks the truce between Crees and Blackfeet will end in "the old thirst for scalps" that will render the country "insecure."[25]

In perpetuating the Hudson's Bay Company's drinking codes, Fleming embodies a European sensibility that likens the North Saskatchewan

---

24 Grant 1970, 43, 117, 129, and 215.
25 Ibid., 215–16, 190, and 132.

River to the "Rhine with its vine-clad slopes near Bingen." Thus, he celebrates stages on his Canadian journey and anniversaries at home in Britain with spirits and wine. On the occasion of camping "before sunset within twenty-seven miles of Edmonton," he brings out "in honour of the event ... our only bottle of claret." He guards a bottle of Noyeau – an almond liqueur – "for some great occasion." This turns out to be his wife's birthday toasted by the group "in three table-spoonfulls a piece." On this occasion, Fleming's taste for plum pudding comes to the fore, a substitute for which he finds in "slap-jacks, mixed with berry pemmican." His making of plum pudding topped with brandy sauce becomes an important bicultural and imperial project. Lacking suet, plums, and a bag in which to boil the pudding, he substitutes "buffalo fat" for suet "and berry pemmican," leading Grant to declare that only "genius could have united plum-pudding and berry pemmican in one mental act." Indeed, Fleming is better at cooking puddings than anyone else. When the group sits down to "the usual *pièce de résistance* of pemmican, flanked for Sunday garnishing, by two reindeer tongues," he disagrees with his fellows that the pudding is a failure, boiling it for another thirty minutes. The result, sauced with a "teaspoonful of brandy on a sprinkling of sugar," leads everyone to hold out their plates for more, making the birthday celebration highly successful. Fleming flamed plum pudding with brandy to gladden his men's hearts and fill them "with old memories."[26]

British signs come to the fore when his band finds a cache near the Thompson River of "Two bottles of Worcester sauce and a bottle of brandy" along with "Half a dozen of Bass Pale Ale, with the familiar face of the red pyramid brand!" The men rejoice that the first two items will furnish "sauce both for the fat pork and for the plum-pudding" the next Sunday. The canned meats, jams, and bottles of claret in the cache evoke "but faint applause." Opening four bottles of ale along with "a can of preserved beef, and another of peaches," they are gladdened by the ale's "kindly" trademark, "'the red pyramid'" touching "a chord in [their] hearts" and Grant imploring "the ascetic and the dignified reader to be a little kind to this ebullition on our part." Leaving the meats,

---

26 Ibid., 156, 169, 203, 216–17, and 270. See Johnson's "Meditation on a Pudding," in Boswell's *Journal of a Tour to the Hebrides* (1785), which, despite its rhetorical wit, shows that Johnson saw food as a basic necessity that defied consumer pretensions (Johnson 1965, 346–7).

jams, and claret for later railway surveyors, Fleming takes the brandy for the baking of plum puddings, which, as we have seen, he often made to recall home. Yet, if, like earlier explorers, he inspires his imperial venture with European gustatory tastes, his criticism of the excessive and luxurious drinking of goldminers near Kamloops reveals a sensibility limiting itself by aspirations for the national future. His dislike of the tasteless excesses of itinerant miners, which counter his hopes for civilized settlement and flourishing local economies, is clear in his description of Lytton. This village's appearance offers no "sign of progress or improvement of any kind." The miners are "dirty looking," their abodes no more than "tumble down little huts." Yet the hotel yields a contrasting image. Inside, miners call for drinks all round, "freely" proffering "claret, champagne, and brandy" and finding the "meat, fish, vegetables, and sweets on the table" to be "all excellent, and well cooked." The explanation of the contrasting living and consuming conditions is "that none of the people came here to stay": they "came to make money and then return home." Hence, "it is not worth their while to build good houses or furnish them expensively; but they can afford to live well." Fleming laments the influx of people into British Columbia: it is not "an emigration of sober, steady house-holders, whose aim was to establish homes, and live by their own industry, but of fever-heated adventurers from all parts of the world – men without a country and without a home." To Fleming the boom-and-bust cycles of the mining industry lead not only to extravagances when miners from the Cariboo wash their feet in champagne or spice pork sandwiches with £10 notes but also to inflation, speculation in property values, and a gambling mentality that harms "the true trading spirit" and "retards the growth" of cities such as Victoria. Arguing that wealth generated by the gold rush should go into financing agricultural and manufacturing production, he dreams of immigrants achieving permanent economic settlements and sound social lives. His wish for imperial order is the stronger for admitting the challenges of itinerant communities and luxurious consumerism.[27]

NEW FRANCE AND BRITISH WINE CODES

The semiotics of the consumption of spirits and wine in eighteenth- and nineteenth-century novels set in Lower and Upper Canada reveals

27 Grant 1970, 266–7, 307–8, and 345.

much about how variably signs function in nation building and imperial history. When characters aspire to refinement through the mannered taking of spirits and wine, the codes they embody gather significations beyond their conscious intentions. Authors, too, who deploy signs of spirits and wine inevitably maintain stances on political history unsteadily. Yet the diverse signs of cultural nationalism that stem from taste for spirits and wine in fiction were ignored by *The Facts of the Case* at the close of the nineteenth century. Unsurprisingly, fiction published in London imposed wine codes on presentations of Canada to celebrate the Cession of New France in 1763. A major example is *The History of Emily Montague*, published in 1769, which, by incorporating the matrices of British codes, delimits the comparative basis of cultural and literary history germane to colonial settlement. Its author, Frances Brooke (1724–1789), in stressing the Conquest, the need to have the habitants assimilated, and a program for establishing Anglicanism, sought to confirm the association of wine with military, genteel, and imperial values but was seemingly resisted by the very signs that conveyed her propaganda.[28]

Her military heroes, Captain Fitzgerald and Colonel Rivers, gain status by translating wine into a hierarchical system of refinement despite their low economic means. When he changes quarters, Fitzgerald leaves "three months wine in the cellars" for a fellow officer, this comradeship giving him a "princely spirit" in the eyes of Arabella Fermor, his witty wife-to-be. When he treats the master of a fast ship to a "bottle of very fine madeira" so that Arabella, now his wife, may be sure of having a letter reach England quickly, Fitzgerald's hospitality signals gentility and sensibility. Further, his wine conveys strategic capacities which show that his impecunious standing is less restrictive than the text claims. The supper Rivers hosts for "the *beau monde* of Quebec" is "admirable" in its "excellent wine." The British community defines itself by keeping "good tables." While the Colonel laments England's "luxury" and enjoys the "homely fare" dressed by the wives and daughters of "lazy, dirty and stupid" French peasants as if he were "feasting on

---

28 Since, according to Scholes, an "author is not a perfect ego but a mixture of public and private, conscious and unconscious elements, insufficiently unified for use as an interpretive base," my discussion focuses on irony which, "of all figures, is the one that must always take us out of the text and into codes, contexts, and situations" (1982, 14 and 76). For an extended historical analysis of political ironies in Brooke's novel, see Merrett 1992.

ortolans in a palace," rank obliges him to keep a "decent table" for friends in his native land. Were he rich, he says, Emily's "suppers" would be "his principal extravagance." The genteel, imperial code that Fitzgerald and Rivers uphold is categorically embodied in the Earl with whom William Fermor, the patriarch, corresponds. The Earl glories in owning the "best claret in the universe." If buying great Bordeaux wines lets him boast supreme hospitality, it signals his habitual conjoining of aesthetic, political, and nationalist referents which, if not wholly complacent, is uncritically conventional.[29]

In the Earl's world, fine wine signifies enjoying economic and social privileges, cultivating a masculine camaraderie that prides itself on sensitivity to women, and supporting policies that advance imperial rivalry with France while appropriating that nation's cultural modes. Wine's significations in Brooke's fiction are exclusive, arbitrary, and aggressive: wine has for her characters functions they neither fully comprehend nor control. In making wine uphold British imperialism, they use it to demean Indians, habitants, and the French. The result is that negative significations recoil on their political and social pretensions. When Rivers asserts Indians are "brutal slaves to their appetites" and that, since the English and French are sober, they did not introduce drunkenness to the Natives, his European perspective is at odds with the testimony of explorers who witnessed the problems arising from consumerism and contact with Aboriginal people. The impulse to homogenize European society is self-defeating: the refusal to differentiate cultural systems is not just arbitrary; it undoes itself. When Fermor scorns the seigneurial system in which "lazy lords" and retainers take brandy together "in a mixture of festivity and inaction," he demeans French hierarchy and Catholicism for impeding productivity and "colonization" with "ignorance and superstition" and "celibacy." Yet his scorn manifests fear of France's economic power. Defending British colonialism, he calls for Quebec's assimilation by Anglo-Americans, not Britons. Not only does anxiety over depopulation at home lead Fermor to speak of New Englanders – often disparaged in the novel – as allies, but fear that colonies erode the domestic economy leads him to call for policies to offset France's larger population, which, like economists of the day,

---

29 Brooke 1985, 87, 309, 111, 110, 297, 18, 313, 380, and 326.

he assigns to intensive "cultivation of vineyards."³⁰ In Brooke's text, French wine does and does not signify Britain's power over France: for cultural appropriation is jostled by political diffidence; colonial power informed by imperial vulnerability; and European solidarity displaced by national competitiveness.

That Brooke's characters would displace French culture from North America – while they partially identify themselves by it – signals how imperialist ideology thrives on unacknowledged conflict between codes, this theme clarified by the irreconcilable semiotic functions arising from those codes. When the usually temperate Fermor rages at habitants' claims to be the "flower of the French nation" and at their belief that France is "the only civilized nation in the world," he retaliates against their denial of the Conquest in asserting that France's military has been assimilated by "savage tribes." But this retaliation clashes with Rivers's view that European mores transcend those of Indigenous peoples. This clash reveals how the interdependence of Canada, France, and Britain subjects characters' prejudices to the fundamental dialectic of social and textual signifiers. Again, when Arabella declares that French gallantry is depraved while English gallantry creates the "peace of families," she differs from Rivers, who holds that French gallantry "debases the mind less than ours," although he groundlessly declares all seigneurs to be illiterate. Arbitrary generalizations on behalf of Englishness are manifest in Arabella's attitudes to alcohol. Holding that Canada lacks "elegant arts" and "Genius" because the severe cold freezes the strongest wines and thickens brandy, she exploits wine and spirits remarkably. For one thing, she gives wine to Indian women who revere the English conquest of Quebec, a gesture belying her professed political indifference and undoing Rivers's claim that Europe has not provided Natives with alcohol. Finding the company of the Indian women "ridiculous," she treats them as "gypsies" and spurns their festive spirit. The subversion of her stance is clearer when she utters a truism typical of rakes in eighteenth-century plays: brandy, she says, makes her speak "like an angel." Her jocularity may lighten the political themes but her wit exposes incoherence in those themes and in the conquerors' cultural system.³¹

---

30 Ibid., 222, 208–9, and 222 a second time. For a full discussion of the economy of vineyards, see Smith 1976, 1:171–4.

31 Brooke 1985, 141, 271, 381, 26, 103, 50–1, and 105.

The transferred meanings Brooke's characters assign to wine drinking are located in lexical fields more diffuse and intricate than they know.[32] When Arabella announces that politics in Quebec are "dregs of old disputes" to which she adopts a "strict neutrality," her transcendent claim is rendered untenable by her words. Dregs are part of wine making: separating them out is not a matter of neutrality but of discriminating taste. Her analogy is reversible: as dregs are organic to wine, so political disputes touch everyone in Quebec. Dividing sumptuary and political signs, Arabella never realizes that signification rejoins them. Such semiotic irony is found in the gap between Emily's trust that she can use Rivers's "inebriation of tenderness" for her to induce him to return to his mother in England and his belief that "inebriation" of passion is not "tenderness." This conflicting metonymy of intoxication confirms that Brooke's characters are not like-minded in romantic sentiments despite their high-flown professions to be so.[33]

IDEOLOGIES OF WINE IN FICTION ABOUT LOWER AND UPPER CANADA

If wine signs in *The History of Emily Montague* expose problems in taste and the ideology of cultural imperialism, this is pointedly the case in nineteenth-century novels such as *Canadians of Old* (1863) by Philippe-Joseph Aubert de Gaspé (1786–1871), *Jean Rivard* (1862–1864) by Antoine Gérin-Lajoie (1824–1882), *The Golden Dog* (1877) by William Kirby (1817–1906), *The Curé of St Philippe* (1899) by Francis Grey (1860–1939), and *The Imperialist* (1904) by Sara Jeannette Duncan (1861–1922), each of which, in their drinking codes, juxtaposes cultural pluralism and political nationalism, similarly highlighting the textual limits of trying to reconcile what and how signs signify. In exposing the contrariety of textual semiosis and the gaps between narrative and social signs, these novels show that literary histories of Lower and Upper Canada encounter challenges in promoting cultural identity through forms of fictional displacement. National sentiments in Aubert de Gaspé's fiction are strong but, in asserting the cultural independence

---

32 To Jacques Lacan, language, "like the unconscious, is an impersonal system outside the subject's control -- a system from which the subject is irrevocably alienated" (Makaryk 1993, 189).

33 Brooke 1985, 98, 212, and 314.

of Lower Canada, the author voices allusions that weaken his claims on behalf of that uniqueness. While he avers that *Canadians of Old* is "Canadian through and through," his depiction of the "manners and customs of the early Canadians" often alludes to British and French literature: to displace European imperialism, he oddly derives Quebec's uniqueness from texts by Walter Scott (1771–1832) and Rousseau, among others.[34] Aubert de Gaspé turns to Scott for a model of historical fiction and a political paradigm: Scott testifies to Scotland's "prosperity" and "peace" after the Act of Union of 1707. Since Scotland prospers from having been absorbed into one of the "mightiest empires of the world," Aubert de Gaspé trusts that Quebec will similarly benefit. But this trust is problematic since Scott saw the Union as one of equal partners and since one of Aubert de Gaspé's heroes is a displaced Jacobite. By not distinguishing between union and conquest and being vague about Scottish nationalism, the novelist unsettles his claims for Quebec's independence. His wish to champion the "sentiments of the human heart" against European social mores draws on Rousseau no less problematically. Since "ancient and modern codes" arise from "barbarous egotism," Aubert de Gaspé proposes that society warps humans, making imperial inferior to primitive peoples. Not only does his political defence of Canada rely on questionable displacement of European codes but his allusions to Rousseau contradict those to Scott: if the former help Aubert de Gaspé to displace French civilization, the latter appear to uphold British imperialism.[35]

Aubert de Gaspé upholds Canada's political and social culture, but, as allusions to Rousseau show, he cannot stabilize relations between textual signs since they are unsettled by a dialectic that exposes Quebec's traditions to ambivalence. Tracing national continuity to the "vivid faith of the *habitants* of New France," he sees in "some of our nineteenth-century Christians ... a shrinking or cowardly spirit" since they do not perform acts of public worship. Involving national and religious traditions, Aubert de Gaspé insists that, if Canadians' identity was strong, it

---

34 Aubert De Gaspé 1974, 11. Remarkably, Aubert de Gaspé takes epigraphs from the following British authors: Burns and Shakespeare; Byron; Tennyson; Scott and Edward Young (1974, 31, 6, 76, 167, and 180). Besides alluding to French and German authors, his text refers to Wordsworth, Shakespeare, Macpherson, and Goldsmith (1974, 130, 145, 173, and 259).

35 Ibid., 19, 30, and 147.

is now weak. To an extent, this contrariness derives from the author's promotion of narrative dialectic. While his hero, Jules D'Haberville, stands up for the seigneurial system, he also stands aside from it. But, to a greater extent, political history imposes on the author unacknowledged paradoxes. Despite lauding Canadians for keeping their nationality "intact," he blames them for seeing themselves as a conquered people and for discovering their history only lately. The clichés in which he presents the external forces affecting Lower Canada illustrate his difficulty in maintaining the independence of Quebec traditions: abandoned by the "mother country, a veritable step-mother," the "fortunate colony" was spared the "horrors of '93" by the "flag of Britain" that gave military opportunities to the habitants to gather "new laurels." Saying the Cession of Canada was a "blessing in disguise," he offsets his accommodation with history by sensationalizing Governor Murray's "vindictive cruelty" and "unreasoning bitterness." This invective equally fails to make the suspension of Britain's policy of assimilation signal the habitants' solidarity. The dénouement – Jules's marriage to a "daughter of Albion" – no more steadily translates paradox into constructive vision: it may betoken Quebec's power to resist assimilation and to absorb Anglo-Saxon virtues, but the renewed affiliation with France is dubious since the "French light-heartedness" that survived the Cession and the Revolution is "disappearing" in "these degenerate days."[36]

If tensions between cultural loss and repair, between rejection by and identification with France, and between dependence on and appropriation of the British empire are unresolved, Aubert de Gaspé's codes, given the wine trade's internationalism, verify this irresolution. In *Canadians of Old*, consumption of wine and spirits is inseparable from Quebec's unsteady displacement of France and Britain. If devastated Canadians are praised for renouncing habitual luxuries and assured the British government will enable them to be "as rich as ... before the conquest," wine signs highlight the cultural dialectic involving imported traditions, Indigenous festivities, and political renunciation. The drinking of brandy and wine involves sets of political signs that convey typologies of consumption – but discrepantly. The signs enhance the dignity of the seigneurial class and the importance of the habitants' festive spirit. Jules is a "connoisseur" of wine who worships "Bacchus." Since

36 Ibid., 94, 13, 167–9, 221–2, 281, and 259.

he enjoys "the privilege of aristocratic descent," he upholds imported French products and modes. But his friend Archie, the displaced Jacobite, is "abstemious," distancing himself from the claret code of Stuart supporters. The aristocratic drinking code is further eroded when Jules praises the habitants' taking of a "few glasses of brandy" with their "warmed-up dishes" as constituting a "more wholesome and natural" taste than that of his class. If they often do not eat well, habitants enjoy brandy because it fortifies the seigneurial class. José, the chief butler of Jules's father, declares his daily allowance to be larger than it is to promote "the honor of his master." Habitants' taste arises from how seigneurs tighten social bonds. If taste for brandy signals solidarity, it compensates for economic failure, too, as when the D'Haberville estate dispenses it to tenants unable to pay rent.[37]

The typology habitants give to brandy stretches tensions between the social and political functions wine codes had in Lower Canada. The "unadulterated brandy" they swallow is a source of pride, its purity conveying their masters' concern for them. They see it as a nutrient: "milk for old men." Enjoying brandy validates a man's honest acceptance of the political order. Still, their code involves paradox as well as metonymy: the "systematic" daily taking of brandy and occasional festive indulgence in it both uphold "propriety." Moreover, appreciation of brandy betokens male prowess by involving contradictory kinds of renunciation. José thinks that to give up the last glass in the world to a friend is the noblest self-sacrifice, whereas at the D'Habervilles' May-Feast the men avoid the wine set at each place since it does not "scratch the throat enough." They take brandy and leave the wine to the women, who go to table only after serving their men, who with brandy imbibe a code upholding their virility, honour, and status in an aristocratic community.[38]

The sexual discrimination implicit in the brandy code makes it less unique than male habitants claim; their brandy drinking is no more socially inclusive than democratic. Despite Aubert de Gaspé's stress on the habitants' plain tastes and unique code, consumption of brandy in Quebec conforms to international modes: women and aristocrats take brandy as an apéritif according to "the customs of all civilized nations." But the habitants' typological distinction between brandy and

---

37 Ibid., 270, 140, 56, 44, 46, 114, 36, and 108.
38 Ibid., 38–9, 259, and 120.

wine is reversed by seigneurs who, if they take brandy "for daily use," prefer purer, costlier unfortified wines on feast days. The "unlimited supply" of "excellent brandy" provided by seigneurs on these days exemplifies their political power more than their taste. This power is imitated by the habitants who control Indians with "fire-water," their brandy code not acknowledging this questionable use. Their code is compromised further by drinking songs that celebrate Bacchus and the divinity of wine in traditional formulas unrelated to their Indigenous cult of brandy.[39]

While the seigneurial wine code is prominent in the setting of *Canadians of Old*, its narrative dominance over the habitants' brandy code reveals the author's commitment to social differentiation and political hierarchy. Yet, because the seigneurial code generates its signs no more consistently than the habitants' code, it implies authorial confusion, the appropriation of foreign culture recoiling on the text. Aubert de Gaspé presents De Beaumont's dining room as a model of civility, but signs in that room undo the model's singularity. Central to the seigneury, the room has a made-in-Canada carpet. It lacks nothing an "Englishman calls comfort" since it also contains "blue Marseilles china" along with "bottles of old wine" and "a silver jar of water" for diluting it in the European mode. At each diner's place are set a "bottle of light wine" and a silver goblet, the range of dishes being such as would "have aroused the envy of Brillat-Savarin." The wine, food, and service reveal more than the importation of luxury goods; they signal a pretension to improve on the imported system of valuing such goods. Yet improving this system involves erasing cultural affiliations. While most habitants were Normans, the finest dish at De Beaumont's feast is "pigs feet *à la Sainte-Ménéhould*," a champenois specialty. This seigneurial meal makes no simple nationalist statement: appropriating French civility, it defends pan-European aristocratic standards. Aubert de Gaspé would displace English and French values by his wine signs but they confirm the international sumptuary and aesthetic standards vital to the institution of the seigneury.[40]

If seigneurs' wine advances aristocratic fellow-feeling, it also emphasizes the cultural origin and economic vulnerability of their society.

---

39 Ibid., 258, 77, 119–20, and 183–4.
40 Ibid., 76–8, 125, and 78.

Their wine code shows the local hierarchy to be subject to what it consumes and rejects: wine signs, in conveying discrepant social and private values, signify that both consumption and renunciation may cut cultural roots. When seigneur D'Haberville, on the birth of son Jules, gives a case of wine to his friend D'Egmont, the gift symbolizes a hierarchy confirming itself in the origins of wine which it displaces. The reception of the wine is no less ambivalent. D'Egmont understands wine: "with great care" he preserves the case for years, aware of the benefits cellarage will confer. Yet, despite caring for it all the years Jules grows up, D'Egmont disclaims connoisseurship. Restricted economic means and antagonism to French policy on New France have led him to renounce wine. The nationalist impulse behind D'Egmont's scorn for wine coexists with the complacency with which Jules, an avowed connoisseur, quaffs the well-aged wine in "several bumpers," treating a vintage wine as a mere beverage. Despite guarding the last bottle for Jules's return from military duty in France, D'Egmont insists that fine wine is but one of "many other useless luxuries." The gap between the domestic and political meanings he assigns to wine is widened by the displacement of his boast that a sofa he built has taken more "elaborate calculations than Perrault required for the construction of the Louvre."[41]

If D'Egmont's renunciation of wine stands for pre-Conquest disgust with France and invites seigneurs to free themselves from French culture, this does not reduce wine's value as a textual sign. Indeed, wine's textuality becomes more important since Aubert de Gaspé turns it into a supernatural omen. As characters devalue and appreciate wine, so do narrative signs. When the toast at the D'Haberville mansion to the victory of the fleur-de-lys is interrupted by a portentous noise and the glasses are left "unemptied in the dining-room," the displaced ritual enhances wine as a signifier. The portent is fulfilled: the English torch the D'Haberville estate. But the displaced ritual, far from stressing the agency of the British army, signifies that Providence has "careless Louis" and his "improvident ministers" as targets. The renunciation of French wine thus involves the would-be fusion of supernatural and nationalist signifiers. Yet, the triangular relations between New France, France, and Britain oppose this fusion, as the rebuilding of the estate shows. At

---

41 Ibid., 140 and 152. Claude Perrault was responsible in 1670 for the exterior reconstruction of the east facade of the Palais du Louvre.

first it is rebuilt with "the absence of more costly appointments." French goods are replaced by indigenous products and British imports: the original drinking cups remain but "sparkling spruce beer" takes the place of champagne, as Spanish does French wine. The new drinks are signs of colonial independence and reliance on Britain's imperial trade. The cultural signs Lower Canada borrows grow more salient the harder the author tries to integrate supernatural and economic signs. For redevelopment of the estate restores French cultural influence. As soon as a legacy permits, the D'Habervilles buy "good wine" – to them this generic noun is specifically French – making it represent supernatural and nationalist power. To Jules, the wine is "the most faithful of presages, for it announces happiness and mirth." The denouement claims that this omen portends the full renewal of the estate in Jules's marriage to a "fair daughter of Albion," and this renewal confirms the D'Habervilles' belief that, far from being subject to Britain, the seigneurial system is enabled by Providence to appropriate English culture. This conclusion, however, is no more self-contained than Brooke's; its propaganda no more consistent. Despite his historical pretensions, Aubert de Gaspé cannot make social change and continuity cohere. Given the tensions between social and textual signs, the marriage with its displacement of British political power makes little semiotic sense. The contrary functions wine has as signifier are not reconciled by the wedding ceremony, an account of which is absent: the contrariety of wine signs resists the transcendent perspective by which Aubert de Gaspé would contain them. The cross-cultural contexts generated by the signs indicate that national dependencies and rivalries cannot be subject to a single-minded narrative conclusion – to the closure as it stands.[42]

Themes of settlement and reconstruction in Quebec in *Jean Rivard* are more consistent than in *Canadians of Old* because Gérin-Lajoie views temperance from a strictly ascetic stance on social reform that anticipates Spence. Gérin-Lajoie presents Jean Rivard, the archetypal settler, as defying urban consumerism and rural custom with a radical sense of temperance. His wish to displace aristocratic, professional, and urban codes leads Gérin-Lajoie to depict habitant virtue with a mythical idealism that displaces Jean's belief in tradition. Hence:

---

42 Ibid., 158, 202, 199, 239, 257, and 281.

Nowhere does the spirit of fraternity exist in such a touching manner as in the Canadian countryside remote from the cities. Here, all classes are in contact with one another. Diversity of profession or condition is no divisive barrier as it is in the cities.

To Gérin-Lajoie, "aristocratic pretensions" in the "social life of cities" are manifest in boring grand balls wasteful in their luxury, as a letter about one from his friend, Gustave Charmenil, addressed to Jean illustrates: "The price of the wines, meats, salads, pastries, custards, and jellies of all kinds consumed on this occasion would certainly have been sufficient to feed several settler's families for an entire year." Since to have voiced this "thought" would not have been "in the best taste," Gustave is "pursued, obsessed, and sickened" by it. Yet Jean is motivated by asceticism when he promotes settlements as self-originating societies that should reject rural tradition. The work bee or *corvée* that builds his house does not serve "Jamaica rum" as of old "before temperance days." This bee is a "religious act," its abstemiousness fortifying communal solidarity after Jean sends back "several gallons of whisky" he had planned to "be drunk to the success and prosperity of the new settlement." Jean's renunciation is supported by an old settler who "feared the treacherous taste of liquor for his sons," convinced of "all the evils, misfortunes, crimes, poverty, and illness brought on by drink." This renunciation of spirits and rural custom may seem odd when guests at Jean's wedding sing drinking songs in the "absence of spirits." Why not invent songs to match Gérin-Lajoie's claims about self-originating communities? The apology for prohibition in Lower Canada reaches its apogee when Jean fixes "a temperance cross" on the wall of his dining room. Yet Gérin-Lajoie sees no discrepancy between the setting up of "temperance societies ... in all the villages and parishes of Lower Canada" and the serving of "raspberry vinegar, spruce beer and in some houses, currant wine" for refreshment in "hot summers." He simply celebrates the displacement of "the strong liquors of 'the good old days'" and the ban on imported liquors in Rivardville. In self-justification, the author has Gustave, Jean's former school friend, report on "the ravages caused by intemperance among the educated youth in our cities" and on the harm done to urban families by "addiction to drink." Certain that the bon vivant is selfish and vain, not liberal and sociable, Gérin-Lajoie makes Jean's biggest challenge that of persuading settlers in Rivardville to spurn the established link between whisky and electoral bribery and to pass severe "regulations" against the sale of alcohol. Despite Jean's ascetic desire as mayor to make Rivardville a "model parish" and "small republic" embodying a "spirit of government" yet to "exist among our people," when he becomes a federal Member of Parliament, he keeps sherry in his wine cellar, "obliged" to serve it to visiting colleagues. If his wife's currant wine signals Quebec's independence, the sherry signals tolerance of sumptuary modes in national institutions and social practice. This compromise heightens Jean's double standards and his creator's questionable stance on cultural independence.[43]

William Kirby's *The Golden Dog* is a sensational gothic romance that deploys wine allusions to project a bourgeois view of Quebec nationalism. It depicts the internal failings of pre-Conquest New France in 1748 to propose that its Christian trading community was thwarted by a colonial administration corrupted by the French court. Pretending that the noblesse assimilated after the Conquest rather than return to France, which the majority did, and claiming, again in a simplistic, unreliable way, that the habitants no less surely, if more slowly, accepted "their new allegiance," the novel attempts to validate through wine signs opposing models of nationalism in Lower Canada. Distinct uses of wine distinguish François Bigot – the evil Intendant who directs the monopolistic trading company whose patron is Madame Pompadour – from Nicholas Philibert, who has put down roots in New France to promote its colonial well-being. Bigot's spirits and wine corrupt those whom he turns into murderous instruments of his greed, while Philibert is "lavish in his hospitality" from true altruism. In bacchanalian orgies at which he serves the "gold and ruby vintages of France and Spain," Bigot ruins the colony's noble youth so that his company's profits will not be impeded by their military courage. While he controls the young man who becomes Philibert's killer by habituating him to the "filth and stench" of a "prolonged debauch" and self-destructive intoxication, the evil his wine creates recoils on Bigot. The "gilded carafe," "silver salver," and "rare wine" by which he gains Angélique des Meloises's admiration lead her to bring about the death of the innocent maiden whom Bigot had intended for his mistress. Despite becoming Bigot's victim, Philibert, as head of "Le Chien d'Or," is a complete foil to the Intendant. His

---

43 Gérin-Lajoie 1977, 58–9, 98–9, 130–1, 143, 139, 205, 197, 207, and 254. Gérin-Lajoie omitted this final wine reference from his novel's later version perhaps because of its inconsistency.

table always welcomes needy guests. His refusal to equate wine with status or to serve it to exercise power means that, far from reserving his "choice wines" to himself, he sends them to the convent and the hospital for the sick. Sympathetic to Huguenots and Jansenist reforms, Philibert is a true bourgeois: against the corruption of the Grand Company, he promotes the circulation of money and commercial growth in the colony by discounting merchants' bills as little as possible. His death leaves the field open to the monopolistic Grand Company, whose plunder for the French court keeps New France militarily vulnerable. Kirby's novel sympathizes with the reforming efforts of the bourgeoisie in Quebec, yet his depiction of the loss of an indigenous nationalism, in stressing the evil of French imperialism, does not so much attack imperialism as a general political phenomenon as promote the British constitution as a firmer foundation of national identity in Quebec.[44]

Francis W. Grey's *The Curé of St Philippe* and Sara Jeanette Duncan's *The Imperialist* flourish an ironic spirit that defies the temperance movement and conventional notions that had accreted to the consumption of spirits and wine by the turn of the twentieth century. In celebrating cultural pluralism, both detail drinking practices – open and covert – and inconsistencies of would-be leaders in Upper and Lower Canada. Each challenges austere temperance to show that drinking habits, attitudes to the liquor trade, and public policy may be ironically, if not rationally, reconcilable. The ironies that Grey and Duncan create acknowledge that everyday and holiday forms of imbibing spirits and wine uphold traditional rites and codes about which full consciousness is neither likely nor feasible. Characters who would stand aside from the stream of history to observe it from an olympian height are liable to sink beneath its flowing moments. Grey and Duncan both admit that products of the liquor trade are metonyms for cultural systems and that spirits and wine can be neither consumed nor prohibited without introducing social problems. To these authors, the liquor trade is a context against which to highlight mixed human motives, altered states of consciousness, and the inevitable diversity of ideologies.

In *The Curé of St Philippe*, the Curé, to raise funds to build a new church, decides to hold "a strictly temperance" banquet but "no ordinary,

---

44 Kirby 1969, 315, 68, 35, 51, 82, 110, and 272. Kirby's novel was first published in 1877 without his permission. A revised and authorized edition appeared in 1896.

every-day supper," to which he knows he must invite as many guests as possible, Protestants as well as Catholics. He knows, too, that the more he feeds his guests the more they will donate. In this realization, the prudent cleric grasps that service to the Church must be advanced by cultural forces that it opposes: neither can his ecclesiastical duty be dogmatically exclusive nor his appeal for funds thrive on communal moderation. Grey heightens tensions between social circumstance and religious creed when he explains why the Church, in upholding its sacramental efficacy, opposes the pledges of temperance "Leagues" and "Societies": institutional and doctrinal rivalries are entangled. In having "grappled with the drink-fiend in the town parishes," the Curé has come to believe more "in grace, penance, and Holy Communion, than in temperance pledges." St Philippe has declared itself a temperance municipality through the efforts of English Methodist bigots who, hunting out illicit saloons, are motivated by the belief that these establishments are patronized by French Canadians. While he supports the town's temperance regulations, the Curé's cultural sense stops him from being taken in by bigots: he will not let his pulpit forward prohibition, for to defend his favourite cause would make him a tool of his people's enemies. Behind his narration of the Curé's paradoxical dilemma lies the author's sense there are two races in the Dominion and that, despite statesmen's prating, they will never be a "homogenous people." By making the Curé face this truth, Grey insists Quebec will never become English and spurns the cultural appropriation common to writing about Lower Canada.[45]

Grey heightens paradoxes in his polemical account of the victory in the municipal election of the anti-prohibitionist Englishman, Fisher, who celebrates by standing "drinks all round" in the outlawed "Shebeen" he patronizes. The electoral campaign shows the Curé that there is social and political solidarity in neither the English nor the French communities. Supporting Bampton, the prohibitionist, in the campaign yet refusing to denounce parishioners who ignore the bylaw against drinking, the Curé befriends the new mayor whose patronage politics he condemns. From this point forward, Grey's drinking signs emphasize how lines of political and cultural affiliation get crossed. In coming to know Fisher and Bilodeau, the French Canadian politician who plays

45 Grey 1970, 18, 62–3, and 67.

federal political parties against each other for his own and his community's good, the Curé learns to live in divided and shifting political worlds. An agent of prohibition, the Curé at a public dinner not only accepts having his health proposed by Bilodeau but also proposes the health of mayor Fisher and the inclusion of "our Protestant brethren." For Grey, the transgressive taking of spirits and wine suggests that creeds are subsumed by a social dialectic that makes and unmakes cultural differences. Whereas liberal and conservative candidates insult one another on the hustings yet drink together amicably in public, Bilodeau – a Conservative who runs for the Liberals – practices a new style of "*de rigeur*" drinking: over drinks he promises government contracts in return for support, while he appeals to voters' religious nationalism by appearing to sever himself from parties. Bilodeau's strategic, élitist conviviality shows the Curé that traditional politics are dubious: the double standards of orthodoxy suggest to him that compromise is important to the evolving identity of his diverse community.[46]

Like Grey, Duncan probes the idealism behind temperance propaganda by making allusions to sumptuary modes unfold the theme that, celebrated or repressed, these modes – transformed into wider cultural signs – expose social and political illusions. *The Imperialist* is a powerful social history because its wine signs satirize Upper Canada's dullness to both British cultural traditions and the involvement of French values in those traditions. Duncan's journalistic style focuses on Upper Canada's nationalist dreams in a sharp manner remote from Aubert de Gaspé's disengagement from contemporary history. By ignoring the Montreal riots of 1837 and the slump in Canada caused by the free trade movement in England that depreciated colonial economies, Aubert de Gaspé weakens his novel, rendering its propaganda more obtrusive than need be. By contrast, Duncan embeds allusions to spirits and wine into her setting to uncover the shallow optimism and cultural blindness of Elgin: its obtuseness about allusions enables her to problematize Confederation. Her focus on the community's failure to make wine signs significant reveals that, more than the other novelists surveyed here, she grasped relations between social history, semiotics, and narrative invention.

Confident in its future, Elgin sees itself as the centre of the empire, able to resist British decadence and to renew imperialism through

---

46 Ibid., 101, 154, and 222.

commerce. Duncan's detailing of its drinking codes questions this vision: its pretensions to create progressive customs and to guard cultural tradition are self-deceived. Elgin thinks it celebrates Queen Victoria's birthday with a "ceremonial festivity" superior to England's bank holiday yet evades festive paradoxes. The town encourages a spirit of "carnival" by issuing permits for eating and drinking stalls in the streets, and citizens agree to tolerate the shouting of drunken Indians as they are taken to the "lock-up." That it requires permits and operates its prison as usual is paradoxical: the holiday is circumscribed by legal refinement, not freed by the suspension of law. Its festive style undoes the town's sense of ritual freedom from old-country political and cultural hierarchies. There is a schism between polite society and popular culture that erodes Upper Canada's claim to appropriate British imperialism. Aloof to the popular festivities, civic leaders stay indoors and drink "raspberry vinegar," royalism displacing the British wine trade with home products. Voicing freedom from custom by appreciating the monarchy, they effect another hierarchy by not participating in street life. Despite its volatile activity, there is a lack of political integrity in Elgin that stems from its divided view of itself as a "little outpost of Empire" and centre of the "growing Dominion." This division arises from cultural blindness that Duncan signals in the town's continuance of drinking codes it believes it has displaced.[47]

The Murchisons, a leading Elgin family with national aspirations, are shattered when Lorne, their lawyer son, fails to add his imperialist tenets to the Liberal Party's platform, a failure prefigured by textual signs that resist the displacement of the cultural past. The Murchisons live in a mansion built by an early British settler. They and their neighbours despise the house's architectural pretensions that include French windows, Italian marble, and a "wine-cellar." Elgin is sure its new modes have displaced the tradition of "six-o'clock dinner, with wine," along with other European customs imported by pioneers. The "old-fashioned French paper" with its "grape-vine pattern" on the Murchisons' drawing room walls signifies nothing to them. They overlook such signs, opining that Elgin has emerged from the past into "sobriety and decorum." But the signs are neither redundant socially nor irrelevant textually. For the refusal of citizens to respect the signs is historically presumptuous. Their

---

47 Duncan 1961, 13–14 and 21–2.

belief that the "gentlefolk of reduced income" who came to the colonies perished of the "readjustment" and were pathetic in the "isolation of their difference and their misapprehension" is undone by the text. While citizens feel that the genteel Anglican "lines of demarcation" have been erased by the society arising out of trading prosperity and while they trust that the "Archdeacon's port" is but a memory, Duncan comically notes that immigrants "from those little imperial islands" not only still come with the "crusted qualities of old blood bottled there so long" but also adapt to and shape the new social order. What Elgin residents see as displaced, the text shows as transmuted and powerful. Miss Milburn, the daughter of another leading family, who despises British immigrants for "getting into debt" and drinking, marries Alfred Hesketh, a London dandy whose decadence fits him for the community. When Dr Drummond, the severe Presbyterian clergyman, weds the Scottish Miss Christie despite her port blood and uncertain past, Elgin's displacement of wine codes and other "inherited anachronisms" is again shown to be illusory. Its blindness to cultural pluralism comes not only from evading wine signs but also from failing to reduce them to empty formality. At a party the Milburns serve a "claret cup" but hide their preparation of the drink from guests: they do not want to seem involved in festive processes. The Murchisons also offer a "dignified service of cake and wine" at a party. Elgin inconsistently acknowledges its importation of wine and strives to pretend it rejects the accompanying rituals.[48]

Upper Canada's pretentious superiority to wine codes is illustrated by the mission that travels to London to request parliament to grant preferential tariffs to Canada at the expense of Britain's larger trading partners. The commissioners' resistance to wine signs stems from a refusal to see the interdependence of commercial and cultural systems. These signs make their pretensions to renew British imperialism risible. The commissioners, "substantial men" and not "total abstainers," stay at a cheap "temperance hotel" to avoid the prevalent "wine habit." Their formal renunciation of drinking and wealth makes them susceptible to the association of the two and less critical of their interaction. Unable to see the relation between sumptuary and social signifiers, they dull themselves to the relation between consumerism and politics. Their mission fails less because of English decadence than because of

48 Ibid., 29–31, 29, 47, 216, 99, 51–2, and 88.

blindness to political meaning in cultural signs. Disgust with British consumption is motivated by whimsy or hypocrisy: one dyspeptic commissioner laments that business negotiations entail "eating and drinking," while another criticizes the "number of courses and the variety of wines" in restaurants to "disguise his gratification." Prejudice blinds the commissioners from seeing what wine codes reveal about Britain's ties to France. They learn nothing from a political leader who prefers trying out his "new French motor" in the countryside to meeting them. Nor, in presenting their imperial critique of free trade to a Mr Chafe, an exporter of decanters to the United States, do they glimpse the meaning of his being "full of Burgundy and distrust." Their journey to London is self-defeating because they detach themselves from the context in which they might read the sumptuary, cross-cultural, and political signs upholding the trading agreements between Britain, France, and the United States.[49]

To the degree Duncan heralds the imperialist cause, she limits her mockery of Elgin's pretensions to progress and refinement. While she reveals that Elgin's narrow-minded displacement of drinking codes is illusory, she does not feel that its unconscious codes always harm public life. The drinking traced in the election process resonates semiotically, however: the hustings where Lorne Murchison wins his candidacy are attended not by voters who have adjourned from a public house as would be so in England. Their stimulants are "tea or cider" and just a hint of whisky. While Duncan insists on national difference, the people of Elgin take stimulants ideologically. The bribery of Indians and electors testifies to a systematic taking of whisky that differentiates between the Canadian and Scottish products: while a "bottle of Canadian" can win over six voters, one of "Scotch" wins ten. The idealistic Liberal Party exploits alcohol strategically: an old Conservative "soaker" renounces whisky and disclaims champagne in order to be fit to vote in the election, but Liberals undo his renunciation to ensure he does not cast a vote. These tactics recoil on their imperialist vision and signal their avoidance of cultural pluralism. But, while Duncan grants that the Liberals are "terrified of Quebec," she does not stress how much young Murchison's evasion of Lower Canada and of Britain's ties to France

---

49 Ibid., 112, 115, 113, and 120.

limits his political vision. His allegiance to England is admirable since it enables him to resist Canadian materialism, yet his remoteness from Elgin's complex history and from the codes that operate in Britain and in Upper Canada reveal a blinkered mentality. The prevalence of her drinking codes suggests that Duncan can no more integrate fresh conceptions of Aboriginal peoples and the Canadian west into her idea of Canada than comprehend Quebec. Thus, she comments that the "signs of civilization" have given Indians a "liquidly muddy eye," a fate to be escaped only by preserving their "savagery" in the west's "wide spaces," without questioning the stereotype's source in Upper Canada's hypocrisy about alcohol.[50]

CODA

Spirits and wine as items of daily consumption and festive celebration in Canadian writing suggest that the physiology of survival and the politics of taste are reciprocal. Not a simple matter of cultural refinement, taste for spirits and wine is expressed in life-and-death survival, imperial expansion, urban development, and medical and culinary history. Both acknowledged and resisted as imported products, spirits and wine generate polyvalent textual signs of tensions between national aspirations and cross-cultural exchanges involving Aboriginal, settler, and immigrant societies. Trade in spirits and wine, besides raising issues of governmental control and ecclesiastical authority, imports foreign significations given its international origins. Hence, the semiotics of spirits and wine affects national identity in Canadian texts, showing it to be inseparable from plural cultures: social and textual uses of wine systematically involve a dialectic between domestic and foreign cultures. Fictional wine allusions that would avoid this dialectic are constrained in ways that erase the boundaries between text and context. Besides challenging nationalist readings of literary history, such allusions show that textual plurality resists narrow-minded political propaganda. If *The History of Emily Montague* proposes the assimilation of French into English culture, it also testifies to their prior inseparability. While wine codes in *Canadians of Old* and *The Imperialist* expose nationalism in

50 Ibid., 191, 239, 224, 259, and 242–3.

Lower and Upper Canada by apparently displacing necessary tensions between English and French culture, confused stances to festivity in these novels lay Canadian colonial signification out for inspection. These novels, in advancing social and textual comparatives, help to renew literary history by strengthening its ties to cultural history.[51]

---

[51] Textuality "takes in what might more traditionally be seen as the purview of the social sciences. Objects of study such as historical events, institutional practices, or cross-cultural relationships may therefore be seen as systems of signs to be deciphered and interpreted, rather than as realities to be recorded" (Makaryk 1993, 641).

4

Cuisine, Eating, and Empires of Taste

I have been assured by a very Knowing American of my acquaintance in London, that a young healthy child well nursed is at a year old a most delicious, nourishing and wholesome food whether stewed, roasted, baked, or boiled, and I make no doubt that it will equally serve in a fricassee, or a ragout.[1]

ROMANTIC SENSIBILITY AND IMPERIAL METAPHORS

Before taking up Swift's "new world" tastes in *A Modest Proposal* that deflate British imperialism, it is worth repeating that Canadian writing was marked for two centuries by imperial drinking codes. Before and after Confederation, authors questioned the equation of temperance with abstinence and renunciation of communal rites yet disregarded the physiology of taste. Relying on drinking codes traditionally, Brooke's romantic sensibility in *The History of Emily Montague* adopts transferred political signs, as a survey of "empire" and "taste" in her text reveals. Empire, far from conveying Britain's expansionary goals in the Seven Years War, denotes the rule by which women govern men. John Temple, Rivers's correspondent, yields to his friend "the whole empire of sentiment." To Rivers, while a true lover grants the "power of the sex," an indifferent one is a "rebel to their empire." Arabella Fermor, whose quips find "no politics worth attending-to but those of the little commonwealth of woman," lets men quarrel over "everything else" if she can "maintain" her "empire over hearts." Limited female power is upheld by Rivers when he says that, while Indian women become "coarse and masculine" after marriage from losing "the power as well as the desire of pleasing," they acquire "a new empire," are consulted in "all

---

1 Swift, "A Modest Proposal" (1960, 441).

affairs of state, chuse a chief on every vacancy of the throne, [and] are sovereign arbiters of peace and war." His claim that the only way to "civilize" savages is "to *feminize* their women" is sexist and racist. The disjunction between femininity and politics suggests that romance embodies an ideology of bourgeois aspiration, since taste, far from denoting gustatory pleasure, signifies innate refinement and gentility. Hence, Rivers declares that "I love the pleasures of the table, not for their own sakes, for no man is more indifferent on this subject; but because they promote social, convivial joy, and bring people together in good humor with themselves and each other." As a colonist, he promises he will "taste ... creation, and see order and beauty gradually rise from chaos." His translation of taste into sensibility matches his opposition to the beau monde's urban modes that drive the market economy, a point underscored when he declares "taste for rural scenes is the taste born with us." Ideologically he suits Emily; she has "little taste for the false glitter of life" and rejects the "insipid" Clayton, a formal lover. Romance propels Brooke's taste imagery: when Emily sees Rivers, she loses "all taste for other conversation," having a "lively taste" only for his discourse. Their marital happiness will hail from a "conformity of taste and sentiment" that subjects physiological taste to a psychologically simplistic aesthetic.[2]

SWIFT'S USES OF DISTASTE AND DISGUST

The History of Emily Montague shows that bourgeois gentility defines itself over against gustatory experience: it stipulates that bodily appetites be subject to codes of personal refinement. Given this flight from Epicureanism, there is little recognition of the body's alimentary needs except as they are subsumed by a narrow sociability: literary texts usually display small regard for food and drink, little imaginary engagement with meal preparation, and sparse discursive relish of comestibles, taste being disjoined from savouring. Modish ingestion rarely entails training the gustatory senses. The physiology of taste as theorized by Brillat-Savarin was generally avoided. Nussbaum studies the "ideational factors" and "cognitive component" of this avoidance.[3] Civilization's tenuousness

---

2 Brooke 1985, 8, 158, 98, 12, 118–19, 380, 4, 327, 95, 142, 167, and 130–1.
3 Nussbaum 2006, chapter 2 "Disgust and Our Animal Bodies," 71–123, especially "The Cognitive Content of Disgust," 87ff.; and Nussbaum 2010, 33–6.

appears to her in the self-evasion inherent in our not wanting to admit our animality. Since, if we can eat other animals, we know we can be eaten; we create lower, impure social orders, denying them humanity to protect our own. Since things that recall our animality are contaminating, we project such things onto others, turning them into underclasses. This "projective disgust" which treats some classes as the "other" involves "irrational, magical thinking" and "self-repudiation" that explain why upper classes hire servants to obviate awareness of their bodily functions.

In the epigraph above, Swift presents tensions between refinement and appetite to probe the psychology and politics impelling callousness and barbarity. Before analyzing how he converts physiological distaste into ideational disgust in *A Modest Proposal* by making the projector absurdly refined, we treat two works which, though published later, occupied him long before his satire on Ireland's subjection to English imperialism appeared in 1729. *A Compleat Collection of Genteel and Ingenious Conversation, According to the Most Polite Mode and Method Now Used at Court, and in the Best Companies of England* saps "pedantry, vanity, ill-mannered raillery and straining after wit."[4] This compendium of breakfast and dinner-table chatter links the inanities of urbanites to evasion of gustatory pleasure. Their slang, jargon, cliché, and stale maxims reveal the beau monde's shallow consumerism. Their words about what they ingest are literally and metaphorically tasteless; fashionably dining at 3:00 p.m., they consume "Oysters, Sirloyn of Beef, Shoulder of Veal, Venison-Pasty, Pigeon, Cucumber, boiled Pudden, Claret, Cyder, Burgundy, Fritters and Pullet," their table service without structure and any sense of culinary preparation. Swift more obliquely saps genteel pretensions when presenting domestics in *Directions to Servants*. Instructions to butler and cook encourage laziness, dirtiness, waste, and theft, below-stairs practices degrading upper-class modes. Not changing glasses and making guests call for drink, the butler is to shake beer bottles into effervescence and wipe them with his palm after tasting them. He will leave opened wine bottles on the table at meal's end so that fellow servants will get their fill and not be accused of stealing. At the sideboard, he is to mix ales and beers. Managing the candles

---

4 Swift 1964a, xxviii and xxxii. This work, published in Dublin by George Faulkner in 1738, was begun in 1704.

for the benefit of his fellows as well as breaking bottles and glasses and damaging cutlery to curry favour with retailers, he will manage hogsheads in the cellar by spitting on spigots to make them easier to reinsert; he will seal bottles after putting corks in his mouth while chewing tobacco. By not draining clean bottles, he will let water dilute wine and pass what is leftover to the cook and his fellows. Instructions to the cook include blaming pets for lost legs of fowls and not reminding the mistress about leftovers so that the servants may eat as well as upstairs. To uphold family honour the cook will maintain her superiority by leaving roasting and boiling to the kitchen maid. She will also stint work by letting larks and wheat-ears be basted – and their savour ruined – by having fat drip on them from roasts on the spit. Satire on debased culinary taste mounts when she is told to send raw meat upstairs so that it will be returned to the servants' hall. Besides purloining delicacies by feeding sweetbreads from breasts of veal to her lover, the butler, and claiming they have been eaten by family pets, she is to disregard cleanliness when managing the spit, pots, pans, and condiments.[5] In mocking table conversation and domestic service, Swift shows that gentility, not being verbally precise, culturally sensible and culinarily refined, leads to economic waste, social strife, and communal decline.[6]

A Modest Proposal intensifies this criticism by inviting readers to a satura – to taste a hodgepodge cooked up by one who speaks from within ill-matched agricultural, fiscal, culinary, and genteel registers.[7] Seemingly appalled by English imperialism and Irish apathy, Swift's persona tells how beggar children are "sound and useful members of the commonwealth" if rendered into products for kitchens. Despite his "melancholy" at the "deplorable state of the kingdom," he is cruel. While tears and pity, he feels, will be moved "in the most savage and inhuman breast" since the poverty of Irish mothers makes them sacrifice

---

5 Swift 1964b, 17–18, 22–4, and 28–30. This work was published by Faulkner in Dublin in 1745.

6 See Swift 1964a, 5–21, for his resistance to linguistic modes. Like Addison, Swift attended to the fracture of spoken cadences and the infelicity of verbal contractions. *Spectator*, no. 135, shows how English words are degraded by contractions and shortened verbs (Briggs 2005, 164).

7 In the OED, the Latin noun *satura* refers to "a discursive composition in verse treating of a variety of subjects." Signifying a "medley," or indiscriminate lump, it is an ellipsis for "a dish containing various kinds of fruit, and for food composed of many different ingredients."

"poor innocent babes" to abortion or infanticide, luxurious consumption outstrips pork and venison production because landowners neglect their farms. The "propagation of swine's flesh" and "the art of making good bacon" need improving. Items of agrarian economy, mothers are "breeders" and dams who annually drop a "fat yearling child, which roasted whole will make a considerable figure at a Lord Mayor's feast, or any other public entertainment."[8] The persona, thinking to be inclusive, projects turning children of the poor into food on American advice qualified by his gust for French cuisine. His refinement of new-world barbarism implies class strife, however. For he is sure that among "persons of quality and fortune" there are "one thousand families" in Dublin who "would be constant customers for infants flesh" and yearly consume "twenty thousand carcasses." A professor of demographic "computation" familiar with upper, middle, and lower classes, he claims that a "child will make two dishes at an entertainment for friends, and when the family dines alone, the fore or hind quarter will make a reasonable dish, and seasoned with a little pepper or salt will be very good boiled on the fourth day, especially in winter." Ingratiating himself with merchants by claiming "the addition of some thousand carcasses" will boost "exportation of barrelled beef," he allays British fears of Irish interloping by saying "this kind of commodity will not bear exportation, the flesh being of too tender a consistence to admit a long continuance in salt." The more he lists his proposal's benefits, the more his inconsistencies expose the ills of Irish society: the more the persona affects moderate tones, the more Swift prods readers to outrage by changing distaste to disgust. Obsequious to merchants, gentlefolk, and yeomen, the projector defers to America, Britain, and absentee landlords. His project is delimited by mercantile views that children are "no saleable commodity" before the age of twelve, Swift hinting that exporting Irish indentured slaves is usual with merchants. If the cost to landlords of babes' flesh will be high, this is fitting since the former have devoured parents. Here metaphorical justifies literal eating, the inversion of standard rhetoric in which the literal precedes the metaphorical heightening the disgust. That mothers' marketing of babes will reduce domestic violence since husbands will care for wives as much as for farm animals exposes mercenary violence and sustains the irony of humans being equated with animals: the

8 Swift 1960, 439–40 and 444.

proposal would have husbands stop beating pregnant wives to treat them as tenderly as "their mares in foal, their cows in calf, or sows when they are ready to farrow."[9]

The projector defends his proposal's source in a new-world perspective by politely refuting another patriot's refinement, itself American advice that further erodes British imperialism. This patriot holds that twelve- to fourteen-year-olds near starvation from lack of work might be butchered to fill the demand for venison caused by Irish gentlemen gluttonously over-killing deer. But this advice is bad because the projector's American acquaintance tells him from "frequent experience" that the "flesh" of boys at that age is "tough," its "taste" being "disagreeable." Rejecting his fellow patriot's view, the projector still upholds American barbarity through the claim of Psalmanazar, a fictional native of Formosa, that the carcasses of those executed be sold to persons of quality as "a prime delicacy," citing the case of a fifteen-year-old girl who, having tried "to poison the emperor, was sold to his Imperial Majesty's Prime Minister of State, and other great Mandarins of the Court, in joints from the gibbet." This satirical redundancy makes the gullibility of the fellow patriot and his supposed tale of distant cannibalism brilliantly subvert imperialism close to home.[10]

Tensions between catering to culinary luxury and diversifying the economy reinforce the connection between modish tastes and dehumanization. Bent on introducing a "new dish" to "the tables of all gentlemen of fortune in the kingdom, who have any refinement of taste," the projector thinks this consumption will improve social harmony because squires eager for luxurious meat will treat their tenants kindly and those whose corn and cattle have been seized will live comfortably on the profits realized in their children. Landlord and tenant will equally benefit since the new meat will not be seasonal like that of farm animals that are not overwintered given the high cost of feed stocks.[11] Since Catholics in Lent conceive many offspring, their flesh will glut the market in winter, rendering it both affordable and effective in reducing the Catholic population. The unstable relations between high and low

---

9 Ibid., 441, 445, and 444.
10 Ibid., 442–3.
11 Ibid., 444. On Gilbert White's sense of new foodstocks arising from the agricultural revolution see below, and on Defoe's discussion of meat marketing see chapter 5.

cost as well as the genocidal prejudice against Catholicism guide readers to interpret British and Irish economic policies. To the projector, his plan will diversify the economy: "thrifty landlords" will flay the carcasses of babes to produce "admirable gloves for ladies, and summer boots for fine gentlemen," and public works will boom from the need to build slaughterhouses. While self-sufficient landlords independent of the market economy will buy "children alive" and dress them "hot from the knife" like roasting pigs, the proposal will help retain the circulation of money in Ireland since gentlemen of refined taste will lay out money for the new dish rather than spend it abroad. Tavern custom will grow since vintners will "procure the best receipts" for this dish, "dressing it to perfection" for "gentlemen, who justly value themselves upon their knowledge in good eating." The hodgepodge of tonal variations and cultural implications in Swift's essay makes it a dystopia, implying that the projector is subservient to English colonial policy and its declared objective of keeping the Pretender from invading Ireland. Despite professed altruism and patriotism, the projector accepts the consumer luxury and refined culinary tastes of the ruling and mercantile classes that dehumanize common folk. The extremity of his proposal to save the commonwealth by making its poorest members consume their offspring and posterity and by making common-sense policy alternatives seem hopeless in the face of British imperialism reveal a powerful deployment of taste. The absurdity of the projector's solutions endows taste with an ideational force that converts distaste into disgust at what imperialism does to communal life.[12]

CUISINE AND THE SCRIBLERIANS

Swift and members of the Scriblerus Club formed in 1713 invented Martin Scriblerus, "a man of capacity" whose stupidly pretentious scholarship embodies "all the false tastes in learning."[13] Food and eating motivated his creation given the club's wish to link scholarly redundancy to cultural decadence and political hegemony. One sign of this linkage

---

12 In 1709, four Indian sachems from the Mohawk Valley near Albany met Queen Anne as agents of British imperialists who wanted New France destroyed. Swift draws on this context to level the reader with the proposer and his American adviser (MacPherson 1994, 109–10 and 115).

13 See Aitken's introduction to Arbuthnot's life and works (1892, 57).

appears in a letter to Swift sent from Whitehall in September 1726, written by Gay, who voices in a poem by Pope their joint regrets about their friend's absence in Ireland. The letter contains a recipe as a token of amity. The recipe is also a word game with political allusions in a key that illustrates the Scriblerians' wide-ranging humour and concern to heighten the significance of daily life.

A Receipt for Stewing Veal

Take a knuckle of veal;
You may buy it, or steal.
In a few pieces cut it:
In a stewing-pan put it.
Salt, pepper, and mace
Must season this knuckle;
Then * what's join'd to a place;
With other herbs muckle;
That, which killed king Will †;
And what never ‡ stands still.
Some § sprigs of that bed
Where children are bred
Which much you will mend, if
Both spinnage and endive
And lettuce, and beet,
With marygold meet.
Put no water at all;
For it maketh things small.
Which, lest it should happen,
A close cover clap on.
Put this pot of ½ Wood's mettle
In a hot boiling kettle,
And there let it be
(Mark the doctrine I teach)
About – let me see, –
Thrice as long as you preach ¶:
So skimming the fat off,
Say grace with your hat off,
O, then! with what rapture
Will it fill dean and chapter!

* Vulgo, salary; † Supposed Sorril; ‡ This is by Dr *Bentley* thought to be time or thyme. § Parsley; ½ Copper; ¶ "Which we suppose to be four hours."[14]

Here culinary expertise requires meat, vegetables, and herbs to be cooked without water above a steamer for four hours. The recipe's archaism reflects a jocular familiarity with cookbooks, its word games adapting the genre by emphasizing herbal lore and glancing at literary pedantry and political history in allusions to Richard Bentley, William Wood's copper halfpence, and the death of King William after falling from his sorrel horse. The topical references,

---

14 Pope 1963, 475–6; Gay 1926, 213; Sherburn 2002, 2:403–4. Richard Bentley (1662–1742), distinguished classical scholar and linguistic critic, was belittled by the Scriblerians.

acknowledging that Swift's exile in Ireland owes something to the British government's proscription of the Drapier, one of Swift's personas, exemplify the scope for irony offered by cookbooks to the Scriblerians.

Another example is chapter fifteen of Pope's *Peri Bathous: Or, Martinus Scriblerus, His Treatise of the Art of Sinking in Poetry* (1728), a work obliquely upholding neoclassical theory. The chapter, "*A Receipt to Make an* Epic *Poem,*" asserts that epics may be made by "mechanical Rules" and "*without a Genius,* nay without Learning or much Reading." Turning Molière's remark about "making a Dinner, that any Man can do it with Money" into an analogy for poetic creation, Pope's persona holds that a "profess'd Cook" who cannot make a meal without money has "his Art for nothing," adding "the same may be said of making a Poem, 'tis easily brought about by him that *has* a Genius, but the Skill lies in doing it without one." The "plain and certain Recipe" for a "grand Performance" in "the *Bathos*" is as follows: the ingredients – fable, manners of the hero, machinery of the gods – may be taken out of old books, thrown down and let work together. When the mixture is strained, "Consistency" matters less than laying everything "*on a Heap*" so the moral is extractable. Scenes of tempests require mixing, foaming, thickening and brewing. Battle scenes, picked "from *Homer*'s Iliads" and "with a Spice or two of Virgil," are then seasoned with similes.[15]

The Scriblerians influenced Henry Fielding (1707–1754), who called himself Scriblerus Secundus. His work best illustrating Scriblerian irony is *The Life of Mr Jonathan Wild the Great* (1743). This mock biography of a gangster imitates the linkage of the criminal underworld and the affectedly polite realms of commerce and politics in *The Beggar's Opera* (1728). A dinner in *Jonathan Wild* generates a motif common to later texts. The scene is set in the home of the Snaps, a disreputable family operating a private prison. "Nothing very remarkable passed at Dinner. The Conversation (as is usual in polite Company) rolled chiefly on what they were then eating, and what they had lately eaten." A "military Gentleman, who had served in *Ireland,* gave ... a very particular Account of a new manner of roasting Potatoes, and others gave an Account of other Dishes. In short, an indifferent By-stander would have concluded from their Discourse, that they had all come into this World for no

---

15 Tillotson, Fussell, Waingrow, and Rogerson 1969, 631–3.

other purpose, than to fill their Bellies; and indeed if this was not the chief, it is probable that it was the most innocent Design Nature had in their Formation."[16]

MARTINUS SCRIBLERUS, A CULINARY AND COGNITIVE ICON

Memoirs of the Extraordinary Life, Works and Discoveries of Martinus Scriblerus by John Arbuthnot (1667–1735), published posthumously in 1741, epitomizes the Scriblerus Club's satire.[17] The *Memoirs* claims that Martin, a self-serving hack, annotated the *Dunciad* and wrote *Peri Bathous*, hinting he is the implied author of *Gulliver's Travels* and the projector in *A Modest Proposal*.[18] A meta-text, the *Memoirs* depicts Martin's acquisition of learned twaddle about diet that makes him susceptible to materialistic ideas of identity. Its absurd theory of ingestion and reductive expositions of mind–body relations are motifs germane to *Imperial Paradoxes*. Cornelius, Martin's father, bullies the nurse about "the nature of aliment," denying her "some dish or other, which he judged prejudicial to her milk." He bans beef since the ancients thought it caused "an irregular and voracious appetite." Eating it would make her milk "hebetate and clog" his son's "intellectuals." An esoteric theorist and model for Walter Shandy in *Tristram Shandy* (1759–1767), Cornelius agrees with Horace that bad diet throws the mind into "too violent a fermentation" or "short madness." His son's "suction" would "imbibe many ungovernable passions, and in a manner spoil him for the temper of a philosopher." To Cornelius, beef makes the English "phlegmatic and melancholy"; "cheese and leeks" make the Welsh "hot and choleric"; "soups, frogs, and mushrooms" induce "levity" in the French. The diet of Italians makes them "jealous and revengeful"; if that of Spaniards yields an approved "profound gravity," it produces the "intolerable vice of pride." Learning classical languages, Martin eats and drinks "according to Homer." Cornelius turns his son's "love of gingerbread" into a pedagogical device by stamping it with the Greek alphabet so that his

---

16 Fielding 2003, 37. On Fielding as a Scriblerian, see Rawson's introduction (2003, x).
17 Arbuthnot 1892, 307–59.
18 Ibid., 342, 331, 354, and 358.

"child the very first day eat as far as Iota."[19] Martin's dullness ends in materialism, a Scriblerian mind–body dualism travestying *A Discourse of Free-Thinking, Occasion'd by the Rise and Growth of a Sect Call'd Free-Thinkers* (1713) by Collins. Deists in the *Memoirs* treat Horace, Cicero, and Seneca as free thinkers and, while they praise Martin's "inquisitive genius," pity his belief in "that theological nonentity commonly called the soul." To them, "self-consciousness cannot inhere in any system of matter, because all matter is made up of several distinct beings, which never can make up one individual thinking being." The text then degrades consciousness by a grossly risible analogy to a kitchen spit:

In every jack there is a meat-roasting quality, which neither resides in the fly, nor in the weight, nor in any particular wheel of the jack, but is the result of the whole composition: so in an animal, the self-consciousness is not a real quality inherent in one being (any more than meat-roasting in a jack) but the result of several modes or qualities in the same subject. As the fly, the wheels, the chain, the weight, the cords, &c., make one jack, so the several parts of the body make one animal. As perception or consciousness is said to be inherent in this animal, so is meat-roasting said to be inherent in the jack. As sensation, reasoning, volition, memory, &c. are the several modes of thinking; so roasting of beef, roasting of mutton, roasting of pullets, geese, turkeys, &c. are the several modes of meat-roasting. And as this general quality of meat-roasting, with its several modifications as to beef, mutton, pullets, &c. does not inhere in any one part of the jack; so neither does consciousness with its several modes of sensation, intellection, volition, &c. inhere in any one, but is the result from the mechanical composition of the whole animal.

Thus, free thinkers reduce the "power of thinking, self-moving, and governing the whole machine" to an infinite chain of particles that preserves "the unity of the system." They deny individuality, indifferent to "how a man is conscious to himself that he is the same individual he was twenty years ago; notwithstanding the flux state of the particles of matter that compose his body." They link "the several modes of thinking" to the "structure of the brain." From their stance "the brain is a congeries of glands, that separate the finer parts of the blood" into "animal spirits" and a gland is "nothing but a canal of a great length,

---

19 Ibid., 320–3.

variously intorted and wound up together," and from "the arietation and motion of the spirits in those canals, proceed all the different sorts of thoughts." Simple ideas come from single canals; "when two of these canals disembogue themselves into one, they make ... a proposition; and when two of these propositional channels empty themselves into a third, they form a syllogism, or a ratiocination." While free thinkers reduce memory to the operating "vessels" in the "primary parts of the brain" and trace wrong thinking to "the bad configuration" of cranial glands, Arbuthnot traces this reductionism to Lockean epistemology. Poor thinkers "are born without the proportional or syllogistical canals." In "dull fellows" the canals, being too long, retard "the motion of spirits"; "in trifling geniuses" they are too "weak and small," and in "over-refining spirits, too much intorted."[20] If irony assails Locke's disciples, the derisory treatment of lactation, children's diet, and mind–body relations confirms that Scriblerians do not pretend to have the last word on cognition.

CULINARY DISCOURSE, FASHION, AND GOOD EATING

In *Evelina* (1788), Fanny Burney (1752–1840) has Lord Orville and Evelina Belmont confirm their affinity when met by a "conversation turned wholly upon eating" at Bristol Hotwells.[21] A lord and two gentlemen, like "professed cooks," display "much knowledge of sauces and made dishes, and of the various methods of dressing the same things." Since they "have given much time, and much study, to make themselves such adepts in this *art*," Evelina will not decide "whether they were most to be distinguished as *gluttons*, or *epicures*; for they were, at once, dainty and voracious, understood the right and the wrong of every dish, and alike emptied the one and the other." In her scorn, she is a model of a gentility that held housewifery to be unladylike and saw cooking as an

---

20 Ibid., 350–3.
21 Burney 2000, 421. The Blooms claim "Sensuousness is in fact erased by spiritual compatibility" (Burney 1982, Introduction xxii). Mrs Selwyn, the manly satirist, finds "Quixotism" in the unworldliness of Berry Hill and romanticism of Orville and Villars (Burney 2000, 512–13).

occupation of the lower orders.²² Performed in 1779 a year after *Evelina* appeared, *The Times* by Elizabeth Griffiths (1727–1793) also scorns modish culinary discourse. To Mr Bromley, a moneylender, "Eating is the rage, the high *ton*, at present, and indeed is one of the most refined of our modern studies." Of one knight, Bromley says "No man tempers a salad like Sir Harry"; he is "a perfect compendium of the whole art of cookery, and has more good receipts in his pocket-book, than ever were published by the celebrated Hannah Glasse." But to Colonel Mountfort, Sir Harry is that "ridiculous compound of affectation and epicurism! who ruminates upon every meal, and tries to preserve the relish of his sauces by a repetition of their ingredients in every new company that admits him."²³ Talk of cooking while dining ruins aesthetic eating and good manners.

The keenest apologist for culinary discourse was Lord Chesterfield (1694–1773), who would have spurned Lord Orville's claim that "the prevalence of fashion makes the greatest absurdities pass uncensured."²⁴ Chesterfield's *Letters to His Son* (1774) justifies the "fashionable kind of *small talk*" that in "mixed companies" at diplomatic assemblies "keeps off certain serious subjects, that might create dispute, or at least coldness." On "such occasions it is not amiss to know how to *parler cuisine*, and to be able to dissert upon the growth and flavour of wines." Such topics "are little things that occur very often" and "should be said *avec gentillesse, et grace*." To Chesterfield, French modes and "delicacy of diction" are "characteristical of a man of fashion and good company." If Burney's names imply she displaces French modes when exemplary characters naturalize them, his claim that cuisine is a trifling topic does not match his hiring of the grand Vincent La Chapelle (1690–1745), the *chef de cuisine* whose *The Modern Cook* (1733) appeared first in English then in French.²⁵

An admirer of Burney who with her attended banquets at the Thrales' home in Streatham, Johnson could not have treated cuisine more

---

22 On the falling status of female cookbook authors, see Lehmann 2003, 62. Upper- and middle-class women who easily afforded cookbooks often acted as culinary directors, handing the books off to servants. Lehmann describes the exclusion of cooking from models of gentility (2003, 66).
23 Finberg 2001, 172 and 155.
24 Burney 2000, 429.
25 Chesterfield 1774, 2:283–4.

differently than his protegée and Chesterfield, his would-be patron. He regarded "good eating with uncommon satisfaction."[26] According to Hester Lynch Piozzi (formerly Thrale, 1741–1821), his ideas of eating "were nothing less than delicate." His "favourite dainties" were "a leg of pork boiled till it dropped from the bone, a veal-pye with plums and sugar, or the outside cut of a salt buttock of beef."[27] James Boswell (1740–1795) records that Johnson minded his "belly very studiously, and very carefully," since "he who does not mind his belly will hardly mind anything else." Boswell was surprised at such vehemence, recalling when Johnson scorned those who gratify their palates and thinking of *Rambler*, No. 206, which argues "against gulosity." Yet he thinks that no one "relished good eating" more than Johnson.

When at table, he was totally absorbed in the business of the moment; his looks seemed riveted to his plate; nor would he, unless when in very high company, say one word, or even pay the least attention to what was said by others, till he had satisfied his appetite, which was so fierce, and indulged with such intenseness that while in the act of eating, the veins of his forehead swelled, and generally a strong perspiration was visible. To those whose sensations were delicate, this could not but be disgusting; and it was doubtless not very suitable to the character of a philosopher, who should be distinguished by self-command. But it must be owned, that Johnson, though he could be rigidly *abstemious*, was not a *temperate* man either in eating or drinking. He could refrain, but he could not use moderately.

Johnson's companions were startled at how much he ate while claiming to be "a man of very nice discernment in the science of cookery."[28] But he recollected "minutely" those dishes he liked or disliked, either "*palates*" or a "*made dish.*" Having dined at "good tables," he saw himself as a "much better judge of cookery, than any person who has a very tolerable cook, but lives much at home." The latter's palate is habituated to "the taste of his cook," whereas in enjoying a range of tastes, he can

---

26 Hemlow 1958, 105–15; Doody 1988, 66; Bate 1975, 256–8.
27 Piozzi 1786, 102.
28 At one inn where Johnson is "exceedingly dissatisfied with roast mutton we had for dinner," in ill-humour he scolded the waiter, saying, "It is as bad as bad can be: it is ill-fed, ill-killed, ill-kept, and ill-drest" (Boswell 1953, Thursday, 3 June 1784, 1285).

"more exquisitely judge." When invited out, he expected "something better than a plain dinner" and loved being catered to. He praised the housekeeper of his neighbouring landlord in Bolt Court for a dinner that could not have been better had "a *Synod of Cooks*" prepared it.[29]

Boswell, surprised to be invited to dine with Johnson one Easter, had supposed that he never entertained at table. He had told Boswell that on Sundays he usually ate a "meat pye" that is "baked at a publick oven," so that his servants might go to church rather than dress dinner. Having dined with Rousseau "in the wilds of Neufchatel," Boswell was curious about dining "in the dusky recess of a court in Fleet-street" after "Divine Service at St. Paul's." Like Foote, the actor-dramatist who said the repast would be "*black broth*" in sly reference to Francis, Johnson's negro servant, Boswell feared having no "knives and forks, and only some strange, uncouth, ill-drest dish." But he "found every thing in very good order." The "bill of fare" was "a very good soup, a boiled leg of lamb and spinach, a veal pye, and a rice pudding."[30] Johnson proudly showed off "handsome silver salvers" as serving dishes. His table manners could be gracious as on the occasion of being seated next to John Wilkes (1725–1797), the radical politician whose principles he despised. Wilkes, knowing Johnson liked "nice and delicate" food, treats him with "much attention and politeness." Wilkes helps him to "some fine veal": "Pray give me leave, Sir: – It is better here – A little of the brown – Some fat, Sir – A little of the stuffing – Some gravy – Let me have the pleasure of giving you some butter – Allow me to recommend a squeeze of this orange; – or the lemon perhaps, may have more zest." At first, Johnson looks at Wilkes with "surly virtue" but is soon won over to "complacency."[31]

Regarding cooking, Johnson boasted of writing "a better book of cookery than has ever yet been written": one based on "philosophical principles." As medicinal prescriptions have been simplified by compounding fewer ingredients, so cookery may be simplified by better knowing the nature of ingredients. Since bad cannot be made good meat, he would tell "what is the best butcher's meat, the best beef, the best pieces; how to choose young fowls; the proper season of different vegetables; and then how to roast and boil, and compound." Dilly, the cookbook publisher being at table, asserted that "Mrs Glasse's *Cookery*"

---

29 Boswell 1953, Friday, 5 August 1763, 331–2.
30 Ibid., Friday, 9 April 1773, 511–12.
31 Ibid., Sunday, 15 April 1781, 1136, and Wednesday, 15 May 1776, 768.

is the best but was "written by Dr. Hill," as the trade knows. Johnson disagrees, "for, in Mrs. Glasse's *Cookery*, which I have looked into, salt-petre and sal-prunella are spoken of as different substances, whereas sal-prunella is only salt-petre burnt on charcoal." Hill will have known this. Granting that, since cookbooks are made "by transcription," Johnson attributes Glasse's mistake to careless copying. He will be more careful in his book. So, he will "agree with Mr. Dilly for the copy-right," since women cannot make good cookery books.[32]

COOKERY, MENUS, AND TABLE ETIQUETTE AS FICTIONAL AGENTS

Speaking as "one who keeps a public Ordinary," Fielding in *Tom Jones* (1749) treats readers as diners who insist "on gratifying their Palates, however nice and whimsical," and "challenge a Right to censure, to abuse, and to d–m their Dinner without Controul." As victualler, he offers a "general Bill of Fare to our whole Entertainment" with "particular Bills to every Course which is to be served up in this and the ensuing Volumes," that is, prefatory essays. He extends the analogy between dining and reading; his single "Provision" may be "Human Nature," but a knowing reader, "though most luxurious in his Taste" will relish it since, "besides the delicious *Calipash* and *Calipee*," a turtle "contains many different kinds of Food." If readers find his cooking vulgar – epicureans spurn "exquisite Viands" sold in "paultry Alleys" – they should recall that "true Nature is as difficult to be met with in Authors, as the Bayonne Ham or Bologna Sausage is to be found in the Shops." Knowing how foreign food is imitated and how carcasses are distributed to vendors, he reminds diners that an animal dressed for a duke is also sold at the "vilest Stall in Town" and that, since an ox or calf may be eaten by noblemen and porters, the sole difference in the eating is "the seasoning, the dressing, the garnishing and the setting forth" of the flesh. If cooking for dukes "provokes and incites the most languid Appetite"

---

[32] Ibid., Wednesday, 15 April 1778, 942–3. Edward Dilly (1732–1779) and Charles Dilly (1739–1807), book trade partners, published Boswell's *Life of Johnson*. Boswell does not specify which brother was present. Presumably the elder. Johnson thinks to do what cookbooks were already doing. For example, the Dilly brothers had published Jenks's cookbook in 1768.

and that for porters may pall "the sharpest and keenest" hunger, he adopts "the highest Principles of the best Cook which the present Age" has produced: "all Lovers of polite eating" are reminded this "great Man" sets "plain Things before his hungry Guests, rising afterwards by degrees, as their Stomachs may be supposed to decrease, to the very Quintessence of Sauces and Spices." So, he serves rural human nature before hashing and ragouting it "with all the high French and Italian seasoning of Affectation and Vice which Courts and Cities afford."[33]

Don Quixote (1605–1615) by Miguel de Cervantes (1547–1616) is a model for Fielding. With stomach craving, the don one meagre day reaches an inn that offers baccalao while he imagines "troutlings." His knighthood, preferring veal to beef and lamb to mutton, means his taste is doubly thwarted; the baccalao is "wretchedly watered, and villainously cooked," the loaf accompanying it is "as black and greasy as his ... armour." Moreover, he frustrates his delicacy by leaving on his helmet as he is fed. Less affected, Sancho Panza's appetite is ultimately thwarted. While he carries an onion, a slice of cheese, and crusts of bread in his satchel, the don claims to "abstain whole months together from food," knights errant not only fasting until sumptuous meals magically appear but choosing field herbs over Sancho's edibles. Still the latter's taste in wine is exquisite: savouring it, instinct tells him its origin, growth, and vintage. Kinsmen in La Mancha once drank from a hogshead, one detecting iron and the other goat leather. When emptied, the barrel contained a key on a leather thong. Yet his culinary dreams dissolve. When the Squire of the Wood rejects his story of living on dried fruits and herbs, his stomach unable to digest "sweet thistle, wild pear and mountain roots," he urges Sancho to content himself with bread rather than fine dishes. The fantasy of being governor leads to dissatisfaction, for Pedro Positive de Bode-well snatches from him roasted partridges, stewed rabbits, veal *à la daube*, and an *olla podrida*, urging him to take confected waters and thin slices of quince. An archetypal scene of frustration occurs when Sancho comes to an inn whose landlord offers everything but delivers little. He first commands two roasted chickens, then, in sequence, a pullet, veal or kid, eggs and bacon. When the last is denied, he calls for a dish of cow-heel with peas, onions, and bacon, said by the landlord to be as fine as calves' feet. But he spurns

---

[33] Fielding 1973, 25–7.

the landlord's inflated words and asks for the cow-heel, cursing the calves' feet to the devil.[34]

Cervantes inspired Fielding's comedy about inn menus in *Joseph Andrews* (1742) and *Tom Jones*, both anticipating satire of haute cuisine in *The Journal of a Voyage to Lisbon* (1755). Robbed and having eaten nothing for a day, Joseph at the Tow-wouses' inn accepts Parson Adams's cautious recommendation of a poached egg or chicken broth despite craving boiled beef and cabbage. The narrator coyly supposes Joseph eats something lighter, perhaps rabbit or fowl. Yet next day Joseph sits down "to a Loin of Mutton." Such dishes demonstrate the superiority of appetites for bread, cheese, and beer at country inns over those "found at the most exquisite Eating-Houses in the Parish of *St. James's*," since "Hunger is better than a *French* Cook." Scorn for haute cuisine makes the Wilsons Fielding's surrogates. Retired from London's corrupt wine trade, they grow "Necessaries" in their garden. Mrs Wilson, a "notable Housewife" who knows "Cookery" and "Confectionary" better than professional housekeepers, has discarded these "Arts."[35]

Cervantes lies behind inn scenes in *Tom Jones*: Mrs Honour puts on airs when ordering food at a country inn, thinking eggs and bacon at midnight hard fare, but Tom eats "an excellent smoking Dish of Eggs and Bacon" with as hearty an appetite as Partridge. In *Tom Jones*, romance does not displace healthy appetites: a lover may well relish "a good Piece of well-powdered Buttock," and "Hunger is an Enemy which partakes more of the *English* than of the *French* Disposition; for tho' you subdue this never so often, it will always rally again in Time." So, Partridge makes "a very hearty Breakfast" of "an excellent cold Chine." Tom differs from him since, like Sancho, Partridge asserts rather than represses his appetite. As a landlord at St Albans puts a "Joint of Mutton" to the fire, Partridge admits to having eaten thirty times more than Tom, who says

---

34 Smollett 1755, vol. 1, bk 1, chap. 2: 11; vol. 1, bk 2, chap. 2: 52; vol. 2, bk 1, chap. 13: 72–3; vol. 2, bk 3, chap. 15: 285–6; vol. 2, bk 4, chap. 7: 374–5. Hume in "Of the Standard of Taste" cites Sancho's story of his kinsmen's exquisite taste to illustrate the principle that "A good palate is not tried by strong flavor, but by a mixture of small ingredients, where we are still sensible of each part, notwithstanding its minuteness and confusion with the rest" (1965, 10–12).

35 Fielding 1999, 102, 110, 189, 254, and 233–4.

"Love is a very rich Diet." But they both feast on "the excellent Shoulder of Mutton that came smoking to the Table."[36]

Like Cervantes, Fielding mocks aristocratic talk of haute cuisine. The "polite Conversation" of Lady Bellaston and Mrs Fitzpatrick is a "mental Repast" inaccessible to those excluded from "polite Assemblies," as are "the several Dainties of *French* Cookery, which are served only at the Tables of the Great." By contrast, Sophia's tastes enhance her character and advance the plot, her "most favourite Dainties" being the "Eggs of Pullets, Partridges, Pheasants." In "sublimest Grief," she dissects the cooked pullet filled with eggs that Black George brings and finds Tom's letter in its belly. She is her father's daughter in culinary taste. Squire Western is a plain eater. For dinner at The Hercules Pillars near Hyde Park he orders "a Shoulder of Mutton roasted, and a Spare-rib of Pork, and a Fowl and Egg-Sauce." The wedding feast at his Piccadilly lodgings requires the newlywed Sophia to surrender her retiring inclination, Fielding endorsing English cookbook etiquette; she "officiated as Mistress of the Ceremonies, or, in the polite Phrase, did the Honours of the Table."[37]

Joint literary and cultural history marks Fielding's philosophy of table manners in "An Essay on Conversation" (1743), which upholds Shaftesbury's patrician values.[38] After giving the etymology of conversation as men's ability to turn round together, the essay asserts that humans are the only truly sociable animals since "the Art of Conversation" is the "Art of pleasing or doing Good to one another" and constitutes "*Good Breeding*," defined as "the Art of pleasing, or contributing as much as possible to the Ease and Happiness of those with whom you converse." Hence, "we must be profitable Servants to each other: we are, in the second Place, to proceed to the utmost Verge in paying the Respect due to others." Fielding illustrates this ethic by ceremonial greetings and titles. Such formalities are valuable: "these Ceremonies, poor as they are, are of more Consequence than they at first appear, and in Reality, constitute the only external Difference between Man and Man." His "Rules" that govern the conduct of hosts clarify this point:

---

36 Fielding 1973, 409–10, 488, 498, 517–18, and 521. Like Cervantes, Fielding opposes "Writers of Romance" who hold that a "Man can live altogether on Love" (1973, 543).
37 Ibid., 535, 648–9, 684, and 758–9.
38 See chapter 1, "Training the Senses and Exploring the Inner Realm."

When an expected Guest arrives to Dinner at your House, if your Equal, or indeed not greatly your Inferior, he should be sure to find your Family in some Order, and yourself dress'd and ready to receive him at your Gate with a smiling Countenance. This infuses an immediate Cheerfulness into your Guest, and perswades him of your Esteem and Desire of his Company.

After "the first Ceremonies" in the "Drawing-Room," the guest should be invited to refresh himself before dinner "for which he is never to stay longer than the usual or fixed Hour."

When Dinner is on the Table, and the Ladies have taken their Places, the Gentlemen are to be introduced into the Eating-Room, where they are to be seated with as much seeming Indifference as possible, unless there be any present whose Degrees claim an undoubted Precedence. As to the rest, the general Rules of Precedence are by Marriage, Age, and Profession.

The "placing your Guests" should regard "Birth" not "Fortune." Serving them is to be regulated by their placement at table. Thus, "the Lady at the upper End of the Table" must "distribute her Favours as equally, and as impartially as she can." Fielding prescribes this rule from having "sometimes seen a large Dish of Fish extend no farther than to the fifth Person, and a Haunch of Venison lose all its Fat before half the Table has tasted it." On the other hand, hosts are not to press guests more than once "to eat of any particular Dish, how elegant soever." Opposing "all earnest Solicitations," Fielding forbids hosts complaining they themselves have "no Appetite"; such complaints "are sometimes little less than Burlesque, and always impertinent and troublesome."[39]

Table etiquette shapes Richardson's *Pamela* (1740), his heroine's domesticity making her an ideal wife so that Mr B. places her at the head of tables to signal her precedence. Trained in "Family Oeconomy," she assisted Mr B.'s mother as "Treasurer" and "Almoner." Used to genteel food preparation in the office not the kitchen, she continues to aid the housekeeper "in the making of Jellies, Comfits, Sweetmeats, Marmalades, Cordials; and to pot, and candy, and preserve, for the Uses of the Family." She was also taught to be "so dextrous a Carver" that, when asked by Mr B to cut up a "boiled Turkey," she does so "in

---

39 Fielding 1972, 123, 126, 127, and 128–9.

a trice," uniting proficiency and elegance as cookbooks urged ladies to do. If she is unused to precedence, when Mr B asks her "to govern the Tea-table" and "grace" the supper table by sitting at its "Upper-end," she is a stylish hostess. Since Mr B. takes "great Delight" in seeing her "carve and help round," she sits at "the Upper-end of the Table" from where she passes ladies their dinner. That Mr B. and Pamela serve each other and that Lady Davers's resistance to sitting at the same table is overcome when Mr B. sits between wife and sister shows how table service marks Richardson's awareness that cookbooks incorporate conduct manuals.[40] Open to the "vegetarian ideology" of George Cheyne (1671–1743), he no doubt well knew of the relation of diet to sensibility and of the tradition of etiquette in cookbooks from those of Hannah Woolley in the 1660s to John Nott's in the 1720s.[41] Rituals of hospitality reached an acme in 1788 when John Trusler (1735–1820) published *The Honours of the Table, or, Rules for Behaviour during Meals; With the Whole Art of Carving. Pamela* symbolizes the developing association between the polite serving of meat and the confirmation of middle-class gentility.

Crude aspirations for upward mobility are decried in *Evelina* when the culinary sloth of the trading class is depicted. Emblems of city vulgarity, this class lacks the aplomb of the Mirvan family who attend theatres and pleasure gardens in the West End. Lodging with a hosier in Holborn, Evelina finds this district a "desart," its inhabitants "illiterate and under-bred." Dinner with them at Snow-hill exposes their ugliness. Living above a large shop in a small, inconvenient house, the Branghtons serve dinner "up two pair of stairs." The dinner is "ill-served, ill-cooked, and ill-managed," the maid forgetting things downstairs and family members rising "from table themselves, to get plates, knives and forks, bread or beer." They make matters worse by disputing propriety. They lack Evelina's cultural sense: at the opera house, they "made no allowance for the customs, or even for the language of another country, but formed all their remarks upon comparisons with the English theatre." They justify her guardian's view that London is "the general harbour of fraud and of folly, of duplicity and of impertinence." Despite learning

---

40 Richardson 1971, 226, 252–3, 262, 266, 279, and 353.
41 Stuart 2007, 181 and 186–91. Hannah Woolley lived from 1622 to 1675. John Nott's dates are unknown. He is the author of *The Cook's and Confectioner's Dictionary: Or, the Accomplish'd Housewife's Companion* (London: C. Rivington, 1723).

to dress according to the spatial conventions of the theatre and opera house, Evelina feels "there ought to be a book of the laws and customs *à-la-mode*, presented to all young people, upon their first introduction into public company." Her feeling is provoked by fops such as Lovel, who, assuming she is a rustic unable to speak French, fills his mouth with clichés such as "*vrai goût*" and "*les gens comme il faut*." Like Sparkish in Wycherley's *The Country Wife*, Lovel "has no time to mind the stage" since "one merely comes to meet one's friends"; besides, "a play requires so much attention."[42] By contrast, Lord Orville models Fielding's concept of conversation. Not only like Evelina does he studiously enjoy plays, but also his manners are "so elegant, so gentle, so unassuming, that they at once engage esteem, and diffuse complacence. Far from being indolently satisfied with his own accomplishments ... he is most assiduously attentive to please and to serve all who are in his company; and, though his success is invariable, he never manifests the smallest degree of consciousness." From the Reverend Villars's viewpoint, Orville is "a better order of beings" who matches his ward's refinement, as confirmed when they are disgusted by the decadent courtiers at the home of Mrs Beaumont, the latter described by the satirical Mrs Selwyn "as an absolute *Court Calendar bigot*." It is a pointed moment in cultural history when Orville shares Evelina's distaste with the gluttonous manners of those courtiers because it reveals Burney's desire to reform the aristocracy with upper-middle-class moral standards.[43]

Jane Austen testifies to the mores of cuisine and hospitality arising from social stratification at the end of the century. Her *Letters* are full of domestic economy. Her family employs a cook and a housemaid; it raises pigs; it cures "the sparibs, the souse, and the lard" and sends meat to distant members. She relishes toasted cheese for supper; distributes expensive fish – "four pair of small soals" – to friends, worried about sending them in a basket that held poultry; enjoys the luxury of eating ice cream and drinking French wine, yet "vulgar Economy" enjoins her to make "Orange Wine" and "Spruce Beer." She snacks by the fire on

---

42 Sparkish: "Gad, I go to a play as to a country treat: I carry my own wine to one, and my own wit to t'other, or else I'm sure I should not be merry at either" (Wycherley 1996, 226).

43 Burney 2000, 288, 289–91, 195, 223, 185, 216, 182, 172, and 416.

a cold day and consumes widgeon and preserved ginger, but home-made black butter is nearly inedible, most of it not offered to guests.[44]

While *Northanger Abbey* (1803) mocks Catherine Morland's gothic obsessions, Austen more pointedly assails General Tilney's acquisitiveness and treachery. Owning an elegant "breakfast set" to impress guests, he pretends having bought it to encourage national industry. Claiming to have an "uncritical palate," he says the tea made in "the clay of Staffordshire" is as fine as that in teapots from "Dresden or Sève." He also claims that his set is old-fashioned, that the manufacture has much improved, that he saw "some beautiful specimens when last in town," and that, "had he not been perfectly without vanity," he might have ordered a new set. Forcing notice of the old one on Catherine, supposing her a wealthy young woman and eligible bride, he is enchanted that she approves of it. In saying he may yet buy a new set, he hints Catherine may soon be his daughter-in-law. Amusingly, she is deaf to his hint. Before learning she is poor and dismissing her, he makes her tour the abbey in his pride at its grand dining room, which he thinks will impress her and deepen her love for his son, Henry. But gothic taste renders her indifferent to Northanger's modern amenities. While the kitchen's massy walls are intact, its smoke, sad to say, is lost to "stoves and hot closets." That "every modern invention" eases the cooks' labour in their "spacious theatre" maddens her. Having applied genius and great expense to designing the kitchen after experts failed him, the general is vain about making his servants comfortable and is sure Catherine will approve since he assumes she is as acquisitive as him. But she is appalled by the "mere domestic economy" that has modernized the Abbey without concern for architectural history: she is not really impressed by the many offices and the servants' spacious quarters. While her home has "a few shapeless pantries and a comfortless scullery," the Abbey's kitchen is "commodious and roomy." Its many servants clash with her notion that the dirty work of large houses may be effected by "two pair of female hands."[45]

Cuisine figures largely in *Emma*. Hospitality early signals that the heroine and George Knightley will marry given their appreciation of social eating. They value food production. On this topic Emma opposes

44 Austen 1979, 99, 57–8, 165, 177, 209, 235, and 241.
45 Austen 1969, 175 and 183–4.

her father, who treats guests with a hypochondriac fussiness that affects his other daughter, Isabella, who laments that her cook cannot make thin gruel. When John Knightley is irritated by his father-in-law, he calls gruel wholesome to keep the peace. Judging suppers "unwholesome," Mr Woodhouse eats "only a small basin of thin gruel." He tells guests to take "a *little* bit of tart" while his apple tarts are free from "unwholesome preserves." Emma supplies "visitors in a much more satisfactory style." Noting her wish to attach Mr Elton to Harriet Smith, Knightley tells her to invite "him to dinner" and serve "the best of the fish and chicken."[46]

Emma shares her community's culinary aspirations. The Coles, recent arrivals, establish themselves by hosting fashionable dinners. Adding "to their house, to their number of servants, to their expenses of every sort," they display a "style of living, second only to the family at Hartfield." A "new dining-room" marks their "love of society" and "keeping dinner-company." But their table suffers from formality; in their dining room, Emma and Frank Churchill are stopped from discussing Jane Fairfax's pianoforte since they "were called on to share in the awkwardness of a rather long interval between the courses, and obliged to be as formal and as orderly as the others." Emma renews her scandal mongering "when the table was again safely covered, when every corner dish was placed exactly right, and occupation and ease were generally restored." Her similar modishness balks Knightley's probing of Frank's dream – a lie invented to cover his secret correspondence with Jane: "Knightley must take his seat with the rest round the large modern circular table which Emma had introduced at Hartfield, and which none but Emma could have had power to place there and persuade her father to use, instead of the small-sized Pembroke, on which two of his daily meals had, for forty years, been crowded." Far from mediating good conversation, dining rooms may serve duplicity.[47]

Emma's hospitality does not stop her matchmaking for Mr Elton and Harriet. Never "indifferent to the credit of doing every thing well and attentively," at suppers she does "all the honours of the meal," recommending "the minced chicken and scalloped oysters with an urgency

---

46 Austen 1971, 95, 124, 21, and 11.
47 Ibid., 186, 196, and 313. According to the *Encyclopedia Britannica* a Pembroke table is a light, drop-leaf table designed for occasional use, probably deriving its name from Henry Herbert, ninth Earl of Pembroke (1693–1751), a noted connoisseur and amateur architect.

that she knew would be acceptable to the early hours and civil scruples of their guests." Ignoring her father's strictures, she hands muffins round twice. Providing a "plentiful dinner" to Mrs Bates and Mrs Goddard when they dine with her father, she compensates for the "unwilling self-denial" he imposes on them "by helping them to large slices of cake and full glasses of wine." Supervisor of Hartfield's kitchen, she serves "roast mutton and rice pudding" at lunch to John Knightley and sons after their rural exercise. The charitable lady who carries pitchers of broth to poor cottagers, she undoes her benevolence: breaking a lace to lag behind Elton and Harriet to thrust them into romantic talk, she is disappointed, on catching up with them, that they are discussing "the Stilton cheese, the north Wiltshire, the butter, the cellery, the beer-root and all the dessert" at the Coles' supper party.[48]

Emma can forget that foodstuffs may create inclusive bonds. Her scorn for the Martins as tenant farmers is absurd given their food sharing. They send Mrs Goddard "a beautiful goose: the finest goose that Mrs. Goddard had ever seen," declares chatty Miss Bates. Hoping to sever Robert Martin from Harriet, Emma forgets that in the neighbourhood "poultry-yards" abound, most villagers raising farm animals. Mrs Weston has a "poultry-house" from which "all of her turkies" are stolen, to Mr Woodhouse's discomfort, a fact that makes him accept a son-in-law living at Hartfield. While Emma and father raise pigs, he is not generous in donating pork. Speaking of Emma's wish to supply the Bateses, he says of a just killed "porker," she "thinks of sending them a loin or a leg." His pride in Hartfield pork lies in its being "very small and delicate." He eats it as steaks "nicely fried, without the smallest grease," saying "no stomach can bear roast pork" and deciding to "send the leg" to the Bateses. But Emma sends "the whole hind-quarter," sure the leg will be "salted" and the loin dressed as they like. He protests the leg must not be "over-salted" and "thoroughly boiled"; if "eaten moderately of, with a boiled turnip, and a little carrot or parsnip," it will not be "unwholesome." Lacking a "salting-pan big enough," the Bateses guard their preferences; Mrs Bates loves nothing better than "a roast loin of pork." Since Mrs Goddard likes nothing "but boiled pork," Miss

---

48 Ibid., 20, 152, 191, 99, and 80–1. Note that Emma asks her housekeeper to examine her stores for arrowroot of a superior quality to send to Jane Fairfax. Not surprisingly, given Emma's scandalous suspicions of Jane which will have been conveyed to her by Frank, the arrowroot is rejected and returned (Austen 1971, 354).

Bates will not call on her; when they "dress the leg it will be another thing." The Bateses hold to their cooking preferences. In their small apartment, they serve sweet cake from a "beaufet."[49]

Austen deploys the Bates's disjointed chat to stress Knightley's culinary generosity. While Emma exploits meals, she is irritated by Miss Bates's talk of Jane's diet: Emma finds "the tiresome aunt" unendurable in her "description of exactly how little bread and butter she ate for breakfast, and how small a slice of mutton for dinner." Miss Bates's concern for Jane reports that Mrs Wallis, the local baker, prepares their baked apples. When Jane is hungry at midday, after eating nothing for breakfast, she finds those apples "extremely wholesome." Miss Bates recalls that Mr Woodhouse thinks baked apples "thoroughly wholesome," but her aunt and she like "apple dumplings" prepared by their cook, Patty, their taste wider than his. They serve him baked apples, which he obligingly judges "the finest looking home-baked apples [he] ever saw in [his] life." Yet Miss Bates cautiously admits that, while he advises them "to have them done three times," they never do them more than twice. The apples they send to the baker come from Donwell, "some of Mr. Knightley's most liberal supply." From his carefully tended orchard he sends "a sack every year; and certainly there never was such a keeping apple any where as one of his trees." He even sends extra apples, keeping none, according to William Larkins, his estate manager; Mrs Hodges, Knightley's housekeeper, is unhappy that "her master should not be able to have another apple-tart this spring."[50]

Baked apples continually draw readers' attention to ironies of food and diet. When Frank sits next to Emma at the Bateses to hide his closeness to Jane and to incite Emma's speculation about the illicit source of Jane's pianoforte, he is "sufficiently employed in looking out the best baked apple." This ruse heightens Knightley's honesty. At the ball in the Crown, baked apples gather dramatic irony. Miss Bates recalls a dinner at Hartfield when her grandmother dined with Mr Woodhouse. She reports that, while the baked apples and biscuits were "excellent in their way," also served "was a delicate fricassee of sweetbread and some asparagus," which he sent back thinking the latter not "quite boiled enough." While grandmother was disappointed since fricassee

49 Ibid., 24, 439–40, 153–54, 156, 158, and 138.
50 Ibid., 150 and 213–15.

is a favourite dish, Mrs and Miss Bates tactfully do not mention it to prevent it getting back to Emma as a complaint. Given their limited diet, a limitation to which Mr Woodhouse is blind, Miss Bates would distract Jane and herself by remembering the dishes served at the ball so she can entertain grandmother with the names. Yet, prompted by the aroma of the soup, Miss Bates cannot resist her hunger, starting to eat it as soon as it is placed before her.[51]

This impoliteness is nothing as bad as the ill manners of Mrs Elton and Frank, which are challenged by Knightley and Emma, whose culinary views converge in the denouement. Knightley's hospitality is conveyed by lucid self-sufficiency as a brewer of spruce beer. Firm of mind, he resists Mrs Elton's bossiness about conducting a picnic at Donwell. Pretending to be "Lady Patroness," she wants an outdoor picnic of "pigeon pies and cold lamb." After having his guests eat strawberries in their beds, he upholds his "idea of the simple and natural" by having "the table spread in the dining-room" since gentlemen and ladies should have "meals within doors." Boasting about cultivating varieties of strawberries such as hautboy, chili, white wood, she not only degrades them by declaring her preference for cherries and currants but also complains about bending down to pick them, having to retire to the shade from fatigue. Frank is similarly reprimanded by Emma after a confrontation with Jane makes him surly with the one he has long deceived. Chiding his rudeness, Emma directs him to be sociable and take another "slice of cold meat, another draught of Madeira and water."[52]

Sterling in Colman and Garrick's *The Clandestine Marriage* prefigures Austen's Tilney; his hospitality is hostile, exemplifying the typology by which Restoration comedy degraded capitalism and confirming that mid-eighteenth-century theatre exploits cuisine and consumerism. Sterling, prizing luxurious display, reduces himself to his name. A trader of stocks, currants, soap, and Madeira on the Exchange, he abuses superiors and inferiors but submits to a termagant sister. He enjoys making impoverished aristocrats eat off golden plates and drink from golden goblets. He has a cook and a butler in his country house, its pond supplying carp and tench when turbot and mackerel do not come

---

51 Ibid., 216 and 297.
52 Ibid., 319–321, 324, and 330.

from London. He serves turtle, venison, and home-grown pineapples. Champagne asserts his wealth to obsequious guests who would marry his money. His strong port oversets claret drinkers. Dutch tulips adorn his gardens, as do serpentine walks, ruins, a cascade, and Chinese bridge. An artificial spire terminating his prospect fulfills the "rule of taste."[53]

Hospitality and fashion are also mocked in Goldsmith's *She Stoops to Conquer* through the trickery of Tony Lumpkin and Kate Hardcastle. When Marlow and Hastings, fortune-hunting beaux from London, arrive dressed like Frenchmen, they think Hardcastle, their host, an innkeeper. His "old rambling mansion" is like an inn, his old-fashioned domesticity unused to company. Kate, his daughter, pleases him by wearing housewife's clothes in the evening but pleases herself by donning French gauzes and silks of a morning. The beaux, inattentive to Hardcastle's militarism, treat dress as martial strategy; it is ammunition in the campaign of courtship, embroidery affording retreat. They command "the bill of fare" for supper with effete insolence. Typical of country fare, the bill offers two courses and a dessert; light eaters, they want two or three "little things" whereas the first course lists "a pig, and prune sauce" at table top with "a calf's tongue and brains" at the bottom, the second course naming a "pork pie, a boiled rabbit and sausages, a florentine, a shaking pudding, and a dish of tiff-taff-taffety cream!" This "exquisite" fare daunts the beaux, who hate "made dishes." That they equate rural dishes with French cuisine exposes their sartorial elegance and cultural pretensions.[54]

ECCLESIASTICAL EATING

Since the Church of England's ten thousand pulpits mediated culture, clerical attitudes to eating are historically important. Sterne funded public feasting in the king's name; George III's coronation "cost" him "the value of an Ox" that was "roasted whole in the middle of the town" of Coxwold for parishioners' merriment.[55] They liked Sterne despite his sojourns on the continent. At Coxwold – its benefice granted by

---

53 Wood 2007, 86–7, 92, 142, and 103–4.
54 Ibid., 171, 166, 178, and 180–1.
55 Sterne to Lady [Anna Pratt], Coxwold, 21 September 1761 (Sterne 1935, 143).

Lord Fauconberg – he felt "as happy as a prince" given his "princely" living: "'tis a land of plenty. I sit down alone to venison, fish, and wild fowl, or a couple of fowls or ducks, with curds, and strawberries and cream, and all the simple plenty which a rich valley ... can produce, – with a clean cloth on my table – and a bottle of wine on my right hand ... I have a hundred hens and chickens about my yard – and not a parishioner catches a hare, or a rabbet, or a trout, but he brings it as an offering to me."[56] The fame of *Tristram Shandy* meant his calendar in London was filled with "14 Engagements to Dine ... with the first Nobility." He won entree to court banquets, as when Prince Ferdinand, the Marquis of Rockingham, and Earl Temple were installed as Knights of the Garter on Tuesday, 6 May 1760. Their "grand retinue" to Windsor permitted him the contentment of attending in Rockingham's "suite."[57] Needing sunny France to relieve consumptive lungs and to stretch his income, Sterne carefully assessed the cost of accommodations and dining. In preparing his wife for life in Toulouse, he told her to bring from England such hard-to-acquire things as a "strong bottle screw," a "silver coffee-pot" for serving "water, lemonade, and orjead" as well as a copper "tea-kettle, knives, cookery book."[58] Her housekeeping was gratifying: she "keeps an excellent good house, with *soupe, bouilli, roti,* etc, etc, for two hundred and fifty pounds a year" which is "extreme cheap."[59] He is proud their Toulouse house "consists of a good *salle à manger* above stairs, joining to the very great *salle à compagnie* as large as the Baron D'Holbach's."[60] His familiarity with cookbooks is evident when he details a medical-culinary receipt prescribed for his lungs which ends in sexual whimsy: "My physicians have almost poisoned me with what they call *bouillons rafraichissants* – 'tis a cock flead alive and boiled with poppy-seeds, then pounded in a mortar, afterwards pass'd thro' a sieve – There is to be one crawfish in it, and I was gravely told it must

---

56 Sterne to A. L–e, Esq, Coxwold, 7 June 1767 (Sterne 1935, 353).

57 Sterne to Catherine Fourmantel, London, 1 April 1760 and Sterne to Stephen Croft, London, c. 1 May 1760 (Sterne 1935, 104, and 107).

58 Sterne to Mrs Sterne, Paris, 14 June 1762 and Paris, 17 June 1762 (Sterne 1935, 174 and 176–7).

59 Sterne to John Hall-Stevenson, Toulouse, 19 October 1762 (Sterne 1935, 187).

60 Sterne to Robert Foley, Toulouse, 14 August 1762 (Sterne 1935, 83).

be a male one – a female would do me more hurt than good."⁶¹ His taste for fine cuisine and wine was formed among English and French grandees in Paris but also in Lyons, Dijon, Montpellier, Avignon, on the banks of the Sorgue, and at the Fontaine de Vaucluse. In Lyons he had "a joyous time," and he found Dijon "a delicious part of the world," its dry climate allowing his "inner man" to be "inspired twice a day with the best Burgundy that grows upon the mountains."⁶²

Gilbert White's *The Natural History of Selborne* (1788–89) and James Woodforde's *The Diary of a Country Parson 1758–1802* reveal how rural clergy improved natural history and culinary practice, their travelling, unlike Sterne's, limited to English villages. Biology and geology inspired White (1720–1793) to study the history of agriculture, horticulture, and food. He admired John Ray (1627–1705), the famous ornithologist who, before election in 1667 to the Royal Society, made botanical tours of Europe. For White, Ray's notes on diet in Italy improved English eating: in 1663 he noted that "the Italians use several herbs for sallets, which are not yet or have not been but lately used in England, viz., *selleri* (celery), which is nothing else but the sweet smallage; the young shoots whereof, with a little of the head of the root cut off, they eat raw with oil and pepper." Intriguingly, Ray had added that "curled endive blanched is much used beyond seas; and, for a raw sallet, seemed to excell lettuce itself." For one notion White stresses is the rarity of leprosy once common in England and Europe. That it is almost "eradicated," he attributes to "the much smaller quantity of salted meat and fish now eaten in these kingdoms" and to better bread and "the profusion of fruits, legumes and greens, so common in every family." Like Defoe, he claims that, since enclosures are highly productive, they yield "sown-grasses, field-turnips, or field-carrots, or hay" so that summer-fattened cattle are no longer salted for winter eating, fresh meat being available in the winter and spring. To White, "agriculture is now arrived at such a pitch of perfection, that our best and fattest meats are killed in the

---

61 Sterne to Mrs F[enton?], Montpellier, 1 February 1764 (Sterne 1935, 210). Paul-Henri Thiry d'Holbach (1723–1789), a prominent philosopher in the French Enlightenment.

62 For his knowledge of Provençal culture, see Sterne to Isaac Panchaud, Beau Pont Vosin, 7 November 1765; Sterne to John Hall-Stevenson, near Dijon, 24 May [1766]; and Sterne to Lydia Sterne, Old Bond-street, 23 February 1767 (Sterne 1935, 262, 277, and 301).

winter; and no man need eat salted flesh, unless he prefers it, that has money to buy fresh." The "good wheaten bread" now "found among all ranks of people in the south, instead of that miserable sort which used in old days to be made of barley or beans," sweetens their blood and bodily juices while "inhabitants of mountainous districts, to this day, are still liable to the itch and other cutaneous disorders, from the wretchedness and poverty of diet." His optimism about garden produce yielded by the agricultural revolution is extensive:

Every middle-aged person of observation may perceive, within his own memory, both in town and country, how vastly the consumption of vegetables is increased. Green-stalls in cities now support multitudes in a comfortable state, while gardeners get fortunes. Every decent labourer also has his garden, which is half his support, as well as his delight; and common farmers provide plenty of beans, peas, and greens, for their hinds to eat with their bacon; and those few that do not are despised for their sordid parsimony, and looked upon as regardless of the welfare of their dependents.

He is glad that, "in this little district" of Selbourne, the poor have "within these twenty years" begun to esteem potatoes whereas they "would scarce have ventured to taste them in the last reign." That there are no boundaries in his mind between science, utility, and aesthetics is clear when he says that, since the aristocracy and gentry have taken up "the study of horticulture," gardening has "made such hasty advances" because "the first people of rank that promoted the elegant science of ornamenting" did so "without despising the superintendence of the kitchen quarters and fruit walls."[63]

Natural history led White to study economic and political ideas, entomology, and ornithology, exposing the challenges posed by insects to food production and culinary hygiene. He often notes how insects and birds damage orchard fruit and kitchen gardens. For example, he details the depredations of the cheese-fly (*Piophila casei*). After "getting into chimneys, and laying eggs in the bacon while it is drying," this fly's eggs turn into "maggots called jumpers," which, after "harbouring in the gammons and the best parts of the hogs, eat down to the bone, and make great waste." Like Austen knowing the importance of pork to the

63 White 1977, 201–2.

rural diet, White's concern for communal food supply leads to esteem for estate and game management. He lamented that Selbourne's manor was not "strictly looked after." Previously, it would "swarm with game." If "hares, partridges, and pheasants abound," woodcocks are no longer "as plentiful." Regretting that hunting and poaching have rendered the red deer extinct, he surveys the migrations and habitats of birds such as quail and landrail from a culinary sense of game: bird spotting involves social analysis. On one occasion he reports not having seen a single wheat-ear, but he knows they abound in the autumn when they are a "considerable perquisite" to shepherds who capture them. During the wheat harvest, "they begin to be taken in great numbers; are sent for sale in vast quantities to Brighthelmstone and Tunbridge; and appear at the tables of all the gentry that entertain with any degree of elegance."[64]

Like White, Woodforde (1740–1803) was a practical clergyman: he tended orchards and brewed beer. His diary details institutional meals. Besides describing those at his Oxford college, he records how he treats vestry officers and tithe-paying parishioners, feeds house guests, hosts local gentry, and enjoys banquets at the bishop's palace. Fellow of New College, he took up a stewardship in November 1762, his task to oversee the weighing of meat in the kitchen. In 1763 he became deacon of the college in which role he observed Oxford's celebrations of Britain's imperial success in the Seven Years War. If the chaplain's table turned him against "roasted Tongue and Udder," he relished the annual venison feast when high table served "a neck of Venison and a Breast made into a Pasty, a Ham and Fowls and two Pies." High-table dinner typically consisted of "two fine Codds boiled with fryed Souls round them and oyster sauce, a fine surloin of Beef roasted, some peas soup and an orange Pudding for the first course, for the second … a lease of Wild Ducks rosted, a fore Qu: of Lamb and sallad and mince Pies." For college guests he had prepared green pea soup, a chine of mutton, New College puddings, a goose, peas, and a codlin tart with cream. At supper he served cold mutton. Culinary experience at college habituated him to link parish duties to food for himself, parishioners, and guests. One day after riding six miles to his curacy, he dined on "a Sheep's heart" he had carried in his pocket. That he bought a "compleat Table service of cream coloured ware" at Norwich shows that culinary modes

---

64 Ibid., 84, 22, 16, and 154.

structured his meals. But his hospitality was tested by problems of food preservation like White's. At one Rotation Day dinner he serves parish officers "a bad Leg of Mutton boil'd scarce fit to be eat by being kept too long," capers, green peas, "a Pigg's face, a Neck of Pork rosted with gooseberries, a plumb Pudding, with Carrots, Turnips" compensating. At another, he serves "part of a Ham, the major part of which Ham was entirely eat out by the Flies getting into it." Happily, this dinner included three boiled fowls, "a Leg of Mutton rosted, and an excellent currant Pudding," the supper offering "a couple of Rabbitts smothered in Onions, some Hash Mutton, and some rosted Potatoes." He did well at parties for friends and relatives. At one, he served tench from his brother's pond, a ham, three boiled fowls, a plumb pudding, followed by two roast ducks, a roasted neck of pork, one plumb and one apple tart, and pears, apples, and nuts. Supper consisted of hashed fowl, duck, eggs, and potatoes. Access to ponds let him serve freshwater fish. At another dinner, he pleases guests with "my great Pike which was rosted and a Pudding in his Belly" and "some boiled Trout, Perch, and Tench, Eel and Gudgeon fryed, a Neck of Mutton boiled and a plain Pudding." He was proud the pike laid over two plates was "prodigious fine eating, being so moist." Dinners for tithe audits could be as elaborate: one offered "a Leg of Mutton boiled, and Capers, some Salt Fish, plenty of Plumb Puddings and a Couple of Boiled Rabbitts, with a fine large Surloin of Beef rosted"; another, "Salt Fish, a Leg of Mutton boiled and Capers, boiled and rost Beef and plenty of plumb and plain Puddings."[65]

Like other country residents, Woodforde aimed at independence from food markets: besides stocking fish ponds, he raised pigs and grew vegetables and fruit. This involved him in charity and social networks: he sends "four Breasts and Hands of my two Piggs, with one of the Loins" to poor neighbours, and, when Mr Custance, the parish's major landowner, sends him "some beans and a Colliflower," he sends back dozens of apricots, accepting in return "another Piece of Parmesan Cheese." His range of food production appears in one day's offering to nine house guests. Dinner offers nine dishes: "some Pyke and fryed Soals, a nice Piece of boiled Beef, Ham and a Couple of Fowls, Peas and beans, a green Goose rosted, Gooseberry Pies, [and] Currant Tarts," and supper offers "fryed Soals, a Couple of Chicken rosted, cold Ham &c." At

---

65 Woodforde 1978, 13–15, 19, 24, 69, 86, 98, 131, 133, 150, 170, 217, and 289.

both, there are strawberries, cherries, almonds, and raisins. When the Custances visit, he serves the usual two courses: the first contains "a Couple of Chicken boiled and a Tongue, a Leg of Mutton boiled and Capers and Batter Pudding," the second "a couple of Ducks rosted and green Peas, some Artichokes, Tarts and Blancmange." For afters, he offers "Almonds and Raisins, Oranges and Strawberries. Mountain and Port Wines." That the peas and strawberries are from his garden in early June signals proficient gardening. Dinners at the Custances do not far surpass his efforts, if some dishes required special kitchen skills and rare produce. The first course of one such dinner contains "some common Fish, a Leg of Mutton rosted and a baked Pudding" while the second offers "a rost Duck, a Meat Pye, Eggs and Tarts." Supper that day consists of "a brace of Partridges rosted, some cold Tongue, Potatoes in Shells and Tarts." Another dinner at their home is more impressive, the first course offering "a Calf's Head, boiled Fowl and Tongue, a Saddle of Mutton rosted on the Side Table, and a fine Swan rosted with Currant Jelly Sauce." The second course intriguingly offers "a couple of Wild Fowl called Dun Fowls, Larks, Blamange, Tarts ... and a good Desert of Fruit amongst which was a Damson Cheese." Killed three weeks prior, the swan was the first Woodforde had tasted; he enjoyed this dish harking back to Robert May (1588?–1664?). The Custances' table is noble. Their dinner of 10 June 1784 matches the fine dining of May's aspirational cuisine: it consisted of "Soals and Lobster Sauce, Spring Chicken boiled and a Tongue, a Piece of rost Beef, Soup, a Fillet of Veal rosted with Morells and Trufles, and Pigeon Pye for the first Course – Sweetbreads, a green Goose and Peas, Apricot Pye, Cheesecakes, Stewed Mushrooms and Trifle" in the second.[66]

His love of traditional dishes, such as hashed goose, "Piggs Pettytoes," and "Sweetbreads," drove Woodforde to scorn the table of the Custances' fashionable friends whose nine dishes in each of two courses were "spoiled by being so frenchified." Feasts with fellow clergymen at Norwich and at the Bishop's palace are another matter. One meal of the first sort served fresh salmon and oyster sauce, boiled turkey and oyster sauce, a fore-quarter of London lamb, and mince pies. On that occasion, the "handsome" supper offered two boiled fowls and oyster sauce, a roast hare contributed by Woodforde, a roast duck, a hot

66 Ibid., 178, 205, 232, 253, 171, 148, 159, and 227.

tongue, tarts and Italian flummery, blancmange black caps, and sweet meats. At a feast given by the Bishop of Norwich on 4 September 1783, the two courses contained twenty-nine dishes, each served with Madeira and red and white wines to twenty guests. Among first-course dishes were a "prodigious fine stewed Carp and Tench, and a fine Haunch of Venison," the second course including "fine Turkey poult, Partridges, Pidgeons and Sweetmeats." Dessert offered "Mulberries, Melon, Currants, Peaches, Nectarines and Grapes." Woodforde was taken by a "most beautiful Artificial Garden in the Center of the table." One yard long and half a yard wide, it featured a temple supported by round pillars wreathed with artificial flowers, figurines of a shepherd and shepherdess, and ornamented urns. Still, no snob, he ate in public ordinaries such as the King's Head in Norwich, where, after dining on "a fine piece of boiled Beef and a Saddle of Mutton," he enjoyed "the best Supper I ever met at an Inn – Hashed Fowl, Veal Collopes, a fine Woodcock, a Couple of Whistling Plovers, a real Teal of the small kind and hot Apple Pye." He was no less gratified by "Beef a la mode" at the Thirteen Cantons near Charing Cross.[67] As Stephen Mennell says, the dishes Woodforde ate show the similar diets of royalty and country parsons.[68] Indeed, what the latter ate links the history of cuisine to issues of social hierarchy, self-sufficiency, and aesthetic taste in the period's cookbooks.

THE CONTINENT AND SCIENCE AS CULINARY CONTEXTS

European modes heavily influenced English cuisine in the seventeenth century. Sir Kenelm Digby (1603–1665), on his father's death, went at age fourteen to Spain, where he began a life-long collection of medicinal and culinary receipts. After studying at Oxford and falling in love with a woman of whom his mother disapproved, he was sent off – from 1622 to 1625 – on a Grand Tour of France, Germany, and Italy, which saw his collection expand. After the execution of Charles I in 1649, he advocated for Catholics in England and patronized May, the author of the era's most complete English cookbook. Publishing a treatise on

---

67 Ibid., 194, 208, 210, 212, 261–2, and 275.
68 Mennell 1996, 125.

bodies in 1644, Digby became a member of the Royal Society, to which he presented a lecture on the vegetation of plants in 1661. His collection of receipts, *The Closet of the Eminently Learned Sir Kenelme Digbie, K*^{t}· *Opened*, came out posthumously in 1669. It features recipes from Germany, Holland, Spain, Italy, and France as well as from English ladies. Those for "*Broth and Potage*" and "*Pan Cotto*" exemplify the influence of France and Italy.[69]

The Royal Society received its charter in 1662 and adopted the innovations championed by Bacon in *The Advancement of Learning*. According to Thomas Sprat (1635–1715), the society's first historian, its scientists conducted experiments in medicine and physics to displace theological controversies that aggravated sectarian strife in the Civil War. Observation and measurement were its preoccupations, positivism dignifying such practical skills as cookery and the mechanical arts of making cutlery, tableware, and glassware. A society member who advanced Digby's work on food and agriculture was John Evelyn (1620–1706). A voluntary exile during the Civil War, he enjoyed daily life in France and Italy. Unwilling to preside over the society, he remained a keen member. On 29 April 1675, he delivered *A Philosophical Discourse of Earth, Relating to the Culture and Improvement of It for Vegetation, and the Propagation of Plants*, published in 1676.[70] This text catalogues soils, methods of tillage, manuring and composting, and the growth of domestic and foreign plants. In 1699 he dedicated *Acetaria: A Discourse of Sallets* to Lord John Somers, the society's president. He asks Somers in his role as Chancellor of England to protect the society against "the Malevolence of Enemies and Detracters" and to find it a permanent address. Homeless for forty years, the society, says Evelyn, has been impeded. Once housed, it will extend the "Empire" of nature "beyond the Land of *Spectres, Forms, Intentional Species, Vacuum, Occult Qualities*, and other *Inadequate Notions.*" Nature must be freed from "those Illusions and Impostors, that are still endeavouring to cloud and depress the true, and *Substantial Philosophy*": "*Fantasms* and fruitless Speculations" must yield to the "*specifick* Nature of Things." Since a "*profound*, and thorow *Penetration*" into the "*Recesses*" of nature leads to "the *Knowledge*, and *Admiration* of the *Glorious Author*,"

69 Digby 1669, 166–7.
70 For his citation of Digby, see Evelyn 1676, 67.

learning the structure, growth, habitats, and nutrition of plants is key to *"Natural History."*[71]

Friend to leading members of the Royal Society, such as Robert Boyle (1627–1691), the chemist, and Christopher Wren (1632–1723), the architect, Evelyn grew close to Charles II at the exiled court. He bought his house, Sayes Court in Deptford, from Sir Richard Browne, his father-in-law, the royal ambassador to the French court. Evelyn's ecological concern for food appears in his translation of Nicolas de Bonnefons, *The French Gardiner* (1658) and in his innovative books on urban pollution, *Fumifugium* (1661), and forest management, *Sylva* (1664). The former promotes the cultivation of gardens and urban farms to cleanse London's evil-smelling air. His *Diary* (first published in 1818) describes foreign and domestic eating. At Vienne in the Dauphiné he tasted an "earth-nut" in a "dish of Truffles," finding it "an incomparable meat." He attended royal feasts, one lasting three days put on for the Venetian ambassadors to celebrate the accession of James II. At this banquet there were "12 vast Chargers piled so high" guests could not see one another across the table. He records other eating spectacles, including the Lord Mayor's feast at the Guildhall for Charles II and the French ambassador in October 1664. As gustatory critic, he is nationalistic; dining at the home of the Portuguese ambassador in November 1679, he finds the "Entertainment was exceeding Civile," but, except for a "good *olio*, the dishes were trifling, hash'd & Condited after their way, not at all fit for an English stomac, which is for solid meate." He is not always prejudiced. At the Spanish ambassador's, he is pleased the plentiful meal is "halfe after the Spanish, & halfe after the English way." Yet, at the house of Earl Berkeley dining with Indonesian ambassadors, he complains their food is cooked and served up by "fat slaves" at a separate table. Their naked torsos and legs strike him as "very uncouth, & lothsom." Still, their Muslim masters "eate their *pilaw* & other spoone-meate without spoones, taking up their potage in the hollow of <their> fingers, & very dextrously flung it into their mouthes, without spilling a drop."[72]

His *Aceteria* has "a fine *Receipt* for the *Dressing* of a *Sallet* with an Handful of Pot-Herbs"; what seems a "low and despicable" task is vital to cultural history since it "challenges a Part of *Natural History*." The greatest

---

71 Evelyn 1706, A2r, A3r, A4r, and A4v.
72 Evelyn 1959, 90, 836, 467, 673, 705, and 726–7.

emperors made salads: they "sometimes chang'd their *Scepters* for the *Spade*, and their *Purple* for the Gardiner's *Apron*." They took "their *Names* from the *Grain* and *Pulse* they sow'd, as the Marks and Characters of the highest Honor." Evelyn honours salads to recall the world to its "Pristine *Diet*," which was "much more *wholsome* and *temperate*" than what is "now in Fashion." Informing *Acetaria* with horticulture, even as he demeans himself "as an inferior Member of the *Royal Society*," he presents the "Dressing" of salads as a "clean, innocent, sweet" activity. While epics depict heroes as butcherly meat eaters, he insists primitive times were purer and more peaceable because of the consumption of greens and vegetables. Heroes are described "chining out the slaughter'd Ox, dressing the meat, and [doing] the Offices of both *Cook* and *Butcher*, (for so *Homer* represents *Achilles* himself, and the rest of those Illustrious *Greeks*)," but the "*Sallet-Dresser*" embodies the "best and brightest Age" of a world – one that knew not "the Shambles Filth and *Nidor*, Blood and Cruelty."[73] In cookbook history, Evelyn's *Acetaria* is an encyclopedic work that incorporates literary and antiquarian interests into the natural history of plants.

Sharing Evelyn's admiration for Hindu rules about eating plants and animals, Thomas Tryon (1634–1703) spurned traditional vegetarianism in his scorn for cuisine and professional cooks and in his commitment to mystical analogies between bodily and spiritual realities.[74] Apprenticed in 1652 to an Anabaptist hatter at Bridewell-Dock near Fleet Street, he held that divine principles govern creation, this causing him to study "Physick" and the works of Jakob Böhme (1575–1624) and to abandon the Baptists: "the Voice of Wisdom" made him shun "all intemperance" and "any kind of flesh or fish." Water was his only drink, bread and fruit his only food. The voice later granted him butter and cheese. At age forty-eight he became an author, in eighteen years writing nineteen titles that treat health regimen and housewifery; brewing, farriery, and cookery; education and manners; business and budgeting. His godly readers were to avoid everything made from the violent death of "our fellow creatures" and to rest content with the wholesome "Delicacy of Vegetables."[75] In *A Dialogue between an East-Indian Brackmanny*,

---

73 Evelyn 1706, A4v, [A5v], [A6r], and 119–20.
74 Stuart 2007, 82–8.
75 Tryon 1691b, 246–7. To Tryon, Pythagoras founded Hindu vegetarianism (Stuart 2007, 69).

or Heathen-Philosopher, and a French-Gentleman, Concerning the Present Affairs in Europe, which appeared in 1683, the "Brackmanny" is Tryon's "alter ego."[76] This "bannian" is a member of the Hindu merchant caste that upholds pacifism, liberty of conscience, and anti-conformist thinking. He assails Eurocentrism, especially France's imposition of Catholicism on Protestants. To him, the only valid suppression is self-suppression. While the Frenchman links warfare to "Empire," "Glory," and "Religious points," the Hindu affirms that "Practice is the Life of any Religion" and denies the heroism of Caesar and Alexander, this forcing the Frenchman to admit that French heroes are gluttonous drunkards. The Hindu then declares that:

We all drink Water; and the fragrant Herbs, wholsome Seeds, Fruits and Grains, suffice us abundantly for Food: Our Stomachs are clean, our Appetites sharp, so that we taste the inward Virtue of each thing, and sing Songs of Praise to the Creator.[77]

Tryon's *Health's Grand Preservative* (1682), reprinted as *The Way to Health* (1683), in denouncing improper mixing of foods, stipulates proper compounding. It argues that increasing the number of ingredients in a dish does not create better nourishment: foodstuffs, being of contrary natures, may produce harmful concoctions. Wise men through the ages have recommended "*Simple* Meats and Drinks," but the English are gluttons because of their mixed foods. Their gluttony is made worse by "*Fruits* and *Spices, Liquors*, &c. that are brought from other Countries, and the remote Regions of the World, which serve to gratifie *wanton* and *liquorish* Pallats, and promote *Gluttony* and *Excess*." Tryon complains that ten ingredients are often mixed in cakes fed to children: "*Flour, Butter, Eggs, Milk, Fruit, Spice, Sugar, Sack, Rose-Water* and *Sweet-Meats*, as *Citrons*, or the like." In this mixture, each ingredient "suffers Violence" and loses its "predominant Quality." But two ingredients yield healthy nourishment: "*Bread* and *Butter, Bread* and *Eggs, Bread* and *Fruit, Bread* and *Sack*, or other *Wine*, is very good Food, and a man may use any of them a long time without nauseating Nature." An exclusive culinary nationalism appears in his following statement:

---

76 Stuart 2007, 66.
77 Tryon 1691a, 2, 4, and 8.

It is no ways proper to mix *Fruits* that grow in hot Climates, as Raisins, Currants and Sugar, with Flesh and Fish, as is done frequently in Pies, Sauces, and other sorts of food; for the same disagreeing in their radixes, generally prove of ill Consequence to health, and nothing is so good, so pleasant, and so wholsom to be boyled and eaten with Fish, as our own Country Herbs and Roots.

For Tryon, unsafe eating comes from mixing pre-cooked and uncooked ingredients, as in bread puddings, reheating of broths and potages, and combining several sorts of flesh and fish in one meal. He opposes preparing different foods in the same vessel. His culinary asceticism is illustrated in his opposition to pies since they contain from ten to twenty ingredients: such sumptuous food is more dangerous than drunken debauchery.[78] His recommendations include methods for preparing fish; he prefers lidless boiling and roasting to baking or stewing, discounting frying. He promotes whole wheat bread that does not have the bran removed in the milling process. Less persuasively, he finds dried peas and beans healthier than green ones if boiled in "*River-Water*" over a quick fire with the pot open to the air. He views raw herbs as a "sublime kind of Food" preferable to boiled ones; salads are best made from spinach, parsley, sorrel, sage, pepper-grass with a small quantity of penny-royal and mint. Since the "mixing of *East* and *West-Indian* and *Spanish* Fruits, with our Food and Drinks, have encreased Diseases" in recent years, he objects to nutmegs, cloves, mace, cinnamon, pepper, and ginger as extremely hot and dry. If recommended by physicians and merchants, such foreign spices should not be bought by farmers' wives with their eggs, butter, cheese, and wheat.[79] Writing of "Flesh-Broths," he contends that those made of "Herbs, Fruits, and Grains" are superior since the "Fat, Blood, Gravy, or Juices of all Beasts are exceedingly crude, full of gross matter and dull, heavy, purblind Spirits, with contaminated dolorous Species." Water imbibes the gross juices, the broth being "endued with all the malignant qualitys." The neck and head are the worst part of animals for uncleanliness yet these parts are commonly used in broths. Flesh potages are unhealthy, especially for the sick. But safe ones are made of "Grains, Seeds, Fruits and Herbs, which are all noble and fragrant, *(viz.)* Water-gruel, Rice, Conju, Wheat,

78 Tryon 1691c, 170, 172–3, and 180.
79 Tryon 1691c, 147, 152–3, 162, and 166.

Chocolate, and various sorts of Caudles, made of Wine, Ale, Beer, Cyder, Oatmeal and Sugar; likewise divers Spoon-meats, made of Milk and Water, and such as these may have Butter mixed with them, *(viz.)* Gruels and Paps, which is many degrees finer than the Fat of Flesh." Tryon's vegetarianism regulates meal times: labourers – merchants, citizens, and farm workers – should eat only twice a day, breakfasting about 8:00 a.m. and dining about 3:00 or 4:00 p.m., this time gap enabling complete digestion and obviating gluttony.[80]

COOKBOOKS, HAUTE CUISINE, AND MONARCHY

To Evelyn's contemporaries, Louis XIV's eating rituals were distasteful. After the Sun King ascended the throne in 1661, poets revered him, feasts at court presenting him as Apollo and impressing hundreds of guests with glorifying imagery: the regal hospitality proved subjects did not share the king's divinity, denied courtiers their traditions, and obliged them to embody new standards of deportment and speech as they ate. Versailles was modelled on the Sun Palace in Ovid's *Metamorphoses* (8 AD). After the court moved there in 1682, the king became Louis le Grand, imperialism replacing myth, especially after the Revocation of the Edict of Nantes in 1685. As absolute administrator, Louis had himself depicted in operas as instructor to the gods. The Revocation led to a diaspora of two hundred thousand Protestants with the conversion of many faced by abduction, torture, and pillage. Englishmen related this persecution to culinary history.[81]

Witnessing this imperialism, François Pierre de La Varenne (1618–1678) published *Le Cuisinier français* in 1651. Thirty editions appeared in seventy-five years. It was translated as *The French Cook*, London versions published in 1653, 1654, and 1673. La Varenne was chef in the kitchens of the Marquis d'Uxelles, governor of Chalon-sur-Saône, and in the field, the Marquis a soldier as well as leading courtier. La Varenne recorded culinary changes in the previous one hundred and fifty years, notably in Italy. His recipes altered gustatory taste by favouring herbs over spices and displacing *olla podrida*. Against other medieval dishes

---

80 Tryon 1701, 89–91 and 179–80.
81 See Jean-Marie Apostolidès, "From Roi Soleil to Louis le Grand" in Hollier, 1989, 314–20.

liked in England, he preferred light sauces and treated cuts of meat distinctly, roasting finer ones and putting lesser ones in slower-cooked ragouts. He used almonds, mushrooms, and truffles in liaisons. His cookbook is structured as much by the church calendar's feast and fast days as by kinds of foodstuffs and modes of cooking. While potages dominate it, they do not reflect Louis's taste for spicy olios. His publisher did not view La Varenne as progressive: his book is said to teach "how to correct the vitious qualities of meats by contrary and severall seasonings" and to offer "solid nourishment, well dressed, & conformable" to "appetites, which are in many the rule of their life, and of their looking well." Sound cuisine renders medicine unnecessary since "it is sweeter by farre to make according to one's abilitie an honest and reasonable expence in sauces, and other delicacies of meats, to cause life and health to subsist, [than] to spend vast summes of money in drugs, medicinall herbs, potions, and other troublesome remedies for the recovery of health." La Varenne embodies France's superiority to "all other nations in the world in point of civilitie, courtesie, and comelinesse in every kind of conversation," including its "comely and dainty fashion of feeding." Paris, "the Metropolitan head City, and the seat of our Kings" sets the standard for "all other provinces" in France.[82]

Culinary appropriation and cultural exchange appear in how La Varenne's *Le Pâtissier français* (1653) was treated in England. *The Perfect Cook* (1656) by a Monsieur Marnette is an unacknowledged translation with English recipes interspersed. The translator's stance is curious. Dedicating his book to the wives of London's mayor and sheriffs, he says he was born of French parents in the city and flatters women by dispraising his subject: "every Matron and young damsel are so well vers'd in the Pastry Art" that they "out-vie the best Forreign pastry Cooks in all the World." If his treatise contains "nothing save Out-landish Cates and Junkets," it will gratify his "Mother City" since Londoners will find "divertisements" in studying the "Forreign Cates and Delicacies, happily never as yet tasted within her walls." Seeing patrons as "Political Parents," he lauds the "Honourable places of trust so deservingly conferred" on them: "supporters of this flourishing Cities admirable Government," they will be renowned to "all eternity." Marnette's obsequiousness is broadcast after Cromwell's Protectorate had expelled the English court.

---

82 La Varenne 1654, [A5v], A8r, and [A8v].

While Marnette assigns French court culture to the City of London, he retains La Varenne's address to readers which opposes the secretive, exclusive, monopolistic conduct of Parisian pastry cooks.[83]

The readership May addressed in *The Accomplisht Cook* (1660) differed from that of Marnette. A prefatory poem by James Parry praises May and attacks Marnette. May writes for small and large budgets so that a wide audience may treat "Kindred, Friends, Allies and Acquaintance" to a "handsome and relishing entertainment in all seasons of the year." His patrons were Catholic aristocrats whom he served before the Civil War in the "Golden Days of Peace and Hospitality" when they entertained and nurtured the wider community. The poem praises May as a native cook who upholds courtly traditions going back to Edward III (1312–1377). May's father cooked for the Dormers of Ascott Park in Buckingham, Jane Dormer formerly a maid of honour to Queen Mary I. On entering their service, May was sent to France to learn cookery in the household of Achille de Harlay, president of the Parlement of Paris. Five years there saw him studying Italian and Spanish cookbooks as well as using his French to read manuscript and printed recipes and to observe kitchen practices. He returned to Ascot Park, after cooking for the Grocer's Company and the Star Chamber. *The Accomplisht Cook* records the names of Catholic nobles for whom he cooked up to the Civil War. When it began, he was serving Elizabeth, Countess of Kent, of Wrest Park in Bedfordshire. She was connected to the Dormers. Her cookbook, *A True Gentleman's Delight* (1653), was one of May's sources. The preface to the second edition of *The Accomplisht Cook*, which reached a fifth edition in 1685, recognizes La Varenne's culinary changes while celebrating hospitality of the past. May organized spectacular feasts because he despised monopolistic cooking guilds. Scorning English preference for French cooking – "Epigram Dishes, smoakt rather than drest" – he thought only aristocratic patronage could endow eating with social cohesion.[84]

The confluence of the haute cuisine of France and the plain style of English roasts, pies, and puddings is evident in such popular cookbooks as *Le Cuisinier royal et bourgeois* by François Massialot (1660–1733). He was chef de cuisine to aristocrats and members of Louis XIV's family.

---

83 Marnette 1656, A3r–A5r. *Le Patissier françois* was published at Paris by J. Gaillard in 1653.

84 May 1678, A3r, A4r, [A4v], [A5r], and [A8v].

Like May, Massialot wrote for chefs. His book was published anonymously in 1691, his name not on the title page until the 1712 edition. The English translation, *The Court and Country Cook*, appeared in London in 1702. Depicting the structure of court meals, it was the first cookbook to be organized alphabetically as an encyclopedia with cross-references and a detailed index. Massialot's famous recipes include chicken with green olives and herbs, ragout of salmon head with white wine, verjuice, capers, and mushrooms, and soufflé fritters flavoured with orange-flower water served hot and sprinkled with sugar. His English publisher is confident that Massialot attests to the culture that "may only be said to Preside in *Europe*, where the best Ways of Seasoning and Dressing all sorts of Provisions, which that Continent affords are well known; and where Justice is done, at the same time, to the wonderful Productions, caus'd by the happy Situation of other Climates." Calling French and English cookery the highest European achievement, the publisher insists that, if Massialot's dishes have been served at "the Court of France, or in the Palaces of Princes, and in the Houses of Persons of great Quality," they are easily adapted by all save "the meaner sort of Country-People."[85]

The influence of French on English cuisine was ubiquitous despite naysayers. Vincent La Chapelle's *The Modern Cook*, a three-volume tome, came out in England before France, a second English edition appearing in 1736. La Chapelle drew on Massialot and the grand court style. Proposing a lighter, more intimate style and emphasizing artful rather than professional cooking yet requiring sauces for everything, Menon published *Les Soupers de la Cour* in 1755, translated as *The Professed Cook* (1769). More influential was his *La Cuisinière bourgeoise* (1746). This was the first French cookbook to address female cooks and readers. Although the translation, *The French Family Cook: Being a Complete System of French Cookery* (1793), did not appear until after the French Revolution, it was early cited by English cookbooks since it adapted recipes to middle-class households, as did *A Complete System of Cookery* (1759) by William Verrall (1715–1761), which presents the recipes of Monsieur de St Clouet, chef to the Duke of Newcastle, under whom Verrall worked in the 1730s and 1740s. A remarkable feature of Verrall's book is its

---

85 Massialot 1701, [A2v–A3v].

preface, which mocks his clients' ignorance of culinary hygiene, cooking equipment, and modern French cuisine.

Growing aristocratic power in the seventeenth and eighteenth centuries gave court cookery a long history in England, as shown by the career of Patrick Lamb (1650–1708), a chef famed for *grosses entrées, olios, bisques,* and *terrines* – dishes of several meats with savoury, broth-based sauces. In 1661 at age eleven, he entered the pastry department of the royal household. The following year he became "youngest child of the pastry" and then "a child of the queen consort's kitchen," a post in which he received board wages and collected fees. In 1677 he was appointed master cook to the queen consort, becoming "sergeant of his majesty's pastry in ordinary" that November. In February 1683, he moved up to be master cook to Charles II, retaining this post under James II, William and Mary, and Anne until his death in 1708. As such, he held contracts for the pastry and kitchen departments, supplying flour, eggs, and condiments. He inherited his father's warrants in purveying wine, spirits, and tobacco. High points of his career were ceremonial meals he prepared for the visit to Westminster of the Venetian ambassadors in December 1685 and for the coronation feasts of James II in 1685, William and Mary in 1689, and Anne in 1702. His *Royal Cookery; or, the Compleat Court-Cook* appeared posthumously in 1710, being reprinted in 1716, 1726, and 1731. Lamb's "*chief Aim*" in recipes "*was to represent the* Grandeur *of the* English *Court and Nation.*" His "*publick* Regales" for princes, peers and ambassadors were debts to "*Custom and Decency*" and to Great Britain's "*frank and hospitable Genius.*" He presents thirty-five plates of table settings, including dinners for Queen Anne in 1704 and 1705 and for King William in 1700. The plates indicate the visual and spatial value of table design and of the hierarchy and symmetry of dishes.[86]

NATIVE HOSPITALITY: THE BEDFORDS AT WOBURN ABBEY

If May lamented the decline of English hospitality, new standards of estate management revived it, as when William Russell (1613–1700),

---

86 Lamb 1710, A4. The plates and their placement in Lamb's text are listed on [A8r–A8v].

the fifth Earl of Bedford, spent money on food carefully yet lavishly. Having made his Grand Tour in 1632–34, he inherited in 1641 the dilapidated Woburn Abbey, along with Bedford House (a London mansion), Covent Garden, an estate in the Cambridge fens, and property in and near Tavistock, Devon. A Parliamentary General, he surrendered this post in 1642, the chattels of Bedford House seized as a penalty. Since managing his estate mattered more than politics, he had the architect Inigo Jones (1573–1652) build on Italian principles a ninety-room mansion on the site of the old abbey. Educated as a Puritan, he inclined to the monarchy. Thrice in the Civil War Charles II stayed at Woburn. Yet the Earl lived there quietly, enjoying his large family and becoming a country gentleman. Sound management saw him pay off family debts. When the piazza at Covent Garden became fashionable in the 1640s and 1650s, he garnered high rents from modish residents. He rode in the cavalcade that oversaw Charles II's return to London and, after attending the feast at the Middle Temple, two days later he attended the Coronation in Westminster Hall on 23 April 1661, later securing pardon for his parliamentary sympathies. In 1671, he acquired from the Crown the right to open a fruit and vegetable market in Covent Garden. Like Digby, he had his portrait done by Anthony van Dyke (1599–1641), the painter who dignified the Restoration court. Russell was made Knight of the Garter in 1672, his service to the nation leading him to become the first Duke of Bedford in 1694. If national responsibilities obliged him to stay often at Bedford House, he preferred making Woburn a locus of civic well-being that protected his relatives, servants, and tenants. Drawing resources from his properties, he made Woburn the centre of an economic and social network, as records of its food consumption indicate.

Woburn's accounts record the purchase of many foodstuffs. Mutton, pork, veal, calves' heads, sheep's feet, neat's tongue, tripe, capons, pullets, pigeons, lobsters, and flounders were bought at local markets. Its ponds were stocked with pike and perch brought in tanks from Thorney, the Cambridge estate. Russell supported tenants by buying their poultry and dairy items. He had barrels of oysters sent from Colchester, an overland journey of four days. Besides making bulk purchases of nutmeg and cloves from London grocers, he got dried and candied fruits from confectioners in Paris and London. To improve his orchards and kitchen gardens, he ordered plant stock and seeds from London nurseries. He cultivated pears, plums, and cherries along with peaches, nectarines, and apricots. He imported Westphalia hams. He bought six or seven fat bullocks from June to October so meat could be salted for winter eating. Thorney yielded hundreds of delicately fleshed birds, such as ruffs, reeves, quails, knots, dotterels, and swans. That estate's improvements supplied corn, oats, hemp, and cole seed (the latter introduced by Flemings who used colza oil for cooking). On visiting his married daughter who lived near Cambridge, he held feasts at the Red Lion Inn there. Here is a transcription of the bill of fare for one held on 15 October 1689. *First course*: a large pike with all sorts of fish about it; a surloin of beef; a pasty; a shoulder, neck, and breast of mutton; a couple of geese; a dish of capons and sausages; a ham and eight chickens and cauliflowers; a dish of collared pig; a "frigize" of rabbits and chickens; salading; a dish of mince pies. *Second course*: two dishes of wild fowl; a brace of pheasants; a brace of curlews and partridge; a dish of fat chickens and pigeons; a stand of all sorts of pickle and collared eels; a large jowl of sturgeon with a rand about it; a dish of all sorts of tarts with ladies' tarts about them; a dish of fruit; lemons and double refined sugar; oil and vinegar. *Supper*: a shoulder of mutton; gherkins and capers; a dish of wild fowl. Likely Russell provided the ingredients and staff to prepare this amazing feast. Its diversity, especially the range of fish, seafood, and birds, is matched by the bill at the Red Lion he hosted next day. *First course*: a brace of carp stewed with perches ranged about them; a chine of mutton and a large chine of veal; a pasty; a dish of tongues, udders, and marrow bones, with cauliflowers and spinach; a couple of geese; a hash of calf's head with sweetbreads; a dish of turkeys; a dish of collared pig; a dish of stewed oysters; a couple of pullets with oysters; a grand salad. *Second course*: two dishes of wild fowl; a jowl of sturgeon; a dish of fat chickens and rabbits; a stand of pickles with oysters, anchovies, and tongue; a dish of snipes and larks; a large Westphalia ham with tongues; a dish of tarts; a dish of partridges; a dish of whipped sillabubs; a "solamaguundy"; a dish of fruit; lemons and double reined sugar; oil and vinegar.[87] Note the combination of imported, wild, and farmed produce.

---

87 Thomson 1937, 126-47, 148–62, and 218–20. Salmagundi is a salad, dating from early seventeenth-century England. It might include chopped cooked meats, anchovies, eggs, onions, fruit, nuts, and flowers dressed with oil, vinegar, and spices and arranged on lettuce leaves. A rand is a long slice of sturgeon flesh (OED 1970, V3:137, 2b).

DISSENTING ASCETICS AND ANGLICAN HOSTS: PARADOXICAL EATING

The author of *The Spiritual Quixote* (1773), Richard Graves (1715–1804), embeds cookbook features into his picaresque novel, treating cuisine as a comic and satirical resource. One such feature are bills of fare listing seasonal foods to help housekeepers manage the annual cycle yielded by hunting and fishing and by farm, garden, and market produce. The following periphrastic setting in Graves's novel acknowledges this temporal and systematic culinary planning:

Buttered toast for breakfast now became unseasonable, and gave way to sage and bread and butter. Lamb and sallad ceased to be a Sunday's dinner, or part of the second course, and was an obvious dish at every table. The parson of F–field no longer threw his oyster-shell into the street, ambitiously luxurious! But supped in his garden upon codlins and cream, or a bit of soft cheese and a cucumber. In other words, the spring was far advanced.[88]

In winter and early spring, parsons consume buttered toast for breakfast, Sunday dinners consisting of lamb and salad – things scarce then – and their suppers of barrelled oysters. Comfortable outdoors later in the year, they eat sage, bread and butter with new apples and fresh cream or soft cheese and cucumber for supper. Anglican clerics, implies Graves, have gardens that yield early fruit and allow them to eat well and fashionably.[89] Table designs inspired by French modes were another feature of cookbooks, bills of fare for monthly dinners and suppers stipulating the range of dishes in each course along with settings and sizes of plates, some remaining on the table or sideboard throughout the meal. In this context and the tradition of Cervantes and Fielding, Graves builds a recipe into a mock-heroic battle when Mrs Tantrum, the landlady of a second-rate inn at Tetbury, whose appearance is as coarse as "Pontius Pilate's Cook-maid," throws a dish at Geoffry Wildgoose, the zealous hero, after he berates her for abusing her daughter-in-law for lechery.

---

88 Graves 1967, 18.

89 Codlins could be eaten out of season. Raffald has recipes for "pickled codlins" and "codlin pudding" (1769, 325 and 153). Her recipe for roast pig in imitation of lamb and served with salad clarifies the notion of special clerical Sunday dinners (1769, 99).

The bad-tempered landlady retaliates, Graves's comic timing facetiously suspending the action with this recipe:

There is a certain farinaceous composition, which, from its being frequently used by our ancestors as an *extempore* supplement to a scanty dinner, has obtained the appellation of an *hasty pudding*. It is composed of flour and milk boiled together; and, being spread into a round shallow dish, and interspersed with dabs of butter, and brown sugar fortuitously strewed over it, give one no bad idea of a map of the sun, spotted about according to the modern hypothesis.

With a "dish of this wholesome food, smoking hot ... in one hand, and a plate of bacon and eggs in the other," the furious Tantrum discharges "the hasty pudding full in Wildgoose's face," the "oiled butter and melted sugar" running down and spoiling his plush-waistcoat. She throws the other dish at Jerry Tugwell, Wildgoose's servant, "one of the poached eggs bursting in his face." Their righteous proselytizing thus frustrated, the two men must console themselves with a loaf, cheese, and tankard of ale for the loss of the savoury food that had so tantalized them.[90]

Graves derives comic energy from how Tugwell and Wildgoose eat on the road. A member of the lower classes, Tugwell is self-effacing: all he expects from inns is "a bit of soft cheese and a radish." Yet he is occasionally surprised; at a public house in Cardiff when he seeks "a cup of good ale and a slice of toasted cheese" for breakfast, he has the good fortune to enjoy "a rasher of bacon." He jumps at a "hearty invitation to a fillet of veal ... roasting at the fire" from a landlord at Bath. In his humility, he often fares better than his master. When the landlord of an inn at Tewksbury asserts that his bill of fare contains a "fine leg of veal, an excellent gammon of bacon, and a couple of charming fowls roasted," Wildgoose finds the veal is "only the knuckle, cut pretty close" and the gammon is "the most bony part of the fore-gammon." He relishes neither the "boiled veal" nor discoloured bacon that is "thoroughly tinged with smoak." The fowls "were full-grown, nicely roasted and frothed up, and looked tempting enough" but the "muscles of the leg were so hard, that no human jaw could possibly make any impression

---

90 Graves 1967, 120–1. Recipes for hasty pudding appear in Smith 1728, 86–7, and *The Lady's Companion* 1740, 473. For Johnson's rhapsody on puddings, see Boswell's account (1965, 346–7).

upon them"; they had been "cock-fighting the day before." After "sucking the drumstick, and licking up his parsley and butter," he eats only "a good slice of Gloucestershire cheese and a crust of bread." But Tugwell dines well in the kitchen on a "pan-full of cow-heel fryed with onions." His unpretentious taste is often gratified. When reapers learn he only wants small beer with a crust of bread and piece of cheese, a young farmer cuts "him off a good slice of some boiled beef, and a piece of plumb-pudding" which Tugwell asks Wildgoose to share. The latter's missionary zeal resisting fellowship and co-dependency, the two usually talk at cross-purposes until Tugwell sensibly clarifies things. Lamenting his failure to convert workers in Birmingham, Wildgoose thinks Tugwell gluttonous since his eyes stare at a plum pudding in a shop window that is "smoking hot, just out of the oven." But Tugwell's provocative question, "cannot a man have true Faith, that loves plumb-pudding?" defies Wildgoose's asceticism.[91]

His insistence on salvation by faith evades Tugwell's question, his belief in "the one thing necessary" further roused by an antiquarian whose historical sense is outraged by the modish building of gothic ruins on estates. When Wildgoose spurns the study of ancient coins and medals, the antiquarian, in the style of Addison, argues for gratifying "the imagination or fancy" as well as "the passions and appetites." He supposes that were he to dispute with a Methodist about "luxury in food, or about the necessity of fasting and mortification," he would not have to prove that everything we eat be "absolutely *necessary* to support life." But Wildgoose protests that he pays no heed to "legal observances of fasting or distinction of meats." Rejecting "mortified pretensions," the antiquarian insists that "bread and cheese" is "an hearty, wholesome food" and the "staff of life" while "eating cheese-cake and custard" is "*agreeable*." To him, some arts are necessary for society's subsistence while others are instrumental to the "recreation of mankind." To Wildgoose, only one thing matters: "the knowledge of our fallen state, and of our redemption, as revealed in the Bible." Above higher criticism, he needs "no commentaries, nor any assistance, to understand the Scriptures." A member of the invisible church of believers, he spurns the established church.[92]

---

91 Graves 1967, 111, 265–6, 180, 320–1, 417, and 335.
92 Ibid., 116–18.

His oratory is grossly anecdotal when he preaches to the poor and hungry in food images. After damning those who eat "Welsh-rabbit," he tells of a Catholic who shoots partridges with a Protestant neighbour on a fast day. Driven by a storm to an inn, all they can eat is bacon and eggs. The Catholic wanting only eggs is tempted by the Protestant to order bacon, the latter saying that, not being flesh, it is no more than a red herring, namely, fish. After a clap of thunder, the Catholic sets the bacon aside, thinking his sin has been detected. Upon deriding the Catholic's superstition, Wildgoose dramatizes his own sins. At Oxford, he says, he fasted seven times a day, making himself a skeleton and taking the sacrament every month. But his reliance on liturgical forms lacked saving faith. As his sermon unfolds in imitation of George Whitfield (1714–1770), it incites disorder when scoffers are driven away by faithful "Lambs" with "stones and dirt." The scene becomes more ludicrous when a collier who buys a black pudding at the tabernacle door enters. Having gnawed one end, he hides the rest in his jacket. As Wildgoose rails against "some darling vice; some dark and secret sin, or perhaps some *black* and *bloody* design" in his congregation's bosoms, the collier thinks the black pudding is detected. Wildgoose harangues about vice hidden in a man's bosom "like a delicious morsel" he "flatters himself that no one can perceive." The collier wriggling in anguish, Wildgoose intensifies his rhetoric: "let us not harbour ... this black and poisonous serpent in our breasts; which will sting us to the very soul ... let us drag the accursed thing from our bosom," urging "Out with it!" Sure he has been exposed, the collier blurts out the "devil take the hog's-pudding!," throwing it into the crowd and fleeing "from this imaginary persecution." The bathos is stressed when the real Whitfield and Wildgoose leave "to partake of a comfortable supper."[93]

To promote a middle way in eating and faith, Graves replaces dissent with clerical models, as with Mr Rivers, a college friend of Wildgoose and surrogate for the author.[94] While *The Whole Duty of Man* (1658) told Rivers "the most temperate meal" is "highly sinful" and, while his aunt held that the only end of eating is "to preserve life," he found that satisfying hunger with bread and cheese was "necessarily attended with pleasure." He learns from the "agreeable mixture of mortification and

---

93 Ibid., 249 and 251.
94 See Tracy's Introduction to *The Spiritual Quixote* (1967, xx).

indulgence" in his cousin, Gregory Griskin, a rural clergyman, who is "as hearty at his meals, as at his devotions."[95] Griskin's house moves comfortably "from collects to collations, and from litanies and absolutions to hot rolls in the morning, to tythe-pigs and fat geese at noon, and to rasberries and cream and apple-custards at night." Persuaded by Griskin's "practical religion" of the compatibility of liturgical observance and good eating, Rivers diverts Wildgoose from converting his wife to belief in faith over good works by inducing him to walk out in the garden to catch fish for dinner. On visiting Griskin's rectory, Wildgoose finds a modern parsonage not laid out fashionably "with sunburnt lawns and barren shrubs"; its grounds "contribute to the comfort and convenience of this life," being "inclosed with fruit-walls, filberd-hedges, and codlin trees; with a good pigeon-house, poultry-yard, and fish-ponds." Like Woodforde, Griskin avoids putting parishioners under duress for payment of tithes but treats them kindly by keeping a "plentiful table" at which they dine by turns on Sundays in the parlour, the oldest and poorest eating in the kitchen.[96]

That a Griskin is edible pork shows that Graves does not present clergymen solemnly. Indeed, they are treated satirically as well as facetiously. Mr Powell, the authoritarian vicar of the Cotswolds village where Wildgoose grows up, as a justice of the peace who adjudicates window tax, denies the difference between a window and the glass door by which Wildgoose improves access to his garden. By denying Wildgoose's distinction on the analogy that there is no difference between "a pudding and a dumplin," the vicar goads his parishioner towards Methodism and ignores that cookbooks differentiated puddings from dumplings.[97] The final conversation between Pottle, a self-interested clergyman, and Wildgoose occurs after they meet in the Red Lyon Inn, its sign "a Shoulder of Mutton." Claiming not to frequent the inn, Pottle invites

---

95 A griskin is the lean part of the loin of a bacon pig or pork bones with little flesh on them. Griskin the vicar is little and fat. Graves applies the phrase "the turning of a pork griskin" to the landlord of an inn (1967, 139). According to Glasse, "The best Way to dress Pork Griskins is to roast them, baste them with a little Butter and Crumbs of Bread, Sage, and a little Pepper and salt. Few eat any Thing with these but Mustard" (1747, 4).

96 Graves 1967, 225–6 and 349–50.

97 Ibid., 16. Besides offering twenty-four recipes for puddings, Raffald provides recipes for "Damson and Apple Dumplins" (1769, 158). Glasse has more than fifty recipes for puddings and at least six for dumplings.

Wildgoose to his parsonage where they dine on "a cold shoulder of mutton and cucumbers," with Tugwell relegated to the kitchen where he eats leftovers from the parlour. Having ranted against "Atheists and Sectaries" at the inn, at home Pottle belittles the country folk he serves, much to Wildgoose's disgust at such hypocrisy.[98]

He is predisposed to missionary work by books in his library consisting of "a miscellaneous collection of godly discourses, upon predestination, election, and reprobation." Graves decries them as "crude trash" suited to Wildgoose's "vitiated palate" since they contain "bitter invectives against the clergy." Not "cloyed" with "this crabbed food," his "appetite" grows by "indulgence." Culinary analogies degrade spiritual metaphors in the titles of seventeenth-century "sectaries" such as "the Marrow of Divinity, Crumbs of Comfort, and Honey-combs for the Elect, The Spiritual Eye-salves and Cordials for the Saints, and Shoves for heavy-ars'd Christians." Among these titles are ones by John Foxe (1516–1587) and Samuel Clarke (1675–1729) about reformation martyrs, one of whom, a Mr Carter of Norwich, is renowned for fasting yet called "a mighty lover of Norfolk-dumplins." Religious dissent is mocked by this humble food, recipes for which appear in many cookbooks.[99]

Cuisine shapes Graves's satire of Whitfield's gluttony and female disciples' self-sacrifice. Wildgoose seeks the preacher to advance the "primitive piety and the doctrines of the Reformation, by turning missionary," but, when Tugwell and he reach Bristol, they find him "dressed in a purple night-gown and velvet cap" seated in an elbow chair in a "handsome dining-room." Instead of a Bible or Prayer Book, he has "a good bason of chocolate, and a plate of muffins well-buttered, before him." Having breakfasted with prisoners in the local gaol "upon some tea and sea-biscuit" and dissatisfied with this crude, insubstantial food, he relishes the chocolate. He offers his visitors nothing, disappointing Tugwell whose hunger desires "a bit of his oven-cake, and a drop of his buttered ale, or whatever."[100] Whitfield's luxury distracts "the Saints of Bristol," his congregation including "two or three wealthy dowagers, and as many handsome wives," "pious ladies" who, thinking nothing too good for holy men, provide him and his followers "with chocolate and rolls for breakfast in the morning, biscuits and sack at noon, with

---

98 Graves 1967, 61–3.
99 Ibid., 19. For her recipe for "Norfolk Dumplings," see Glasse 1747, 112.
100 Graves 1967, 29, 229–30, and 233.

turbot, ducks, and marrow-puddings, for dinner, and roasted fowls or partridges for supper at night." Thus, Wildgoose passes "his time in no unpleasant manner" at Bristol. The women would have known *The Experienced English House-keeper* (1769) by Elizabeth Raffald (1733–1781), which shows how to hash a wild duck, boil a turkey, roast pheasants and partridges, and prepare marrow puddings.[101] Lower-class women are also self-sacrificing. Mrs Sarsenet of Gloucester sups on "radishes and some dry bread" since she spends so much treating "Spiritual Bargemen and pious Colliers" to "tea and coffee, and buttered rolls" at breakfast. To Tugwell, who knows that before converting she dined with her mother and sister "upon some good roast mutton and baked pudding," Mrs Sarsenet's asceticism is senseless; creed undermines her health. Formerly, she would have had "a bit of soft cheese, or butter" with the radishes. A down-to-earth Sancho, Tugwell, who "infinitely preferred the smoak and savoury smell of a greasy kitchen to the meagre neatness of Mrs. Sarsenet's parlour," rejoices in Mrs Whitfield's inn, The Bell at Gloucester, where he and Wildgoose find the hostess at supper "alone, upon a brace of partridges, with a large China *bason* of warm punch." Wildgoose eats her food because her brother "sanctified" her. Yet he proves hypocritical, for when the two set out on their journey and Tugwell, the menial cobbler, puts in his wallet "a good luncheon of brown bread, and some Gloucestershire cheese," Wildgoose, like the don, accuses his Sancho of being discontent with "the heavenly manna of meditation" and of lusting "after the garlic and flesh-pots of Egypt."[102] His asceticism stems from domestic frugality as much as principle, his mother breakfasting on sage tea not on "hyson or congo" – delicious green and black teas from China. Sacrificing pleasures to "future ease and happiness" and scorning "fashion," his mother, afraid the costly beverage will harm her health, takes sage tea for its medical efficacy.[103]

Social scenes challenge culinary pretensions because, like May, Graves laments the decline of hospitality among fashionable squires gulled by rural tenants and city shopkeepers. This type defines itself by consumerism, such as getting "a barrel of oysters" from London at Christmas. Mr Slicer, a retired solicitor and hypochondriacal farmer, is one such. Rural

---

[101] Raffald 1769, 65, 20, 55, and 154. On partridge recipes, see Raffald 1769, 119 and 120.
[102] Wildgoose is conflating Exod. 16:3 and Num. 11:4–6.
[103] Graves 1967, 237, 314, 320, 315, 42–3, and 47.

retirement so bores him that his appetite has palled; "even venison [has] lost its relish." When Wildgoose and Tugwell reach his house, they learn from Mrs Quick, his housekeeper, that, since the chimneys have not been swept because of her master's avarice, "a whole heap of soot has fallen down into the fish-kettle, and entirely spoiled the carps." She catches "the loin of veal upon the spit" before it is "covered with dust and ashes." Slicer's indifference to hygiene is aggravated by disregard for cooking times; his late arrival home means "the fowls are boiled to a rag; and the veal is roasted to powder; and there is not a drop of gravy left." Complaining that had she known he was bringing guests home she "would have made a custard-pudding," she offers to "beat up two or three eggs, and a spoon-full of cream, and a little orange flower-water, and make a little pudding, in the catching up of a sausepan." Despite her complaints, she produces a fine meal: "three fine pullets; an excellent Yorkshire ham; a loin of veal; and the custard-pudding" that she "tossed up, adorned with currant-jelly; a gooseberry-tart; with other ornamental expletives of the same kind." Unlike his housekeeper, Slicer understands little of health and diet, Graves presenting the "quack medicines" he takes "with a large bason of veal-broth" as nauseously ineffective. While Slicer promotes Spartan eating, he overloads his stomach. If he will "not touch a morsel of skin, or fat, nor eat any butter with his veal or his boiled fowl," he picks "the very bones of a pretty large pullet, with two good large *vertebræ*, and half the kidney of the loin of veal, not to mention a good quantity of supplemental pudding, goose-berry-tart, and apple-custard." A Scottish guest agrees about preserving health by "plain food" but his claim the English sap theirs by eating "mixtures" since "French Cooks have been in vogue" ignores Slicer's innate gluttony.[104]

Mr Graham, also a surrogate for Graves, scorns "the forms of life" of "paltry little Esquires" like Slicer. To atone Graham performs simple acts of hospitality. Opposing Wildgoose's quixotism and insistence on faith above good works, he will not "pretend to live upon roots and rock-water" since he "can feast upon mutton and potatoes, and a bread pudding." Displacement of hypocritical eating unfolds when Wildgoose visits the estate of Sir William Forester, a man of fine sociability who serves a "cold collation" in his "natural grotto." This consists of "a good

[104] Ibid., 56, 339–42, and 345.

quantity of cold ham and fowls, cold tongue, orange cheese-cakes, and other portable provisions of the best kinds." When he enters Sir William's dining room with its "constant table" and "side-board set out with some degree of splendour," he is served "hashed calve's head" by Lady Forester, the "savoury smell of this dish soon" expelling his "spiritual ideas." Eating this dish much featured in cookbooks, he fancies "himself in the land of promise; and, with a true patriarchal appetite, he feasted most devoutly."[105]

Biblical implications exposing Wildgoose clarify Graves's sense of gentility and cuisine. The exemplary figure is Mr Aldworth, "an opulent country gentleman, and a very worthy Magistrate," whose "way of living gave one the truest idea of that hospitality for which the English nation was formerly distinguished." Not recalling "the days of Queen Elizabeth, when even the Ladies breakfasted upon toast and metheglin, or cold beef," days "semi-barbarous and uncivilized," Graves is mindful of the hospitality of seventeenth-century gentry that lasted to "the Revolution, and continued in some measure in the days of Queen Anne and George the First." It cast aside the "refined luxury" of aristocrats who were "tantalized with a dozen French dishes (which no Frenchman, however, would ever taste), and stared at by as many French servants, dressed better than yourself or their own Master" and involved "being dragged out, the moment you have dined, to take a walk in the shrubbery, and wonder at his Lordship's *bad* taste, and then frightened away with the appearance of cards and wax candles." At Aldworth's, one finds "a ham and fowls, a piece of roast beef, or a pigeon-pye, and a bottle of port-wine, every day in the week; and, if you chose to spend the night at his house, a warm bed, and an hearty welcome." His "primitive merit" is evident in the second course when you eat "a leg and a wing of duckling, and a plate of green pease."[106]

Graves defends the Church of England by linking its efficacy to the golden mean of native cookery. Gastronomic codes in *The Spiritual Quixote* confirm how eighteenth-century fiction adopts culinary discourse. That Graves applies this discourse to humour and satire and to economic, political, and theological commentary reveals his ability to combine high seriousness and comedy. This combination is announced

---

105 Ibid., 137, 367, and 384–5. Raffald offers one of the finest recipes for hashed calve's head (1769, 73–4).
106 Graves 1967, 301–2.

in the mock dedication to Monsieur Pattypan, "Pastry-Cook to His most sacred Majesty George II." Inventing a French cook as patron, Graves names him after a piece of kitchen equipment. In *The English Housekeeper*, Raffald refers to pattypan as a small tin pan in which patties are baked and as the patties themselves. Identifying with his invention, Graves admires Pattypan's "*compositions*" – his recipes for diet bread (a bread for invalids or those under dietary regime), for wigs (buns or small cakes made of fine flour), and for puffs (kinds of light pastry and confectionary). If readers will find no book of confectionary by Pattypan, they will find recipes for wigs and puffs in Raffald, thereby realizing that cooking enhances the ecclesiastical commentary.[107] In Korsmeyer's words, Graves well knew that food is "formative of community, what makes it possible, what it presumes, what it accomplishes."[108] An Anglican apologist, he defends the middle way and civility against imported modes. *The Spiritual Quixote* equates Methodism and asceticism only to displace them, while also spurning the nexus of gentility and consumerism. To Graves, hospitality based on exclusive taste for scarce foodstuffs and French cuisine undermines ecclesiastical administration and social harmony. His depiction of meals that shun abstinence and luxury relates traditional dishes to genteel sociability and national identity. If he holds that bodily and mental tastes interact when gastronomy meets philanthropy, he connects those tastes for both instrumental and aesthetic reasons. Citing "taste" many times, he hardly questions its conventional senses. He grants that ingestion yields primary satisfaction by relieving hunger yet avoids the metaphorical transformation of gustatory taste encountered in Brillat-Savarin and other authors.

107 Ibid., 7.
108 Korsmeyer 1999, 187. On the "slapstick" with which novelists resisted Richardson's moralistic focus, see Hammond 1998, 263. If female readers will have been more familiar with cooking, Graves assigns concern for constructive aspects of food and eating to male characters.

5

Travel, Fashion, and Cultural Exchange

Travel literature had an immense impact on the eighteenth-century arts and sciences; belles lettres fell under its influence as never before, and prose fiction was characterized by a variety of journey plots and traveling protagonists.[1]

THE DIALECTIC OF TRAVELLING: IMPERIALISM AND NATIONALISM

Travelogues dominated the eighteenth-century book trade partly because travel shared with cuisine many cultural ramifications.[2] The genre earned praise and ridicule: recording explorers' adventures and provoking utopianism, it also roused arguments about Britons' educational goals. Occasionally, travelogues detail exotic foods and eating customs. *Travels, Or Observations Relating to Several Parts of Barbary and The Levant* (1738) by Thomas Shaw (1694–1751) is one example. The work of an Oxford fellow, clergyman, and member of the Royal Society who, open to Islam, studied African nomads and Turkish settlers, Shaw's *Travels* adopts anthropology from the Old and New Testaments. His preface, after describing the food of camels, reports that "*Camel's Dung*" is a "*Fuel*" vital to cooking for tourists whose desert crossing lasts two months during which they must carry "*Wheat-Flour, Biscuit, Honey, Oyl, Vinegar, Olives, Lentils, potted Flesh*" and "*Kitchen Furniture*" of a "*Wooden Bason or Copper Pot.*" His group ate "*potted Flesh, boyled with Rice; a Lentil*

---

1 Curley 1976, 7.

2 "Between 1660 and 1800 eight encyclopedic collections and forty-five smaller compilations appeared in England. Besides the major works, there were thousands of individual accounts and miscellanies of local tours, distant expeditions, and Continental travels. If we include publications from the Continent, the number of all European collections of voyages and travels would alone amount to well over a hundred voluminous productions in several editions and translations" (Curley 1976, 53).

Soup; or Unleavened Cakes, served up with Oyl or Honey." It was welcomed in Arab camps with "*Figs, Raisins, Dates or other dryed Fruit*" and "*a Kid, or a Goat; a Lamb, or a Sheep; half of which was immediately seethed ... and served up with* Cuscasowe; *the rest*" being "*usually made* Kab-ab, *and reserved for our Breakfast or Dinner the next Day.*" Shaw details religious calls to meals, eating on the ground, rolling food in palms and using fingers, not knives and spoons, at table. He gives scriptural analogies to Arabs' diet of bread, turnips, and fruit, to their "publick Ovens," and to transportation of "Grind-Stones" for the milling of grain by "*Bedoween* Women," noting their cakes of unleavened bread in "Ta-Jen." He enjoys the "savory" taste of "different Sorts of Fricasees, and of Roast, Boiled, and Forced-meats" and likes how "the richer Part of the Turks and Moors, mix up a variety of Dishes with Almonds, Dates, Sweet-Meats, Milk, Honey"; their feasts offered "more than two hundred Dishes, whereof forty at least were of different kinds."[3]

Shaw's interest in Islamic communal eating irritated Graves's Anglicanism to the extent that *The Spiritual Quixote* distorts North African gastronomy by exaggerating the exoticism of a feast served by the emperor of Morocco. In this travesty, the first course contains at the top of the table:

a dish of fish, consisting of a young whale boiled, and a few sturgeons and porpuses fryed round it. At the bottom, was the hind-quarter of an elephant. On one side, a brace of lions, fricasseed; on the other, the neck of a camel, made *kabab* ... The second course, a brace of ostriches roasted, at the upper end, with the ropes of a toast; at the lower end, a griffin; on one side, a dish of cranes and storks; on the other, a potted crocodile.

The only butcher's meat at the side-table is a "roasted buffalo." The account climaxes when Shaw is said to take "the short ribs of a lion" rather than "the *leg* or the *wing* of the griffin."[4] Graves's travesty matches commentaries that dispute the educational benefits of travel and claim it fosters decadence and immorality. Anticipating this criticism, the fourth book of *The Dunciad*, of which Pope was proud, presents an obsequious tutor who lauds his pupil's improvements on the Grand

3   Shaw 1738, iv–v and 296–7.
4   Graves 1967, 370–1 and 494n2.

Tour and views this "dauntless infant" as a "Rake" fit to take his place in the court of the "great Empress," Dullness. Before the continent's cultural sights, the pupil makes himself a spectacle: "Europe he saw, and Europe saw him too." Visiting "happy Convents, bosom'd deep in vines, / Where slumber Abbots, purple as their wines," he saunters through religious institutions, where he gathers "ev'ry Vice on Christian ground." The tour corrupts him; he surrenders his principles to become a bibulous, gluttonous whoremonger. Having "Intrigu'd with glory, and with spirit whor'd," he "Try'd all *hors-d'œuvres*, all *liqueurs* defin'd, / Judicious drank, and greatly-daring din'd." To crown the abuse of education, Pope has the tutor declare his pupil has lost "All Classic learning ... on Classic ground."[5]

Earlier, *Gulliver's Travels* (1726) mocked travel writing, Swift's rhetorical deployment of Gulliver's utopian literal-mindedness darting irony at British imperialism, partly through narrative distortions of eating and drinking. In the end, Gulliver stands aloof from writers who tell "strange improbable tales"; he has related "plain matter of fact in the simplest manner and style" since his "principal design was to inform, and not to amuse." Not having described "wonderful animals at sea and land," his "chief aim" was "to make men wiser and better, and to improve their minds by the bad as well as good example" in accounts "concerning foreign places." Having "perused several books of travels with great delight" in his youth, he knows from having "gone over most parts of the globe" that travellers make their "works pass the better upon the public" by foisting "the grossest falsities on the unwary reader." Able "to contradict many fabulous accounts from [his] own observation," he has "a great disgust against this part of reading, and some indignation to see the credulity of mankind so impudently abused." A "subject of England," he was expected to inform the Crown about lands he discovered so that conquests might ensue. But those lands would not suffer conquests like the victories of "Fernando Cortez over the naked Americans":

---

5 Citations to Book Four of *The Dunciad* are from Pope 1963, 781–83. Line references are as follows: 281, 284, 286, 294, 301–2, 312, 316–18, and 321. See Gay's fable #14, "The Monkey who had seen the World," which ends: "Thus the dull lad, too tall for school, / With travel finishes the fool, / Studious of ev'ry coxcomb's airs, / He drinks, games dresses, whores and swears, / O'erlooks with scorn all virtuous arts, / For vice is fitted to his parts" (Gay 1926, 246–7).

The Lilliputians, I think, are hardly worth the charge of a fleet and army to reduce them, and I question whether it might be prudent or safe to attempt the Brobdingnagians. Or whether an English army would be much at their ease with the Flying Island over their heads. The Houyhnhnms, indeed, appear not to be so well prepared for war, a science to which they are perfect strangers, and especially against missive weapons.

Far from invading the Houyhnhnms, Gulliver wishes they "were in a capacity or disposition to send a sufficient number of their inhabitants for civilizing Europe, by teaching us the first principles of honour, justice, truth, temperance, public spirit, fortitude, chastity, friendship, benevolence, and fidelity." Another anti-imperial passage says he would not "enlarge his Majesty's dominions" given his concern for "the distributive justice of princes" which he castigates as follows:

For instance, a crew of pirates are driven by a storm they know not whither, at length a boy discovers land from the topmast, they go on shore to rob and plunder, they see an harmless people, are entertained with kindness, they give the country a new name, they take formal possession of it for the king, they set up a rotten plank or a stone for a memorial, they murder two or three dozen of the natives, bring away a couple more by force for a sample, return home, and get their pardon. Here commences a new dominion acquired with a title by *divine right*. Ships are sent with the first opportunity, the natives driven out or destroyed, their princes tortured to discover their gold, a free license given to all acts of inhumanity and lust, the earth reeking with blood of its inhabitants: and this execrable crew of butchers employed in so pious an expedition, is a modern colony sent to convert and civilize an idolatrous and barbarous people.

Here the indignant persona attacks colonization, arguing that travelogues serve political propaganda and constitutional illusions.[6] Thus, Swift's anti-imperial satire relies on keeping readers off-balance and unable to identify steadily with Gulliver, who, far from writing plainly, is inconsistent in his calculations, ratios, and proportions. Swift basically discomfits his persona in eating and drinking scenes to question his physiological taste and the generalizations to which it prompts him. In

6 Swift 1960, 234–7.

Lilliput, he eats "the flesh of several animals, but could not distinguish them by their taste. There were shoulders, legs and loins shaped like those of mutton, and very well dressed, but smaller than the wings of a lark." That he eats "two or three at a mouthful" dulls his discrimination. Yet he writes that Lilliput's "Mutton yields to ours, but their Beef is excellent," also asserting that the twenty or thirty geese and turkeys he puts on his knife for one mouthful "exceed ours." When at a "draught" he drinks the "largest hogsheads" that barely contain "half a pint," he says Lilliput's wine tastes "like a small wine of Burgundy" but is "more delicious." Yet he does not detect the "sleeping potion in the hogsheads." Scales of ingestion render his gustatory pleasures and cross-cultural comparisons dubious. Being twelve times taller than Lilliputians, why are his "victuals" dressed by "three hundred cooks" who prepare "two dishes" each and why is he served by one hundred and twenty waiters? That he eats one hundred and fifty dishes at a meal is absurd. He lacks the self-reflexivity that reversed perspectives in the narrative demand. If he surprises Lilliputian servants on eating joints of meat as Englishmen eat the "leg of a lark," why does his stomach turn when the Queen in Brobdingnag crunches a lark's wing, swallows in a mouthful what twelve English farmers eat at a meal, and drinks a hogshead at a draft?[7]

The reversed scale of Gulliver among Brobdingnag's giants seems initially credible, but his desire to please them sees him comport himself as a toy, a baby, and an infant monkey. Under each aspect, he is discomfited by food. The first dish he tastes is served on a plate "of about four and twenty foot diameter," the farmer's wife mincing "a bit of meat" for him. Struggling to lift a two-gallon "small dram cup" to drink her health, he affectedly insists the "liquor tasted like a small cider, and was not unpleasant." Walking to his master on the tabletop, he stumbles "against a crust" and falls flat on his face. When he would impress lords and ladies of the court with the repartee of a page, the Queen's dwarf drops him into "a large silver bowl of cream" in which he all but drowns. That "malicious little cub," squeezing his legs together, wedges him into a "marrow-bone" up to his waist where "for some time" he makes "a very ridiculous figure." More uncomfortably, a monkey snatches Gulliver from his dollhouse and holds him "as a nurse does a child she is going to suckle." This "frolicsome animal" takes him "for a young one of his

---

7   Ibid., 19, 51, 19, 21, 51, and 85.

own species." Placing him "like a baby in one of his forepaws," the monkey feeds him "by cramming" into him "some victuals he had squeezed out of the bag on one side of his chaps." This episode, anticipating the fierce analogy of apes to humans in the fourth book, alerts readers to elements of dream and fantasy in Swift, elements that in the account of the king's kitchen invite us to note factual distortions in Gulliver's travelogue. The kitchen is a "noble building" about "six hundred feet high." Its oven is "not so wide by ten paces as the cupola of St Paul's." Gulliver will not detail its grate, its "prodigious pots and kettles," and "the joints of meat turning on the spits" to avoid being censured as a hyperbolic travel writer. But this disclaimer only heightens his hyperbolic presentation of number and scale.[8]

Swift exploits mathematics in the third book of *Gulliver's Travels* on mocking the eccentric influence of science and music on food preparation. Laputan meals conventionally offer three main dishes in two courses while turning Royal Society preoccupations into obsessions: the first course at the king's table offers "a shoulder of mutton cut into an equilateral triangle, a piece of beef into a rhomboides, and a pudding into a cycloid. The second course was two ducks, trussed up into the form of fiddles; sausages and puddings resembling flutes and oboes, and a breast of veal in the shape of a harp." Gulliver looks forward to meeting the immortal Struldbruggs, only to be disgusted that at ninety they lose teeth and hair and have "no distinction of taste, but eat and drink whatever they can get, without relish or appetite." Since their appearance proves "most mortifying," Gulliver's "keen appetite for perpetuity of life was much abated."[9]

He promotes the "hard fare" and "insipid diet" of Houyhnhym oats, such fare sufficing many Europeans. But his asceticism is inconstant and reactionary: he varies his diet by catching rabbits and boiling "wholesome herbs" or eating them as salads. He will not copy travellers by detailing meals he supposes of no interest to readers. Yet he explains the lack of salt in the horses' diet by claiming that "the frequent use of salt among us is an effect of luxury" that is but "a provocative to drink." His claim that no animal but man takes salt is incredible. Remarks on English food and drink to his Houyhnhym master lapse into a diatribe.

8 Ibid., 72–3, 87–8, and 98.
9 Ibid., 129 and 172–3.

In describing "costly meats," he enumerates "as many sorts" as come into his "head, with the various methods of dressing them." His critique further declares that ships visit "every part of the world, as well for liquors, as for sauces": "this whole globe of earth must be at least three times gone round" so that a high-class female yahoo may eat breakfast. The "greatest part of our necessary things," he argues, are sent abroad to import goods that "feed the luxury and intemperance of males, and the vanity of females." Thus, the poor are deprived of home-grown produce. Gulliver argues that wine in England is less a beverage than an extravagant drug that induces insensibility, diverts melancholy, and shortens life. Pedro de Mendez, the "courteous and generous" Portuguese captain who rescues the reluctant Gulliver, embodies hospitality that redounds on the latter's unreliability as travel writer. He remains "silent and sullen" before the captain, loath to admit the excellence of the chicken and wine Pedro serves. While Pedro rightly reads Gulliver's tale as "a dream or a vision," the latter's refusal when home again to let his family "presume to touch my bread, or drink out of the same cup" confirms the inhumanity that travel inflicts on him.[10]

TRAVEL AS EDUCATION

That travel hardens Gulliver's heart yet renders his political mentality ironically acute is germane to debates about whether touring is inherently educative or necessitates prior training. Slava Klima's introduction to *Letters from the Grand Tour* by Joseph Spence (1699–1768) claims touring was a "civilizing institution whose primary purpose was to extend university education by travel."[11] As many contemporary authors support this contention as reject it. Addison's *Remarks on Several Parts of Italy, etc, in the Years 1701, 1702, 1703* holds that touring grounds knowledge of Roman history and poetry.[12] Here is his preface's defence of the Grand Tour and classicism:

There is certainly no place in the world where a man may travel with greater pleasure and advantage than in Italy. One finds something more particular

10 Ibid., 188, 203–4, 231–2, and 234.
11 Spence 1975, 1.
12 The first edition appeared in 1705, the second in 1718. Several others appeared in the century.

in the face of that country, and more astonishing in the works of nature, than can be met within any other part of Europe. It is the great school of music and painting, and contains in it all the noblest productions of statuary and architecture, both ancient and modern. It abounds with cabinets of curiosities, and vast collections of all kinds of antiquities. No other country in the world has such a variety of governments, that are so different in their constitutions, and so refined in their politics. There is scarce any part of the nation that is not famous in history, nor so much as a mountain or river that has not been the scene of some extraordinary action.[13]

To Johnson, these "observations" rely too much on the collection of "Roman poets" he assembled before setting out: Addison, he claims, looked at Italy so much through "the eyes of a poet" that his account might as well have been "written at home." Still, Johnson praises his "elegance of language and variegation of prose and verse" which "became in time so much the favourite of the publick" that the price of his volume rose "five times" before it was reprinted.[14]

A mature twenty-eight-year-old, Addison made his tour from 1699 to 1704. A successful poet, he had dedicated to Lord Somers a poem on King William's military campaigns, securing from the Crown a pension of £300 to fund his travels.[15] Enough aware of travelogues to avoid repeating them, he comments on Italy's diverse political cultures and the paradoxes of imperialism. Noting the Milanese would prefer to be ruled from Germany rather than from France, he voices democratic hints against autocratic rule. Thus, the "public good" is more justly pursued by the "body of a people" than by "the nobility and gentry, who have so many private expectations and particular interests" that bias "their judgments, and very possibly dispose them to sacrifice the good of their country to the advancement of their own fortunes." By contrast, the people "can have no other prospect in changes and revolutions, than of public blessings that are to diffuse themselves through the whole state in general." He relates the decay of Venetian trade to a rigid aristocracy: "a trading nation must be still for new changes and expedients, as different junctures and emergencies arise." The too-numerous

---

13 Addison 1890, 357.
14 Johnson 1952, 1:403–4.
15 See the preface by Thomas Tickell (1685–1740) in Addison 1890, v. Bohn reprints Hurd's text.

hospitals and religious festivals limit Rome's "trade and business" and explain its low work ethic. Romans, "so wholly taken up with men's souls, that they neglect their bodies," suffer even more from "natural evils in the government and religion" when avaricious popes cultivate nepotism. Yet had nepotism not impoverished the people, Rome's "splendour and magnificence," its "many glorious palaces with such a profusion of pictures, statues, and the like ornaments," would not have come into being: if "the bulk of the people was more rich and happy in the times of the commonwealth, the city of Rome received all its beauties and embellishments under the emperors." About tax policy in Naples, he observes that the "gabels" and "imposts" on "oil, wine, tobacco, and indeed on almost everything that can be eaten, drank, or worn" crush the poor since they are "laid on all butcher's meat, while at the same time the fowl and gibier are tax-free." Meat being taxed by weight, the "duty lies heaviest on the coarser sorts, which are most likely to fall to the share of the common people": "beef perhaps pays a third, and veal a tenth of its price to the government, a pound of either sort having the same tax fixed on it." Worse yet, gabels are in "the hands of private men."[16]

Addison's sense of political systems being corrupted by private interests is clear when he compares small and large governments. About the tiny states of Modena and Parma, he avers one might assume "a much greater regulation of affairs for the ease and benefit of the people, than in large, overgrown states, where the rules of justice, beneficence, and mercy may be easily put out of their course, in passing through the hands of deputies and a long subordination of officers." He sketches the possibility that it might "be for the good of mankind, to have all the mighty empires and monarchies of the world cantoned out into petty states and principalities, that, like so many large families, might lie under the eye and observation of their proper governors; so that the care of the prince might extend itself to every individual person under his protection." Yet such schemes are false; "petty sovereigns" try "to equal the pomp and grandeur of greater princes, as well as to outvie those of their own rank." Citizens of small commonwealths may live in ease and

---

16 Addison 1890, 375, 387, 421, and 429.

prosperity, but none suffer more "under the grievances of a hard government, than the subjects of little principalities."[17]

If touring aroused Addison's contrarian politics, Spence, professor of poetry at Oxford and friend to Pope, earned academic and church preferments after tutoring three aristocrats on the Grand Tour between 1730 and 1741. His tour with Lord Middlesex saw the latter found the first masonic lodge at Florence in 1733, which soon had sixty members, mostly English grandees.[18] Addressing many letters to his mother, Spence voices a keen interest in commodities and consumerism. Revealingly, he carries his own knife and fork as well as a supply of tea and sugar.[19] This upholds his view that travelling makes one appreciate one's own country, its quality of imported goods higher than that met abroad: "We could never buy even so good Burgundy at Dijon as may commonly be bought in London, and the Florence I have generally tasted in England is better than what we drink now on the spot." Italy may be the country for sightseeing but England is the one to live in. In Italy he "wished in vain ... to sit down to a good piece of mutton." "Florentine beef is not half so good as our English." His nation's trading power means "a man may perhaps be happier in England, not only with liberty and the things of our own growth, but with all the best foreign productions in an higher degree than the foreigners themselves."[20] Writing from Dijon on 12 May 1731 on his first tour, Spence focuses on French modes of eating. He comments on the prevalence of "fowl" on dinner and supper tables, which habituated him to "a pullet or capon" every day. He continues:

At present we never miss of that and pigeons, with two plates of sparagrass – one dressed with oil and vinegar for the good people of the country, and another with <honest> butter for us poor Englishmen. The dinner always begins with a *soupe*, and both that and the supper end with a dessert. As soon as this is set on the table, the servants place a glass for each person and a bottle of Burgundy at each end of the table, make their bows, and retire. The dessert and cloth stay as long as you do – which keeps the table dry and gives you sweetmeats whenever you have a mind for them. In the winter we never

17 Ibid., 505.
18 See Klima's introduction to Spence 1975, 5.
19 Spence 1975, 430.
20 Ibid., 125.

missed of grapes, preserved in the bunches as they grow, and a plate of almonds in their neighbourhood. At present we have generally a preserve which is very much my favourite: 'tis made of barberries in which there is a mixture of sharpness and sweetness that is extremely agreeable. They have now, too, curds and cream in the dessert, but 'tis always sour. The best Burgundy at the taverns costs but eight pence a bottle, and from the finest cellars of the great merchants here but sixteen pence. The common people buy worse sorts cheaper and cheaper, and 'tis matter of fact that the lowest of all is but a halfpenny a bottle. I had almost forgot to tell you that about the beginning of last month I had the pleasure of tasting a fricassee of frogs for the first time. <It had a sort of chickeny taste, but something of an odd sourness at the bottom that I did not quite like.[21]

Writing during his third tour with Lord Lincoln from Turin on 13 April 1740, he gives his mother further details about eating frogs which he would like to try at home. He reports that

of late I have had frequent occasions of revenging myself on those animals, for all the times they have frightened me either in pictures or in their proper persons. We have ever now and then a ragout of them, and I eat them out of spite. They do very well thus at a table; for they are more tender, and have a finer relish than any ragout of chicken I ever tasted; and when we are at Birchanger, if you approve of the dish as much as I do, we will never fail of a handsome dish of frogs on either of our birthdays, and on the great state holidays we may add a plate of stewed snails, as they dress them here in perfection. If you care for it, I'll get you the receipt from the King's cook here, and when I come home will enter it in your receipt-book – if there's ever a half page in that vast folio that is not already written upon.[22]

Since his mother collected recipes, she may well have known that ones for frogs and snails appeared in the two most prestigious cookbooks of the period that promoted the nouvelle cuisine of France: Vincent La Chapelle's *The Modern Cook* and Menon's *La Cuisinière bourgeoise*.[23]

21 Ibid., 46.
22 Ibid., 269.
23 Chief cook to the Earl of Chesterfield, Vincent La Chapelle has this recipe: "*Broths with Snails and Frogs, against a dry Cough*. Take a dozen of Vine or Garden Snails, and the hind legs of two dozen of Frogs; let them have two or three boils, to

Adam Smith spent from 1766 to 1776 on the continent tutoring the Duke of Buccleuch. A leader of the Scottish Enlightenment, Smith belonged to the Select Society of Edinburgh, whose secular concerns exemplified polite conversation and congeniality. Critical of English universities unlike Hurd, Smith, like the bishop, admired Addison's constructive civility. He campaigned for public schooling at government expense so that lower-class parents might send children to work less early. In this, he drew on Greek and Roman militia training and Scotland's parish schools. Unsurprisingly, *The Wealth of Nations* (1776) faults English universities for retrogressive pedagogy. The well-endowed "have chosen to remain, for a long time, the sanctuaries in which exploded systems and obsolete prejudices found shelter and protection," but the poorer ones that depend on teachers for revenue "pay more attention to the current opinions of the world."[24] Hence, he defies the "custom" of dispatching young people to "foreign countries immediately upon their leaving school, and without sending them to any university." If it is assumed that youth "return home much improved by their travels," a young man "who goes abroad at seventeen or eighteen and returns home at one and twenty" must improve "in three or four years." But, if he "acquires some knowledge of one or two foreign languages," he still cannot either "speak or write them with propriety."

take off the skim, then pound them in a marble Mortar; take also the white of four Leeks, or half a dozen good Turnips, which you must scrape and cut small, with a small handful of peel'd Barley. Let the whole boil in two pints of water, till boiled away to one: Then let it run through a Sieve without straining it, and make it serve twice: Before you give it to your Patient, put ten or twelve grains of pounded Saffron into the Porringer. This sort of Broth is taken fasting in the morning, and three or four hours after supper, for a month or six weeks, taking some Purge when requisite" (1733, 1:72–3). Menon in *The French Family Cook* has this recipe: "*To fricasee Frogs like Chicken*. Take the thighs, which is the part only used; let them boil up in water, shift them into cold water, and drain them and put them into a stew-pan, with mushrooms, a clove of garlic, a bunch of parsley and scallions, and a bit of butter; turn them two or three times over the fire, and shake in some flour: moisten the whole with a glass of white wine and a little broth; add salt and whole pepper, and let them stew a quarter of an hour and reduce to strong sauce. Thicken it over the fire with the yolks of three eggs, a little cream, and a bit of parsley shred fine; taking care that it does not boil" (1793, 205).

24 Jacob 2019, 129 and 131–3; Muller 1993, 150–1; Smith 1976, 2:294–5.

In other respects, he commonly returns home more conceited, more unprincipled, more dissipated, and more incapable of any serious application either to study or to business, than he could well have become in so short a time, had he lived at home. By travelling so very young, by spending in the most frivolous dissipation the most precious years of his life, at a distance from the inspection and controul of his parents and relations, every useful habit, which the earlier parts of his education might have had some tendency to form in him, instead of being rivetted and confirmed, is almost necessarily either weakened or effaced.

The discredit of English universities has brought "into repute so absurd a practice as that of travelling at this early period of life." A father only gains from the practice freedom "from so disagreeable an object as that of a son unemployed, neglected, and going to ruin before his eyes."[25]

The periodical with the culinary title *Olla Podrida*, edited by Oxford dons, includes two essays that debate whether the Grand Tour corrupts or educates upper-class youth.[26] No. 27, authored by the Reverend Kett of Trinity College, an acquaintance of Richard Graves, also a contributor, opens with lines recalling Spence's trust in English liberty and democratic freedoms:

So propitious is the British government to the rights of the people, so free is its constitution, and so mild are its laws, that the more intimate our acquaintance with foreign states is, the more reason we find to confirm our predilection for the place of our birth.

Nationalism informs the dismissive tones in which young men on the Grand Tour are said to "launch out into the wide ocean of fashionable indulgence." Their intercourse merely consists of resorting to the most fashionable tailor in Paris, intriguing with a celebrated madame, and appearing before the lieutenant of police for drunkenness. Their refinement involves losing money at the ambassador's card parties, supping in the stables at Chantilli, and being introduced to the

---

25 Smith 1976, 2:295–6.
26 "Olla Podrido, o Cocido Madrileno" is one of the oldest national dishes of Spain. Ingredients include: beef, chicken, bacon, lettuce, cabbage, gourd, carrots, beans celery, endive, onions, garlic, and long peppers. They are cooked in two pots (MacMiadhacháin 1976, 179–80).

monarch at Versailles. They might bring home a Paris watch, a counterfeit Antonio Allegri da Correggio, and a hogshead of champagne. In "a kind of commercial treaty with our polite neighbours," they exchange "simplicity for artifice, candour for affectation, steadiness for frivolity, and principle for libertinism." Contact with "the votaries of fashion" makes them "in manners a monkey, in attainments a sciolist, and in religion a sceptic." Linguistic ignorance makes them poison one another with prejudices against foreigners whom they neither know nor wish to. The essay concludes they should remain at home and study "Brydon's Tour, Moore's Travels, or Kearsley's Guides" rather than undertake the Grand Tour.[27]

No. 36 of *Olla Podrida*, written by Thomas Munro, besides recalling Shaftesbury, cites the "author of the *Tableau de Paris*" for saying "that we are not best acquainted with those things which every day affords us an opportunity of seeing." To Louis-Sébastien Mercier (1740–1814), curiosity grows languid "where access is easy, and gratification is immediate." Munro's premise is that mental alertness is kept vigorous by strangeness. Yet it is "the fashion of the present times to skim over the surface of things, and to dive to the bottom for nothing"; he who pretends to general ideas deservedly "meets with ridicule" by depreciating "intercourse with mankind." Subsequently, Munro offers his model for an ideal youth: after school and university, he should acquire "a solid foundation of domestic knowledge, before the superstructure of foreign travel" is "erected." Domestic knowledge consists of "an investigation of the principles of the constitution, the system of laws, and the administration of justice." It comprises "a general inquiry into the several branches of commerce and manufactures; the state of agriculture, learning, and the arts" and finishes "with an examination of the reasonableness of national religion." Defects in books on these topics are to be remedied "by conversations with intelligent persons," "vague systems of theory" being "rectified by observations on the actual state of things." The ideal youth will diversify "these pursuits" by making "the regular tour of Great Britain, with the double intention of surveying natural and artificial curiosities, and of conversing with those who were eminent for manners, attainments, or genius." When he visits the continent, "a

---

27 *Olla Podrida*, Saturday, 15 September 1787, 143–47. Brydon travelled through Sicily and Malta, Moore through Africa, and Kearsley through the British Isles.

more extensive and interesting prospect" will open "to his view"; he will not "dissipate his curiosity amidst a frivolous and perplexing variety of objects," since his "researches" will have "been long habituated to the acquirement of useful knowledge." After three years, he will return home with manners "refined, but not formal," with dress "fashionable, but not foppish, and with "deportment easy, but not finical." His constitution will have been invigorated by exercise, and his fortune unimpaired by extravagance. Skepticism will not have "undermined, nor bigotry contracted, his religious principles." Thus, he proves "how high a polish the British diamond will take." To Munro, an educated traveller will possess an ardent philanthropy and a "patriotism not less spirited than rational." A "citizen of the world" familiar with "the merits of all cultivated nations," he will make England his "place of his residence," since her merits outweigh all others.[28]

Travel writing, in stimulating dialectic about learning from prescribed routes that saw Britons settle abroad, provoked debates about how humans learn from physical movement, how cognition relates to dislocation, and how individuals experience cultural differences. When he tells a correspondent about *A Sentimental Journey*, Sterne denies that touring generates essential ideas: "You will read as odd a Tour thro' France, as ever was projected or executed by traveller, or travel Writer, since the world began ... 'tis a laughing good temperd Satyr against Traveling (as puppies travel)."[29] As his imperial metaphors show in chapter 1 of this volume, Sterne heightens his sensibility to give lessons in idiomatic and cultural minutiae and to dramatize gaps between cerebration, imagination, and experience. Travel having no single-minded purpose, he delights in mixing romantic feelings with licentious voyeurism to prove the absurdity of cultural translation and the power of synesthesia to realize palate memories that taste a rural supper and dance as embodiments of the Eucharist.[30]

Fielding's satire of travel writing in *The Life of Jonathan Wild the Great* is tinged with Swiftian absurdity. When Wild is sent on his travels by his father, he is, ironically, transported for seven years. No account of the voyage "to his Majesty's Plantations in *America*" being available, the author fills his substance-less chapter with Wild Senior's view of the

28 *Olla Podrida*, Saturday, 17 November 1787, 191–7.
29 Sterne to Robert Foley from York, 11 November 1764 (Sterne 1935, 231).
30 Sterne 2003, 42, 47–8, 71, and 99.

Grand Tour as a pointless institution. To him, North America is "freer from Vices than the Courts and Cities of *Europe*, and consequently less dangerous to corrupt a young Man's Morals." The old man believes the advantages of voyaging there are equal to "those attained in the politer Climates; for travelling, he said, was travelling in one Part of the World as well as another: It consisted in being such a Time from home, and in traversing so many Leagues." He holds that "most of our Travellers in *France* and *Italy*" show "at their Return, that they might have been sent as profitably to *Norway* and *Greenland*." The stance on travel writing later in this mock-heroic work becomes more complex. In the most sustained narrative section of the book, Mrs Heartfree describes her heroic self-preservation in the face of attempted rapes by Wild himself and by pirates, privateers, and brutal sea captains. But then her account descends into bathos and incredulity by abusing natural history. Her group of travellers meets a monstrous elephant the size of Windsor castle with eyes as large as halls. After marching through its body, the group broils a piece of its heart which it finds more unsavoury than "the worst Neck Beef." After avoiding a snake almost a quarter of a mile long, they seize the phoenix expiring in its own flames, expecting an "elegant dish" but, on cooking it, they find it "greatly distasteful."[31]

The mode of travel writing that Ann Radcliffe (1764–1823) offers in *A Journey Made in the Summer of 1794, through Holland and the Western Frontier of Germany with a Return down the Rhine* (1795) aims to be empirical and verifiable since she believes the genre needs intelligent reform. Her original route is far from the conventional one of the Grand Tour, as her stay at Rotterdam attests, from where she examines imperialistic trade. About the "many hundreds of British residents," she concludes that "our language and commerce have greatly the sway here over those of all other foreign nations." There "are nearly as many English as Dutch [vessels] in the harbour," and "if you speak to any Dutchman in the street, it is more probable that he can answer in English than in French." She gives ties between England and Holland a historical context, noting that a church she attends is "within the jurisdiction of the Bishop of London, Parliament having given £2,500 towards its completion in the beginning of the present century."[32]

---

31 Fielding 2003, 24 and 150–2.
32 Radcliffe 1795, 1:19–20.

Comparative costs of living in Holland and England figure in her book. She is not exact about the "prices of provisions in this province" but thinks them "as high as in England." Charges for staying at inns are like those "within an hundred miles of London, or, perhaps, something more." Port is "not so common as wine which they call Claret, but which is compounded of a strong red wine from Valencia, mixed with some from Bourdeaux." After pricing claret, she mentions the daily charge for "*logement.*" The following paragraph shows that she follows methods of guidebooks:

Private families buy good claret at the rate of about eighteen pence per bottle, and chocolate for two shillings per pound. Beef is sold for much less than in England, but is so poor that the Dutch use it chiefly for soup, and salt even that which they roast. Good white sugar is eighteen pence per pound. Bread is dearer than in England; and there is a sort, called milk bread, of uncommon whiteness, which costs nearly twice as much as ordinary loaves. Herbs and fruits are much lower priced, and worse in flavour; but their colour and size are not inferior. Fish is cheaper than in our maritime counties, those excepted which are at a great distance from the metropolis. Coffee is very cheap, and is more used than tea. No kind of meat is so good as in England; but veal is not much inferior, and is often dressed as plainly and as well as with us. The innkeepers have a notion of mutton and lamb chops; but then it is *à la Maintenon*; and the rank oil of the paper is not a very delightful sauce. Butter is usually brought to table clarified, that is, purposely melted into oil; and it is difficult to make them understand that it may be otherwise.[33]

Given her love of natural scenery, this economic survey shows that Radcliffe's stress on the practical indicates that, to her, travel writing was neither a simple nor an unmixed genre.[34]

Take her account of the "Imperial and Electoral city of Cologne," which notes the "feculence of the streets." She then cites Johnson that such "diminutive observations" erode the "dignity of writing" since they are "never communicated, but with hesitation, and a little fear of abasement and contempt." This fear Radcliffe assigns to writers' egoism; they

---

33 Ibid., 1:118–20.

34 Batten differentiates between guidebooks and travel literature since factual elements in travel writing were minimized by century's end (1978, 46). On Radcliffe's travel book and her impersonal techniques, see Batten 1978, 40, 68, and 105.

want to be thought able to command more pleasures and prevent more inconveniences than others, since to do so is a "general passport to respect." In her mind, authors accept this "fallacious sort of respect, that attaches to accidental circumstances" rather than "the real sort, of which it would be more reasonable to be proud." A writer of travels who relates "part of the history of his life" chooses not "to shew that his course could lie through any scenes deficient of delights; or that, if it did, he was not enough elevated by his friends, importance, fortune, fame, or business, to be incapable of observing them minutely." Such authors detail the "curiosities of cabinets and of courts" yet include "as much of every occurrence as does not shew [them] moving in any of the plainer walks of life." Egoism leads them to ignore "the difference between the stock of physical comforts in different countries, the character of conditions, if the phrase may be used, such as it appears in the ordinary circumstances of residence, dress, food, cleanliness, opportunities of relaxation; in short, the information, which all may gain, is sometimes left to be gained by all, not from the book, but from travel."[35]

THE PARADOXES OF IMPERIAL TRAVEL

Travel writing based on commercial enterprise and anthropological curiosity had long anticipated Radcliffe's intentions. James Lancaster, an Elizabethan buccaneer who plundered Brazil, inspired the foundation of the East India Company in 1600, its aim to compete with Dutch trade for pepper, cinnamon, and nutmeg.[36] Failure to gauge the investment needed in ventures to Asia saw European nations using privateers to advance their interests in the New World and the Caribbean – the privateers serving their own interests as pirates. To Niall Ferguson, piracy and empire were entangled: he cites the case of Henry Morgan (1635–1688), whose theft of Spanish gold purchased large areas of Jamaica to cultivate sugar; he took up official posts on the island, becoming acting

---

[35] Radcliffe 1795, 1:177–9. Unlike Radcliffe's criticism of travel writers, Addison critiques them for glibly systematizing antiquities: "In short, the antiquaries have been guilty of the same fault as the system-writers, who are for cramping their subjects into as narrow a space as they can, and for reducing the whole extent of a science into a few general maxims" (1890, 466). He is for full recognition of the diverse imagery of the gods on ancient urns, lamps, lachrymary vessels, etc.

[36] See Fraser and Rimas 2010, 199–203.

governor.[37] At first a buccaneer, William Dampier (1651–1715) later promoted natural history as well as colonization. His *New Voyage round the World* (1697) galled Swift with its navigational details and exploitation of Aboriginal people, but its observations on the isthmus of Panama and elsewhere of the native modes on which the buccaneers depended for survival conveyed otherness to European readers, especially in culinary discourse. So did the account by Richard Walter (1716–1795), *A Voyage round the World* (1748), which featured the plundering of Spanish treasure ships by Anson, who was hampered by the high death rate of crews who succumbed to scurvy. What connects Anson and Dampier is their call for higher standards of exploration.[38] However, by Anson's time, pirates had been crushed, their utopian experiments lost to the power of the Royal Navy, whose success in the Seven Years War had been achieved through the admiral's administrative reforms.[39]

Necessity drove Dampier and Anson to study natural history and ethnology in their imperial ventures. They appropriated exotic eating habits in the face of illness and starvation. When Dampier trades for food with Moskito Indians in South America, he learns that "Peccary" and "Warree" are "each a sort of wild Hogs and Deer" and notes how "Plantain-Trees," yams, potatoes, and bushes of Indian pepper grow. Besides eating monkeys on arduous overland trails, he encounters the "Quaam, a large Bird as big as a Turkey." His men enjoy the "extraordinary sweet, wholesome Meat" of manatees, relishing the tails of young cows and discovering that sucking calves provide "the most delicate Meat." In finding that Guano eggs are "very good to eat," they learn that "Broath" made from Guano flesh is curative. While the lean black flesh of flamingos is "very good to eat," the most excellent morsel is the large "Knob" of fat at the root of their tongues, a dish of which is fit for a "Prince's Table." On the shores of the island of Juan Fernandez, besides catching fine snapper and groper, they turn the fat of sea and land turtles into oil as a substitute for butter on their "Dough boys or Dumplins." The privateers render mutiny less likely by taking strange meats to be equivalent to home dishes: they serve seal as roasted pig, boobies as hens, and penguins as ducks. Still, they stay open to exotic foods: poisonous catfish offer delicious, wholesome flesh, and an island

[37] Ferguson 2002, 11–13.
[38] Curley 1976, 31.
[39] Rediker 1987, 285–7.

off Panama surprises them with its delicate "Sappadilloes. Avogato-pears, Mammees, Mamme-Sappota's, [and] Star-apples." They find that Guava fruit "bakes as well as a Pear" and that, since it "may be codled ... it makes good Pies." Observing natives cooking with coconut milk, they boil fowl in it and mix it with rice. From natives they learn how to bake bread fruit and scorch the rind so that the tender insides resemble the "Crumb of a Penny Loaf." In Cambodia, Dampier and crew enjoy "Mango-Achar" – young mangoes pickled with salt, vinegar, and garlic cloves – as an excellent sauce.[40] Like Dampier's privateers, Anson's men ate monkeys and parrots, preferring the tongues and hearts of sea lions to those of bullocks. On Juan Fernandez, they enjoy watercresses, purslain, wild sorrel, turnips, and Sicilian radish because, along with oats, clover, and cabbage trees, they find these foods anti-scorbutic. Given his horticultural interests, Anson planted lettuce, carrot, and other garden seeds on the island along with plum, apricot, and peach stones. Again like Dampier, he motivated his men by serving seal meat as lamb and sea lion as beef, this pretence offset by abundant fish in the island's waters, such as black fish, cavallies, cod, conger eel, crayfish, bream, gropers, and silver fish.[41] His planting of drupes established fruit-bearing trees that yielded good nutrition to subsequent mariners.

As the years passed, humanitarian challenges to imperial travel grew, as evidenced in chapter 1 of this volume. Before Anson undertook his global mission, Johnson told stories of Elizabethan navigators like Francis Drake (c.1540–1596) to induce Georgian readers to support commercial rivalry with Spain.[42] But he turned against colonial rivalry, as *An Account of the Life of Mr. Richard Savage* (1744) and remarks on Thomson in *The Lives of the Poets* confirm. Treating a poem by Savage (1697–1743) on public works and its expatiation on a ".Kind of Beneficence not yet celebrated by any eminent Poet," Johnson describes the dream of peaceful "Settlement of Colonies in uninhabited Countries, the Establishment of those in Security whose Misfortunes have made their own Country no longer pleasing or safe, the Acquisition of Property without Injury to any, the Appropriation of the waste and luxuriant Bounties of Nature, and the Enjoyment of those Gifts which Heaven

---

40 Dampier 2007, 16, 20, 24, 23, 33, 48, 57, 70, 82, 106–8, 143, 156, 203, 205, and 266.
41 Walter 1748, 45, 124, 117–18, 122, and 125.
42 Curley 1976, 60.

has scattered upon Regions uncultivated and unoccupied." But this dream, he argues, should spur politicians to explore why legislatures do not remedy conditions that lead to depopulation and self-imposed exile. Further, he sees that Savage undoes his utopianism: he does not forget "to censure those Crimes which have been generally committed by the Discoverers of new Regions, and to expose the enormous Wickedness of making War upon barbarous Nations because they cannot resist, and of invading Countries because they are fruitful; of extending Navigation only to propagate Vice, and of visiting distant Lands only to lay them waste."[43] In the life of Thomson, Savage's friend, Johnson questions the propaganda in *Britannia* about the claim that the nation is surrendering its "empire o'er the conquered seas." Thomson offers "a poetical invective against the ministry" that single-mindedly ties sea power to possible loss of growth in imports and commerce.[44] Like Johnson, Goldsmith in *The Deserted Village* (1770) decries the export of native produce so luxurious global products may be imported: "Around the world each needful product flies, / For all the luxuries the world supplies." Such imperial commerce starves and displaces rural populations and allows the anti-agricultural retreats of gentry to dominate landscape topography. Ignoring the need for native independence to be rock-like and permanent, politicians forget that "trade's proud empire hastes to swift decay."[45]

Goldsmith's perspective was shared by Smith, who held that, while "every empire aims at immortality," all "empires, like all the other works of men," prove "mortal."[46] Of course, his stance on the relation of mother countries to colonies was thoroughly argued and less impressionistic than the poet's. To Smith, colonies drain a mother country's resources, providing neither sufficient revenue nor military force for their own defence. They weaken rather than strengthen empires. Exclusive trade with them appears to be the sole benefit to mother countries. Yet, since such trade disadvantages other nations, in the long run it harms the mother country by reducing the number and increasing the cost of imports from excluded nations. Because colonial commerce blocks free trade while affording easy profits, it keeps prices high

---

43 Johnson 1744, 119–21.
44 Johnson 1952, 2:351; Thomson 1908, 474, l. 103.
45 Tillotson 1969, 1256–7: ll. 283–4 and l. 427.
46 Smith 1976, 2:355.

in all markets and misdirects domestic and displaces foreign capital.[47] Trade with the New World, being distant and roundabout, is insecure since it is forced into one channel. Noting the growth of manufacturing and exporting sites far from London, Smith advises government to relax the colonial trading monopoly and to give Americans parliamentary representation proportional to their contributions. He would prefer that the colonies go, but national pride and political interests resist this advice.[48] Like Goldsmith, he blames wealthy consumers: "The inhabitants of trading cities, by importing the improved manufactures and expensive luxuries of richer countries, afforded some food to the vanity of the great proprietors, who eagerly purchased them with great quantities of the rude produce of their own lands."[49]

Paradoxically, concern for domestic geography arose from travel books that dealt with Turkey, India, Indonesia, and China published in England and France and from diplomatic, mercantile, and military rivalries between the East India Companies. As readers became more informed about natural history and customs in the wider world, they called for texts reflecting their homeland. From the 1730s, books on the antiquities of counties such as Cornwall and Norfolk became popular. By the 1770s, readers could buy travel guides that specified postal routes and carriage timetables, facilitating trips to Scotland and the Lake District.

DOMESTIC TRANSPORTATION, MARKETS, AND CONSUMERISM

Early developments in the agrarian and industrial revolutions led Defoe in *A Tour through the Whole Island of Great Britain* to analyze London markets' contrary effects on national and local economies and on regional culture. Consider the 40,000 cattle brought each year from the Scottish Highlands to fatten in the pastures of East Anglia: they "feed so eagerly" and "grow monstrously fat," yielding a beef "so delicious for taste" that it is superior to that of English cattle. Yet, eating in the highlands has improved: three of Cromwell's regiments settled near Inverness where there is "much of the English way of living among them,

47 Ibid., 2:106–11.
48 Ibid., 2:129–40.
49 Ibid., 1:428.

as well in their manner of dress and customs, as also of their eating and drinking, and even of their dressing and cookery." Food there is "much more agreeable to English stomachs than in other parts of Scotland." Enthusing about inventions such as the "penny post" and "a new method of carriage" that lets carts "with four stories or stages" journey overnight to London laden with geese and turkey, Defoe is ambivalent about river and sea transport. The Thames, being "the channel for conveying an infinite quantity of provisions from remote counties to London, and enriching all the counties again that lye near it, by the return of wealth and trade," "sucks the vitals of trade," causing "decay of business" in Ipswich and ports like Southampton, Weymouth, and Dartmouth that are "swallow'd up by the immense indraft of trade to the city."[50]

The capital as the centre of market distribution is problematic yet beneficial. Farmers, "cow-keepers, and grazing butchers who live in and near London" buy Lincolnshire and Leicestershire sheep at Smithfield when graziers sell them cheaply in the autumn. Those, not fattened east of London, are sold as "marsh-mutton" at Christmas for exorbitant prices. Yet, if markets yield easy wealth to entrepreneurs, they aid rural well-being: the city takes "provisions from the whole body of the nation" so that "every part of the island" gains. Supplying London with turkeys governs Suffolk and Norfolk, each season droves of 150,000 arriving via the River Stour. Towns on the Thames such as Feversham depend on transporting fish and oysters to Billingsgate. Dorking's surrounding farms produce "the fattest geese and the largest capons"; "a manufacture to the country people," its produce is in demand at Leaden-Hall. Spalding in the Lincolnshire fens has a new way of moving fish "alive by land carriage" in "great buts fill'd with water in waggons." Perch, eels, tench, and pike are given clean water each night on their way to the metropolis.[51]

Not all speciality foods end up in London. Poole in Dorset sends barrelled oysters to Italy, Spain, and the West Indies, and Winander Meer in Lancashire yields a rare "char fish." This "curious fish" is potted "as a dainty" and "sent far and near" as gifts. Defoe lauds Stilton cheese, "our English Parmesan," and says that, when black cattle are killed in Yorkshire in September and October, their salted flesh becomes a

---

50 Defoe 1974, 1:65; 2:408; 1:341; 1:60–1; 1:174; and 1:43.
51 Ibid., 1:9, 59, 112–13, 153; and 2:100–1.

"smoak'd beef" of a "very great rarity." He reports that subsistence farming is evolving and the seasonal availability of meats changing because of the industrial revolution: London's need for food effects technologies that alter eating habits. Turnpikes let cattle and sheep be driven to market without their flesh wasting from wallowing in sloughs. Since sheep now travel in winter, mutton is cheaper, and graziers do not have to sell at distressed prices. Improved roads and causeways built in the Roman mode afford inland towns the opportunity to receive fresh herring, sprats, and mackerel as well as fine regional cheeses. Transportation binds urban consumers to rural producers, making suburban life more equitable. Thus, commuters in Epsom who work in the city make supper the main meal of the day; their wives cook at night so that families may eat together.[52]

In relating consumerism to taste, Defoe resists the typologies traced in chapter 1. He acknowledges them but treats them freely. Observing the "fashion of the towns" in Hackney, north of the city, as "quite altered," he notes most buildings in Tottenham are new, "generally belonging to the middle sort of mankind, grown wealthy by trade" and adds without innuendo that residents "still taste of London," some owning homes in the city and the country. Disparate prices in metropolitan and rural markets are not necessarily bad since diverse living standards disperse population and prompt resettlement. At Totnes on the river Dart, he buys fresh salmon peal five times cheaper than those sent from Chichester to London. Thus, Totnes offers excellent provisions to families intent on living within their means. On the quay, his servant buys fresh pilchards broiled with pepper and salt for a farthing a person. Next day a friend buys fresh lobster for a sixth of the London price. He also discusses relative independence from the market economy advanced by innovative estate management that produces wall fruit as well as vegetables. At Sir Nicholas Carew's estate at Beddington, he finds

---

52 Ibid., 1:208; 2:269, 110, 199, 100, 127, 131–2; and 1:162. On the improvement to transportation effected by the interconnection of turnpikes, see Szostak 1991, 15 and 60–3. Smith reports that in the 1720s "counties in the neighbourhood of London petitioned the parliament against the extension of turnpike roads into the remoter counties." He adds that fear of productivity from remoter regions was unfounded; land rents near London did not fall; the introduction of "rival commodities into the old market" encouraged "good management" because of the "free and universal competition" that weakened monopolies (Smith 1976, 1:165).

England's only standard orange trees. With "moving houses to cover them in the winter" and having flourished for eighty years, they yield much fruit. He congratulates the Marquess of Annandale for building a walled garden near Edinburgh: its bricks retain the sun's "warmth" and enable the Marquess to grow peaches and nectarines.[53]

Interest in domestic travel and fashion leads Defoe to survey spas and hot springs, an interest extending beyond the cost of living associated with popular diversions to consider bodily and moral health. He types resorts according to the class of visitors. The common folk of London who take the waters for health walk out to Dulwich and Streatham Wells of a morning and back at night; merchants take in Epsom Wells; and gentry and nobility visit or reside at Tunbridge Wells, making it a luxury market. Because of the wealthy there, this resort offers "abundance of wild-fowl," such as "pheasant, partridge, woodcock, snipe, quails" and "duck, mallard, teal." It is famed for delicious "wheatear," the English ortolan, these birds costing much less where they are trapped on the South-Downs. Less polite about this consumerism than White, Defoe claims that Tunbridge is full of fops, fools, beaux, gamesters, and intriguers.[54] He no more praises Newmarket, its horse races drawing people from all over England who are "so intent, so eager, so busy upon the sharping part of the sport, their wagers and bets" that they resemble "horse-coursers in Smithfield," declining from their "high dignity and quality, to picking one another's pockets, and biting one another." Fashion makes them act "without respect to faith, honour, or good manners." Diversions at Bath are worse. This resort is barren; those not taking the waters for health take up raffling, gaming, and visiting, the "gallantry and diversions ... meriting rather a satyr, than a description." The "resort of the sound, rather than the sick," its "bathing is made more a sport and a diversion, than a physical prescription for health." By contrast, Buxton Hot Spring in the Derbyshire Peaks has potential for healthy tourism given the open countryside: everything there is "much more convenient than in a close city as the Bath is, which, more like a prison than a place of diversion, scarce gives the company room to converse out of the smell of their own excrements, and where the very city it self may be said to stink like a general common-shore." Above

---

53 Defoe 1974, 2:2; 1:225–6, 157–8; and 2:312.
54 For White's remarks on Brighthelmstone and Tunbridge, see chapter 4, note 49.

all, Defoe recommends Bury St Edmund's, "the Montpellier of Suffolk, and perhaps of England," its visitors "people of the best fashion, and the most polite conversation": its beautiful, healthy situation lured the clergy, who "always chose the best places in the country to build in, either for the richness of soil, or for health and pleasure in the situation of their religious houses." To "taste the pleasures of the place," the monks moved "the body of [their] saint," increasing their wealth by promoting pilgrimages to his shrine.[55]

From a Scottish stance, Tobias Smollett (1721–1771) features domestic tourism in *The Expedition of Humphry Clinker* (1771), his epistolary and picaresque novel's settings moving from Glamorganshire in Wales to Bristol Hot Wells, Bath, London, the Yorkshire resorts of Scarborough and Harrowgate, the cities of Durham, Edinburgh, Glasgow, and the Scottish Highlands, returning via the Derbyshire Peaks and Buxton Wells. This circuit affords criticisms of consumerism, fashion, class mobility, hygiene, and food processing. His alter ego, Matthew Bramble, skeptical about progress, defies Methodist enthusiasm and French manners, his communitarianism rejecting partisan politics. Concern for diet leads him to praise a substantial Argyleshire breakfast consisting of:

one kit of boiled eggs; a second, full of butter; a third, full of cream; an entire cheese, made of goat's milk; a large earthen pot full of honey; the best part of a ham; a cold venison pasty; a bushel of oatmeal, made in thin cakes and bannocks, with a small wheaten loaf in the middle for strangers; a large stone bottle full of whisky, another of brandy, and a kilderkin of ale.[56]

Matt frequently appeals to readers' distaste and disgust, as in his account of visiting the estate of his friend Baynard, whose wife has almost bankrupted it with her lust for French modes:

At dinner, the lady maintained the same ungracious indifference, never speaking but in whispers to her aunt; and as to the repast, it was made up of a parcel of kickshaws, contrived by a French cook, without one substantial article adapted to the satisfaction of an English appetite. The pottage was little better than bread soaked in dishwashings, lukewarm. The ragouts

---

55 Defoe 1974, 1:160, 127, 75; 2:34, 167–8; and 1:49.
56 Smollett 1984, 243.

looked as if they had been once eaten and half digested: the fricassees were involved in a nasty yellow poultice; and the rotis were scorched and stinking, for the honour of the fumet. The desert consisted of faded fruit and iced froth, a good emblem of our landlady's character; the table-beer was sour, the water foul, and the wine vapid; but there was a parade of plate and china, and a powdered lacquey stood behind every chair, except those of the master and mistress of the house, who were served by two valets dressed like gentlemen.

Dining "in a large old Gothic parlour" recently "paved with marble," Matt, not warmed by the fire, is struck "with such a chill sensation, that when I entered it the teeth chattered in my jaws." Every modish thing is "cold, comfortless, and disgusting."[57] Smollett closes his novel by detailing the renewal of two estates. Matt counters all of Baynard's wife's modishness, refinances the estates, dictates a strict budget, and restores the land to agricultural productivity. Matt is inspired to do so by having learned from a college friend, Charles Dennison, who, having himself inherited a ruined estate, renews it by relying on the economic sense of local farmers. Curiously, he learns to cook "several outlandish delicacies, such as *ollas, pepper-pots, pillaws, corys, chabobs,* and *stufatas.*" His skill with Oriental, Spanish, Italian, and West Indian dishes validates imperial travel.[58]

FASHION AND FOOD IN PARIS AND LONDON

Louis-Sébastien Mercier, a Girondin opponent of the *ancien régime,* regicide, and Jacobins, was, according to Michel Delon, "le prophète des évenements" who foresaw the Revolution in "l'instabilité des modes."[59] Fashion and privilege operating in food markets preoccupy him in *Tableau de Paris (1782–88)* by causing social distress. The exorbitant cost of provisions on the luxurious tables of the rich who consume the best leaves the worst food to the poor. of the profuse entrées and *entremets* served to the rich only a quarter are eaten, the leftovers devoured by servants so that a lacquey eats better than the petit bourgeois. The latter only smell the seafood that sates valets. What stewards

---

57   Ibid., 295.
58   Ibid., 342–3 and 326.
59   Delon's introduction to Mercier's *Tableau de Paris* (1990, 12 and 20).

themselves do not eat, they sell for three times the purchase price. There is no worse-nourished people than Parisians. The diet of 75 per cent is limited: they eat soup for dinner, supper consisting of beef with oil, vinegar, and parsley or a shoulder of mutton. Provincials need not envy those who cannot afford vegetables and fish on Sundays. The poorer the class, the more its food costs. The lowest live on *cervelas* – sausages made from pigs' brains – costing thrice what a prince pays.[60] Pastry cooks and pork butchers exploit the poor. Their shops do a roaring trade on Sundays and saints' days. But families who live in attics and send meat to be cooked in the ovens of pastry cooks are duped; the cooks squeeze juices from the meats with larding pins and sell it back to the poor in succulent meat pies, while the families take home blackened, overdone joints.[61]

To Mercier, fashion distorts markets. Primeur vegetables and fruits are bought up by nobles to decorate their tables, stewards purchasing unripe, tasteless produce obliged to please the eye rather than satisfy the palate of grandees. Nobility seems to identify itself by out-of-season *petits pois*. How is it, Mercier asks, that rank is confirmed by the display of such legumes and why should money flow to table decorators rather than to cultivateurs? He illustrates his point by an anecdote. A water carrier swallows without chewing them a small quantity of peas in a silver saucepan in the kitchen of a prince of the blood thinking them leftovers. But they were primeurs costing six hundred livres. The cook is desperate and the water carrier cries like an infant. When told, the prince laughs; he would not have enjoyed them. But the water carrier thinks he should have had pleasure in committing his sin. Could there be a moral in the kitchen of princes? Especially when the water carrier would have preferred swallowing sixty gold ducats? Mercier reinforces his query by another anecdote. A miser must provide an annual meal to a corporation: to pocket the money for one dish of peas, he offers one dish of peas plus an imitation dish of asparagus tips, asking the steward to let the imitation dish fall to conceal his deceit. The steward, deceived by the dishes, drops the wrong one, leading to exposure of the miser. Mercier again would prefer the money of the wealthy going to a

---

60 Mercier 1990, *Les halles*: 67.
61 Ibid., *Pâtissiers, Rôtisseurs*: 179–80.

cultivateur rather than to a painter, sculptor, or architect – wretched artisans guilty of idolatry.[62]

On Normandy's coast, Mercier sees that Providence amply supplies fish whereas excise taxes render it an impossibly expensive luxury in Paris. The system of privileges condemns Parisians to go without fish: fermiers close off the sea, blaming the lack of fish on the distance of two hundred leagues. The fees these money grubbers demand for transporting fish increase its cost eleven times. The seasons when species abound do not change their stance; the periodical arrival of schools of fish does not soften their fiscal rigour. The sea is not harvested; the resource is wasted by controlled supply. On shore, Mercier stumbles over crabs and readily notes the plenitude of fishes. But the farm controls a healthy food and lets it decompose to stink up the city's gates. Public administration, in betraying Providence, which gives the most common food delicate flavours, cruelly deprives the populace who cannot come up to the farmers' cupidity. To Mercier, the government would gain dignity by suppressing all tax on sea fish; it would thereby value the needs of the hungry more highly than the avarice of farmers. At the same time, it would recognize the risks taken by fishermen and the efforts of couriers to transport fish quickly. Current market manipulations make Mercier think that natural man enjoys a more liberal subsistence than he who lives under state law.[63]

Mercier's views on Parisian food markets are paralleled by Fielding in *The Journal of a Voyage to Lisbon* (1755). Becalmed in Torbay, his vessel takes on supplies from fishing boats whose sole and whiting are so good, fresh, and cheap that he dons his magistrate's hat. After buying a costly john dorée, he decides its firmness and flavour warrant its price but wonders how it is that country gentry enjoy a delicacy unavailable to London fishmongers and chefs. As a public good he ponders the availability of fish: it is most plentiful. If a rivulet feeds more mouths than a meadow, the comparison applies more to the seas, which "abound with such immense variety of fish, that the curious fisherman, after he hath made his draught, often culls only the daintiest part, and leaves the rest of his prey to perish on the shore." Since nature makes fish reproduce faster than land animals and birds, this food should be cheap. How is

---

62 Ibid., *Primeurs*: 314–15.
63 Ibid., *Cherté de la marée*: 335–6.

it then that "not one poor palate in a hundred" knows "the taste of fish" in London? This taste is so excellent that "it exceeds the power of French cookery to treat the palates of the rich with any thing more exquisitely delicate." But, if fish were to become the common food of the poor, "it might put them too much upon an equality with their betters," think those who equate social distinction with exclusive consumerism. Luxury in eating, says Fielding, is always associated with vanity and scarcity, whereas honest appetite feeds on plenty. London fishmongers monopolize the Westminster market by selling only rare fish and keeping its cost out of the reach of the poor. Such market control should be a capital crime since it starves thousands. He doubts this can be effected. Yet fishermen might well be stopped from over-fishing the Thames were magistrates to implement parliamentary acts passed to let fish grow in size and then be caught. In lamenting that legal statutes and sumptuary laws for reforming markets have not been put into effect so that fishermen still deplete the Thames of small fry, Fielding anticipates Mercier's economic and cultural idealism.[64]

CULTURAL AND CULINARY EXCHANGE

Population movements affect culinary fashion. The flight of Huguenots after the Revocation of the Edict of Nantes in 1685 and of Catholics after the Jacobite Rebellions of 1715, 1719, and 1745 along with ongoing emigration to North America saw hundreds of thousands of Europeans crossing seas and national borders. Here is an account of French refugees in England published in 1719 by Francis Maximilian Misson (c.1650–1722), a Protestant born in Lyon who fled in 1685 and settled in Britain.

The *French* Protestants that fled into *England*, are so spread over the whole Country, that it is impossible to be certain, or so much as guess at their Number. Besides, the eleven Regiments which are wholly made up of them, there are some in all the other Troops. A vast many of both Sexes are gone into Service in various English Families; so that there is scarce any considerable House where you may not find some of our Nation. Many have set up Manufactures in the Country, and Churches at the same time: Abundance

---

64 Fielding 1907, 102–6.

went to *Scotland* and *Ireland*, to *Jersey* and *Garnsey*. At present, there are Two and twenty *French* Churches in *London*, and about a Hundred Ministers, that are in the Pay of the State, without reckoning those that are arriv'd at other Means of subsisting. The Royal Munificence, and the Compassion of the People, have been very great towards them; and they can never sufficiently express their Gratitude, and bless a Nation which has so charitably open'd her Arms to receive them. The Earl of *Galway*, a brave and noble Gentleman, if ever there was one in the World, is their Head, their Friend, their Refuge, their Advocate, their Support, their Protector. When he arriv'd from *Turin* some Days ago, his House was so crowded every Morning, that for a quarter of an Hour after his rising it was scarce possible to get so much as to the Bottom of the Stair-case. Of this Multitude of poor exiles, there are not at most above Three thousand that receive Alms, or as we call it, are *au Comitè*, that is to say, upon the List of those who enjoy the Publick Assistance. Many others have Pensions from the King. The late Queen, who was Goodness and Charity it self, succour'd them to the utmost of her Power: And among the rest of the great Kindnesses which she shew'd to them, we may reckon the Vogue she gave to certain little Works which she herself work'd at, and wore, the better to establish the Fashion and Wear of them. This for some Years was like Manna, dropping from Heaven for the Support of infinite Numbers of People.[65]

Appreciating the welcome extended to Huguenots by Queen Anne, King George I and the Earl of Galway, which still left thousands in need of public alms, Misson notes that their assimilation was limited by English eating habits, making his point in an essay on inns that explains why metropolitan taverns are unlike French inns. "There is nothing," he claims, "at *London* like our Inns in *France:* It is not the general Custom for Travellers to lodge in the Houses where the Coaches, Waggons, Carriers, and other publick Vehicles, set up; one or two people might perhaps be furnish'd with a Bed in them, but not three or four; neither have they *Auberges*, where a Man can lie, and eat at set Hours, and at so much a Head. At *London* they hardly so much as know what an *Auberge* is: There are, indeed, a thousand and a thousand Taverns, where you may have what you please got for you; but a publick House, where once or twice every Day, at a fix'd Hour, you may go directly and sit down to

---

65   Misson 1719, 231–3.

Table, at so much a Head, both at Dinner and Supper, as you may in all the considerable Towns in *France*, is not any where in *London*, nor as I know of in any Part of *England*." Misson regrets that fixed-price, set-hour meals are unavailable and that visitors must board in private houses and have food sent in or hire cooks. This informality strikes him as strange. Although there are "Cooks Shops enow in all Parts of the Town, where it is very common to go and chuse upon the Spit the Part you like, and to eat it there," no Frenchman uses them comfortably. While the humblest refugees find this custom scandalous, English aristocrats eat contentedly at cook-shops. Sure that the French spend more of their income than the English on dining out, Misson tells how cook-shops operate: "Generally four Spits, one over another, carry round each five or six Pieces of Butcher's meat, Beef, Mutton, Veal, Pork and Lamb; you have what Quantity you please cut off, fat, lean, much or little done; with this, a little Salt and Mustard upon the Side of a Plate, a Bottle of Beer and a Roll; and there is your whole Feast." Relieved that foreigners in London are setting up *auberges* to cater to French eating habits, he closes his essay by recommending that "Those who would dine at one or two Guineas *per* Head, are handsomely accommodated at our famous *Pontac*'s."[66]

Pontack's was London's first long-lived restaurant, opening in Abchurch Lane off Lombard Street in 1666, the year the Great Fire burned 13,000 houses, public buildings, and churches to the ground, and the year after the bubonic plague carried off nearly a quarter of the city's population of 400,000. Pontack's promoted French cuisine and wine in the heart of the city rather than at the court end of town in Westminster. Both catastrophic events, the Plague and Great Fire, led to urban renewal of which Pontack's opening is symbolic. Its full name was "The Sign of Pontack's Head." While a tavern, it was luxurious, serving the finest food and wine, as shown by its clientele of aristocrats, professionals, and leading citizens. Dinners at Pontack's cost as much as two guineas. Its wine sold for seven shillings a bottle, while

---

66 Ibid., 144–7. John Ozell (d. 1743), translator of Misson, came from an English family of French origin. He earned his living managing the accounts of the City of London, St Paul's Church, and St Thomas's Hospital. From 1711 to 1713 he published *The Works of Monsieur Boileau*, his version criticizing English authors and annoying Pope, who turned Ozell into an image of a hack. Ozell favoured Whig authors who met at Daniel Button's coffee house in Covent Garden.

two shillings was the normal price for generic wine charged at other taverns. Such prices could be afforded by those who worked at the Old Bailey and Mansion House, namely, barristers and lawyers and public administrators. Pontack's was opened by François-Auguste de Pontac, the son of Arnaud de Pontac, president of the Parlement of Bordeaux who lived regally in one of that city's finest mansions. The Pontac family were lawyers and wealthy landowners who rose from being artisans and merchants into the ranks of the nobility. Members of the *noblesse de la robe* and long-term members of the Parlement, they owned the estate of Haut-Brion in Pessac on the outskirts of the city from the sixteenth to the end of the eighteenth century. Sparing no expense to perfect his wines since he understood English tastes, Pontac senior thought a London restaurant would make a good outlet for wines from his Haut-Brion estate, today known by the appellation of Graves, and from his estates in Saint-Estephe, the northernmost region of the Médoc. Until then generic wine from Bordeaux was known as claret. Arnaud de Pontac saw London as the place in which to market estate wines. What he foresaw came to pass since Haut-Brion and Pontac were successfully retailed at Pontack's and other London eateries. The diarist Samuel Pepys (1633–1703) drank "*Ho Bryan*" at The Royal Oak tavern near The Exchange in Lombard Street. He usually ate and drank there: when Sir William Petty's ship *The Experiment* was being readied for sea and supplied with victuals from that tavern, Pepys enjoyed a dish of marrow bones and a chine of beef along with the noble company.[67] Evelyn dined at Pontack's together with fellow members of the Royal Society. He lauded "the famous & wise Prime President of *Bourdeaux*," the "owner of that excellent *Vignoble* of *Pontaque & Obrien*, whence the choicest of our *Bourdeaux*-Wines come." Yet he was unimpressed by the son who ran the restaurant because of his addiction to "Cabbalistical fancies."[68] From 1801 to 1804, Haut-Brion was owned by Charles-Maurice de Talleyrand (1754–1838), a dynamic politician whose influence on gastronomy was enormous.[69]

Although French wines were banned in 1679 and again in the reign of William III, Haut-Brion was sold at Pontack's, perhaps as the result

67 Pepys 1983, 4:100 and 6:38.
68 Evelyn 1959, 974 and 748–9.
69 For further information on the Pontac family and their wine estates, see Johnson 1989, 201–8.

of smuggling or special arrangements. This availability may have enhanced its prestige as an eating place. The Royal Society held dinners at Pontack's shortly after it was opened, according to Pepys and Evelyn. Famous writers such as Dryden, Defoe, and Swift dined there. Later, The Royal Society Club, founded in 1743, held annual dinners there for three years. Pontack's was demolished in 1780, having been renowned for over a century. It served its clientele the best wine of Bordeaux and fine meals for so long that recipes of its dishes appeared in cookbooks appealing to a range of social classes. "*Mutton Cutlets from* Pontack'*s*," "*Veal Cutlets from* Pontack'*s*," and "*How to stew Carp from* Pontack'*s*" appear in Sarah Harrison's *The House-keeper's Pocket Book; And Compleat Family Cook*.[70] These recipes are found verbatim in James Jenks's *The Complete Cook*, a volume written for cook maids.[71] The carp recipe appears in Richard Bradley's *The Country Housewife, And Lady's Director*, a book for middle-class women, its author a member of The Royal Society and professor of botany at Cambridge.[72]

BRITONS IN FRANCE

In 1781, during the American War of Independence, Guy Jean Baptiste Target, "the leading advocate of the Paris bar," while defending the property rights of an English widow, claimed the English live peaceably "in the bosom of our cities; calm social intercourse has not been unsettled by hostilities; soldiers from the two countries fight; citizens remain friendly, and the King's humanity offers Europe the new and happy spectacle of harmony among private persons at a time of official

---

70 Harrison 1735, 39 and 64.
71 Jenks 1768, 107 and 165.
72 The carp recipe, addressed to middle-class women, appears in Bradley 1762, 190. Bradley (1688?–1732) was elected to the Royal Society in 1712. In 1716 he published two articles on botany in its Philosophical Transactions, later publishing in horticultural periodicals. He attracted a patron in James Brydges (1653–1744), first Duke of Chandos, who had him supervise plantings at Canons in Middlesex. Adding to the collections of Sir Hans Sloane (1660–1753), Bradley dedicated texts to him. Sloane likely helped him to the professorship of botany at Cambridge, where he published *Ten Practical Discourses* (1727) and *A Course of Lectures upon the Materia medica* (1730).

conflict."[73] That Britons had long resided in France is evident in its press, which details their influence on urban geography. The *affiches* record English names of streets, buildings, and districts. Hotels, shops, gardens, and factories being also so designated, property was occupied by Britons whose activities raised values and created urban landmarks. They affected rural life, too, influencing regional consumerism by mediating agrarian and industrial revolutions.[74]

According to the *affiches*, luxury thrived on foreign trade; British manufacturers, merchants, shopkeepers, tradesmen, and artisans were instrumental in this. While the population and economies of port cities grew twice as fast those of inland regions, tax revenue in Angers and other hinterland towns accelerated from levies on international trade, which changed the taste of urban elites through the mediation of English residents and visitors.[75] The *affiches* show that, when Parisian retailers of luxury items, such as jewels, cosmetics, wigs, clocks, and porcelain, passed through or set up shop in the provinces, they faced the stylish goods of British competitors. Newspaper advertisements by domestic and British tradespeople attest to strenuous commercial rivalry. Customer services, retail techniques, new forms of credit, as well as

---

73 Doyle 1989, 90; "Les Anglois vivent paisiblement dans le sein de nos villes; les communications de la paix n'ont pas été troublées par les hostilités: les soldats des deux pays se combattent; leurs citoyens se rapprochent, & l'humanité du Roi donne à l'Europe le spectacle heureux & nouveau de la concorde entre les particuliers, au milieu des divisions publiques" (*Journal de Provence*, vol. 1: Mélanges [1781] 169).

74 Philip Benedict calls for study of the ties between urban growth and consumerism. To him, cities in the *ancien régime* affected daily life more than their small, unstable populations suggest. If the populace lived in the countryside where wealth was generated, riches were displayed in cities. In mid-century, migration of administrative elites and other nobility into cities accelerated; urban development was reshaped by aristocratic culture that knit urbanity to aesthetic refinement and social distinction. Luxury trades formed round elites so that cities established informal institutions in the absence of regular governance. Although towns were centres of noble residence and fashion before 1700, this increased when growing agricultural profits of bourgeois landowners were diverted to towns and when industries owned by merchants left cities to be replaced by trades catering to fashionable consumers. If urban renewal was sped by the demolition of city walls demanded by the Crown, it was exploited by nobles who built townhouses and promenades as arenas of display in imitation of the Parisian *beau monde* (Benedict 1989, "French Cities from the Sixteenth Century to the Revolution: An Overview," 7–68).

75 Benedict 1989, 45–6.

wholesale methods stemming from London's financial revolution figure as much in advertisements as do imported consumer and producer goods. Since shops selling British goods and operated by British tradespeople became landmarks in Lyon, Bordeaux, and other centres, one sees how commerce affected fashionable life in France.

In 1750, the first year for which there are extant copies of the *affiches* of Lyon, Mme Legendre, a perfumer, advertised a depilatory wax at her shop on rue Galande at the corner of the rue des Anglois, this name a guide to customers. In the next decade, the *affiches* manifest more significant institutional effects of British commerce on Lyon. Northeast of the Town Hall where aldermen regulated trade, a quarter grew around "the London Exchange" on St Catherine Street, one block to the north of the place des Terreaux on the south side of which the Town Hall had been built and on which cafés and shops formed meeting places for merchants. The London Exchange was some distance from the Exchange built in Vieux Lyon in 1749 as a business centre. Yet the official exchange featured less in city life than the London Exchange, which centred a neighbourhood based on trade, industrial production, and fashionable consumption. Its radiating influence was the wider because urban space was at a premium; there was little scope for expansion given the restrictive presence of religious institutions and aristocratic townhouses. In 1785 Lyon covered no more ground than in the sixteenth century, its population having doubled to 140,000. This growth was met by taller buildings, increased density, and the housing together of the bourgeois and lower classes. The London Exchange was so refashioned. Like others nearby, it combined domestic accommodation, work spaces, warehouses, and shops, functions made important by the sluggish economy. Lagging behind Bordeaux, Lyon was burdened by municipal debt, a slump in employment, and problems in the silk trade. An informal institution, the London Exchange addressed long-term problems.[76]

As an edifice, it was advertised as modern; it had five stories, with large rooms and apartments, capacious attics and cellars, as well as "souillardes" (rinsing rooms) and toilets. It may have had single owners, but leases were held by residents and non-residents, who rented out portions of the building as apartments and shops for which there was a strong if variable demand. On 5 November 1760, a widow, Madame

---

76 *Affiches de Lyon*, 24 February 1750; Gravejat 1980, 198 and 200.

la veuve Duverney, living on the third floor, offers shops and apartments for rent on the next St-Jean-Baptiste Day. The lead time of seven months implies that her rental agreements are long term and that demand for leases is strong. The widow does not mind if renters take the shops and apartments separately. In the event, she seems not to have rented all her spaces, for, on 14 May 1761, she advertises as immediately available a shop on the street and an eight-room suite on one level with two bathrooms, cellars, and attic. The Duverney family likely retained property in the Exchange after her decease, for, on 7 September 1768, a non-resident M. Duverney advertises the rental of three shops on the ground floor, a room on the fourth floor with a cellar. Owning property in the London Exchange was desirable economically and socially. The son of the Servants, a merchant family resident there, on 26 March 1761 listed for rent a room and office on the second floor, stressing that the latrine was exclusive to the renter. As merchants and property owners, the Servants did well; nine years later, on 21 November 1770, they sought a head gardener for their château fifteen miles out in the Dauphiné. They sought an unmarried man of thirty-five to manage orchards and kitchen garden: a horticulturalist, able to graft and espalier trees and bushes and to cultivate mulberries for the manufacture of silk. No longer residents, the Servants end their advert with the note that their company office is close to the Change de Londres.

Notices in the 1760s and 1770s confirm the London Exchange was popular as residential and commercial property among merchants. Giving it as their address, MM. Jean-Jacques Aunant & Compagnie advertised for a two-seater carriage drawn by two horses to take them speedily to and from Geneva. Non-resident and resident merchants continued to rent out property in the Exchange and nearby. M. Rigolet, a "Marchand Fabricant" living on rue Sainte Catherine, listed for rent three shops and an apartment on the third floor, while MM. Chapeaurouge & Compagnie, négociants who resided there, offered for rent two attractive shops in the "maison de la Charité" on the "place des Carmes."[77] M. Claude Bourne, who lived on rue du Bât-d'argent, offers five large rooms, a rinsing room, and two shops on the first floor, with

---

77 *Affiches de Lyon*, 29 July 1767; 30 December 1768; 10 July 1771. In his advert, M. Rigolet says that a M. de Vial owns the Change de Londres, thereby suggesting that, while the building may have had one title holder, property in it was likely held by way of leasehold.

three rooms on the third floor, a cellar and attic, and a bedroom on the fifth floor. Renters could take the property whole or in part. Six weeks later, now giving his address as the London Exchange, he offers a first-floor apartment of five rooms with closets decorated with mirrors and paintings along with two shops and three rooms on the third floor and four rooms on the fourth floor: availability was six months later on Saint-Jean-Baptiste, 1772.[78]

The London Exchange's suitability for gracious living and attractive business quarters is clear from an advert of 6 May 1772 listing a large *magasin* with a rear shop in the apartment on the first floor and five rooms on the same level as well as cellars and attics. The social importance of the London Exchange created demand for fashionable shops and apartments in buildings nearby. Thus, an apartment for immediate rent consisting of three rooms, one of them very large, with partitions, rinsing room, cellar, and attic is said to be close to the place des Terreaux opposite the London Exchange. Three months later, an apartment on the second floor of a building opposite the Change de Londres is listed as having six rooms, closet and rinsing room, two cellars, and an attic, with two rooms on the fourth floor, with a rinsing-room and two attics above, along with three shops two of them in the front of the building. This ensemble is available for occupancy the following year on St-Jean-Baptiste, the early announcement implying much about the terms of notice and duration of contracts on which leases were sold. Emphasis on the size, stylishness, and distinctiveness of apartments conferred by proximity to the London Exchange leads to colourful adverts. One apartment for rent on the second floor of a building beside it on the hill called la Glacière with three rooms, a mezzanine floor, a cellar, and an attic is called "very smiling."[79]

Cloth manufacturers with their families, servants, and staff lived and worked in and near the London Exchange. Suites with workrooms and offices with terraces overlooking the hillside centre of the silk trade were often listed in the *affiches*. One placed by occupants of the first floor on 19 September 1770 offered two fine shops and a work room giving onto a beautiful terrace and three rooms on the fourth floor. Stressing that the London Exchange is situated at the corner of rue

---

78 *Affiches de Lyon*, 6 November 1771 and 28 December 1771.

79 *Affiches de Lyon*, 23 December 1761; 31 March 1762; 15 March 1769, "très-riant."

Sainte Catherine and "la montée de la Glacière," the occupants have for sale chests for money, scales, and tools of the clothmaker's trade. Probably, the shops and rooms were rented without the equipment, for the occupants put up for sale the next month small, medium, and large scales, chests, cupboards, and manufacturing equipment. Clothmakers were also landlords in nearby buildings. M. Combe, a stocking merchant with a shop on the place des Terreaux, advertised three rooms with cellar and attic in a building close to the London Exchange that gave onto the Gardens of the Capucins.[80]

While the *affiches* of Lyon reveal the London Exchange to have been a centre for property transactions, fashionable residences, and elegant shopping in the 1760s and 1770s, French residents, merchants, and artisans esteemed this building since they respected British influence on the silk trade in Lyon and the city's openness to the industrial revolution and to consumer goods based on British modes of production. That trade valued English-style scales for weighing quantities of silk, also preferring English iron coffers for guarding money.[81] When Mr Mason, an Englishman, under royal licence established a manufacture of brass and iron mesh, he produced grillwork of from ten to sixty filaments an inch that warded off flies and other insects from domestic food and that preserved goods in shops, books, and papers in libraries and animals in cages. Of greater importance to silk manufacturers were his steel combs.[82] The silk trade welcomed English operatives. A factory

80 *Affiches de Lyon*, 24 October 1770 and 9 January 1771.
81 *Affiches de Lyon*, 1 July 1761: "On demande à acheter une bonne Balance à l'Angloise propre à peser de 150 à 200 marcs; on remettroit en échange une grande Balance à peser des soies, & une plus petite à la Françoise, propre à peser 120 à 150 marcs"; 3 March 1762: "Une caisse de fer à l'Angloise, propre pour fermer de l'argent; une grande balance & une petite aussi à l'Angloise, avec leurs poids, bonne l'une & l'autre pour peser la soie."
82 *Affiches de Lyon*, 17 July 1771: "Le Sieur Mason, Anglois, Pensionné du Roi, vient d'établir une Manufacture à l'Angloise, où il fabrique des Grillages en fils de laiton & de fer, depuis dix jusqu'à soixante fils par pouce, utiles pour Magasins, Bibliotheques, Cages, & Gardemangers, où les mouches ni autres insectes ne peuvent pénétrer; enfin pour toutes sortes de Tamis d'une grande utilité pour tous les grains, drogues, épiceries, farines, &c. Il donne avis à MM. les Marchands & Maîtres Fabricants en étoffes de soie, que sa demeure qui étoit ci-devant dans la maison de M. Barmont, rue de la Vieille Monnoie, est maintenant dans la maison de M. Roux, rue Royale, dans l'allée du Serrurier, au quatrieme étage, où il fabrique les Peignes d'acier pour toutes sortes d'étoffes en soie."

for printing calico at Oullins in the outskirts of Lyon was founded by a Mr Bradley, as announced on 15 May 1765.[83] Printing linen and cotton with the techniques and colours of India, Bradley offers dyeing and printing services to producers of raw silk. M. Palleron, a French dyer in Lyon, claiming to have discovered a method for dying silk black in a finer way than that of Genoa, offers raw silk dyed black in the manner of England. The retail trade was familiar with English cloth and clothes. M. Catalan, an upholsterer on the place des Jacobins, sold calicos from a new English factory suitable for furniture and apparel given the solid beauty of its colours. By 1766, a shop opened on the quai de Saint Antoine selling hats made at the English factory under royal licence at Grigny.[84]

The semi-institutional status of the London Exchange is clarified by French artists who offered to enhance domestic life there by emphasizing their foreign training. M. Voisin, in Lyon to sell medals and plaster plaques depicting Roman emperors and monarchs of France and Europe along with other ornaments, presents himself as a moulder trained at the Academy of London. His moulds are the more desirable since he learned to make them there.[85] Visiting aristocrats helped link London to luxury. When an English lord with a large family advertises for a big house in an elegant quarter, his rental request that stipulates the need for a garden, coach house, stables, and modern conveniences is embedded with signs emanating from consumption of English modes.[86] Two other landmarks near the London Exchange confirm

---

83 *Affiches de Lyon*, 15 May 1765: "Le sieur Bradley, Indienneur, a établi sa Fabrique d'Indienne à Oullins, près de Lyon. Il indienne pour tous ceux qui s'adressent à lui; sur toile soit de lin soit de coton, en véritables couleurs des Indes & à nouveaux desseins. Il fait indienner aussi sur toile de lin ou de coton, des Mouchoirs façon de la Compagnie des Indes, en rouge, véritables couleurs des Indes, qui résistent à tout lavage; & des Mouchoirs ordinaires, en bleu, à deux faces, au plus juste prix. Il avertit MM. les Fabricants qui voudroient faire fabriquer des Etoffes en soie cru, propres pour indienner, qu'il les indiennera, soit en Mouchoirs façon des Indes, ou en Robes à desseins du meilleur goût & en bon teint."

84 *Affiches de Lyon*, 28 October 1767; 22 May 1766; 28 December 1765.

85 *Affiches de Lyon*, 4 November 1762. M.Voisin calls himself "ci-devant Mouleur à l'Académie de Londres." Notably, he operates out of the house of a merchant on the place des Jacobins ("Il est logé chez M. Lasage, Marchand Faiancier, place des Jacobins").

86 *Affiches de Lyon*, 5 February 1767.

the informing presence of English people and goods. When the master of a boarding school tries to secure employment for a student as secretary to a nobleman or in an office, he directs potential employers to his premises on rue du Bât-d'argent vis-à-vis the Cheval Anglois, knowing this inn was a landmark. While buying and selling horses in French cities conveyed appreciation of Britain's superior animal breeding, this inn's name testifies to a local wish to appeal to visitors and tourists. A second landmark – one cited more often in the *affiches* – is the English Shop, which opened on the first floor of new premises built by M. Tolozan on the grand place du Plâtre. This square, to the east of the place des Terreaux, gave onto the Rhône on the quai St Clair. The Tolozan family, who built magnificent houses on that quai and on the place du Plâtre was the most prominent in Lyon. Louis Tolozan de Monfort was born there in 1726, the son of Antoine Tolozan, a peasant from the Dauphiné who arrived wearing clogs and with 24 sous in his pocket. The father's story is one of rags to riches; he made a fortune in the silk trade in which he established his family's name. Louis Tolozan was not only a merchant and manufacturer of silk but a banker, squire, and proprietor of the fief of Monfort. He served as director of alms from 1763 to 1767 and later, after leaving his bank and commercial enterprises to successors whom he financed, he was city treasurer from 1776 to 1784. When provost of merchants in January 1785, he presided over the silk industry, but over much more, for the provost and four aldermen who comprised the city government administered the police and justice in the king's name.[87] In 1789, when patriotic payment to the Revolution was fixed at a quarter of income, Louis Tolozan was inscribed for 20,000 livres, the largest contribution from the four hundred members of the merchant community. When the English

---

87 *Affiches de Lyon*, 11 October 1769; 23 May 1770. See Wahl 1974, 6, 7, and 33. "Mais Lyon est surtout ville municipale et bourgeoise. Les bourgeois comme ceux de Paris, même lorsqu'ils ne possèdent pas la noblesse personnelle, sont plus que des roturiers, ile ne payent ni les tailles ni less accessoires. Le prévôt des marchands et les quatre échevins qui composent avec lui le Consulat ne président pas seulement à l'administration de la cité, ils en ont la police et le commandement pour le roi" (Wahl 1974, 9).

Shop linked itself to the Tolozans, it stood for economic and social power in the city.[88]

Goods in this shop were luxurious. Its first advertisement, in May 1770, offers English jewellery. The following August it announces strings of pearls ornamented with diamonds in the form of earrings, necklaces, and hair ornaments. Business must have been good since a year later the shop moved from the first floor of Tolozan's house to its ground floor in the great courtyard. By this time, the shop had become a service centre; contact with proprietors wishing to rent out country houses was effected in it, even as it expanded imports of household furniture, including blue, green, and unpainted straw armchairs, dressing tables, writing tables, chests of drawers, commodes, iron cooking stoves, and carriage-horse harnesses. It imported all sorts of games and speciality items as New Year's gifts. A centre of refined consumerism, the English Shop reminded elegant customers of possessions such as inscribed parasols that they may have left behind.[89]

If differently from Lyon, Bordeaux was also influenced by Britain. Regarding the city in his *Review* of Thursday, 18 July 1706, Defoe foretells Target: "that Town has a great Deal of *English* Blood in it; the *English* were Masters of it above 300 Years, and of all the Country round it, and their Progeny are blended there with the *French*, as they are with all the rest of the World at home."[90] Since familial and commercial ties

---

88 The Tolozan name signalled bourgeois power: "Cette riche bourgeosie, dans les mains de laquelle sont les gros capitaux, le haut commerce, la fabrique, la banque, qui possède la plupart des immeubles de la ville, avec des maisons de campagne, des fermes, des châteaux, des seigneuries dans tout le pays d'alentour, est la véritable aristocratie, la classe régnante" (Wahl 1974, 7). No wonder Louis Tolozan was an object of hate and destruction in the Revolution (Wahl 1974, 95): attacks on him conveyed resistance to the consulat. Early in the Revolution, he retired to his chateau at Ouillins. His role in commerce and municipal government made him the leader of a privileged urban elite: "le corps municipal tel qu'il est constitué ne représente qu'une oligarchie: les quelques douzaines de familles, nobles ou bourgeoises, qui tiennent le haut commerce et la banque, occupent les principales charges de justice et de finance et la plupart des bénéfices ecclésiastiques, et qui sont vraiment les familles consularies de Lyon" (Wahl 1974, 16).

89 *Affiches de Lyon*, 20 August 1770; 20 November 1771; 18 September 1771; 1 May and 2 October 1771; 28 December 1771; 30 December 1772; 17 October 1770.

90 *A Review of the Affairs of France*, Thursday, 18 July 1706, 3:342.

remained strong during the War of Spanish Succession, Defoe emphasizes that British and French blood had mingled there for centuries. What he does not say is that Bordeaux was home to "nations," or groups of European merchants. One was an Irish community that fostered the vignoble, wine trade, and banking through Jacobite immigration. Irish institutions such as the Catholic College and the regiment sustained by the Dillon family flourished until the Revolution. The ennoblement of Irish families and the fact the Lynch family provided a long-serving mayor testify to an impact rendered weighty by political, economic, and religious conflicts within Britain that were tempered by Bordeaux's ethnically diverse merchant community.[91] Its urban development was shaped by German, Dutch, Flemish, Anglo-Saxon, Swiss, and Russian traders who were obliged to reside in the outskirts. One obstacle to the city's growth, however, was the Château-Trompette, a fortress modernized by Louis XIV to coerce the loyalty of the Bordelais. Its cannons threatening vessels on the Garonne, the castle monitored wine exports, the route across the river to northern France, and the livelihood of citizens. It slowed growth by cutting the city into three, blocking communication between the old one inside the medieval walls to the south, the Saint-Seurin quarter to the west, and the district of the Chartrons to the north reserved for the nations.[92] Vital as redistributing exporters of goods to northern Europe, the nations enjoyed liberal living conditions, appointing their magistrates and consuls. Since their energy drew many immigrants from France and attracted the financial expertise of Portuguese Jews, they persuaded intendants to modernize the city by freeing it from its medieval walls and reducing the blockading effects of Château-Trompette.[93] Claude Boucher (1673/5–1752), Louis-Urbain-Aubert de Tourny (1695–1760), and Nicolas Dupré de

---

91 Ennobled Irish families were widespread in France. The *affiches* of Angers reveals the economic and cultural influence of Lords Southwell and Walsh. Owners of estates, they not only created local employment but encouraged the importation of luxury goods. When Southwell's property was put on the market the range of his influence was apparent (*Affiches d'Angers*, 22 April 1785; 2 and 16 December 1785; and 7 July 1786). When Irish regiments were disbanded at the Revolution, Lord Walsh who had recruited and financed one for years, emigrated, his reluctant departure revealing how great had been his influence on the local economy and culture (*Affiches d'Angers*, 12 and 26 June 1788; 4 May, 15 May, and 31 August 1790).

92 Desgraves 1960, 21.

93 Ibid., 34.

Saint-Maur (1732–1791) made changes, resisting public opinion voiced by the Jurade and the Parlement: Boucher supervised construction of the Bourse and the Place Royale, breaching the medieval walls; Tourny built the city's facade on the Garonne, created the *allées* that bear his name, and widened principal streets; and Dupré de Saint-Maur began the demolition of Château-Trompette. The Grand Theatre gave form in the 1770s to a district where West Indian merchants rivalled one another in building elegant *hôtels*.[94] Trade and social refinement had begun to be linked by 1755 when the Place Royale with its Hôtel des Fermes and Bourse became modish in Bordeaux's new commercial centre.[95] Sixty-five stone benches invited people to take in the fine buildings and river scenery undisturbed by the port's noisy activities. Tourny, following his predecessor in replacing the medieval gates with triumphal arches and spacious squares, created *cours* and airy promenades.[96] Perhaps his major decision was to integrate the Chartrons into the city by making the allées de Tourny lead into the Jardin Public which in 1746 opened in the faubourg Saint-Seurin. Wanting the garden to improve the health and entertainment of the Bordelais, he devised it so that merchants might conduct business there. It was a second bourse – a bourse of the evening.[97] The route linking the city, the garden, Saint-Seurin, and the Chartrons bypassed Château-Trompette. Next Tourny embellished the quai with an elegant facade and extended the Chemin de Roi so that the road to and from Paris cut through the quarter: interior and exterior routes made the Chartrons vital to the city.[98]

These urban changes matched its growing maritime and commercial status. In 1681, it had become the entrepôt for Caribbean tobacco; in 1684, a reduced excise on sugar favoured this import; the Chamber of Commerce was established in 1705; the city received a monopoly on the slave trade in 1710; letters patent authorized the port to arm ships for West Indies trade in 1717 and permitted it to export, import, and re-export goods in a tax-favoured situation. Its shipbuilding flourished;

---

94 Ibid., 36.
95 Ibid., 166.
96 Ibid., 37.
97 Ibid., 353: "C'est en quelque façon une seconde Bourse, une Bourse du soir."
98 Ibid., 39.

fourteen vessels were built in 1754 with thirty-four completed in 1782.[99] Throughout the century, Bordeaux had the fastest-growing population in France, moving from 45,000 in 1715 to 110,000 in 1790. In these years, the wine trade grew by 50 per cent, and colonial trade rose by twenty times to represent a quarter of French commerce.[100] The British community numbering over three hundred persons when the Seven Years War started accelerated this growth. Half were Protestants, half exiled Jacobites. Eighty-eight family heads were active in trade, twenty-five as company owners and twenty-seven as managers.[101] With merchants and tradesmen from other nations, they infiltrated the city. Britain's monopoly on first-growth wines had long encouraged nobles to develop estates and *chais*, and modes of British business had altered dining customs by arranging meals of twenty *couverts*.[102] Yet Britons, in marketing producer and consumer goods, influenced daily life beyond the modes of aristocrats and merchants. The city's newspapers show that it had many British residents and visitors, such as medical doctors, industrialists, and teachers.[103] Members of the Parlement employed 450 servants, many being British. Of the eight thousand servants working during the American War of Independence, a lot had crossed La Manche.[104]

British visitors admired Bordeaux, its European image and cultural dynamism. Mrs Craddock and husband, touring France between 1783 and 1786 to observe industrial growth, in June and July of 1785 stayed

---

99 Ibid., 33. Shipbuilding accounted for one out of every five registered French vessels ("Bordeaux: An Eighteenth Century Wirtschaftswunder" in Crouzet 1996, 2:45). Crouzet downplays institutional changes in Bordeaux; the city shared with twelve others the privilege of exporting to the colonies with customs exemptions. To him, Bordeaux's ability to export agricultural goods, including flour, wine, and brandy, from its hinterland and to re-export salted beef from Ireland accounts for its competitive advantage (1996, 2:46–9).

100 Doyle 1974, 2; Butel and Poussou 1980, 21–4.

101 Butel and Poussou 1980, 24.

102 Ibid., 169–71, 188, and 71.

103 I follow Jean Sgard, ed., *Dictionnaire des journaux* (Paris: Universitas, 1991), in calling the Bordeaux newspapers the *affiches*. The actual titles are: *Annonces, Affiches et Avis* (1758–59); *Annonces, Affiches, Nouvelles et Avis divers pour la ville de Bordeaux* (1760-63); *Annonces, Affiches, et Avis divers pour la ville de Bordeaux* (1764–84). The successor, *Journal de Guienne*, which appeared daily, ran from 1784 to 1790.

104 Butel and Poussou 1980, 40.

at the refurbished Hôtel d'Angleterre on the cours de Tourny.[105] They admired the stylish white-stone houses overlooking the cours and facing Europe's grandest theatre. In summer heat, they found the promenade on the quai des Chartrons refreshing. From their windows, they enjoyed, like thousands of spectators in the cours, a military parade the manoeuvres of which were overseen by the Duke and Duchess de Mouchy, the intendant and his wife.[106] In the region to study the vignoble – cultivation of vines, structure of soils, and classification of estates – Thomas Jefferson (1743–1826) attributed the wine trade's success to British merchants.[107] The city's commerce, wealth, and magnificence exceeded Arthur Young's expectations. He faulted the lengthy quai for lacking order and style: ships could not dock, the shore sloping, muddy, and obstructed by barges. Admiring the place Royale, he was more impressed by the Chapeau Rouge, the merchant quarter with houses of white stone, the building material favoured throughout the city, even in the outskirts where tradesmen built small houses after the peace of 1783 at the end of the American War of Independence. He was excited by plans for the extension of Chapeau Rouge into the area to be left vacant by the razing of Château-Trompette and the

105 The Cradocks were typical tourists in visiting factories that manufactured luxury items. They took note of English workers and manufacturers in France. On visiting the glass factory at Sèvres on 7 June 1784, they met a compatriot, one of the workshop heads, who got angrier and angrier about fellow workers and France. This skilled man had been persuaded to immigrate on the promise of being well recompensed for revealing his manufacturing secrets. But, since English law proscribed him as a traitor and banned him from returning to his native land, the factory defaulted on its promise and disparaged his skills and work (Balleyguier 1896, 39–40). A happier Parisian visit was to Mr Arthur's factory, which produced exquisite wallpapers. Mrs Cradock admired the illusions produced by papers imitating flower-embroidered tissue, stone sculptures, and ornamented glassworks (Balleyguier 1896, 72). The Hôtel d'Angleterre was founded on 12 April 1777. It was directed by Stevens and Jacob, two Englishmen. It was praised by Arthur Young as well as by Mrs Cradock. Frederick Augustus, son of George III, travelling under the name of Count Delphios, stayed there in 1791 and addressed the municipality on 30 May, hoping commercial ties between Bordeaux and England would remain strong. In 1793, the hotel was renamed the Hotel Franklin, reverting to an earlier appellation (Desgraves 1960, 346).

106 Balleyguier 1896, 201–15. The intendant and his wife were executed on 27 June 1794. The Revolution, as Crouzet explains, was hard on Bordeaux's economic life (1996, 2:56).

107 Jefferson, "Memoranda taken on a Journey from Paris into the Southern Parts of France, and Northern of Italy, in the year 1787" (1903, 18:122–6).

construction of a square, new streets, and 1,800 houses. Enthusiasm for "private exertion" as the main cause of prosperity led him to blame the French court and Britain's merchant community for sponsoring wars that hindered the city's development, the building boom having ended from fear war might be resumed.[108]

Still, cultural forces impelling Bordeaux's economic development had been present for years, the tastes of residents long catered to by merchants and tradesmen who imported products from Britain or imitated its manufacture in local factories and workshops. In turn, caterers and suppliers extended their services beyond the British community, modifying the supply of goods and services in the city and its hinterland. Hotels were rivals in appealing to Britons. M. Batut opened his Grand Hôtel d'Angleterre on the place du Chapelet, west of the Grand Theatre and southwest of the allées de Tourny in 1781. He wanted guests of the first quality for meals or lodgings, catered to individual diets, and took pensioners by the month or year. With a coach house, stables, and a range of facilities, his hotel opened before the peace was signed at the end of the American War. Batut competed with the Hôtel d'Angleterre on the grand cours de Tourny nearby and a little to the northwest. Founded in 1777, the hotel while still operating went up for rent in October 1785. Described as a modern building near the Jardin Royal, it had two storeys with finished attics, an underground kitchen, an office, a wine cellar, and a small cellar, courtyard, and well; on the ground floor its staircase with iron railings was notable, as were a large dining room giving onto the garden, its stable, coach house, corn-loft, and panelled, nicely laid-out apartments. This floor plan was repeated on the second storey, with bedrooms in the attic. The hotel, like Batut's, hosted English visitors in the American War, as shown by an advertisement for a four-wheeled English coupéd carriage with four springs.[109]

Horses and carriages of owners coming to the city were put on sale at the Hôtel d'Angleterre, Stevens, the hotelier, making it a transport centre.[110] Theodore Martell, a *négociant* in the Chartrons, made available for inspection there a nearly new carriage.[111] The hotel's

---

108 Young 1970, 1:60–1.
109 *Affiches de Bordeaux*, 10 May 1781; 30 May 1785; 9 August 1781.
110 *Journal de Guienne*, 16 June 1785 and 22 November 1787.
111 *Journal de Guienne*, 16 March 1790.

integration into the local economy is evident when Stevens rents space to London négociants for temporary shops.[112] His advertisements in the *Journal de Guienne* show he was close to the populace. As a transport centre, the hotel advertised on behalf of British residents and visitors seeking carriage seats for specific destinations. One Englishman, claiming to be well known and wishing to set out for Nantes and the Orient, asked to share a carriage.[113] The hotel's integration is clear from how Stevens made it serve as an exchange for employers and job-seekers. One visitor wished to hire a fifteen- to eighteen-year-old apprentice cabinet- and artificial flower-maker to train in English modes. Another wanted to hire a certificated, native English male servant. Yet another wanted an attendant able to shave and speak English whom he intended to take to Dublin. One young unmarried English woman used the hotel as a contact place when advertising services as a governess or lady's companion. The hotel's proximity to the Jardin Public and to a major axis of communication between the old city and the Chartrons gained it informal institutional status. This was admitted by city officers when they called a meeting of foreign négociants to discuss how their status had been affected by the Revolution.[114]

The Hôtel d'Angleterre's closeness to the Jardin Public, the Grand Théâtre, and Bourse suggests the policy of containing Britons and their goods within the Chartrons failed. The reach of British négociants, merchants, and tradesmen beyond the Chartrons signals their cultural influence. Operations in the Chapeau Rouge and factories and warehouses inside the medieval walls and in Bordeaux's hinterland confirm that they satisfied demand and fashion. As in Lyon, shops purveyed commercial and aesthetic standards to the Bordelais. The goods in English shops, particularly in the 1780s, signify industrial provenance. While shops still flourished in the Chartrons, their reach into main business districts increased property values and sped development in central neighbourhoods. According to adverts in the *affiches* and *Journal de Guienne*, English shops arose and prospered between July 1776 and October 1781, the period of actual fighting in the American War. The adverts of M. Tessa, an optician, during and after the war reveal how

112 *Journal de Guienne*, 3 July 1787.
113 *Journal de Guienne*, 2 June 1787.
114 *Journal de Guienne*, 11 February 1788; 24 February 1788; 11 July 1789; 31 March 1787; 19 January 1790.

English goods affected shopkeepers and consumers. Tessa sold imported luxury goods in the Bourse and on the place Royale before moving to the rue Richelieu on the quai south of the Bourse. On 1 January 1778, he announced, as just arrived from London, Moroccan leather wallets decorated with penknives and scissors, fruit baskets, cruets, sugar bowls, coffee and tea pots, writing desks, candle holders, soup spoons, ladles, and warming plates. He extended his luxury goods that year when he offered for rent or sale fairy lights for holiday illuminations along with other novelties from London, such as large vases and crystal goldfish bowls. Three years later, when he sold fairy lights made of coloured English glass and advertised raw imported English silk, he named his premises the English shop. After the Eden Treaty of 1786, he expanded his optical and marine instruments by adding Ramsden of London's telescopes, opera glasses, binoculars, microscopes, and lenses. Bent on novelty, he sold lamps for purifying air in hotels, offices, and shops. His widow imported, unimpeded by the Revolution, all kinds of stuffs and hardware as well as hydrometers, barometers, and thermometers.[115]

Tessa's shop reveals a growing retail dependence on Britain. After 1776, the sale of producer and consumer goods was often marked by Englishness, which stood for utility and luxury, efficiency and style. The desirability of English tools appears in many adverts. Lathes for cabinetmakers and toolkits for smiths and clockmakers are said to excel because English.[116] Craftsmen imitated British manufacturing styles: a locksmith offers English-style furniture locks and a jeweller sets diamonds in the latest London as well as Paris modes.[117] English foodstuffs were increasingly available. The Irish shop in the Chartrons listed Gloucestershire and Cheshire cheese, mustard, and London bottled beer. Such goods were aimed not simply at British residents; nobles were invited to provision grape pickers with English cheese. When M. Bernière took on "l'*Hôtel du Prince de Galles*" on rue Capdeville in Saint-Seurin, he heightens its appeal by stressing its spacious rooms,

---

115 Jesse Ramsden (1735–1800) was honoured by the Royal Society for his optical inventions. *Affiches de Bordeaux*, 22 October, 1778; 15 November 1781; *Journal de Guienne*, 17 October 1787; 6 November 1787; 19 February 1790.

116 *Affiches de Bordeaux*, 24 September and 29 October 1778.

117 *Affiches de Bordeaux*, 23 November 1780; 13 September 1781.

pleasant gardens and terraces, and fine food and wine by saying he worked as a "Cuisinier en Angleterre."[118]

While Bernière's hotel shows British goods and services traversing the medieval city, John Howison's shop, situated in the building on the Chapeau Rouge near the Grand Theatre out of which the *affiches* operated, proves his economic power. He sold clothing materials for ecclesiastics and ladies, eyeglasses by Dolland of London, and high-quality English razors.[119] He also offered English pencils, Whitechapel needles, London bedspreads, and loads of tin plate. Besides listing English boots, buckles, lacquered candlesticks, and Irish flannel, he offers sideboards decorated with paintings by Benjamin West (1738–1820) and Thomas Gainsborough (1727–1788). Selling beer and porter in bottles and barrels alongside tin cooking pots, he evades restrictions on French retailers. His marketing was aggressive: in an announcement of tableware, including knives with ivory handles, silver-plated cutlery, scissors and razors, he offers a 15 per cent discount to those paying cash, while in another offering textiles, pottery, chinaware, men's outfittings such as boots, swords, saddles, and bridles, he admits that, by buying up failed shops, he is not limited by reserve prices.[120]

Such retailing illustrates the competitive success of English shops. Mr Murphy operated one on St Catherine Street that marketed all sorts of merchandise and drove up the price of houses nearby.[121] Spencer and Company had an English shop on the Chapeau Rouge in M. Barthez's house. Located amid residences of the richest merchants, it sold engravings by Hogarth and William Woollett (1735–1785) as well as the finest crystal and chinaware.[122] The English shop of M. Milhas

---

118 *Affiches de Bordeaux*, 5 July 1781; 6 September 1781; *Journal de Guienne*, 1 August 1786.

119 John Dollond (1706–1761) was recognized by the Royal Society for his optical and astronomical instruments. He patented and commercialized achromatic doublets.

120 *Journal de Guienne*, 15 October 1787; 21 October and 17 November 1787; 20 and 29 December 1787; 2 May 1788; 25 July and 30 October 1788.

121 *Journal de Guienne*, 5 June 1787; 29 May 1788. Trade with England was known to affect property values. One advertisement for the sale of a fine large house in the Chartrons rented out in 1761 for 1,350 livres announced that the rent would increase to 2,500 livres on the day that "la paix avec l'Angleterre sera publiée" (*Affiches de Bordeaux*, 16 April 1761).

122 *Journal de Guienne*, 9 November and 11 December 1787; 22 April 1788.

on the Chapeau Rouge sold flannel, cottons, wool stockings, as well as oven-proof pottery and anchors.[123] Competition among English shops was keen in the Chartrons. M. Constantin's English shop sold Cheshire cheese, and in hers Mrs Connell stocked superfine chinaware: plates, terrines, oval and round serving dishes, white and coloured coffee cups, and many stuffs, including rare oriental cloths.[124] The influence of such shops is clear from their increasing diversification of goods. In his shop on the place de la Comédie, Mr Sykes sold the thermometer invented by Josiah Wedgwood (1730–1795) on which he wrote for the newspaper, recommending its utility to distillers. When Mr Maynard assumed Sykes's shop at the Revolution, he increased the supply of English goods, making sure, however, to stock up on French products so as to appeal to rural customers.[125]

Official efforts to block imports by setting up 'English factories' in Bordeaux were effective only in tightening bonds between English industrialism and French consumerism. In 1764, Mme Brabant opened a factory to make English wallpaper outside the city near a water supply. She staffed it with a designer, engraver, dyer, metalworker, and woodworker whom she hired locally and lodged at the plant. Her tasteful shop was situated on the quai Bourgeois near the Porte du Caillou, a gate south of the Bourse that opened the city to the port.[126] A few years later, English merchants also set up factories. James Wilson established one in the Chartrons for the production of paper and velvet wall hangings in the English mode, appealing to the taste of négociants and basing his reputation on aggressive pricing.[127] The next month, Duras, a newly arrived Englishman, announced his factory on the square near the Porte Dauphine. To exploit the housing boom, he offers wall hangings for all domestic spaces, including ceilings. His coverings include gold and silver tissues, Chinese materials, and Chinese patterns. Some have Indian designs, others presenting rural landscapes with the embossed appearance of stucco. At no extra charge he hangs his own coverings. His advertisements acknowledge the encouragement given him by Messieurs les Jurats and magnify the health benefits of wallpapers

---

123 *Journal de Guienne*, 22 April 1788; 24 January 1789; 15 March 1789.
124 *Journal de Guienne*, 10 February and 21 February 1788; 24 January 1790.
125 *Journal de Guienne*, 3 March 1788; 24 July 1789.
126 *Affiches de Bordeaux*, 26 April 1764.
127 *Affiches de Bordeaux*, 23 April 1772.

that reduce dust and fleas. He matches the designs of wall hangings to coverings of furniture and draperies. All his products are numbered and marked with fixed prices. Renewing his advert the following December, he claims to have made a breakthrough in lowered production costs that he passes on to customers. He has ordered a new machine from England that will produce all kinds of wallpapers more cheaply than anywhere in Europe.[128]

Neither an industrial centre like Lyon, a rival to Paris, nor a port like Bordeaux that was vital to France's economy, Dijon is a third example of British influences on urban geography. Despite its size, Dijon gained regional and international prominence in the pre-revolutionary era. From 1730 and 1770 "une ville moyenne," it had no more than 23,000 inhabitants.[129] Far from letting its medieval walls restrict its urban spaces, the city transformed them to appeal to residents and tourists. Unimpeded by a static population, it became Burgundy's capital with a strong institutional life. As an administrative, legal, and political centre and home to the Parlement, 20 per cent of its inhabitants worked directly or indirectly "au service de l'État."[130] A guardian of educational and cultural tradition, the city gained a faculty of law in 1723 and a bishopric in 1731.[131] Its seminaries, renowned Jesuit college, and famous Academy of Sciences, Arts and Belles-Lettres gave Dijon a conservative tone, ingraining daily life with "une forte culture classique."[132] Municipal policies enhanced the city's advantages as a transportation centre, opening it up to visitors, especially those on the Grand Tour. Dijon's location at the crossroads of "sept routes royales" exploited transportation advances: improvements in roads, carriages, horses, canals, and "coches d'eau" brought it closer to Paris, between 1765 and 1780, the journey each way falling from six to three days.[133] As many as five thousand Britons resided in Paris in the 1760s. Many visited Dijon and environs in the 1770s and 1780s.[134] Burgundy was known by Britons to be an

---

128 *Affiches de Bordeaux*, 7 May 1772; 10 December 1772.
129 Ligou 1981, 143–4.
130 Ibid., 150.
131 Ibid., 161 and 157.
132 Bourée 1932, 214. Bourée reports there were "seize monastères d'hommes et de femmes" in Dijon (1932, 209).
133 Braudel 1984, 3:316–17.
134 Black 1985, 4–5; Lough 1987, 11, 25, 131–5, 152–3, and 161–3.

inexpensive, agreeable place in which to live. When, on 20 December 1757, John Carmichael, a Jacobite, wrote from Fontaine Gaillarde near Sens to James Edgar, an agent for the exiled Jacobite Court, to request credit from his "Royal Sovereign" to provide for his family, he underscores his frugality by saying that he has "taken a house and a small farm in Bourgogne where the ground is not very dear" and where he expects, once clear of debts incurred from furnishing his home, to be self-supporting.[135]

Edward Southwell the younger, an experienced European traveller who became secretary to the Council of Ireland in 1730 and was elected MP for Bristol in 1739, recorded his sense of Dijon in October 1725. The rebuilt Logis du Roy, the Palais with its Chambre du Parlement, the churches of St John, St Michael, and St Stephen, and the tombs of the Dukes of Burgundy with their architectural marble and sculptural beauties were impressive. He was also taken with "the first vintage of all France."[136] On his stay from January to May in 1731, Spence upheld Southwell's views of institutional and church architecture; he found the city "handsome," its streets "broad and well paved," its walks "grand, and those on the ramparts very agreeable." Among the 150 people who attended concerts and masquerades in Lent, Spence met Jacobite exiles.[137] If British residents were few, their impact on Dijon was significant. In 1730, sixteen English families were in residence. By the Revolution, this number reached fifty, including prominent aristocratic clans.[138]

According to Claude Courtépée, Dijon's promenades made the city unique.[139] The relation between spaces outside and on the city walls was visually and socially stimulating. Citizens took the air in the shade of allées formed by hundreds of chestnut trees and by arbours of linden trees, leaning on the parapet to enjoy the prospect of the plain, the river, the city, and its fauxbourgs. From the turn of the century, civic pride came from using the ramparts as public spaces. The section

---

135 Tayler 1939, 224.
136 Black 1985b, 47–8.
137 Spence 1975, 34–6.
138 Mead 1914, 239; Giroux 1981, 215. Other provincial cities had numbers of English residents. In 1787, Horace Walpole says sixty English families were resident in Nice (Faber 1975, 113).
139 Courtépée 1986, 2:87.

between the Saint-Pierre gate and the river Ouche, an 852-metre-long portion of the south and southwest walls known as the Beau Mur or Beau Rempart, featured in the city's maintenance budget. The year 1716 saw the "bastion d'Ouche" mounded with soil, Mayors Labotte and Baudinet having it planted with trees in the shape of a star, called the Quinconce, in the middle of which a Vauxhall or English-style pleasure garden was built. This Vauxhall, inaugurated on 3 June 1769, was a large, open-air hall surrounded by loges. Dancing started at five p.m. to the music of a symphony orchestra, and, after midnight fireworks, the hall was illuminated by thousands of lanterns visible to the promenades. Dancing went on until three a.m.[140] When M. Ferry, director of the theatre and Dijon's entertainment director, named the summer fêtes Vauxhall, his initiative testifies to a receptivity to English visitors and even to anglomania.[141] The original pleasure park, Spring Garden, opened on 2 July 1661 at Lambeth, soon taking on the name of Vauxhall, the district of London in which Lambeth finds itself.[142] This name became the generic title for pleasure gardens in and beyond England. While the opening of Dijon's Vauxhall followed hard on the one opened by M. Terre at St Cloud in Paris, that the name touched Dijon the same summer as Paris confirms Burgundy's openness to Englishness.[143] This is reinforced by an English circus's visit to Dijon to perform at the Jardin de l'Arquebuse in 1769.[144]

The conversion of ramparts and the operation of the Vauxhall show a municipality keen to benefit from wealthy British residents and visitors. Competition for Vauxhall's directorship and lesser posts, such as

140 Marc 1898, 10 and 31–2.
141 Micault 1887, 206.
142 Rudé 1971, 73.
143 The origins of Vauxhall Gardens are likely bicultural: the original may have been either founded by a Frenchman, Français de Vaux, or established on the site of the château of a Norman baron called Faulk de Brand (Marc 1898, 30–1). In *Le Mercure Dijonnais*, Dumay cites M. Fyot de Mimeure, *Notice sur la ville de Dijon et ses environs* (Dijon: Gaulard-Marin, 1817, 20), as saying that the pleasure gardens "conserva [le nom de Vauxhall] tant que les Anglais nous apportèrent leur argent et leur personnes; quand la Révolution nous en priva, il prit le nom de Tivoli à l'imitation d'un établissement de ce genre dans la capitale" (1887, 206).
144 For this and other popular entertainments, such as jugglers and puppeteers, see Perrenet 1920, 15–16. He insists the Vauxhall was so named to honour English visitors.

the right to teach dancing and to hold balls, confirms this economic reality. When in 1775 M. Virot, a firework-maker in town, won a ten-year contract to manage the Vauxhall, he invested in an elegant refreshment hall and covered walk. He highly decorated his coffeehouse, shrewdly providing liqueurs and bonbons.[145] It benefited M. Haitray, a dancing master, in 1787 to win the right to organize balls and banquets in the Vauxhall, the licence issued by the Marquis de Gouvernet, Bourgogne's commandant-in-chief.[146] The significance of Dijon's Vauxhall, as with others across France, came from integration into political and ceremonial life. When in 1777 Dijon welcomed the king's brother, Louis-Stanislas-Xavier, Comte de Provence, it sanded and carpeted streets, fired canons, rang city bells, feasted him, and closed his day with a visit to Vauxhall at 11:30 p.m. On the Prince de Condé's visit in 1778, Dijon decorated the ramparts with "pyramides de lampions" and lit the covered walk in the Vauxhall with "une double bordure de pots à feu" to protect the huge crowds from injury. On other visits, the prince's days culminated in the Vauxhall.[147]

Le Mercure Dijonnois, Claude Micault's account of spectacles in and beyond the Vauxhall, shows that English residents and visitors often participated. Thus, he reports that when the wife of an Anglican gentleman, a certain "madame Clartie," bears a son in 1768, the baptism is attended by the noblest local dignitaries: it is heralded by "une descharge de canon," a regiment of the watch, and a troop of soldiers marching before the Duke of Burgundy's carriage, which is surrounded by a company of horse guards. Up to the Revolution, English residents and visitors of social standing initiated events and dignified major occasions with their presence. Micault records that in March 1785 "tous les Anglois qui étoient à Dijon" gave a ball to honour married and unmarried ladies, that "l'assemblée fut brillante," and that the Dijonnaises, responding to the English, "firent parfaitement bien leurs honneurs." To celebrate "l'ouverture de la vendange de Dijon" in 1787, M. de Montigny hosted

---

145 Micault 1887, 274. The opening of the Vauxhall was one setting for public rejoicings over the re-establishment of the Dijon Parlement by the young Louis XVI in 1774. Virot's name is given as Viret in the notice in the *affiches* for 28 May 1776 on the occasion of that season's opening of the Vauxhall on Sunday, 2 June.
146 Marc 1898, 31–2.
147 Micault 1887, 280–1, 284, 291, and 318.

a supper and ball; the splendour was confirmed by the attendance of thirty-two local ladies and by "une partie angloise et beaucoup de jeunes miss."[148] When the Prince de Condé arrived in Dijon on 10 November 1787, ten of the fifteen ladies presented to him were English. That evening among the two hundred guests attending the dinner put on by the intendant for the prince the same ten ladies were among the thirty women present. When English patrons ignored codes in diplomatic and aristocratic functions, their faux pas amusingly illustrated the licence they were afforded. On 11 March 1776, "mylord Craunn, de la maison de Monrose" gave a fête at the Intendance, comprising a supper, ball, and "un grand jeu" but mistakenly invited "bourgeoises" as well as ladies of quality.[149] The latter, hearing the former had been invited, would not go, while the former, refusing to demean themselves by staying away, went, thereby reducing the brilliance of the fête.[150]

While English nobility were welcomed by Dijon, all English residents and visitors benefited property owners. Where English people resided had advertising appeal: when Abbé Roux of the Sainte Chapelle offered for rent a residential pavilion owned by his order in the district of Saint Nicolas, he clinched his *annonce* in the *affiches de Dijon* by declaring the property was "où demeuroient des Anglois."[151] In the Revolution's early years, property in the environs was promoted for being associated with Englishness. An English garden in the Fauxbourg d'Ouche behind the General Hospital with pavilion, coach house, stables, and outbuildings was presented as desirable because of its walled enclosure planted with fruit trees and poplars. In the commune

148 Marc-Antoine Chartraire de Montigny was the "trésorier général des États de Bourgogne," a powerful authority who was nicknamed "le vice-roi de Bourgogne" (Bourée 1932, 206).

149 To Henri Giroux, Milord Craun's "fête" was not peculiar in including gambling; some inhabitants of Dijon counted on winning large sums from foreign visitors (1973–75, 202).

150 Micault 1887, 199, 321, 333–4, and 277.

151 *Annonces et Affiches de Dijon* (Dijon: Jacques Causse, 1770–76), 14 April 1770. Later titles were: *Affiches, Annonces et Avis Divers de Bourgogne* (Dijon: L.N. Frantin, 1776–83); *Affiches de Dijon* (Dijon: J.B. Capel, 1783–95). On this press, see A. Ronsin, "La librairie et l'imprimerie en Bourgogne d'après une enquête de 1764," *Annales de Bourgogne* 32 (1960): 126–37. For ease of reference I call these newspapers by the same name: *Affiches de Dijon*.

of Saint-Martin-du-Mont, a pond called "des Anglois" went for sale without having its name changed.[152]

The lasting effect of English residents on real estate appears in the listing of houses and apartments near the Vauxhall. Even with the political turbulence and closure of the pleasure garden caused by the Revolution, citizens with properties overlooking the ramparts did not drop its name from adverts in the *affiches*. A merchant candlemaker offers two large gardens, one with access onto the ramparts and the other into rue Maison Rouge. The latter had a hot house. The former was a summer house consisting of two large salons with two small rooms, a kitchen with an earthen floor, and a cellar. Apartments on streets close to the ramparts were advertised on the assumption that English occupants were available: one landlord on the rue du Chaignot offered three partially furnished apartments suitable for lodging English people. After the Revolution when the English had supposedly left, property development exploited the renown of the Vauxhall. One newly built small house with a charming garden led to by a promenade of linden tress was put up for sale on 16 August 1791. In 1793, the year the Vauxhall was dismantled, adverts of property were common: apartments with gardens giving on to the ramparts were advertised on 26 February 1793; they boasted good views from galleries overlooking gardens, and one had a billiard room. Such adverts did not cease when citizen Piget, who won the right to dismantle the Vauxhall, sold as building materials the planks of oak, rafters, casements with window panes, and rooms and closets garnished with floor tiles and covered with roofing tiles which he despoiled along with the plum, apple, and cherry trees "en plein vent & en quenouilles." Later, gardens with flower beds and vegetable plots giving on to the ramparts of Vauxhall became available. They had been developed with an aesthetic sense of English appreciation for outdoor living, gardening, and exotic plants such as pomegranate and orange trees. Galleries overlooking parterres and orchards figure prominently in such adverts.[153]

---

152 *Affiches de Dijon*, 28 September 1790; 30 November 1790.
153 *Affiches de Dijon*, 19 May 1789; 20 April 1790; 19 March 1793; 4 June 1793 and Tridi brumaire de l'an troisième.

BRITISH EXPORTS AND FRENCH CONSUMERISM

By enterprise of its agrarian and industrial revolutions or by accidents of war, Britain's produce became habitual to French consumers. The Atlantic seaboard being accessible in war and peace, English seafood penetrated the hinterland. In 1750, oysters from England with ones from Marennes and La Rochelle were sold in Lyon; salt salmon from Aberdeen and cod from the Grand Banks of Newfoundland also marketed there in 1770.[154] Shipping reports in the coastal cities of Rouen, Nantes, and La Rochelle show that English meat, dairy produce, and grain were provided by licensed traders, smugglers and privateers. During the Seven Years War, English boats from Chester took flour to Le Havre, the traffic accelerating when peace preliminaries were signed in late 1762.[155] Before the signing of the Treaty of Paris in 1763, vessels from England, Scotland, and Ireland carried flour and corned beef along with lead, tobacco, and candles to Le Havre.[156] Ships seized by Dunkirk frigates put onto the market hundreds of barrels of English flour destined for Portugal.[157] English and French biscuit from a seized vessel was earlier marketed for grape pickers and soldiers at La Rochelle, showing that English food was institutionally useful.[158] When cargo from the *Fox Hunter* was sold in Nantes in February and March of 1781, the sale was overseen by the consul of France, the vessel having been taken by a royal frigate.[159] Since the cargo was food, drugs, edge tools, hardware, tin and copper dishes, and prohibited dry goods, this sale highlights English food-related goods, the press lauding pirates who made Cheshire cheese and English beer available in Nantes and Orléans.[160]

Forty years before the Eden Treaty of 1786, a trade balance favoured England five to one, many imports related to eating.[161] In emergencies

---

154 *Affiches de Lyon*, 17 November 1750; 14 February 1770.
155 *Affiches de Rouen*, 17 December 1762.
156 *Affiches de Rouen*, 8 April 1763.
157 *Affiches de Rouen*, 19 November 1762.
158 *Affiches de La Rochelle*, 3 September 1779.
159 *Affiches de Nantes*, 2 February 1781.
160 *Affiches de Nantes*, 24 August 1781; *Affiches d'Orléans*, 19 March 1779.
161 For editorials on the trade imbalance, see *Journal de Guienne*, 31 July and 18 August 1785. Mercantilist fear of England was aggravated by the sense that the

after the Treaty, as when the *affiches* at Caen reported on English ships delayed by the cold in the face of a desperate need for grain in early 1789, reliance on English foodstuffs was acute.[162] But the flood of imports after 1786 reflects a long-standing trend as much as the effect of the Treaty. The bottled and barrelled beer, the mustards, cheeses, and best Chinese teas sold in the English shops of Bordeaux after 1787 were offered by English and French traders, including courtiers, who had long promoted English food along with faience, casseroles, saucepans, and cooking pots at London prices.[163] English mustard was sold as condiment and medicament in fashionable shops in Angers, Dijon, and Lyon as well as Paris and Versailles before 1770: its long keeping and restoration of invalid appetites was heralded.[164] Reports of butter, cheese, and mustard after 1789 reveal such products were used in culinary sauces.[165]

English agriculture changed farming and eating in coastal regions, being promoted from Paris. Potatoes arrived before the Eden Treaty. A bordelais growing best English, Irish, and American potatoes marketed them in 1785, claiming his potato flour had the properties of sago.[166] High-grade English potatoes were sold wholesale and retail after the

Eden Treaty would speed imports that were rated at 53 million livres while French exports to England were rated at 10 million. See François Crouzet, "England and France in the Eighteenth Century: A Comparative Analysis of Two Economic Growths" in Hartwell 1967, 139–74. France's economy grew but suffered deflation in food prices since it lacked Britain's "national market" (Crouzet 1967, 163).

162 *Affiches de Caen*, 18 January 1789.

163 The following issues of *Journal de Guienne* illustrate competition between English shops in Bordeaux: 2 September 1787; 2 November 1787; 20 January 1788; 10 February 1788; 2 May 1788; 27 June 1788; 21 July 1788; 9 September 1789; 24 February 1790.

164 *Affiches de Lyon*, 22 February 1769; *Affiches de La Rochelle*, 28 January 1774.

165 *Affiches de Nantes*, 19 October 1781; *Affiches de La Rochelle*, 8 June 1787 and 1 January 1790. The *Affiches d'Orléans* reprinted an essay on sauces from the *British Magazine* on 30 November 1764.

166 *Journal de Guienne*, 14 December 1785. On resistance to potatoes in France, see Fink 1995, 171–2, and 1983, 19–27. Chesterfield advocated them, having served as lord-lieutenant of Ireland. He told his son from Leipzig on 2 January 1748: "I cannot say that your suppers are luxurious, but you must own they are solid; and a quart of soup, and two pounds of potatoes, will enable you to pass the night without great impatience for your breakfast next morning. One part of your supper (the potatoes) is the constant diet of my old friends and countrymen, the Irish, who are the healthiest and the strongest bodies of men that I know in Europe." He uses standard medical

Eden Treaty in Bordeaux.[167] At the start of the American War, experimental English potatoes were donated to a curious public by Parisian authorities. Requiring more space and planting depth, they were distributed for superior nutrition to a hungry peasantry in the regions.[168] Vegetable and horticultural produce was advanced in the provinces by English seeds and plants sold by peripatetic merchants and language teachers. A tree merchant in Orléans, partner of a court botanist, sold English cauliflower seeds in 1775.[169] After the war, a nurseryman near Paris who had been honoured by academies bred "des vrais choux d'*Yorck* & à *pain-de-Sucre* d'Angleterre ... estimables par leur délicatesse & leur précocité." He offered seed of fast-growing English cabbage in identical adverts in the *affiches* of Angers and Auxerre.[170] Typical of astute English teachers, Mr Gosse promoted plant breeding in the *affiches* of Orléans. Appealing to taste and variety, he sold vegetable and fruit seed yielded by specimens at the Royal Gardens at Kew: Cyprus and early-season melon, three kinds of Chelsea broccoli, four kinds of Savoy cabbage, climbing and green beans, late-season cauliflower, Gibraltar artichokes, three kinds of lettuce, round peas, Minorca parsnips, carrots, and oranges. Confident such enhanced seeds were new to the region's kitchen gardens, he keenly promoted the broccoli since, if originally from Italy, it had been so bred that it could be planted in spring and eaten from November to April.[171] Fruit trees from England had been bred before the American War deeper in the country. A nursery at Sens advertised Butter and Bergamot pear trees along with Royal and Golden Pippin apple trees.[172]

French horticulture was informed by English gardening. Adverts in Angers and Auxerre about *The Gardeners' Dictionary* by Philip Miller (1691–1771) in the summer of 1784 stress that this Fellow of the Royal Society and Keeper of the Chelsea Physic Garden is an authority on kitchen, fruit, and flower gardens. Proposing a five-volume French

---

advice in telling his son to eat sago, barley, and turnips to counteract weakness in his lungs (Stanhope 1901, 42, and 185).
167 *Journal de Guienne*, 28 January 1787.
168 *Affiches d'Orléans*, 23 December 1774.
169 *Affiches d'Orléans*, 14 April 1775.
170 *Affiches d'Angers*, 14 February 1783; *Affiches d'Auxerre*, 14 February 1783.
171 *Affiches d'Orléans*, 22 May 1789.
172 *Affiches de Sens*, 10 November 1774.

edition with supplements on the medicinal properties of plants, the adverts celebrate his methods for improving vegetables, fruits, and flowers.[173] They also exalt the aesthetic benefits of agriculture to landowning classes by praising his advances. However, provincial readers were used to innovative, compendious books on agriculture, for Henri Louis Duhamel du Monceau (1700–1782) published *Traité de la Culture des Terres, suivant les principes de M. Tull, Anglois* and *Le Gentilhomme Cultivateur, ou corps complet d'Agriculture, tiré de l'Anglois de M. Hale*, both sold at Lyon in 1750 and 1762 respectively.[174]

Besides recognizing essays on field tillage, manuring of orchards, and crop production for animal feed, the press lauded English engines that milled grains for cattle feed and pumped water. English metallurgy entered domestic life as tableware and kitchenware. An article in the *affiches* of Bordeaux in 1763 laments that superior English cutting tools and hardware cause local merchants to pass off French and German hardware as English to inflate prices for their supposedly banned goods. The article urges metal-gilding factories in Charité-sur-Loire and Talende to hire English workers and managers and to copy Birmingham's industrial acids.[175] In the 1760s, private sales in Lyon listed new cruets, platters, and drinking fountains of Cornish tin and unsharpened silver and steel table knives with porcelain handles.[176] By the late 1770s, English tableware made of laminated steel was in fashion at Aix-en-Provence: trays for holding twelve cups, sets of twenty-four saucers, and fruit baskets were advertised in its *affiches*.[177] Silver and crystal adorned tables in

---

173 *Affiches d'Angers*, 4 June 1784; *Affiches d'Auxerre*, 14 July 1784. Miller was Keeper from 1722 to 1771, his book appearing in 1724 and its eighth edition adopting the Linnaean system in 1768. English gardeners operated horticultural services in regional France, even at the height of the American War: see, for example, *Affiches de Bordeaux*, 18 November 1779.

174 *Affiches de Lyon*, 5 May 1750; 31 March 1762. Miller published his translation of *The Elements of Agriculture* by Henri Louis Duhamel du Monceau (1700–1782) in 1764. Jethro Tull (1674–1741) is best known for *The New Horse-Houghing Husbandry: or, An Essay on the Principles of Tillage and Vegetation* (London: 1731). Smollett's Dennison renews his estate by joining recommendations from "Lyle, Tull, Hart, Duhamel" to the experience of a local farmer (1984, 327).

175 *Affiches de Bordeaux*, 21 April 1763.

176 *Affiches de Lyon*, 6 July 1763; 13 November 1765; 3 January 1766; 11 January 1769.

177 *Affiches d'Aix*, 3 March and 19 May 1777.

provincial households. Adverts of table and coffee spoons and forks in Bordeaux featuring their weight and English style testify to demand for luxurious silverware.[178] At the end of the American war, crystal was carried by itinerant English merchants to centres like Orléans: carafes, regular and convex wine glasses, trays, glass stands, and wine buckets were offered for sale.[179] The success of such imports is clear when the Lasalle Glass Company promoted itself in Orléans by comparing its crystal to the transparency, weight, and sonority of English crystal.[180] It boasted tableware in the style of English manufacturing. Dining-room furniture also adopted Englishness. Advertisements for large tables confirm the trend to place dishes before diners rather than serving them from sideboards.[181]

Although English hard-paste porcelain reached an acme only in the 1780s, fire-proof dishes were available in France earlier. Sets reveal how traditional meals and serving styles were evolving. One second-hand set offered in Aix had forty-eight plates including salad bowls, soup tureens, wine-glass holders, cream and mustard pots, sugar bowl, sauce boat, and other serving dishes including one for boiled beef, showing the various shapes and sizes of English tableware and the design of meals. The platters on which serving dishes rest suggest how diners moved food from one to another: they saw the distinct plates and used them without the aid of servants.[182] The more decorated the dishes, the more worthy of being observed and moved they were.[183] After 1786, this articulation of meals will have become clearer since many English shops that opened after the Eden Treaty focused on porcelain. Poitiers and Angers were flooded with coffee and tea as well as dinner services by Britons who imported chinaware from Staffordshire. If competition drove French merchants to order from the potteries and to employ new retail and wholesale methods, it also defined eating modes. The advertisement of a French merchant in Caen shows that importing English porcelain let him offer it attractively. Besides English crystal

178 *Journal de Guienne*, 25 July 1786.
179 *Affiches d'Orléans*, 28 January 1785.
180 *Affiches d'Orléans*, 29 June 1787.
181 *Affiches de Bordeaux*, 15 May 1777.
182 *Affiches d'Aix*, 23 June 1777.
183 To Elias, proliferating forms of tableware confirm an evolving pattern of manners (1978, 105).

tableware, he stocks gold ornamented, white porcelain because such easy-to-handle, fine crockery is socially desirable.[184] The proliferation of shops specializing in porcelain says much about this desire. Widow Bellier's adverts in Poitiers are good illustrations since they typify the widening range of table services. She orders "la véritable Faïence d'Angleterre, manufacture royale de Londres" being "autorisée à vendre cette marchandise beaucoup au dessous des prix qui avoient été annoncés." Three months later, she receives another shipment: embossed soup and dessert plates, wine coolers, plate racks, oil and vinegar cruets, covered dishes for vegetables and stews, and decorated fruit baskets stand out. Four months later, she gratifies customers more cheaply "parce que le cassage est devenue beaucoup moins considérable depuis qu'il a été pris de nouvelles précautions pour la sureté de l'emballage & du transport."[185] Demand for fine English pottery was fixed during the American War in Orléans. Travelling salesmen took blue and white tableware there in the 1770s.[186] Thus, by 1790 five shops rivalled one another in the Orléans press for the sale of faience. Also selling crystal dishes and ornaments from France and Bohemia as well as England, they favoured English porcelain sets.[187] One resident English merchant proved the safety of his porcelain by testing it with boiling water in front of customers.[188] A French rival imported the finest English porcelain after the Revolution, dispatching his wares to all provinces.[189] Demand was so strong that French merchants in Orléans deferred to English taste in faience.[190]

The effect of Britain's agrarian and industrial revolutions was not well grasped by official France. Scorning anglomania, bureaucracy in the *ancien régime* thought English technology could be appropriated without risk, having no measure of anglophilia. But English producer and consumer goods strained the French economy. The Eden Treaty of 1786 worsened the strain. Confidence from military and diplomatic success in the War of American Independence led France to seek free trade

184 *Affiches de la Basse-Normandie*, 16 September 1787.
185 *Affiches de Poitiers*, 24 April, 14 August and 11 December 1788.
186 *Affiches d'Orléans*, 9 April 1779; 14 April 1780.
187 *Affiches d'Orléans*, 14 March 1788; 27 February 1789.
188 *Affiches d'Orléans*, 30 January 1790.
189 *Affiches d'Orléans*, 27 May 1790; 15 October 1790.
190 *Affiches d'Orléans*, 5 January 1791.

with England. Bent on making policy serve imperialism by upholding trade restrictions, England stalled on clauses in the 1783 Treaty of Versailles. When France signed the Treaty, unawareness of how English imports had eroded its economic and social structures was deep. France was blind to the inundation of goods that was the more overwhelming because of lowered duties on hardware, cottons, woollens, and cambrics. Had officials scanned their court-censored press after 1760, they would have seen that protection of domestic industrial production was not effectual; they might have glimpsed the coming depression that struck so hard in 1788 and 1789; they might have guessed that England's agrarian and industrial revolutions would cause growing political unrest.

FASHION AND IMPORTED BODY STYLES

Gilles Lipovetsky's *The Empire of Fashion: Dressing Modern Democracy* holds that fashion's very ephemerality makes the public critical yet tolerant. Collective life, he says, is unstable when fashion validates novelty, assigning prestige to new modes while degrading old ones. Further, imports cannot disturb a society unless domestic rules elevating fashion to taste already exist. To Lipovetsky, declining sumptuary laws led eighteenth-century European aristocrats to identify more with status than nationalism: they evaded restrictions on imports since they needed new ways of displaying their wealth. Louis XIV had made French fashion dominant, but the dynamic by which modes renew themselves undermined that imperial dominance.[191] How, then, did English fashions change France?

In the 1770s, Rouen's press, facing industrial decline, demanded that sumptuary laws be upheld, calling the taste for English jewellery and fabrics an unpatriotic mania.[192] Equating fashion to frivolity, it asked that courtiers and merchants who defended that taste be punished. It might not have complained had the rapid cycle of modes been limited to domestic produce. But that was not the case. So, the press tried to discourage imports by labelling English modes eccentric. Hence, satires on English funeral pomp. Newspapers in Orléans and Montauban wrote that funerals bankrupt aristocrats and starve the lower classes, who

---

191 Lipovetsky 1994, 10, 18, 20, 24, and 30–7.
192 *Affiches de la Basse et Haute Normandie*, 6 September 1771.

imitate their betters by passing to the grave in horse-drawn carriages. The English, it was said, adorn dead rather than living bodies.[193]

Since the court neither understood nor controlled fashion, its propaganda erratically blamed and encouraged women. One of Louis XVI's speeches after ratification of the Eden Treaty, admitting executive powerlessness, blames fashionable imported luxuries on women: their fantasies accelerate modishness, heighten demand for prohibited stuffs, destroy the customs system, and have eroded sumptuary laws for thirty years. Until they adopt a national costume, there can be no remedy for the trade imbalance or for the court's humiliating subjection to merchants who promote "perpetual revolutions in the costumes of the Court and the City."[194] Since inept French negotiators of the Eden Treaty did not block silk blends and lace, the cloth-manufacturing towns begged female consumers to imitate English aristocrats and hold subscription balls the proceeds of which would foster cloth production. Troyes's factories need to follow those in Normandy and Flanders by copying English technologies and banning imports. Female patriots must get menfolk to renounce English modes.[195]

That its press saw France as the centre of the fashionable world in which women were trendsetters made their bodies sites of ideological conflict. In 1789, when the *Journal de Guienne* praises French women for giving Europe its civilized tone, it validates ever-changing modes and the appropriation of foreign styles.[196] In the 1760s, newspapers idealized female whimsy since exported Parisian modes benefited commerce: boosting the wearing of rapidly changing styles in bonnets and shawls aided French imperialism. At the same time, the press reprinted Addison's articles about the harm done to English bodies by French

---

193 *Affiches d'Orléans*, 18 September 1778 (reprinted from the *Affiches de Montauban*).

194 The speech printed in *Affiches d'Orléans*, 10 November 1786, was extracted from the *Journal d'Agriculture*.

195 *Affiches de Troyes*, 9 and 16 January 1788, extracted from the *Journal Général de France*, which took Normandy's Chamber of Commerce's criticism from the *Journal de Normandie*.

196 *Journal de Guienne*, 12 January 1789. The list of modes includes the following styles: dresses *à la Polonaise, à l'Anglaise, à la Circasienne, à l'Insurgente, à la Turque, à la Musulmane, à la Czarine, Demi-Négligente, Lévite, Fourreau à l'Agnès, Chemise à la Jesus, Juste à la Suzanne, Caraco Zélandais*. The names witness women's inventive and exhaustive nomenclature.

fashion. Pieces in the Orléans paper dissect a petit-maître's skull and a coquette's heart; the man's pineal gland smells of orange water and his frontal lobes are stuffed with ribbons, lace, and embroidery, the woman's heart no less curious, being as cold as ice, as hard as steel, and as light as a feather.[197] Another translated article in this paper derides sots, coxcombs, and fops as they parade French modes through London's fashionable districts.[198] That the French press decried and praised English modes while chiding the foreign tastes of female readers and urging them to advance national styles reveals fashion's contrary and bicultural impulses. From September 1784 on, the *Journal de Guienne* reprinted rules from *Le Magasin des modes françaises et anglaises* for styles fitting to rank and gender, articles combining French and English modes in clothes, hats, and riding equipment.[199] The grand style for men prescribes moss stitching for ruffles, plum satin with pink and green embroidery for the suit, and white satin for jackets and culottes. A woman dressing *à l'ingénue* must wear a tall straw hat *à l'anglaise*, the brim decorated with violet ribbon, gauze, and four white feathers overtopped by a large violet one.[200] This mode also mandated a ribbon necklace with a medallion. French and English female fashions equally require foundation garments. Parisian tailors sold English and French corsets and bodices to correct anatomical defects and enhance spectacular aspects of figure and costume. Corsets *à l'anglaise* were recommended for scoliosis because they did up on both sides of the torso.[201] Tailor-made whalebone English corsets were approved by London and Paris surgeons; they were quilted in a manner that constrained the body without seeming to.[202] Parisian tailors promoted them because they could be easily made to measure so as to go under tight- and loose-fitting dresses *à l'anglaise*.[203]

Body image concerned French merchants in textile centres; they valued English flannel's curative and aesthetic effects. Alleviating gout

---

197 *Affiches d'Orléans*, 16 and 23 June 1769. The accounts are from *The Spectator* for Tuesday, 15 January 1712 (Addison 1963, 2:318–21).
198 *Affiches d'Orléans*, 21 September 1791.
199 *Journal de Guienne*, 3 September 1784.
200 *Journal de Guienne*, 26 November 1785.
201 *Affiches de Lyon*, 18 November 1767.
202 *Affiches de la Haute et Basse Normandie*, 30 July 1773.
203 *Affiches de Nantes*, 28 April 1775; *Affiches d'Auxerre*, première quinzaine September 1777 & deuxième quinzaine January, 1782.

and rheumatism, its patterned reversibility when striped and damasked appealed to fashion designers.[204] The incursion of English fabrics into textile centres is evidenced by the sale of English lace in Lyon after 1763: suits with headdress, ruffles, and capes were sold alongside ones from Valenciennes and Alençon.[205] In the 1770s, English lace clothes grew popular because of their stitching. English lace cuffs, bonnets, lappets, and palatines were so sought after that the repairing and restitching of English-style lace became part of female education. Tailors in Lyon used English silk for clothes, headdress, and shawls of the latest French fashion.[206] Before the Eden Treaty, illicitly imported textiles were common. From 1770 on, wool, nankeen, and printed and quilted cottons were sold wholesale in Bordeaux along with knitted and silk clothes.[207] After the Treaty, English textiles flooded in. Black cotton velvet was hailed in Troyes for the solid dye that made it desirable for the latest style of men's and women's clothes.[208] English merchants in La Rochelle imported kalmucks, Turkish satins, prunella, muslins, and cotton along with silk blends such as bombazine.[209] Caen's press promoted English gauzes, velvet cottons, muslins, and casimirs, saying the latest fashion depended on materials and blends manufactured in England.[210] English shops habituated the Bordelais to brightly patterned chintzes and white cashmeres as well as to corduroys and knitted wools. The Royal Velvet Manufacture at Sens, operated by Englishmen, produced ribbed silks, satinettes, and cottons by importing innovative methods from Manchester.[211]

French fashions drew on English medicine and cosmetics, the press often reporting the Royal Society's physiological experiments. The cataract surgery of William Cheselden (1688–1752) was broadcast, as were essays on British ophthalmology and spectacle makers.[212]

---

204 *Affiches de la Haute et Basse Normandie*, 4 January 1765.

205 *Affiches de Lyon*, 2 March 1770. See also *Affiches de Bordeaux*, 7 March 1771.

206 *Affiches d'Angers*, 6 October 1775; *Affiches de Bordeaux*, 11 February 1779; *Affiches de La Rochelle*, 7 January 1780; *Affiches d'Auxerre*: deuxième quinzaine May 1790.

207 *Affiches de Bordeaux*, 26 November 1772; 4 March 1779; 1 June 1780.

208 *Affiches de Troyes*, 14 November 1787.

209 *Affiches de La Rochelle*, 14 December 1787.

210 *Affiches de la Basse-Normandie*, 17 August 1788.

211 *Affiches de Poitou*, 6 December 1787.

212 *Affiches d'Orléans*, 22 June 1764; 17 August 1781.

Translated medical texts were reviewed, reaching an acme with the *English Journal of Medicine* when Sir Joseph Banks, its founder and president of the Royal Society, was celebrated for making London the centre of medical research with a network of European correspondents.[213] From the 1750s, the press heralded English pharmaceuticals for removing pimples, freckles, rashes, and eruptions of all kinds.[214] English pearl water was said to improve the complexion and prevent wrinkles, persons of rank in England and France using it to whiten skin and reduce razor burn.[215] Pomades for dermatological applications and for nourishing hair sold well in Paris and the provinces.[216] The press did not hesitate to lift hair-dyeing recipes from the English press. English dental practices were featured for ameliorating facial appearance. In 1772, a female dentist in Aix boasted her ability to clean, whiten, separate, equalize, fill, transplant, and extract teeth, also claiming expertise in the installation of dentures operating by gold or silver hinges and springs. She had served the English court for which the Queen awarded her a pension.[217] Notices from English newspapers provided recipes for dental opiates and advice about oral hygiene. Related is news about English smallpox inoculators; losing one's life, limbs, and eyesight from ulceration brought them to the notice of readers afraid of disfigurement.[218]

British fashion accessories also contributed to French body styles. Besides perfumes and jewellery, snuff boxes were promoted as New Year's gifts: long, boat-shaped, and ornamented with mythical figures, the finest ones appealed to aristocrats, as lost property adverts attest.[219] Gold tobacco holders with polished hinges were popular. Double-barrelled pistols for pocket, saddle, and coach, steel-hilted swords with gold or silver handles, ornate sword-belts and leather scabbards, imported from England or made at Paris in the English style, were in demand.[220] England's superior leather and metallurgical trades figure

213 *Affiches de La Rochelle*, 2 December 1785.
214 *Affiches de Bordeaux*, 24 August 1758.
215 *Affiches de La Rochelle*, 24 September 1773.
216 *Affiches d'Angers*, 7 July 1780.
217 *Affiches d'Aix*, 5 April 1772.
218 *Affiches de Nantes*, 10 February 1775.
219 *Affiches de la Haute et Basse Normandie*, 30 November 1770.
220 *Affiches de La Rochelle*, 10 September 1779; *Affiches de Lyon*, 29 January 1772; *Affiches d'Orléans*, 25 November 1774; *Affiches de Bordeaux*, 17 June 1779.

in adverts of riding equipment, such as boots, silver spurs, and whalebone whips with silver handles. Versailles told women to buy English-style parasols and gold double-cased watches, sculpted, engraved, and decorated with carved rock crystal and agate.[221]

Paradoxically, fashionable court culture of the *ancien régime*, which distinguished itself by shunning accessible consumer goods, popularized the modes by which it sought exclusivity. The privileging of English styles, despite political, economic, and aesthetic rules that belittled them, lured administrations and aristocrats into weakening their cultural power: modes that distinguished the body in ballrooms, on promenades, in sickrooms, on city streets, and in the countryside became popular. Cultivating English styles in public and domestic spaces, the beau monde made them imitable in the act of displaying them. The culture that appropriated English fashions, even as it recognized other foreign styles, turned Englishness into a recognizable international category. If French society, from some English viewpoints, diseased Britons, it enhanced Britain's industrial and aesthetic modes. Ironically opening France to material and corporeal Englishness, French aristocrats made themselves vulnerable – diseased themselves. If French consumerism enfeebled aristocratic identity, France's illicit trade with England won imperial markets for its rival. Such paradoxes of consumerism are relevant to English literary history because they unsettle national typologies and uphold the applicability of interdisciplinary and comparative procedures. Since England's industrial and commercial expansion needed unofficial exchanges with France, we may wonder how much national stereotypes in the conventional narratives of literary history undo their exclusivity.

---

221 *Affiches de La Rochelle*, 4 April 1777; *Affiches d'Aix*, 8 April 1788; *Affiches de Bordeaux*, 30 October 1777.

6

Comparative Imperial Aesthetics and Viticulture

By habit, objects become insipid to us, as we do to others. Let us then change our country, and we shall become new beings; and though men are the same every where, their passions and their manners, which we study under new forms, rouse our attention, and engage that curiosity which employs the minds of young people so agreeably.[1]

COMPARING CULTURES

In the words above, Anne-Marie du Bocage (1710–1802), a native of Rouen and renowned poet and dramatist in Paris, endorses comparative travel in an enthusiastic yet philosophical style that opens up cross-cultural relations in the 1770s. Honouring Addison as "a divine moralist," she thought the Earl of Chesterfield's French cook a "misfortune"; English nobles generally follow the advice of doctors whose self-interest destroys patients' stomachs. Lamenting that France's "senseless luxury" is "by degrees" corrupting "all nations," she is witty about English politics: in "this country the love of Liberty seems to make slaves of its defenders." She clearly senses the dialectic of change and continuity, as she ponders the divide La Manche imposes on the two nations: "We have different meats, different manners, and different prepossessions: even the practice of physic is here so different from what it is with us, that as I cannot conceive how the distance of a hundred leagues is able to produce such a variation, I am tempted to think that it is a science founded entirely upon hypothesis." Hence, the comparative experience travel afforded her:

---

1 Du Bocage 1770, 2:169.

When we take a view of the world, of books and of life, we easily perceive, that the different ways people have of dressing themselves, of impairing their constitutions, of curing their disorders, of lodging, of eating, of gaining each others favours, and of cheating, are all in effect much the same. You will then very probably say, it is unnecessary to give one's self the trouble of travelling. Excuse me, it is an advantage to have it in our power to convince ourselves by experience of what by reason we could only conjecture: in fact, we see that both extremes are in all countries much the same: the want of bread amongst people of the lower class, and of honours amongst Courtiers, reduces them to the same meanesses.[2]

By contrast, Jean-Pierre Grosley (1718–1785), a magistrate of Troyes and historian lauded by European academies and the Royal Society of London, turned his 1765 stay there into occasions for single-minded criticism of food production. Decrying the low consumption of bread and the disgusting inferiority of meats, he declares that "the flesh of English animals, being of a substance less firm, less compact, and less solid, than that of animals in France, is not equally able to bear the operation which prepares the best dish in French cookery." Like Evelyn, he finds London's "garden-stuff" has a disagreeable taste, since "impregnated with the smoke of sea-coal." He repeats truisms that London's red wines are brewed with "sloes and blackberries" and the "juice of turneps." On visiting Charles Hamilton's Painshill at Cobham, Grosley notes the vineyard features Burgundian grapes and is properly exposed to the sun but faults the vine-props that, taken from hop grounds, rot and weaken the vines. He dislikes Hamilton's white wine: "to the eye, it was a liquor of a darkish grey colour; to the palate, it was like verjuice and vinegar blended together by a bad taste of the soil." However, having made two Grand Tours, Hamilton knew much about wine production and vine varieties, eventually making marketable white wines with the help of David Geneste, a Huguenot immigrant from Clairac near Bordeaux who taught himself to be a vintner.[3]

As the century unfolded, imperial rivalries led authors to compare political institutions and cultural modes with equanimity or animus. Consider *A Comparative View of the French and English Nations in Their*

---

2 Ibid., 1:38–9, 42, and 46–7.

3 Grosley 1772, 1:69, 71–72, 81, and 83. See also Hodges 1974, 77–80, and Clarke 2016.

Manners, Politics, and Literature (1785) by John Andrews (1736?–1809).[4] With Addisonian moderation, Andrews gives an account of taste that links government to aesthetic theory. His introduction sketches how Armand Jean du Plessis, Cardinal Richelieu (1585–1642), Jules Raymond Mazarin (1602–1661), and Jean-Baptiste Colbert (1619–1683) advanced French absolutism. Asserting that the dissolution of national assemblies "annihilated all regard for the public good," he says the French court's absolutism aided by clerical and military nobility impeded literary progress and alienated the populace, making it compliant and easy to rule: "deserted by the nobility and upper clergy, and by no small a proportion of their own body, the French commons grew dispirited, and tamely retreated from the scene of action." The clergy and nobles ruling the state embroiled it in "religious persecutions" and fomented divisions from which they expected "personal benefit." Factionalism coincided with a nation-wide focus on manners. Under Louis XIV, France's "reigning passion" became "a studious refinement in those arts and improvements his patronage had so powerfully countenanced." Since "grandeur and elegance" could be carried no further, great ingenuity and invention were applied to "the manifold productions which genius and capacity had already brought forth." Every "subject wherein fancy could strike out new forms" was studied minutely: "where the appearance of things could not assume an air of absolute novelty; no attention was, however, spared to throw in that difference which is communicated through the channel of taste; a word that became the motto of the times, and was appropriated to those embellishments that happened to meet with approbation." Taste was "unanimously adopted by all who laboured to signalize themselves in those departments where brilliancy was chiefly sought, and striking disposition of ornaments, was the object principally consulted. Poets, orators, and even historians, became solicitous to versify, speak, and write according to what was called the standard of purity and taste; and palaces, furniture, equipage, and dress, were all regulated by the same test." In hope, Andrews says "the iniquitous spirit of malevolence, envy, and detraction" has failed to displace the previous age's refinement: today's "spirit of judgment

---

4 This volume is a reworking of *An Account of the Character and Manners of the French; With Occasional Observations on the English.* 2 vols. (London: E. and C. Dilly, J. Robson, and J. Walter 1770). It has many verbal changes as well as distinct pagination and typesetting.

and criticism" in "many judicious performances" will "transmit it to future times as of equal utility with the former."[5]

Andrews's first essay considers the relative size of London and Paris, contrasting the politics of their urban geographies. An English traveller will note, he says, that Paris is not equal to London in size, the latter comparable to "the real magnitude of ancient Rome." He explains that Richelieu induced Louis XIII to impose limits on Paris, since large cities are "dangerous impediments in the way of tyranny, by the freedom of speech and the communication of sentiments, unavoidable in crowds." Richelieu's sense that the urban press hastens private and public information led him to "remove every obstacle to the establishment of despotism that might accrue from the size and populousness of the capital." Such a policy had been adopted by Queen Elizabeth I, who set limits to London to hinder inhabitants' independence from the court and her authority. Charles I also tried to dissuade the nobility and gentry moving to London when Parliament was not in session, but he met with resistance. Hence, the different rates of poverty in the cities: London's poor enjoy plentiful nourishment unlike the poor of Paris. That city's populace below the "middling of the industrious classes" is miserable, if apparently so only in "apparel." Moreover, the wretchedness of French countryfolk is lamentable in contrast to the semblance of gaiety "so much affected in the capital." Britons who assume "the blessings of a free government (as too many are apt to do among us, ...) would do well to pay a serious visit, not to Paris, where the exterior glare of things will dazzle them, but to the provinces of France, where the inhabitants, even of such as are less harrassed and oppressed, are beneath all comparison, inferior in every consideration of circumstances, to the peasantry of England: a race of mortals far happier than any of their degree, in any other part of the world." While foreigners admit "the superior excellence of our political constitution," Frenchmen dare not do so in private or public: "silent on affairs of state, and the intrigues of court," they fear "discovery, through those multitudes of spies, commissioned by the lieutenant of police at Paris, that swarm in coffee-houses, and other places of public resort."[6]

---

5 Andrews 1785, 12, 14, and 33–6.

6 Ibid., 37–8, 39–41, and 42–4. On court spying, see "The King's Secret," the network set up by Louis XV and ended by Louis XVI (Kates 1995, 61–4, 78–9, and 216–17).

Andrews's essay comparing English and French food and touching on mind–body relations considers national types only to reject them. If the French eat more frequently at set meals than the English, a possible conclusion is that French nutrition is "a lighter quality" that induces "an easier and less unequal flow of animal spirits." Another may be that "the greater substantialness" of English food, "though it may render us less lively and jocund, is, in all likelihood, the real cause of our more solid way of thinking." Andrews accepts this notion in so far as "vigour and fortitude of heart" are more often found in those who consume heavy flesh than those who live on lighter meat. But he doubts that "the intellectual faculties receive the same proportion of advantages from the greater substantialness of our food." Such a claim is refuted by "the sentiments of numbers that have treated elaborately of the human system": the "lightest, as well as the most moderate quantity of food, is, in their judgment, the most conducive to freedom of spirits, a clear head, and a depth of reflexion." Sir Isaac Newton (1643–1727) created his theory of light and colours by consuming bread with a little sack and water, and John Law (1671–1729), projector of the Mississippi scheme, ate only half a chicken and a pound of bread, a diet that let him earn "considerable sums." A more likely cause for "the solidity of our thinking" than "our substantial food" is "our political constitution." Still, "external comeliness, and an air of bodily vigour and prosperity" are more diffusive in England than France, as shown when natives of England reared in France contract complexions that displace English looks. The look of exterior physique stems from the "equal repartition of property among the subjects of this free government, and the greater diffusion of business and occupations, which enables the very lowest classes among us to procure sufficient and regular supplies of wholesome food." Starvation, little known in England, explains why the poor of Europe are slovenly and filthy.[7]

The next essays stringently address the cultural implications of French politics. To Andrews, both republican visitors and men of independent thought will be disgusted by the "intellectual bondage" that fetters the French mind to "the thinking of the multitude"; few "individuals in France live for themselves, and can be said to follow the bent of their own inclinations in such things as must necessarily come under the

---

7 Andrews 1785, 60–6.

cognizance of public observation. This complying humour extends from the most material, to the most common occurrences and transactions of private life ... fashion is the word of command in its fullest acceptation. The various modes of living, ways of diversion, topics of conversation, compliments, dresses, and whatever belongs to appearances, are in a manner, so strictly and minutely regulated by what they have thought proper to call the *bon ton*; that to deviate from it, in any particular, always subjects the transgressor to the censures and criticisms of the world." This "conformity to established manners and customs, constitutes as essential a difference as any subsisting in the character of the French" compared with that of the English; they act totally from "pure, native, unrestrained impulse," whereas no other nation than the French "more tamely" submits to "the guidance of the mode, in every respect."[8]

Andrews recalls Chesterfield's view of French modes in that the diplomat cultivated airs and graces but spurned amateur performances. So, Andrews finds disparate manners in "the excessive and absurd regard shewn" by the French "to secondary qualifications, such as skill in singing, dancing, musical instruments, and other accomplishments of less merit": they value too highly a man's skill in presenting himself socially. Granting such "inferior qualifications" should not be ignored, he finds exasperating "acclamations of respect" paid to "mere outside." Having argued that political machinations cause the French to be too charmed by trifles and to take them as essential to knowing how to live, he decries the term "*savoir vivre*" as the "pompous denomination given to that experience and dexterity some folks possess, in the usual intercourse and common offices of society": "To make a bow, enter a room, or offer anything gracefully; to accost a lady, or run over the alphabet of compliments, with an air of facility, and without the least appearance of bashfulness or inexperience, is *savoir vivre*." He accepts ties between conduct and public discourse and grants that to "excel in knowing the various reports and transactions in the gay world, is an agreeable recommendation every where in persons otherwise liberally qualified; but in France, it is a passport to the most insignificant characters. The curiosity of the French is insatiable, it treasures up every tale and story that is offered. Things that with us are no more than transient subjects of discourse,

---

8 Ibid., 77–9.

will here engross a very material portion of time and attention, and live many a long day in the remembrance of people, as the frequent recalling of them to notice in conversation but too evidently proves." Politics in France leads to obsessive conversation about "uninteresting objects": the "minds of men in arbitrary governments, are designedly diverted from any freedom of exertion, and forced to keep their distance from speculations of national importance. These the ruling powers will always labour to secure from too nice and prying an inspection, through a consciousness of the danger resulting to their authority from a public reciprocation of sentiments on affairs of state." If state absolutism explains "the amazing frivolity of speech that reigns in the generality of French companies," Andrews admits that "it is but justice to acknowledge that, notwithstanding the futility of the matters treated of, the method of handling them makes one almost forget their unworthiness to employ our thoughts. Gracefulness and facility of expression seem to characterise the French when thus engaged. However we may prefer the sterling, instructive discourses that are certainly more frequent among people of education in England, we should not at the same time refuse a due share of praise to those capacities, which are able to erect such pleasing edifices from such paltry materials; which can amuse at the same time that we despise the subject of our amusement; which, in short, can enslave our attention in spite of our understanding; and may with the utmost propriety be said in the language of Swift, to raise the gaudiest tulips from the poorest soils."[9]

Andrews's final essay exemplifies even-handedness: initially, it satirizes French travel accounts but, in the end, assails English travellers and the Grand Tour, like Foote, Hurd, and Smith. He first avers that the French are keen to be "considered as travellers, and examiners of mankind," despite "very circumscribed" excursions. Their travelogues, claiming to have visited places they have never seen, offer "ample descriptions." They list the civilities of celebrities whom they never met. They claim "intrigues" and amours with virtuous women. "In the career of his imaginary adventures, a Frenchman of this stamp willingly makes free with female names, in order to establish his fame in the regions of gallantry." This habit of "traducing absent characters" incurs dangers. When travel writers discuss domestic matters, they are more reserved

---

9 Ibid., 79–84.

but still have an "unaccountable propensity to pry into them," and, given their "most impatient, restless indiscretion," they publish to "the world every disparaging story, true or false," that they have "either heard or invented." This exposes them "to the very serious eclaircissements with the friends of the parties thus calumniated; but on no occasions more frequently than those where a man boasts of favours from the fair sex." While men who boast of such favours and whom distance places out of danger are found in other nations, especially in those who think a tour of France "an appendage of genteel education," France itself is "the native soil where such beings mostly flourish, and whence the science of assuming airs of gallantry" has been propagated across Europe. Thus, Andrews repeats the long-standing complaint that "swarms of travellers" visit France "with no other intent than to form a practical collection of those ways and manners that render the French and their imitators equally disagreeable and ridiculous." This applies to English gentlemen returning from countries where they spend large sums of money with no credit: disgraceful extravagancies dishonour them and their country. Travellers are "representatives of their countrymen abroad" and should behave in ways that add "to the reputation of the community to which they belong." He is bitter that British travellers do not reflect their nation's "capacity or power"; what they display is "national opulence." Far from proving "intrinsic merit," they "leave not infrequently the most disadvantageous impressions of their countrymen, through the irregularities and follies in the commission of which some of them seem to glory." As in Hurd's impersonation of Locke, Andrews laments that lads, "inexperienced in civil life," set out on their travels. Having learned nothing at home, such "juvenile ramblers" appear ridiculous to "judicious, intelligent foreigners" who pity uneducated abuse of travelling. Andrews closes in indignation "at the absurd rage of thrusting mere youths of no experience into a strange world, at a time of life when the passions are in their most uncontrollable state, and where every temptation will be thrown in their way that need or avidity can suggest."[10]

Andrews's reflexive, even-handed comparativism differs from the nationalism of Joseph Warton (1722–1800), who, when a student at Oriel College, Oxford, penned "Fashion: An Epistolary Satire to a

10 Ibid., 323–4, 325–6, and 327–30.

Friend." To Warton, the English have been turned into "social Herrings" by fashion which constitutes a "Fool-o'erwhelming Flood." Fashion has displaced "Taste," the aesthetic sense of the upper classes, leading aristocrats to run "Picture-mad" over Dutch "Dawbings" as well as to prefer the landscapes of Claude Lorrain (1600–1682) to the art of Guido Reni (1575–1642). Rather than eat beef and brown bread, aristocrats prefer a "hundred Dainties" smoking on their tables, happy to have "Earth, Air, and Ocean's ransack'd for a Feast." "Truffles and rich Ragouts" take pride of place in "this Sauce-enamour'd Age." Warton chides France for subjugating England:

O France, whose Edicts govern Dress and Meat,
Thy Victor Britain bends beneath thy Feet!
Strange! That pert Grasshoppers should Lions lead,
And teach to hop, and chirp across the mead:
Of Fleets and laurel'd Chiefs let others boast,
Thy Honours are to bow, dance, boil and roast.

His catalogue of French modes expresses disgust that English life devalues military victories and maternal direction of family life. His satire ends by calling for the rediscovery of "*Nature*'s Rules" in pastoral retirement.[11] His scorn of France in "Verses Written at Montauban in France, 1750" is more single-minded than anything Andrews wrote. On a tour of the southwest, he begins his poem looking out at the vineyards visible from the banks of the river Tarn:

TARN, how delightful wind thy willow'd waves,
But ah! They fructify a land of slaves!
In vain thy bare-foot, sun-burnt peasants hide
With luscious grapes yon' hill's romantic side;
No cups nectareous shall their toils repay,
The priest's, the soldier's, and the fermier's prey:
Vain glows this sun in cloudless glory drest.
That strikes fresh vigour through the pining breast;
Give me, beneath a colder, changeful sky,
My soul's best, only pleasure, LIBERTY!

---

11   Warton 1742, 3–4, 6–7, and 11.

The beauty of land and climate cannot hide the poverty and hardships suffered by peasants working the vineyards. The scene may be romantic and its product luscious but the working poor are unable to taste the fruits of their labour. They are oppressed by the court system in which priests, soldiers, and fermiers thrive. Despite the sunshine, they pine in want. Warton prefers cold, grey England, the land of liberty free from Catholic persecution. France is no model. So, he celebrates the resistance of native chiefs who sacrificed themselves in resisting Roman invasions, closing his lines by beseeching Albion to ensure England remain the home of liberty.[12]

TOURISM AND WINE

Andrews and Warton, as tourists to France, were doubtless motivated in their comparative efforts by a mass movement to which travelogues catered. According to Horace Walpole, at the end of the Seven Years War from 1763 to 1765 about 40,000 Britons set out for the Continent. This is what he wrote to Lady Ossory on 8 November 1789:

I made a random calculation above 20 years ago (and calculation is not my bright side) that the English wasted annually in France above £500,000. When I was there in 1765 their late King said that by the returns from Calais forty thousand English had passed through there, though but two years after the peace – if half were tradesmen, cooks and barbers *pour s'instruire*, not one went and returned for so little as five pounds. Though that was a tide that had been dammed up, I believe the emigrations of late years have been as numerous. Two years ago there were above 60 English *families* at Nice; and a year ago there were said to be 40,000 English in France and Lorrain – numbers indeed from economy, but thrift itself does not live in France on French money, not on what it proposes to save, nor is it easy to save, where everything is charged so high to a *Milor anglais*.[13]

---

12 Warton 1750, 217–18.
13 Walpole 1965, 34:78–9. Robert and Isabelle Tombs say that, after each war, peace witnessed "a rush to visit the former enemy." They see "an annual figure of 12,000 British visiting the Continent in the late 1760s, rising to over 40,000 in the mid-1780s" (2007, 63–4).

If some Britons travelled to save money and health, Walpole knew that many indulged in modish consumerism. As he says, the French knew how to fleece Britons. Hence, travel guides instructed travellers in the wise purchase of accommodation and comestibles as well as in the etiquette of wines. Recommendations about how to live comfortably in Paris, Dijon, Lyon, and Bordeaux reveal that wine was a major amenity enjoyed by British residents and tourists. Readers were trained to see that wine constituted essential knowledge: impure water made it a hygienic beverage, and its digestive, anaesthetic, and intoxicant functions involved it in many social transactions.

One early guide is *The Grand Tour* (1749) by Thomas Nugent (1700?–1772). Published before the Seven Years War at a time of travel restrictions, it was expanded and republished several times. Its preface bases the educational value of travelling on classical examples. To Nugent, travellers are philosophers and scientists – the first to enter the "republic of letters." They diffused science, their "relations" critical to deep history: they "did not think it beneath their care to consult stones, metals, barks of trees, and every other monument, whereby they were enabled to acquaint us with many surprising facts, of which the inhabitants themselves had lost all tradition."[14] The moderns, including "the great Lord *Anson*," have imitated the ancients, bringing to the public those "useful discoveries which have contributed to improve the conveniencies and elegancies of life" that "render human society more happy." Nugent offers his book as a "guide and companion," describing roads and routes, the "nature and price of carriages, the conveniency of accommodations," and information about coinage and money. His sense of utility is broad: his travel details aim to "enrich the mind with knowledge, to rectify the judgment, to remove the prejudices of education, to compose the outward manners, and in a word to form the complete gentleman."[15]

The fourth volume's first chapter on France deals with geography and climate, listing rivers, regions, and districts. It surveys levels of governance, including tax collection, next offering commentaries on manners, the class system, leisure, and entertainment along with institutions of learning and science. This chapter finally describes the ease of

---

14 On "deep history" and the work of Daniel Lord Smail (2008), see chapter 2 in this volume.
15 Nugent 1778, 1:i–v and xi.

travelling in France, detailing kinds of carriages with their costs. The second chapter covers the journey from Dover to Paris by packet boat, the "farce" of being examined by customs officials, the need to "have your trunk plumbed with a leaden stamp for *Paris*," a list of the best inns at Calais, a warning to be not "too free with their small wines" for fear of "flux." He explains how to hire a trustworthy manservant on arriving in Paris, then lists the "many very good inns at Paris, where you are sure of being extremely well accommodated, according to the figure and expence you intend to make." He recommends:

the *Hôtel Imperial*, in the *rue Dauphin* and *Faubourg de S. Germain*; the *Hôtel d'Anjou*, the *Hôtel d'Hambourg*, the *Hôtel d'Orleans*, and the *Hôtel de Picardie*, in the *rue Mazarin*; the *Hôtel d'Espagne*, in the *rue de Seine*; the *Hôtel Imperial*, in the *rue de Tour*; the *Doge of Venice*, in the *rue de Boucherie*; the *Grand Hôtel de Luine*, and the *Little Hôtel de Luine*, on the quay *des Augustins*; the *Croix de Fer*, the *Croix Blanche*, and the *Croix Dorée*, in the *rue S. Denis*.

Visitors aiming to sojourn in less expensive accommodations may contract for furnished lodgings the usual terms of which he details. Short-term lodgers who stay up two pair of stairs receive a "bed and bed-linen, water-bottle, bason, and towels." Servants hired as housekeepers provide "a tin tea-kettle, some charcoal and a dish, a tea-pot, some tea-cups, saucers, milk-pot, a decanter, and about half a dozen glasses." For breakfast they buy "*French* rolls and sugar, and good hyson tea." Those who rent apartments in families are told to contract with cooks to dress and send in dinners and suppers from a tavern. "For eight livres a day, you may have for dinner two good dishes and a soop, which will serve four in company, and servants." His culinary advice includes such comments as that Parisian mutton is better than its beef or veal, and that its hare, partridges, and wild fowl are excellent. Such renters should avoid beef and veal but order hare, partridge, wild fowl, and mutton. Since fast-day soups are disgusting, Nugent recommends "plain gravy, with a roll and vermicelli in it." If travellers request "partridge, pigeon, chicken, or a bit of fish" for supper, they will pay extra. Single lodgers should eat at public ordinaries where they are served a variety of dishes at reasonable prices and where they will benefit from enjoying company from many nations. Finally, those who board with families get a neat, furnished room, a hot dinner and supper (breakfast excluded) with a pint of wine at each meal. He repeats his warning that readers not drink "much water, or too plentifully of their small wines, for this will assuredly throw you into a looseness." Hence, travellers should know what the common wines drunk at Paris are and be sure to mix them with water: the safest are: "1. *Bon vin vieux de Beaune,* and *De Volne L'Année passée*, 2. *Preignac,* a tolerable common white-wine; 3. *Frontignan,* excellent for a glass or two, especially with walnuts; 4. *Champagne*; 5. *Cote Rotie* ... a light pleasant, drinking wine, and more used to sit over than any other; 6. *Hermitage,* for those who can bear a strong wine ... As to claret they have none at *Paris*; and good *Burgundy* is very dear, and hard to be got."[16] Besides listing manufacturers of carpets and plate glass such as the Gobelin tapestries that are worth visiting, Nugent looks beyond Paris to towns in the Loire valley, such as Orléans and Blois, and to the Atlantic seaboard from Bordeaux to Nantes as well as Lyon and towns in Provence on the route into Italy.

Nugent follows Addison, whose interest in classical architecture covered industrial and wine technology in *Remarks on Several Parts of Italy* (1718). Addison turns from coins and statues to vineyards when describing the benefit of St Marino's natural cellars to growers. Besides pondering the chemistry of fermentation and the vapour of stum dowsing flames, he treats how water transportation facilitates wine production and refines Swiss life.[17] Thus, Addison became a model for writers who linked wine production to cultural life beyond metropolitan centres. Travel books concentrating on the arts or politics, such as *The Present State of Music in France and Italy* (1771) by Charles Burney (1726–1814) and *An Account of Corsica ... And Memoirs of Pascal Paoli* (1769) by Boswell, present the role of wine in tourism, consumerism, and cultural exchange. Setting out from London in June 1770 with a sense that music and musicians have been neglected by cultural historians, Burney thirsted for "draughts" from the "source" of music in Italy. Not to be distracted by pictures, statues, and buildings, he was "determined to hear with [his] *own* ears, and to see with [his] *own* eyes; and, if possible, to *hear* and *see* nothing but *music.*" His critique of musical entertainments on the boulevards outside Paris gates is scathing; performances of Italian music are ill-executed, feebly imitating London's Vauxhall and Ranelagh. Yet, at Montefiascone on route to Rome to visit Signor Guarducci, whom

---

16 Ibid., 4:20–1 and 33–6. Preignac is a village in the Sauternes, and Frontignan is a naturally sweet wine produced near Montpellier.

17 Addison 1890, 1:403, 437, and 520.

he heard sing in London, Burney is impressed by the singer's house built with "great taste" in the "English manner" and by his hospitably loading Burney's chaise with "exquisite wine" from his vineyard, Montefiascone wine famed throughout Italy.[18]

Boswell's tasting of wines leads to a sense of the economic future. In conversation with the affable, if austere, General Paoli, the "illustrious commander of a nation," he appreciates his host's republicanism. While the general treats the island's leading men to "a table of fifteen or sixteen covers" and an "Italian cook who had been long in France," he himself chooses "a few plain substantial dishes, avoiding every kind of luxury, and drinking no foreign wine." The general's nationalistic restraint alerts Boswell to Corsica's natural resources so that he foresees that it could "carry on a pretty extensive commerce." The Corsicans might "make plenty of admirable wines, for their grapes are excellent. They make in Capo Corso two very good white wines; one of them has a great resemblance to Malaga." It is exported to Germany as Malaga. Some exported from Leghorn to England "passes equally well for the production of Spain." The other white is like Frontignac. Touring the island, he sees that at "Furiani they make a white wine very like Syracuse, not quite so luscious, and upon the whole, preferable to it." In "some villages, they make a rich sweet wine much resembling Tokay. At Vescovato and at Campoloro, they make wine very like Burgundy; and over the whole island there are wines of different sorts. It is indeed wonderful, what a difference a little variation of soil or exposure, even in the same vineyard, will make in the taste of wine. The juice of the Corsican grapes is so generous, that although unskilfully manufactured, it will always please by its natural flavour." Corsica might produce wine of "a good sound moderate quality, something between Claret and Burgundy, which would be very proper" for England. Although "the Corsicans have been so harassed for a number of years, that they have had no leisure to improve themselves in any art or manufacture," their annual export of oil worth two and a half million French livres and of chestnuts worth a hundred thousand crowns of "the same money" persuades him they will likely become a commercial nation in the long tradition of republican governments, like Holland.[19]

18 Burney 1771, 2, 6–7, 16, 255, and 257.
19 Boswell 1769, 317 and 213–15.

Travelogues that relate viticulture to life in the French provinces include *The Gentleman's Guide in His Tour through France* (1766) by Philip Playstowe and *A Tour through the Western, Southern, and Interior Provinces of France* (1774) by Nathaniel William Wraxall (1752–1831). Playstowe's visit to Burgundy compares Auxerre and Dijon. Finding the former mean and dirty, he advises those passing through to wait for the stage coach at the best inn, the Petit-paris, and to contract for meals with good Burgundy so as not to be charged double. Because French is spoken with propriety at Dijon, he knows no "town in *France* preferable to this, for the residence of any gentleman, 'till he has perfected himself in the *French* tongue." His praise is comprehensive:

It is a parliament town; ever neat and clean; situated in a most pleasing, healthy, and extensive plain, and hath delightful walks both within and without its walls; many curiosities are to be seen there, and for six hundred livres, you may lodge and board in the greatest decency, with the counsellors of the parliament. There are abundance of gentry live here on slender fortunes, with the greatest comfort; all kinds of provisions being extremely cheap: the young gentlemen of the town are very polite to strangers, and have many agreeable amusements which are not expensive; in short all its inhabitants shew an hospitality, and generosity, that I met not with, in any other part of *France*."

His sense of the moderate cost of living in Dijon is heightened by his denigration of the famous monastery of Cîteaux, "the richest body of monks in the kingdom" with a revenue "supposed to be half a million of livres annually, about £11,375." The monks are obliged to treat strangers hospitably and politely, and, while they never eat meat, "you will see at their table perhaps fifty dishes of fish, eggs, and garden stuff, served up in the most elegant and delicious manner; with the most exquisite wines that *Italy* or *France* can produce." Contrasting with how these "useless muck-worms live" are the "half-starv'd" beggars "prancing after you in wooden shows" when you leave the convent.

Playstowe's accounts of Lyon and Bordeaux emphasize their suitability as tourist sites and places of residence. Lyon, more costly than Paris, is suitable for short stays. He recommends the Park and the Palais Royal as the city's most elegant inns where travellers are certain to meet other Britons. This city's commercial and industrial energy sustains luxurious lifestyles: its "manufactures consist of gold and silver stuffs, all manner of silks, velvets and laces; silk stockings, and various sorts of woollen goods." He is impressed by how inhabitants resort to the Dauphiné countryside: they calmly walk out of a morning with cold collations and return at dusk "singing, capering, and dancing." It is "highly entertaining" to observe "the various inventions" by which citizens amuse themselves. Such scenes of pastoral tranquillity will convince any phlegmatic Englishman who happens to be a spectator that the French know how "to taste the enjoyments of this life; into which we are most certainly sent to be more happy than we, too frequently, make ourselves." Britain's "dark gloomy atmosphere," heavy foods and liquors "add greatly to our unhappy hypocondriack disposition."[20] Bordeaux's best inns, the Hotel de Prince, Hotel d'Orleans, and the Hotel de Condé, "where you are always sure of meeting some of your countrymen," equally move his social and aesthetic senses. Noting this "town is large, populous, and extremely commercial," he admires how it tolerates the nations who frequent it and the privileges enjoyed by "the Scotch" on "account of the services they formerly rendered to France." Given Bordeaux's slow urban redevelopment, he doubts its military defences and port's navigability but applauds its tolerance of Protestants.[21]

On 7 October 1775, Wraxall writes in a manner unlike Warton about the appeal of vineyards near Bordeaux: "The adjacent country, more particularly the 'pays de Medoc,' which produces the finest clarets, is exceedingly pleasant; and at this season when the peasants are all engaged in the vintage, forms one of the most delicious landscapes in the world." To Wraxall, the aesthetics of the wine and its vignoble are equivalent. Similarly, his sense of the prospect of the city's beautiful crescent of modern buildings on the Garonne involves politics, economics, and taste. The "favourable impression" Bordeaux makes on a stranger on arriving is confirmed by residence. "Pleasure seems to have as many votaries here as commerce; luxury and industry" reigning "within the same walls, and that in the most extensive degree." The prospect is bettered nowhere in Europe since the city uniquely joins industry and luxury. Whereas court cities are "effeminate, seducing, and voluptuous" and commercial cities, spurred by love of gain, shun the softer passions, in Bordeaux luxury and dissipation are "more openly

20 Playstowe 1766, 40–8.
21 Ibid., 90–2.

patronized, and have made a more universal conquest" than in most European cities. In this, Bordeaux represents the genius of the French nation's rejection of superstition. If at the accession of Louis XIV, the city was "ill built, badly paved, and dangerous" given a lack of police and municipal regulations, it has changed in the last thirty years, now boasting noble public edifices, handsome streets, and safe, attractive promenades. Thus, Wraxall declares "I am never tired of walking on the banks of the Garonne. The quays are four miles in length, and the river itself is considerably broader than the Thames at London bridge. On the opposite side, a range of hills, covered with woods, vineyards, churches and villas, extends beyond the view."[22]

Major accounts of the aesthetics and economics of viticulture were voiced by women. Hester Lynch Piozzi's *Observations and Reflections Made in the Course of a Journey through France, Italy, and Germany* (1789) is compellingly reflexive. Passing through the Beaujolais in September 1784 on route to Lyon, she found the ordinary country wine "deliciously cool and sharp," if lacking body for long keeping and power to produce "sensible effects." Yet beautiful, expansive views of a productive countryside make her rhapsodize "where vineyards swell upon the rising grounds, and young wheat ornaments the valleys below; while clusters of aspiring poplars, or a single walnut-tree of greater size and dignity unite in attracting attention, and inspiring poetical ideas." She is moved by the "ceaseless variety of colouring among the plants," namely, "the cerulean willow, the yellow walnut, the gloomy beech, and silver theophrastus." The scenery unites "that sublimity which a wide expanse always conveys to the mind, with that distinctness so desired by the eye; which cultivation alone can offer and fertility bestow." She is upset by clashing rural and urban scenes; towns which should "adorn these lovely planes" exhibit "misery; the more mortifying, as it is less expected by a spectator, who requires at least some days experience to convince him that the squalid scenes of wretchedness and dirt in which he is obliged to pass the night, will prove more than equivalent to the pleasures he has enjoyed in the day-time, derived from an appearance of elegance and wealth – elegance, the work of Nature, not of man; and opulence, the immediate gift of God, and not the result of commerce." Ideas of human and divine agency seem to trouble an economic sense that might

---

22 Wraxall 1774, 73 and 67–9.

blame French laziness. She continues: "Content, the bane of industry, as Mandeville calls it, renders them happy with what Heaven has unsolicited shaken into their lap; and who knows but the spirit of blaming such behaviour may be less pleasing to God that gives, than is the behaviour itself."

She again questions her own perspective when encountering Lyon's stateliness, its fine site on the Rhône, and its powerful cloth mills. She discountenances truisms about French economic laziness in the face of the artistry of double-faced velvets made in the city. Not surprised that "many English families reside" upon La Montagne d'Or, she offers remarks about aesthetics that transcend economic notions and vulgar consumerism:

It is observable, that the further people advance in elegance, the less they value splendour; distinction being at last the positive thing which mortals elevated above competency naturally pant after. Necessity must first be supplied we know, convenience then requires to be contented; but as soon as men can find means after that period to make themselves eminent for taste, they learn to despise those paltry distinctions which riches alone can bestow.

There follow sensitive remarks on the hospitality of Lyon merchants with whom she resides. From eighteen to twenty-two persons dine on thirty-six dishes, and sup on twenty-four. Luxurious table service is matched by genteel manners and entertainments. She is caressed by kindness as never before or since; Lyonnais hospitality could not be more pleasingly and less coarsely expressed. Hence, she invokes "wealthy traders"; they should "unite to pour the oil of commerce over the too agitated ocean of human life, and smooth down those asperities which obstruct fraternal concord."[23]

As Piozzi moves to Italy, her travel account precisely registers impressions of food and drink. Near Mont Cenis the pale colour of lake trout is not attractive; the fish at Venice that "wait one's knife and fork" abound in "perfection"; "Fresh sturgeon, *ton* as they call it, and fresh anchovies, large as herrings, and dressed like sprats in London," are "incomparable: turbots, like those of Torbay exactly, and plentiful as there, with enormous pipers, are what one principally eats." New culinary experiences

---

23 Piozzi 1789, 17–19 and 20–3. For Mandeville, see page 338.

do not upset her comparative sense: she enjoys the "fried liver, without which an Italian can hardly go on from day to day." It is "so charmingly dressed in Milan, that I grew to like it as well as they; but at Venice it is sad stuff, and they call it *fegao*." About Italian fruit and flowers she is enthusiastic: figs are so perfect that "it is not easy for an English gardener to guess at their excellence; for it is not by superior size, but taste and colour, that they are distinguished; small, and green on the outside, a bright full crimson within, and we eat them with raw ham, and truly delicious is the dainty. By raw ham, I mean cured ham, not boiled or roasted." Sadly, Italy does not cultivate strawberries and seems to lack peaches, nectarines, and greengage plums. A keen gardener, she cannot but be overwhelmed by flowers in Florence: "how rich they are in scent here! How brilliant in colour! How magnificent in size! Wallflowers perfuming every street, and even every passage; while pinks and single carnations grow beside them, with no more soil than they require themselves." After finishing *Anecdotes of the Late Samuel Johnson, LL.D. during the Last Twenty Years of His Life*, she persuades her husband to let her play the housewife near Pisa so that she may relish "the new wine" running "from the cask" and caress "the meek oxen that drew it to our door," feeling "sensations so unaffectedly pastoral, that nothing in romance ever exceeded my felicity."[24]

Radcliffe's account of viticulture on the Rhine abounds in empirical, sociological, and aesthetic ideas. Despite the Rheingau's "rugged projections," the "labour of cultivating" vines on the steep banks and "expressing the wine, supports a village at least at every half mile." Cultivation reaches up the banks "with the help of steps cut in the rock," soil held back by "walls of loose stones" which impede erosion by rain. The "small patches" contain as few as "twenty vines." If the summits require "excessive labour," the soil lower down affords the "most luxuriant vegetation."

It might be supposed from so much produce and exertion, that this bank of the Rhine is the residence of an opulent, or, at least, a well-conditioned peasantry, and that the villages, of which seven or eight are frequently in sight at once, are so superior to the neighbouring towns by the state of their inhabitants, as they are by their picturesque situation.

24 Ibid., 31, 142–3, 193–4, and 253.

Such is not the case, "the inhabitants of the wine country" being "said to be amongst the poorest in Germany." One reason is that landowners know the value of "every hill ... so that the tenants are very seldom benefited by any improvement of its produce." If farmers pay rent in money, they are left with only so much as will let them live and pay their workmen. Stewards extract as much income for landlords from the vineyards as if they themselves were invested in the estates. But, since "rent is frequently paid in kind, amounting to a settled proportion of the produce" and since "this proportion is so fixed," while "the farmer is immoderately distressed by a bad vintage, the best will not afford him any means of approaching to independence." The "severity" of this "agricultural system" sustains itself by "continuing the poverty, upon which it acts." The system prevents tenants from revising their contracts as they might in other countries. With no opportunities in industry, vineyard workers either labour under masters or at best become masters of day labourers. Most farmers are stewards for princely and ecclesiastical owners, most workers mere servants. Wealth is not distributed. Since the celebrated vineyards mandate that rent be paid in-kind, proprietors hoard wine to drive up the market. The "sure proof of the wretchedness of the inhabitants" is that, "in a month after the wine is made, you cannot obtain one bottle of the true produce, except by the favour of the proprietors, or their stewards. How much is the delight of looking upon plenteousness lessened by the belief, that it supplies the means of excess to a few, but denies those of competence to many!" The pleasure of vineyard scenery is undone by knowing the few enjoy an excess that denies a competency to the many. Indeed, "the bounteousness of nature to the country is very little felt by the body of the inhabitants."[25] Still, her second volume returns to the "astonishingly grand" valley, celebrating the outlook on the Rheingau towards Mentz and the westward course of the Moselle towards France. Sure of what readers want, she lists the "uncouth names" of the Rheingau's famous villages, using another guidebook's remarks about full-bodied versus brisk and spirited wines and adding notes about the soils where Hockheim wines are produced and their esteemed flavours.[26]

---

25 Radcliffe 1795, 1:262–6.
26 Ibid., 2:28 and 48–52.

EXPERIENCING VITICULTURE

A century before Radcliffe, experience in winemaking and technical knowledge of vines entered literary awareness, the Grand Tour inducing travellers to relate wine to aspects of foreign culture such as art history and landscape forms. Italy and France taught Evelyn to recognize grape varieties and to judge those worthy of export to England. On a winter stay in Padua, he bought "3000 weight of excellent grapes," pressing them into an "incomparable Liquor." This led him to take pleasure in the scenery of vineyards and to get involved in importing French vines and establishing them in England. In 1654 he rejoiced over a vineyard planted in Lady Brooks's gardens at Hackney. As garden designer, in 1670 he made sure his specifications for a vineyard at Albury were met. Yet Colonel Thomas Blount's vineyard made him sad that most vines were only garden specimens.[27]

Horticultural challenges of growing vines taught gardeners and connoisseurs to study how different varieties rely on soil and climate. Since Sir William Temple (1628–1699), Swift's mentor, imported several species of vine for table fruit, he could describe the relation of light, heat, and air circulation in the best French vineyards and classify their grapes. In 1685 he reports that, of the four French vines he imported, the Chasselas grows best while the Burgundy is surest to ripen.[28]

Touring France between 1675 and 1679, Locke made systematic observations on Hautbrion, President Pontack's famous vineyard. He noted its topography: "It is a litle rise of ground, lieing open most to the west. It is noe thing but pure, white sand, mixd with a litle gravell." The land did not appear fruitful, seemingly with no single method of cultivation: "Some of the vines are about 4 or 5 foot high & have stakes. Others are direct along upon the ground, not above a foot from it, between litle, low stakes or laths, soe that the old branches stand on each side the root like a pair of armes spread out towards the south."

---

27 Evelyn 1959, 240, 336, 546, and 364.
28 Temple 1983, 27 and 25. On 15 June 1706, Swift wrote from Dublin to John Temple, a nephew of Sir William's: "I was desired by a person of quality to get him a few cuttings of the Arbois and Burgundy vines mentioned by Sir William Temple in his Essay on Gardening, because they ripen the easiest of any. Pray be so kind to order your gardener to send some against the season, and I will direct they shall be sent to London, and from thence to Chester" (1912, 1:58).

Lacking the "Gascoin" tongue, he could not learn from workmen "this different way of culture." To his surprise, the vintages yielded not twenty-five but fifty tuns of grapes, which gave Pontack large profits from harvests. To his bafflement, Locke learned that neighbouring vineyards with equal soils and climates produce wine that is "not soe good."[29]

Locke studied grape varieties in Provence. At Montpellier, he inspected soils, sites, grape blending, and styles of fermentation. His diary records the crushing of grapes, the time taken for wines to gain colour and aging properties, and the care of butts. His interest in regional vineyards other than those of Bordeaux was moved by anger at how English demand had almost doubled the price of claret in the 1670s; "fashionable" buyers had given "orders to have the best wine sent them at any rate." He was glad when prices of Bordeaux fell in France because of limits imposed on the carrying trade by Navigation Acts and because of the prohibitions Parliament devised on learning of Charles II's treaty with Louis XIV in 1678. Rather than admire Pontack's estate wine, he praises the wines of St Chinian, Hermitage, Pouilly, and Saumur, if unhappy with customary processes of fermentation that included adding wood shavings. If disgust with lack of hygiene reveals ignorance of the disinfectant power of alcohol, more importantly it marks his resistance to foreign culture and wine's symbolic functions. Still, in a text prepared for his pupil, *Observations upon the Growth and Culture of Vines and Olives: The Production of Silk: The Preservation of Fruits. Written at the Request of the Earl of Shaftesbury, To Whom It Is Inscribed* (1679), he makes sound remarks: he sees that the "soil about Frontignan, where the best muscat grows, is so stony, that one can see no earth at all." He adds that vineyards "about Montpelier" yield good and bad wines. He describes the region's ways of pruning and tells how layering replaces dead vines. After noting fining by pigeons' and hens' but not horses' dung, he says how passionately vintners in Gaillac defend their reputation. He lists forty kinds of vines around Montpellier, saying which are good for eating and which blend well. He understands that a "vineyard, from its planting, will last fifty, eighty, or an hundred years" and that the "older the vineyard, the fewer the grapes, but the better the wine."[30]

---

29 Locke 1953, 142–43. See chapter 1 of this volume for Locke's tour and chapter 5 for President Pontack.

30 Locke 1953, 51, 117; Locke 1823, 10: 329–32. The latter text was kept by Shaftesbury's family until it was published in 1766.

Visiting France in 1765 and 1766 at the height of his fame allowed Sterne "a joyous time" dining with the commandant of Lyon and being hosted in a chateau near Dijon with the best Burgundy from nearby mountains affording inner inspiration twice a day. On an earlier visit he had got to know untrustworthy aspects of the wine trade, being alerted to risks taken by his betters in importing wine. About to return home from Montpellier, he could think of nothing better to send Lord Fauconberg than two hogsheads of best Provence red. Since the Bordeaux vintage of 1763 had been destroyed by hail, he knew Rhône wines were being bought by London merchants as substitutes for claret. Friend to a wine agent, he could buy the best at the lowest price and send his patron a shipment that would free him from the over-priced London market. Thus, on 20 September 1763, he proposed:

I would gladly send you over a Hogshead as a specimen – You must know, my Lord, That the Vintage this Year about Bourdeaux is quite destroyd by a terrible Hail wch cut up all the Vines throughout the whole district which furnished you w^h so my much good Claret in England [*sic*] – This I find has set many Commissions a going in this neighbourhood, to purchase up the strong ordinary Wines which as they will bear the sea, & can be shipped for 40 Shillings a Hogshead at Cett near this town and landed at London for 20 Shillings more – will not be drunk at more than 2 Shill^s a Bottle – but y^r Lord^p understands this Calculation better than I – this I am persuaded of, That many 100 Tuns will be both given & bought <from> for french wine – wch they truely are in one sense, tho' not in another – If upon the whole Y^r Lords^p thinks a couple of Hogsheads worth the Duty, I sh^d [be] very happy in being allowed to present you with them, which I will warrant shall be the best of their kind – as I am in particular friends with a Person here, who has a large Commission for the wines of this present Vintage – to ship to London."[31]

To Sterne, the issue for English consumers was misrepresentation and fraudulent pricing.

Authors often made images of the wine trade metonyms for society's ills. Without reference to personal taste, Fielding alludes to it in *Joseph Andrews* to distinguish between corrupt urban life and rural sufficiency.

---

31 Sterne 1935, 200.

The Wilsons retreat to the countryside after Mr Wilson realizes that he cannot reform the trade. Unwilling to adulterate imported wines, he cannot compete with vintners whose adulterated wines are cheaper than his and whose profits are double. The Wilsons' cellar in the country is stocked with home-made wines, an emblem of their frugal independence, less from foreign wines than from corrupt trading practices.[32] In *Tom Jones* Fielding employs motifs of adulterated wine and corrupt hospitality at country inns as tropes exposing economic and political propaganda: rural inns proffer indigenous liquors as foreign wines. The landlady at Upton whose Worcestershire Perry answers to the "Name of every Kind of Wine" is not just greedy. To her, sober, good clients are those who without dispute buy her Perry as if it were champagne, her service an illusion.[33] Fielding often scorns English-made wines because he holds that the public unthinkingly consumes propaganda along with wine. His posthumous *The Journal of a Voyage to Lisbon* reveals, in the face of death, that he shunned English coastal inns by way of resisting the Methuen Act of 1703. Moreover, he transported claret so that he would not have to drink port in Portugal.[34]

IMAGES OF THE WINE TRADE, THE VIGNOBLE, AND BURGUNDY

Through Matthew Bramble, Smollett treats the wine trade as an institution that debases public taste. Wine at Bath is "not the juice of the grape" but "an adulterous mixture, brewed up of nauseous ingredients, by dunces, who are bunglers in the art of poison-making." Blaming Oporto merchants for adulterating port further spoilt by the London trade, Bramble imports "claret of the best growth" via a trustworthy agent. Yet he complains that Londoners once content with port entertain with the "richest wines of Bourdeaux, Burgundy, and Champagne." He wants sumptuary laws to stop their consumption driving up the cost of fine wines. Wishing social hierarchy fixed, he expects urban citizens to tolerate adulterated port out of respect for the exclusivity of landed gentry. Curiously, *The Expedition of Humphry Clinker* instills free-market ideology in one who would block middle-class desire for healthier

32 Fielding 1961, 188.
33 Fielding 1974, 2:533–5.
34 Fielding 1907, 66 and 73.

wine.[35] It is further curious that in his earlier travelogue, *Travels through France and Italy* (1766), Smollett says London's wine trade is superior to that of France since English travellers are duped. What is served at Boulogne is a "very small and meagre" wine from Auxerre: Boulogne's inhabitants "drink no good wine; nor is there any to be had, unless you have recourse to the British wine-merchants here established who deal in Bourdeaux wines, brought hither by sea for the London market." With not a "drop of generous Burgundy" there, "the aubergistes impose upon us shamefully when they charge it at two livres a bottle." In Dijon to see the vendange and sample the wines, he is disappointed: the generic wine is so "weak and thin" one would not drink it in England. The "very best" sold in the "capital of the province" is inferior in strength and flavour to that available in London. Supposedly "all the first growth is either consumed in the houses of the noblesse, or sent abroad to foreign markets." He himself has drunk "excellent Burgundy at Brussels" at a reasonable cost but that sold at Paris is a disgusting, "very thin kind of Burgundy."[36]

On setting out, Smollett expected to be pleased by "the vintage, which is always a season of festivity among all ranks of people"; he assumed the vendange would dispel his sense of political economy. But, while the "mountains of Burgundy," covered with vines and oriented to sunshine, were beautiful, a late harvest and unripe grapes banished all "signs of festivity." Holding Burgundy to be the ideal wine, he cannot avoid the poverty of French peasants. Just as Locke sought substitutes for Bordeaux, Smollett hunted for wines that might stand in for Burgundy. Near Lyon he found "hermitage" from the Dauphiné a "tolerable small wine." But, if it is cheap, commonly taken at meals and "remarkably strong," its flavour is "much inferior to that of Burgundy." Neither is the country wine in the region of Montpellier a substitute; it is strong, harsh, and must be mixed with water. The wines of Tavel are almost "as good as Burgundy." But local connoisseurs who make their own wine choose "grapes from different vineyards and have them picked, pressed, and fermented at home." Travellers who cannot make their wine should buy it on the recommendation of peasants whose wine is "generally genuine" whereas that of wine merchants is brewed and

---

35 Smollett 1984, 47, 118, 120, and 88.
36 Smollett 1981, 23, 65–7, and 44.

balderdashed. About the vintage at Nice in 1764, Smollett writes as acutely as Locke. He details the fermentation process: grape selection, the first pressing, the vats, the second pressing, and the addition of quick lime and pigeon dung to compensate for meagre grapes. He follows Locke in liking "Hermitage and Cote-roti" – the wines of Dauphiné – and in disliking Provençal wines. His descriptions of the Nice wine trade and British wine houses in Boulogne exhibit economic and political criticism like Locke's. But Smollett is conflicted and inconsistent. While he voices personal tastes and wine's cultural importance, he spurns it as a beverage by claiming that the French in the wine-growing districts are diminutive and unhealthy unlike the English who live on "small-beer." Despite understanding improvements in wine classification and production, he holds that "wine, and all fermented liquors, are pernicious to the human constitution."[37] His erratic images of the wine trade raise questions about relations between political and aesthetic issues. When Bramble scorns the "taste and organs" of those who prefer "adulterate enjoyments of the town to the genuine pleasures of a country retreat," Smollett, like Rousseau and other contemporary social critics, suggests that so-called progress and modern urbanization pervert the "very organs of sense" and cause citizens to lose "every relish of what is genuine and excellent in its own nature."[38]

The emblematic effects of the wine trade are expressed diversely in travelogues that, as a whole, present the aesthetics of vineyard landscapes in terms of opposing ideas of nationalism. Mrs Thrale admired French vineyards in fruit but, from personal and national pride in ale, found dormant vineyards less attractive than hop gardens.[39] Writing to his mother from Rheims on 21 June 1739, early in the growing season, Thomas Gray (1716–1771) viewed the countryside as "one great plain covered with vines, which at this time of the year afford no very pleasing prospect, as being not a foot high." Still, pleasures denied to sight are made up "to the palate; since you have nothing to drink but the best champaigne in the world, and all sort of provisions equally good."[40] Johnson enjoyed the landscape of the vintage but qualified his liking

---

37   Ibid., 15, 68, 75, 103, 161, 183, 325, 165, 31, and 314–15.
38   Smollett 1984, 118.
39   Thrale 1932, 87.
40   Gray 1955, 97. At the table of his friend, Thomas Warton the younger (1728–1790), Gray was used to drinking fine burgundy (1955, 138).

by saying it was France's only natural advantage over England. Subjecting appreciation of wine to economic contrasts between England and France, he contends in *The Idler* that travelogues are pointless when writers regale their palates with vintages: such records are insignificant since the "great part of travellers tell nothing, because their method of travelling supplies them with nothing to be told. He that enters a town at night and surveys it in the morning, and then hastens away to another place, and guesses at the manners of the inhabitants by the entertainment which his inn afforded him ... may gratify his eye with variety of landscapes, and regale his palate with a succession of vintages; but let him be contented to please himself without endeavouring to disturb others." In *Further Thoughts on Agriculture*, comparing the imperialism of Spain, France, and England, he asserts that France's vineyards are more than equivalent to Spain's Indian gold and Peruvian silver the main purpose of which is "to procure the wines of Champaigne and Burgundy." He asserts that France will always do better than Spain, its viticultural productivity less subject to imperialism's contingencies. Yet England's productivity is more reliable: "the valleys of England have more certain stores of wealth," for, whereas wines are "chosen by caprice" and not always "equally esteemed," there "never was any age, or people, that reckoned bread among superfluities, when once it was known."[41]

Opposing views of Burgundy among English travellers reflect domestic politics. Burgundy often figures as a metonym for competing nationalisms. In the 1700s, it was the oenological aristocrat. Chambertin was the only wine Louis XIV drank, other top burgundies favoured by the French court throughout the period. Burgundy wines were preferred by the Hanoverians. Unlike generic claret consumed in England as a beverage, best Burgundy was an exclusive rarity, subject to privileged importation outside the wine trade: it was steadily imported, being served at court banquets, at the tables of wealthy aristocrats, and at Vauxhall's pleasure gardens. Passions roused by its consumption could be regarded as a "treasonable offence."[42] Burgundy intensified debates

---

41 Thrale 1932, 221; Johnson 1824, VII:387 (*The Idler*, no. 97, Saturday, 23 February 1760); Johnson 1824, 2:396. His charge that tasters' notes are often senseless is matched by Thomas Warton's sketch of a lazy university don whose brain is addled by bottling and cellaring his Port and Madeira (*The Idler*, no. 33, Saturday, 2 December 1758, Johnson 1824, 7:129–32).

42 Younger 1965, 369–70; Simon 1927, 72, 75, and 149.

about the trade and class hierarchy. In her letters, Lady Mary Wortley Montagu uses European travels to question England's reliance on French modes that saw the trade as exploiting consumers. Treating wine as a necessary beverage, she writes from Cologne in 1716, claiming the admirable Lorraine wine she drinks there is sold as Burgundy in London. In a letter from Chamberry in 1741 she opines that Savoyard wine is as good as best Burgundy. Her relish of Bulgarian peasant wines reflects a wish to defy the wine trade's propaganda and poor English taste. In extending her Italian dining room onto a shady, terraced, and productive vineyard, she displays an inventive application of landscape and architectural forms.[43] In this she freed herself from her husband's avarice and luxury as well as distanced herself from the English wine trade's dubious reliance on French fashion.[44]

Its low quality and high price in London often caused travellers delight with Burgundy available in France. In 1700, Congreve, future Commissioner of Wine Licences, relished fine champagne and burgundy at Calais, impressed that the former cost only twelve pence a quart and the latter only fifteen pence.[45] Edward Wright, on his Grand Tour in 1720, was bowled over by the countryside and wine of Burgundy. He was so struck by "the pleasing Appearance of the Vineyards" near Auxerre that he left the "*Coche d'Eau*" to walk through them to the city. He was less impressed by its streets which he found "abominably pav'd." But he so loved the wine that he joked about bad paving being a necessary check on a man's drinking.[46] At Dijon in 1731, Spence reported costs of best Burgundy in taverns at eight pence a bottle and that from great merchants at sixteen pence. While the poor buy the cheapest for halfpenny a bottle, he says that what he drinks would cost three times more in London.[47] Since importing Burgundy via the trade was not trouble free, diplomats and aristocrats had to be proactive. Chesterfield bought wine from growers and transported it in a second carriage.

---

[43] Montagu 1906, 364, 315, and 110.
[44] Reporting Wortley Montagu's death, Gray recounts how the latter "every day drank ... half a pint of tokay, which he imported himself from Hungary in greater quantity than he could use, and sold the overplus for any price he chose to set upon it" (Gray 1955, 245).
[45] Congreve 1964, 13–14.
[46] Wright 1730, 1:7.
[47] Spence 1975, 46.

Having received one shipment of spoiled Burgundy from a wine merchant in Mannheim, he refused the offer of a shipment of Rhenish, opting to purchase old Hock from a vintner when abroad. Tasting wine on site reconciled him to transporting it: in 1753 he told his son he would buy wine at Liège or Aix-la-Chapelle on his way to Spa and bring it home.[48]

A precursor of Andrews in outlook, Philip Thicknesse (1719–1792) continued the work of Nugent by offering advice to travellers not in Chesterfield's rank. Thicknesse's *Observations on the Customs and Manners of the French Nation*, published after Smollett's ill-tempered travelogue, tells how to get bargains in French inns by contracting for accommodation fees. While warning about the "many disagreeable circumstances" met travelling in France, he argues that complaints by Englishmen arise from wrong expectations and ignorance of cultural practices, this obliging him to state that they may be "the foulest feeders in the universe." Thus, he defends dining etiquette: "At elegant tables in France, to every cover is set a large deep glass, three parts full of water, wherein the bowl of your wine glass is inverted, to keep it cool and clean." He also praises the "easy address of people of fashion in France," finding it "captivating." His critical balance is evident in the following sentences: "Nothing is so disagreeable as a low bred Frenchman; no man is more agreeable than a well bred Frenchman: A low bred Englishman shocks you with his vulgarity; a low bred Frenchman sickens you with his impertinence." Stressing the "many instances of good breeding" that "French gentlemen have shown to the English in peace and war," he insists that such "humanity as well as politeness ... ought to have deterred a man, who has established the character of an historian, from stigmatizing a whole nation, abounding with polite arts, ingenious men, and beautiful women, as a parcel of painted dolls of one sex, and hottentots of the other." Mocking Smollett, he says that "the very dirtiest and lowest beggars" in France "would find a good sale for their old cloaths in the kingdom of Scotland." He also retorts that eating at a table d'hôte in Paris may be done more affordably than in London, given the "pint of excellent wine" served. He has eaten the best roast beef ever at such a table and upon plate even if not "very clean."[49] In *A Year's Journey through France*

---

48 Stanhope 1929, 274.
49 Thicknesse 1766, 84–9.

and Part of Spain (1777), Thicknesse admits that Smollett was not in good health or temper when writing his travelogue, "the least entertaining of his works." To Thicknesse, travel writers are "either all panegyric, or all censure": what they say "cannot be just; for all nations are governed by men, and the bulk of men of all nations live by artifice of one kind or other." He himself strives to balance praise and blame. Delighted at Rheims with "the most delicious wine in the world," he visits a wine merchant whose cellars are like underground streets filled with thousands of bottles. He buys a couple only to be disappointed but catches himself up: the champagne he drinks in England is likely "adulterated" with sugar. So, he offers readers a test to see if their champagne has been sugared.[50] His comparative sense persists. Leaving a genteel family at Rheims who made his stay comfortable, he is somewhat unhappy. Once in Dijon, he finds "*Bourgogne* is, however, a much finer province than Champaigne." Yet praise of the city's urban geography does not result in unqualified praise of Burgundian wine. Dijon may be "pleasantly situated, well built, and the country round about it as beautiful as nature could well make it," but, if the province's wine is excellent, he has had better in London. After reporting various growths, he says "the quality is not in proportion to the price." He also describes problems with exporting Burgundy to England, costing hampers, casks, bottles, freight, and duties. He advises sending as strong a wine as possible in casks so that it will "mellow, and form itself in the carriage." The casks must be doubled to prevent "the frauds of the carriers." Still, he praises France as "a great and mighty kingdom, blest with every convenience and comfort in life," including its good wine, which taken moderately as the French do is "an excellent cordial to the nerves" that "contributes to long life, and good health." He claims that you "seldom meet a drunken peasant, and never see a gentleman (*except he be a stranger*) in that shameful situation"; the cheap availability of wine and brandy is the explanation. English prejudice among people of fashion against the French nation is "illiberal," given national drinking habits: a Frenchman drinks wine with food, mixing water with his "*genuine* wine," while an Englishman "drinks much stronger, and a variety of fermented liquors, and often much worse, and sits *at it* many hours after dinner": "While the Englishman is earning disease and misery at his bottle, the

---

50 Thicknesse 1777, 1:2–3 and 30–1.

Frenchman is embroidering a gown, or knitting a handkerchief for his mistress." Another visit renders him less positive about Burgundy's wines. Travelling from Beaune to Autun, he says of the mountains covered in vines that they "*did* produce the most delicious red wine in the world; I say *did produce*, for the high goût and flavour of the Burgundy grape has for many years failed, and perhaps so as never to return again."[51]

A sentimental, more dissociated stance is adopted by John Moore (1729–1802), the medical doctor, on considering Burgundian vineyards in *A View of Society and Manners in France* (1781). Although peasants in the vignoble are poverty-stricken and emaciated, he insists that in the vintage they enjoy a "happy enthusiasm, a charming madness, and perfect oblivion of care." Were they allowed to enjoy the fruits of their labour, they would live Arcadian lives.[52]

The writer whose shrewd and systematic account of France's wine trade was most fortified by cultural comparisons is Arthur Young. He grants "there is scarcely any product so variable as that of wine": its seasonal yields are unsure; the availability of casks is uncertain; and unsteady prices "menace with poverty all who are concerned in it." His national survey of vignobles rejects prejudices and stresses paradoxes; he discards the prevailing notions that "the wine provinces are the poorest, and that the culture is mischievous to the national interests," showing that much wine is produced on land unsuited to growing wheat. He thinks that government policy discourages wheat production, that the desire to own rural properties keeps vineyards small, and that small-scale proprietors depend on larger estates for work, this stopping them tending their own vines properly.[53] A farmer himself with a small income and little influence, Young does not protest the association of rank and consumption of fine wines, accepting that Burgundies were beyond him. To him, in the district of Nuits the vineyards with "the greatest reputation" were "those of St. George, Romané, La Tashe, de Vaume, Richebourg, Chambertin, and Côte roté." Trusting ranked *domaines*, he celebrated "*Clos de Veaujeau*" as the "most famous of all the vineyards of Burgundy," it commanding the highest prices. Yet he objects to the fiscal disparity between growers and merchants: "mere merchandize, and not cultivation" sees the latter with good cellars buying and

51 Ibid., 1:35–6, 47–8, 67, 98–9; 2:139.
52 Moore 1781, 1:347–8.
53 Young 1794, 2:1–2 and 20.

storing wines for three or four years as prices rise by 20 to 30 per cent. This disparity caused him, like other travellers, to seek alternative wines. On discovering *Vins de Cahors*, he shipped it home as substitute port. When he learned that merchants added Cahors to Bordeaux, selling the blends as Bordeaux, he was shocked that vintage Cahors did not come up to the price of casks. Unlike port, he enjoyed Cahors as a "full bodied" wine which had "great spirit, without being fiery."[54]

Young's middle-class consumer's view of the wine trade led him to comparative insights into English and French cookery. The English, he says, "have about half a dozen real English dishes, that exceed any thing, in my opinion to be met with in France." These are "a turbot and lobster sauce – ham and chicken – turtle – a haunch of venison – a turkey and oysters." But "after that there is an end of an English table." He excludes roast beef, "for there is no better beef in the world than at Paris." French cuisine is more extensive, cooks dressing "an hundred dishes in an hundred different ways, and most of them excellent; and all sorts of vegetables have a savouriness and flavour, from rich sauces, that are absolutely wanting to our greens boiled in water." This difference, not applicable to aristocratic tables of either nation, "is manifest, in an instant, between the tables of a French and English family of small fortune. The English dinner, of a joint of meat and a pudding, as it is called, or *pot luck*, with a neighbour, is bad luck in England; the same fortune in France gives, by means of cookery only, at least four dishes to one among us, and spreads a table incomparably better." In England, dessert "is expected, at a considerable table only, or at a moderate one, when a formal entertainment is given; in France it is as essential to the smallest dinner as to the largest; if it consist of a bunch of grapes only, or an apple, it will be as regularly served as the soup." Tables in the whole of France, says Young, have a sobriety that comes from proper wine service; new glasses are always to hand for later in the meal when richer and rarer wines appear. Even in houses of "a carpenter or blacksmith, a tumbler is set to every cover." French hygiene is clear from the fact people think it absurd to dine without napkins, while English "of tolerable fortune" do not use them. His tour of Italy further exercises his comparativism. He claims that dining well at a London coffee house, with a pint of bad port, and a poor dessert costs as much as staying a

---

54 Ibid., 2:16–17 and 4.

day in Venice. The art of cookery in Italy and France sees ordinary families spreading their tables at half the cost of doing so in England. Luxury in Italy and France is directed more at "enjoyment, than consumption." Thus, observations on the "trifles" of food and wine are better marks of "the temper of a nation" than "objects of importance," the tables of the French symbolizing their "good temper."[55]

WINE IN COOKBOOKS

Young's view of French cuisine is confirmed by the translation of Menon's *La Cuisinière bourgeoise* (1746): *The French Family Cook: Being A Complete System of French Cookery* came out in 1793, a year before Young's *Travels*. Addressing female readers and cooks of middling fortunes, Menon has thirty-four recipes for sauces.[56] In its many ways of cooking beef, veal, pork, fish, and fowl, the text mixes traditional French with English names. It does not refer to claret, burgundy, or port and mentions champagne only once, but scores of recipes call for generic white wine and a few for red wine. This aspect of cookbooks is held over from the days of Robert Smith and Charles Carter. In the former's *Court Cookery: Or, The Compleat English Cook* (1723), while over sixty recipes call for white wine, thirty-eight require claret, sometimes in pints and quarts (for example, a quart is used to preserve barberries). Smith does not mention burgundy; only twice does he refer to champagne and thrice to Rhenish. Carter, having offered court-style food to aristocrats at home and abroad, sought to popularize his art among aspiring families in *The Complete Practical Cook: Or, A New System of the Whole Art and Mystery of Cookery* (1730). While his book offers copperplates of table settings for meals served to royalty and grandees and of sets of dishes for the seasons, plates celebrated by "*Mr. Austin, Master of* Pontack'*s in Abchurch-Lane*," only six recipes call for claret and four for "Rhenish-wine," forty-five others calling for generic red and white wine with which

---

55 Ibid., 1:290, 230, and 75. He decries imperialism in all nations but appropriates the imperial metaphor to cultural achievement in saying of Italians that an "exquisite sensibility has given them the empire of painting, sculpture, architecture, poetry, and music" (Young 1794, 1:193 and 233).
56 Menon 1793, 278–89.

Carter stews, bakes, roasts, poaches, fricassees, marinades, and boils meats and vegetables.[57]

Britons throughout the century were made aware of the culinary status of wine by cookbooks. *The Whole Duty of a Woman*, published anonymously in 1737 and republished in 1740 as *The Lady's Companion*, specifies cooking with French wine. Fifty recipes call for claret, and there are fourteen references to champagne, a bottle required when dressing salmon, turbot, sole, or pheasant.[58] While eight recipes stipulate Rhenish wine in the cooking of pigeons and celery, there are no references to port. Likely written by a man, this cookbook was the one most plagiarized by Hannah Glasse (1708–1770). Her self-published *The Art of Cookery, Made Plain and Easy* had twenty editions before 1800, its success due to a marketing strategy that secured an impressive list of subscribers. What makes her book stand out, apart from the fact that 287 of its 972 recipes were lifted from *The Lady's Companion*, is that, in her anti-French stance, she conceals her appropriation of French cuisine. About 120 recipes call for generic wine, only six requiring claret: fricassee of pigeons, stewing a rump of beef, stuffing a leg or shoulder of mutton, stewing cucumbers, making "plum-Porridge for Christmas," which requires a quart, and collaring beef.[59] There is only one reference to burgundy in a recipe for making a sauce for partridges or pheasants, but none to port.[60]

William Verrall (1715–1761), master of the White-Hart Inn at Lewes and understudy to St Clouet, chef to the Duke of Newcastle, might have been expected in *A Complete System of Cookery* (1759) to champion French wines but does not. Thirty of his recipes call for generic white wine, while only another ten specify champagne or Rhenish. One in particular is striking: fricassee of eels with champagne. His sole reference to claret and burgundy is when he tells how to prepare truffles by soaking them in French wine. Interestingly for a book that makes a wonderful introduction to nouvelle cuisine, he calls for a hare to be stewed in three half-pints of port and follows traditional recipes for preparing turtle in Madeira. The following recipe demonstrates his skill and style:

[57] Smith 1723, 58; Carter 1730, A4v.
[58] Anon. 1740, 221, 222, 225, 256, and 394–5. This text prescribes claret for the making of a lip salve (1740, 689).
[59] Glasse 1747, 15, 220, 26, 63, and 128.
[60] Ibid., 54.

Des bignets de peches, au vin de Rhin. / Peach fritters, with Rhenish wine.

This must be done with peaches of the fleshy sort, and cut in two, put them to some Rhenish wine as long as you please, with plenty of fine sugar, cinnamon, and lemon-peel; dry 'em. and fry them without flour, strain your wine into another stewpan, and boil it to a caromel; dish up, and pour it over with the kernels of the peaches blanched, split, and thrown in.[61]

Nationalism dominates *The British Housewife* (1760?) by Martha Bradley (fl. 1740s–1755). If she promotes circular French dining tables and symmetrical location of plates and dishes to please the eye and make guests comfortable in serving themselves, her recipes do not mention claret, burgundy, or champagne. Despite often referring to generic white and red wines and giving recipes for home-made wines using turnips or raisins, she favours fortified sweet wine, calling ten times more for port than other wines. Here are a few: she would boil a rump of beef in the French way with a quart of rough port; fry beefsteaks in port; stew a turkey and boil woodcocks in port; prepare mutton "Venison fashion" with port; and bake a calf's head in port. She employs port in baking an ox cheek, making a ragout of lamb or ham, and dressing a hare the Swiss way. She would stew a neat's tongue with white port, Madeira, or Malaga wines. Promoting savoury Mediterranean ingredients such as anchovies, capers, caviar, and cayenne pepper and decrying English substitutes, she would improve English wines, which she finds "unpalatable." Taking sugar as wine's basis, she senses what coopers do to port; they know how to produce, since "People like Port to be deep coloured and rough[,] that Taste and Colour; for the true genuine Wine of Oporto is not of that Sort: Every one knows genuine Port Wine is quite a different Thing from what is commonly sold under that Name; therefore the Colour and Taste, and also the Brightness, and in some Degree the Richness of Port Wine, are owing to Ingredients" added by the English trade. She wants to "find what those Ingredients are, and imitate the Art in putting them together."[62] In similar vein, Elizabeth Raffald (1733–1781), an entrepreneur with commercial and industrial interests in the Manchester region, published *The Experienced English*

---

61 Verrall 1759, 70, 189–90, 236, and 203.
62 Bradley 1760, 52, 162–3, 171–2, 178, 225, 234–5, 326, 348, 451, 544, 663, and 462.

House-Keeper, for the Use and Ease of Ladies, House-Keepers, Cooks, etc. in 1769. Calling for generic white and red wines, she gives recipes for making wine from flowers, bush berries, and tree fruit. Her gooseberry wine, she claims, is like champagne. Calling for Madeira and preparing turtle and mock turtle soup with it, she also uses it in stewing partridges and making calf's foot jelly as well as in such desserts as apricot pudding and floating island.[63]

ADULTERATED WINE: POLITICAL DUPLICITY AND TASTE

In *A Review* for 18 July 1706, Defoe, unhappy that ties between England and France remain firm in the War of Spanish Succession, opposes influential consumers with a "Gust" for "French Claret": "high Duties" on it should be retained to protect manufacturers. Trade with Bordeaux must not be free; the outflow of bullion for French wine would slow exports. The Methuen Treaty, which initiated exchange of Portuguese wines for British cloth, must be upheld. The proposed "Act against Sophisticating of Wines" must not pass. The "dark Doings of our *Vinteners, Wine-Coopers,* and *Brewing Merchants*" do less harm than would a return to "the old Channel of Trade." To import the "best Wine in *Europe*" would forfeit England's economic advantage over France. The "few City and Court taverns" that "demand their dear *French* Wines, with hard Names, only because they are dear, and have hard Names" should be ignored.[64] Thus, Defoe opposes his own taste. Before French wine was embargoed, he was in the trade. Importing up to seven hundred pipes of Oporto a year, he sold tons of "as good French *Claret* as is in the World." That he embodied a double standard is clear from his service for the Union of Scotland and England in 1707. Demanding that Robert Harley (1661–1724) heed the revenue that would be lost to the Crown by London merchants buying French wine imported duty-free into Scotland, he trusted his palate for Bordeaux enough to use his location in Scotland to offer Harley a tun of "Rich Claret" for the same cost as a mere hogshead in London.[65]

---

63 Raffald 1769, 300–1, 12–14, 119, 167, 149, and 176.
64 Defoe 1965, 3:342.
65 Defoe 1955, 206.

Duplicity marks Steele's views on claret, *The Tatler* charging vintners with exploiting the demand for French wines piqued by embargoes: they manufacture "under the streets of London the choicest products of the hills and valleys of France." Honest vintners who laid in French wine before the War of Spanish Succession cannot sell it since the English are habituated to cheap substitutes made by adding chemicals to diluted port to yield a "most beautiful pale Burgundy," a "perfect Languedoc," a "florid Hermitage" or a "very deep Pontac." These "wine-brewers," this "corporation of druggists," vitiates the "nation's palate" by squeezing "Bordeaux out of the sloe." He concludes that taste for false claret degrades discourse in pamphlets, speeches, sermons, and daily conversation. He heightens wine's political meaning when, in 1714, he reverses his position on claret in *The Reader*: he argues against Bordeaux as England's "*national Drink*," claiming that at the height of its importation it was mixed with Spanish wine and that port is cheaper, healthier, and morally beneficial. By debating French and Portuguese wines and advancing the Whig promotion of port, Steele, like Defoe, provoked later writers to grasp the semiotics of wine.[66]

How to shun adulterate and take genuine wines by sensing *terroir*'s qualities preoccupied medical doctors who thought wine essential to the healthy diet of the elderly. Such experts held that the unregulated market degraded wine by treating it as a cash commodity. One such was Sir Edward Barry (1696–1776), whose *Observations Historical, Critical, and Medical on the Wines of the Ancients and the Analogy between Them and Modern Wines* (1775) praises the wines of Champagne and Burgundy as France's best, their fine "texture" and distinctive "flavour" rendering impurities immediately detectable. Barry details fine wines to train readers to taste their purity. The "*Champaign river* Wines are more delicate and pale" than "*mountain* grey Wines." Both keep well in cellars, but, guarded too long in cask, the former "acquires a taste from the wood; but in flasks is durable from four to five, and six years." The firmer structure of mountain wines lets them be kept for two to three years in cask before they are bottled; they are suited to exportation because they travel better. Best mountain wines have a "grateful pungency, and balsamic softness." While fine champagne has a light generosity and

66 Steele 1953, 164–6; 1959, 173–5.

sub-astringent taste, sparkling wines bottled early effect a "depravity of taste." There is a danger of contracting gout and gravel from drinking them as they ferment.[67]

Barry drew on *Dissertation sur la situation de bourgogne* written in 1728 by Claude Arnoux (1695–1770), a priest from Beaune who taught English and sold wine in London. He classified burgundies by distinguishing between "vins de garde" and "vins de premier."[68] He noted the varying maturity and longevity of wines from the villages of Volnay, Pommard, Chassagne, Nuits, and Chambertin. While Volnay's grapes require a short fermentation because of their delicacy – a vintage lasting only one year – those of Nuits and Chambertin are so "rough, hard, and tart" they must be kept "till their second, third, fourth, and fifth year." As "their tartness and roughness go off, they acquire a perfume and balminess, very delicious." Possessing "all the good qualities of the other wines, without any of their faults," Chambertin commands twice the price of any wine in Burgundy.[69]

While Barry trusts the regulatory efficacy of Beaune's wine commission, he distrusts Bordeaux wines on the London market. Once, only the wealthy could afford Pontac, Haut-Brion, Margaux, Lafitte, and Latour, the first growths available in taverns and inns and renowned for their "favourable soil and situation" that gave them "superior qualities, and a taste peculiar to each." But the Bordeaux trade let those growths lose their distinctive flavours by mixing them with "*Spanish* wines, particularly the *Alicant*" to give them "more strength, and an equal, or higher flavour" to inferior growths. French merchants ignored the law forbidding such a practice and led people from England and Ireland to come to Bordeaux "as *Factors*, with a view, at first, of acquiring the profit arising from the large commissions, which before had been always consigned" to them. These factors became merchants who employed their own "*Tasters*, after the vintage was over, to examine the new wines" and buy up those that would meet English expectations, adding to them Spanish wine to increase their strength, flavour, and price. This need not have degraded claret had the addition been natural and the "union and transparency" of the French been preserved, "but this cannot be obtained without *forcing* them into a new fermentation,

---

67 Barry 1775, 422–3, 425, and 427–8.
68 Francis 1972, 159 and 147.
69 Barry 1775, 430–3.

which adds more *spirit* to the *Spanish* Wine, while it enervates the *French* wine, dissipates entirely its native flavour, and gives it a tendency to an *acetous* kind of acrimony." Growers in Bordeaux asked Parlement to establish a system for authenticating wine, but factors and merchants opposed the call. Even worse for taste is the fact that "these Wines are often more injured, after they are imported, than they had been in *France*, by committing them to the conduct of our modern artists, who mix them with other fermented liquors, and unite them by a repeated fermentation." By "these arts we have been almost entirely deprived of any genuine claret Wines, which had been so long esteemed for their grateful, and salutary qualities. Few now can even recollect the peculiar taste of their first growths, in their former genuine state, or drink them in their present depraved state."[70]

Barry sees no end to the decline of taste: port may be preferable to claret, but rising demand and higher prices are increasing its adulteration. It is already heavier and taking longer to mature because of excessive fortification. Since the chief vineyards are owned by British and Irish merchants whose local privileges have been curtailed, their sole profits derive from exporting to England. They doubly adulterate their wines – once in Portugal and again in England. This is a crisis, says Barry, because port is essential to the diet of the elderly, whose health will decline if they have to leave it off. He ends his survey of modern wines by urging the wealthy to plant vineyards like his friend, Charles Hamilton, who produces a white wine superior to French champagne. He thus looks beyond skepticism to the day when English gentlemen will make pure "native Wines" commercially.[71]

As we saw in chapter 1, twenty years after Barry, John Wright's aesthetic response to port was ambivalent. Having tasted Hamilton's wine, he held out no hope for English vineyards. Rather, he thought, since port was on the decline given adulteration in the wine trade, Britain should develop viticultural enterprises abroad. The problem is paradoxical: it is not that more port is imported than other wines but that far more is consumed than imported, that much being "beneath mediocrity." Once "used only at the tables of the opulent," it was a better beverage, but "now it is common where ale only was to be found," it is losing its "purity."

70 Ibid., 434–8.
71 Ibid., 439, 472, and 479.

Wright's objection to port is that most consumers who think themselves rational guzzle it without taste or reflection; ignorant, avaricious, or parsimonious, they will not develop their palates. Were they to detect adulteration, they would avoid the illnesses it causes and render "the social felicity of social festivity ... more pleasant."[72]

Wright's hope for importation of port was not fulfilled, so says *A History and Description of Modern Wines* by Cyrus Redding (1785–1870), writing fifty years later with a sense of the political history of the marketing of Portugal's second-rate wines. After recalling that every pipe of eighty-one gallons brought into England contains twenty-four of brandy, Redding vociferates: no "wine is worthy to be drunk in a highly-civilized country which is not made of grapes alone." He is angry that coarsened taste was "forced on us by our rulers," the monopoly granted the Douro Company in 1756, ensuring that low-quality wines were further adulterated in England. This coarsening has worsened in the last thirty years since incentives to adulteration have increased. To Redding, far from constituting a sound cultural tradition, port stands for government interference and corrupt patronage. He is sure that taste for strong, sweet port led to the adulteration of claret with brandy and with the heavy wines of Hermitage and Cahors. Damning port as dull, heavy, and excessively alcoholic, he praises claret for being cool, light, and exhilarating and hopes it will again be favoured by the "refined and wealthier classes." Sadly, Englishmen have by "long usage" come to believe "port wine the only real red wine in the world," and they shiver "whenever Romanèe Conti, or Lafitte" is named. Oporto wine, "which is naturally of a good character," might have become first class from "generous and honourable competition with French wines"; with "perseverance, and a liberal outlay of capital," it could have approximated burgundy, Côte Rôti, or Bordeaux.[73]

NATIONAL WINE?

To late seventeenth-century diarists, English vineyards seemed hopeful. In his *Diary*, Pepys enjoys red wine from Lady Battens's estate at Walthamstow in 1660, relishing it again in December 1667 and noting

72 Wright 1795, v–vii, ix, 19–20, and 43–5.
73 Redding 1851, 240, 239, and 237.

it ages well. Naturally, he exploited his privilege as a senior naval officer to import wine free of duty and to build a substantial cellar. In 1665, his held two casks of Canary along with single casks of Sack, Tent, and Malaga as well as two forty-two-gallon casks of claret. Like Evelyn, Pepys most prized claret, also, like Evelyn, finding Haut-Brion unique. Proud that friends could not match his cellar, Pepys joined them in importing wine, relying on vintners and coopers for advice about managing his cellar.[74] Still, the period's interest in English vineyards was serious, as clear from William Hughes's *The Compleat Vineyard* in 1665 and John Rose's *The English Vineyard Vindicated* in 1669, the latter appended to Evelyn's *The French Gardiner* that year.

Interest in English vineyards was sustained but became contentious. In a letter of 1740, Aaron Hill (1685–1750) wrote to Samuel Richardson, full of what he saw as a "new spirit for vineyards." Hostile to vintners' mixing of wines and adding raisins or sugar, Hill insists that English will soon outrank French wines for quality because he has developed a technique that compensates for under-ripened English grapes. This involves boiling a proportion of must, that is, unfermented grape juice, and adding it to unconcentrated must. The result, he claims, is a wine with "true English firmness of heart." He calls his wine English burgundy, promoting its alcoholic strength as exceeding that of the oldest port. His goal is to cultivate French grapes and to vinify them according to the methods of Oporto, thereby displacing claret and burgundy. Hill's dream of a strong, national wine savours of economic and cultural imperialism.[75] Adam Smith agreed that Britain could produce fine grapes with the aid of hotbeds and garden walls, granting that good wine could be made. But he questioned why anyone would want to make native wines costing thirty times more than imported ones. To him, it was inconceivable that foreign wines might be banned to foster the domestic production of claret and burgundy. His promotion of free trade recognizes distinct yet complementary geographical advantages and recommends employing labour and capital as efficiently as possible.[76]

---

74 Pepys 1983, 1:317; 8:341–2; 1:277; 4: 100; 3:14; 4:171. Evelyn thought the "excellent *Vignoble* of *Pontaque* & *Obrien*" produced "the choicest of our *Burdeaux-*Wines" (1959, 749).
75 Richardson 1966, 1:44 and 50–1.
76 Smith 1976, 1:480.

FRENCH VINEYARDS AND NATIONAL IDENTITY

While Britons generalized about the wines of France, that country's viticulture was regional in orientation. Debates about wine there resembled those in England: views on adulteration and marketing reveal similar conflicts about regulatory controls. Probably, foreign markets' demand for its wines sped France's sense of nationalism. On this Arthur Young was insightful: he thought French vintners "often incorrect" by not regarding the wine economy "in a national light."[77] What limited their political sense was confusion about the nature of wine and resistance to studying soils and microclimates. When the *Affiches d'Orléans* declared in 1770 that wine is "the spiritous fermentation of no matter what substance" and that the flavour of wines depends only on "the particular properties" of grapes, it treated soils and climates as "accidental things," as did Martha Bradley.[78] Such a view, which encouraged adulteration in the wine trade, was not challenged until Monsieur Maupin wrote a series of books digested in the press across France between 1770 and 1785. From a national perspective, Maupin berates vignerons for claiming to know everything about their vignobles. Addressing "less vain and more judicious" vignerons who admit the inadequacy of viticulture, he promotes experiments that vary space between rows of vines, that prune grape bunches to improve the per-acre quality, and that reduce fertilizers. He argues that vinification should be modified according to the different rates at which vines mature and grapes ripen. Fermentation should not always be "long and slow" or aimed at producing the strongest possible wine: it should be "prompt, rapid, and uninterrupted."[79] He offers his theory in a letter sent to the publisher of the *Affiches d'Angers*: admitting his methods are not well known, he declares they are practised successfully "in the largest number of wine-producing provinces." Still, there remain in France five or six thousand proprietors who should improve their practices. To their great detriment and that of society, they spoil their vines and wines. This spoilage cannot be too much decried; while it harms proprietors, it damages the public interest of provinces, consumers, and

---

77 Young 1970, 2:1–2 and 20–6.
78 *Affiches d'Orléans*, 7 December 1770.
79 *Affiches d'Angers*, March and April, 1775.

the nation. If critical in order to sell books, reviews support his view that backward-looking viticulture is a problem for the state.[80]

Analyzing Maupin's *Théorie, ou Leçon sur le temps le plus convenable de couper la Vendange dans tous les Pays & dans toutes les années* (1782), the *Affiches de Troyes* admits that its wine-growing district is struggling. It upholds Maupin: while chemists insist fermentation should be long and slow to render wine strong, his contrary view is based on observation. His advice suits Troyes since local vignerons do not draw from its fertile vignobles "the finesse and the qualities the different terroirs are able to produce." Maupin's empiricism inspires the *affiches* to propose administrative reforms about declaring dates for the vendange given the relative maturity of grapes. The harvest should not be declared when the Pinot is ripe, for this grape always matures first, leaving the others still green and worthless for production. Uniform calls for the vendange displace pickers, reduce the potential grape yield, increase the costs of transportation, and encourage gleaning among rival growers. Were those who time the harvest salaried, they would make it more productive.[81]

Some months later, citing Maupin's titles, the *Affiches d'Auxerre* also faults its region's viticulture: "The low quality of wines, the high cost of the culture of vines, and the poor use of land, are public ills which it would be well to remedy." District proprietors and growers should, it declares, heed his works.[82] While press responses to Maupin were mostly positive, he admitted the inefficacy of his works: promoting them elicited resistance to a national sentiment for the wine trade. To define this sentiment, he used observations in Champagne and Burgundy, not in the advanced wine trade of Bordeaux. Still, reviews of his works expose problems in the commerce of wine more than do harvest reports in newspapers.[83] While it promoted his reforms, the press did not advance national viticulture since it was implicated in a

---

80 *Affiches d'Angers*, 1 August 1783.
81 *Affiches de Troyes*, 4 September 1782.
82 *Affiches d'Auxerre*, première quinzaine de décembre 1782.
83 "Burgundy had no experience like the boomtime of 18th century Bordeaux. No new wines were invented, no new district planted. The Bordeaux Picture is all expansion and creation; the Burgundy one of evolving tastes and techniques, of new market forces, and overall of slowly progressing definition: a more precise notion of the character, style and value of the wine from each corner of the Côte" (Johnson 1989, 267).

secretive trade. From 1765 to 1775, no vintage in Auxerre was successful, but this is not revealed in the press. Its harvest reports are misleading or contradictory. The one for 1781 heralds an abundant, long-keeping wine, but says that scarcity of barrels will oblige proprietors to dig vats in the ground. Far from blaming monopolistic coopers, the report turns to past market problems: much wine remains from "the last three harvests" since buyers were put off by a rumoured lack of wine. Were a long-keeping wine produced, would it not lower the price of the stock without gaining new custom, and were former customers to buy the stock, who would buy the new wine? The next year the *Affiches d'Auxerre* no more intelligently predicts that the "hardworking vigneron" will share in the "communal happiness" of the vintage. Autumn's fine days, after "abundant rains," have doubled the crop, creating an embarrassment of riches. Vignerons will not have to store wine since merchants are coming from afar in homage to the vintage. The anticipated prosperity is deluded, the press too much an agent of boosterism. The 1788 report in the *Affiches d'Auxerre* expresses "sweet hopes" for the vintage by reminding vintners how to extract maximum colour while preserving bouquet. Vintners must sustain Auxerre's renown by ensuring their wines will travel well and improve with age. That Auxerre's "excellent cordial renews exhausted strength, fortifies the stomach and re-establishes digestion" has been attested by Chevalier Lynch, English ambassador to the court of Turin, and his lady when they stayed in town for eighteen months to recover their exhausted health. Vintners must remember that "English gentlemen agree that it is the drink which most suits their temperaments." If France is to incorporate wine into its identity, it will have to recognize the influence of the English market.

WINE AND FASHION IN ENGLISH LITERATURE

George Crabbe (1754–1832) links champagne to the court, port to the Church, and burgundy to the military. His "Inebriety" blames clergymen for toadying to atheistic patrons for the sake of drinking fine vintages and boasting expertise in tasting; they are pagans who make wine their divinity. In "The Patron," a young poet dies from expecting preferment. In advancing a lord's political career, he grows used to luxury but wins no post, his father having warned him against developing a liking for French wine. On the poet's death, the lord haughtily disclaims responsibility, denying he should have nurtured the poet with champagne.

Crabbe refuses to equate wine and sensibility in *The Parish Register* when he deflates a youth's marital expectations. At his wedding, the young man rejoices in Psalm 128, likening a wife to a fruitful vine and children to its branches. But his wife proves too fruitful and his children too numerous: the vine overgrows their cottage, blocking out all light.[84]

Wine allusions in plays after the Restoration formed a typology that deepened the reflexive power of seemingly trivial scenes. Susanna Centlivre (1667–1723) has Scoredouble, the deceitful innkeeper in *A Gotham Election* (1715), admit that, while his trade in port to poor customers is small, his business thrives on gentry who demand claret. That Tickup, a candidate for election, buys wine from the local inn for constituents yet disclaims bribery shows that corrupt politics defines the classes.[85] Garrick uses this insight in *A Peep behind the Curtain* (1767) when Wilson affirms that claret is what a landed gentleman with a seat in Parliament drinks.[86] Farquhar had made the nexus of privilege and hedonism farcically apparent in *Sir Harry Wildair* (1701) when the hero, attacked by a gang intent on getting him drunk, insists on the gentlemanly privilege of being stifled with claret rather than with brandy like a bawd.[87] The contrast between drunken rakes and necessitous prostitutes exposes the double standard encoded in the typology. In Restoration comedy, misogyny and pretensions to rapacity are implicated by the gendering of wine. Hazzard, the rake in *The Miser* (1672) by Thomas Shadwell (1642–1692), says of a young woman that she looks as if she would melt "like an Anchove in Claret," making her the object of luxurious eating. Farquhar exploits such sexism in *The Recruiting Officer* (1706) when Worthy reserves "the Maidenhead" of a "fresh Pipe of choice *Barcelona*" for Captain Plume's piercing, implying that men take women as greedily as they drink wine.[88] More dramatic plays see female characters questioning the wine code and its social and economic prejudices. Thomas Otway (1652–1685) has Victoria in *Friendship in Fashion* (1678) expose the mechanical lovemaking that obsesses men who yield to "powerful Champaign," and Oriana in Farquhar's *The Inconstant* (1702) mocks men who,

---

84 Crabbe 1834, 2:302; 4:245, 247, 259; 2:160.
85 Centlivre 1872, 3:158.
86 Garrick 1980, 2:72.
87 Farquhar 1930, 1:92.
88 Shadwell 1927, 2:22; Farquhar 1930, 2:51.

intoxicated by claret, presume to judge women but, in toasting their healths, destroy their reputations.[89]

Shadwell documents the semiotics of wine. In *The Sullen Lovers* (1668), while recording how urban gentry define themselves by eating à la mode and drinking champagne, he depicts a rural gentleman who hypocritically spurns as marital partner a woman who wants a "Sellar full of Champaign, Chablee, Burgundy."[90] Like other rural men, he enjoys luxurious wine as a sexual rite in London brothels but spurns it as a sign of domestic refinement. Shadwell often bases dramatic conflict on hypocritical consumption and devaluation. *The Humorists* (1671) widens the gap between citizens who devalue and townsmen who appreciate wine. While Crazy holds that wine destroys health to hide his diseases caused by sexual indulgence, Raymund lauds burgundy's healthiness, promoting it as a social bond and inspirer of humane and divine thoughts. Taking wine as an instrument of reform, the manly Raymund despises those who drink claret for the conventional reason of increasing virility. That men debase themselves in brothel rites is clear when Friske and Striker, rival strumpets, tell how customers compete in drinking wine in which they have washed.[91]

Shadwell turns brothel rites upon men. In *The Miser*, Timothy, Squire Squeezum's son, shows his familiarity with brothels when courting his intended. He asks Theodora to get Sack from a tavern where she has credit, saying he carries sugar with him since innkeepers charge too much: insultingly, he asks her to play the rake. By satirizing avarice and lechery in country gentry, Shadwell makes the wine code uphold typology. Timothy swallows the gamblers' slogans about claret making a drunk a great king. Yet, champagne so oversets him on his wedding day that he is unconscious at the ceremony. In contrast, Theodore the hero, far from succumbing to burgundy or whores, uses luxury wines to provoke his father to expose his avarice and the lechery with which he would attach his son's lover.[92] The goal for excusing and blaming the uses of wine are similar in *Epsom-Wells* (1673) where Shadwell reforms town wits who espouse "lusty Burgundy" as a generous discipline but treats Clodpate, a rural justice who hates London wine because it is too

89 Otway 1932, 1:354; Farquhar 1930, 1:227.
90 Shadwell 1927, 1:38 and 88.
91 Ibid., 1:195–6 and 226.
92 Ibid., 2:36, 54, and 69.

expensive, roughly. The wits praise debauchery until they meet women who make them recant, but Clodpate is undone. After criticizing "foolish *French* kickshaw Claret" and getting drunk on ale, he sings a song comparing his mistress's lips to two brimmers of claret, her breasts to two bottles of white wine, and her eyes to two cups of Canary. Such wine imagery holds that town wits are more reformable than country gentlemen.[93] Satirizing the gross consumerism of country knights, Shadwell wins new dramatic and moral ironies, the role of his women in challenging wine codes influential by 1700 for mocking aristocrats. In *The Woman-Captain* (1680), Sir Humphrey Scattergood inherits an estate with cellars full of choicest wines. If "very good *Langoon* and *Burdeaux*" that satisfied his father are fit only for menials, his wines are rarer: "*Vin d'aye*, high Country Wine, *Frontiniac*; all the delicious Wines of *Italy* and *Spain*; the richer wines of *Greece* and *Sicily*." He buys "*Celery, Champaign* and *Burgundy*, with *Vin de Bon, Vin Celestine*, and *Hermitage*, and all the Wines upon the fruitful *Rhine*." He dresses his steward as "*Bacchus*" and has him squeeze "twined Wreaths of Grapes" so that guests and he may bathe in floods of "Poetick Juyce." Giving his overworked bawd mere sack, he tries to rape the wife of Gripe, the jealous financier who incites Scattergood's luxury but eschews wine. While the knight uses wine for sex and Gripe for strategy, Mrs Gripe's heroism saves her from both men. Shadwell binds libertinism and capitalism to misogyny so that his females may ridicule wine codes. Only when his estate is about to fall does Scattergood reform: he takes wine enough to have an appetite for a woman and woman enough to have an appetite for wine. This indulgence does not move his companions; to them, only fools are merry without wine. His estate is saved by his whore.[94]

Mid-century comic wine imagery narrows; Garrick uses it to censure aristocratic decadence. In *Lethe* (1740), Lord Chalkstone ignores his habitual indulgence. He will not "abstain from French wines" to save his life, needing them to kill time! In *The Male-Coquette* (1757), Chalkstone's nephew, Daffodil, is too refined to ruin women: he trifles rather than make love, just as he daintily sips but does not swallow Tokay. In *Bon Ton* (1775), Lord Minikin's headache makes him feel he "must absolutely change" his wine merchant since one taste of poor

---

93 Ibid., 2:150 and 152.
94 Ibid., 4:23–4, 64, and 70.

champagne renders him ill for a week. Minikin, like Daffodil an effete philanderer, will not give up that wine. In *The Clandestine Marriage*, the target remains aristocratic decadence, even if wine images are voiced by a servant and a businessman. Brush, Lord Ogelby's valet who would seduce a chambermaid, excuses his grossness by pretending the port served him is too strong for a "claret-drinker." Brush shows that sex, like indulgence in French wine, descends the social scale. Even the money-grubbing Sterling, who hates aristocrats, must outdo them in fashionable consumerism. That he feels obliged to serve aristocratic guests champagne better than that enjoyed by dukes signals the negative influence of nobility.[95]

Foote, like Garrick, not only makes French wine convey aristocratic decadence but joins it ironically to patriotism. In *The Englishman Returned from Paris* (1756), a baronet so affected by Paris culture prefers French *chansons à boire* and pleasures of the table to the formality of English meals from which, he derisively claims, the lady departs "drenched with a bumper," as the husband treats male guests to port and politics. In fact, this play denounces French manners sarcastically and champions British political rights uncritically. Foote is less doctrinaire in *The Knights* (1754). Objecting to the English habit of equating wealth and virtue, Hartop urges Englishmen to imitate French concern for birth and character rather than for fashion. He claims the English aggravate their decadence by valuing a man only if he can afford to drink French wine. Foote's contempt for French wine as status symbol is conveyed by Mrs Cole, the old bawd in *The Minor* (1760). When a whore, she drank Burgundy with clients. But, a reborn Christian, she will not touch French wine, although she buys Burgundy for her girls and enjoys old Hock and strong liquors. Mrs Cole's hypocrisy is treated so indulgently that her questionable antipathy to French wine signifies her nationalism.[96]

Wine images in the plays of Goldsmith and Sheridan confirm that satire of drinking codes is limited by sentimentality and nationalism. In *She Stoops to Conquer*, Tony the drunkard equates drinking and genius as well as frankly enjoying sex. Yet, since he is good-natured and instrumental to the plot, his drinking is no matter for reform. While Marlow's pretentious sensibility is the target of the plot, his attitudes are not

---

[95] Garrick 1980, 1:28–31, 152–3; 2:264; 1:321, and 271.
[96] Foote 1968, 1:20–1, 9, and 30.

probed; he enjoys Hardcastle's claret cup but is not a serious drinker. Rather he sends his servants to drain Hardcastle's cellar. While Marlow is too occupied by French fashions to like drinking, his sexual double standards and use of wine imagery to seduce Kate prove that he embodies the drinking code. Evading his imagery, Kate is more interested in winning him for a husband than analyzing his faults. When he asks to taste the "nectar" of her lips, she pretends that is a French wine. To his retort that the nectar he wants is of true English growth, she claims it is strange she has not heard of it since they "brew all sorts of wine in the house." Gentle satire of rural inns and its implicit nationalism show the play avoids probing drinking codes.[97]

Reforming those codes is no concern of Sheridan's *The School for Scandal*. Charles Surface, an extravagant imbiber, satirizes society through wine images: to him, contemporaries are degenerate since they do not drink. Their luxury abstains from wit and wine: according to Careless, there is no "social spirit of raillery ... to mantle over a glass of bright Burgundy." Conversation, his friend continues, is like spa water; it has "the pertness and flatulency of champagne, without its spirit or flavour." Implying that wine heightens moral awareness, Charles cavalierly yet conventionally asserts that he takes champagne to dull his sense of gambling losses and to discover which of his mistresses he loves. He excuses indulgence in burgundy on the grounds it neither corrupts nor improves a man's character but simply reveals it. Sir Oliver, who likes good wine and dislikes prudence in young men, ignores Charles's drinking excesses given their sentimental bond. This bond makes reform of the drinking code irrelevant, even though it is a questionable aspect of that bond.[98]

Wine imagery in the plays of Hannah Cowley (1743–1809) is less satirical than in Goldsmith and Sheridan; she was more intent on imitating earlier plays than testing contemporary manners. In *A Bold Stroke for a Husband* (1784), she imitates Shadwell and Cibber by having a husband unknowingly reveal his addiction to debauchery and burgundy to his wife, the satire being weak: the code holding that a "woman without prattle, is like Burgundy without spirit" is not unsettling. In *The Belle's Stratagem* (1782), sexual ethics are not probed; when Letitia

97 Wood 2007, 202 and 197.
98 Moore 1933, 911–13.

disguises herself to distract Doricourt, her reluctant lover, from his bottle, the debt to Goldsmith quells critical implications. The ritual use of wine in the denouement does imply reform: Letitia's father orders his "Forty-eight" to be drunk by the parish to celebrate her marriage, keeping a dozen bottles back for an eventual christening. If this imagery displaces rakes' use of wine, it does so gently. When Cowley gives her imagery bite, it singles out aristocratic vices. Tippy, impersonating an aristocrat in *The Town before You* (1795), gets invited to the best dining parlours and wine cellars, having become a connoisseur of art and wine: knowing what grapes go into what wines, he can pass judgment on Tokay and old Hock. He shows fashionable aristocracy to be a mirage since its modes can be so easily imitated.[99]

Negative images of aristocratic drinkers and sentimental ones of middle-class drinkers abound in the plays of Thomas Holcroft (1745–1809). In *Seduction* (1787), Sir Frederic Fashion proudly seduces women and injures fathers and husbands. To him, enjoying a wife is "A turtle feast without French wines." He takes wine only after making a prospective father-in-law in despair "foam and bounce like a cork from a bottle of champaigne." Yet Fashion turns out to be ineffective: the plot dismisses his evil rather than treat it as a serious problem. On the other hand, Harry Dornton in *The Road to Ruin* (1792), is a good-natured gambler willing to marry a rich widow to restore his father's fortunes. He drinks "three bottles of Burgundy" to get in an amorous frenzy to court the widow but wins her by admitting his drinking. Containing his self-sacrifice, he rescues a friend from prison, sensitively encouraging him with champagne. His drinking, then, is virtuous when excessive and moderate. That this play derives from Centlivre's *The Platonick Lady* explains why its sentimental presentation of wine prevents it from contributing to generic and satiric renewal.[100] The undramatic social fantasy towards which comedy moves is evident in Holcroft's *The Man of Ten Thousand* (1796), where a whimsical, unworldly character, Hairbrain, who, ignorant about business, feels inferior to an aristocratic friend, Dorington, wins a lottery, which he gives to the aristocrat to enable him to restore his fortune by marriage. Dorington's

---

99 Cowley 1979, 1:3, 82; 2:22.
100 Holcroft 1980, 1:26, 33, 65, and 75.

superciliousness is undermined by his dependence on Hairbrain and by Hairbrain's more appreciative taste for the aristocrat's burgundy.

MYTHS OF CLARET AND BURGUNDY

In *The Art of Preserving Health* (1744), John Armstrong (1709–1779), the poetical doctor, calls burgundy "gay, serene, good-natured" – the "divinest gift." While cider, "Pomona's juice," matches "the sprightly genius of champaign," he will not praise the British beverage to the exclusion of foreign wines. Still, in "A Day: An Epistle to John Wilkes," he blames addiction to port and the nation's resultant ill health on policies furthering it. Anticipating Redding, he holds that trade with Portugal has so dispatched health and pleasure that the English are "muddy brained." Their only remedy is "time and burgundy." Hence, French wine is a trope of personal and social health – of a healthy beverage and of healthy trade – whereas port is a "black poison" and a "double, treble curse." The choice of wine figures in "Taste," his poem that stresses discrimination's role in sustaining theatrical values. So, he likens those who prefer Rowe's to Shakespeare's plays to tasteless people who take "flat Minorca's dose" before claret. He spurns those seeking oblivion in "poison'd nectar sweet"; rejecting the divine gift of burgundy, they wish heaven had withheld the grape from humans: in so rationalizing their unrefined drinking, they deny wine's mythopoeic value.[101]

The wine codes of comedies are tested by novelistic dialectic, as in Richardson's *Pamela*, which adds psychological depth to class ideology. Trapped in Mr B.'s Lincolnshire house, Pamela is forced to serve burgundy to her master so he may display prestige by demeaning her. His coercion stems from weakness: he demeans her partly because she prefers the company of fellow servants. His emotional weakness is a foil to her mental strength. Her serving of burgundy, despite spilling it, betokens agonized self-control. Deferential to social rank, she suffers from loss of self-respect. To her, it is an honour to serve the wine, but she stands out of sight behind Mr B.'s chair as he drinks to protect herself. When commanded to pour a second glass, she is mocked for spoiling the wine with tears. Again, her signs of weakness revert to his susceptibility. Finding beauty in her tears, he would hide his confusion

---

[101] Gilfillan 1858, 34, 97, 74, and 55–6.

by calling artificial what he knows to be natural. Mr B.'s burgundy is transformed from a sign of misogyny into one denoting Pamela's capacity to grow in personal suffering and to uphold household order. Her powerlessness embodies a moral intuition: unwilling to serve him, she resists wordlessly his connection of sexual and social power. Yet once a member of the gentry, she not only drinks wine to be polite but upholds the etiquette of serving wine: her support of the ritual of toasting healths proves domestic and social capability. On asking Pamela's father to take wine with him and giving Pamela champagne to calm her wedding-night nerves, Mr B.'s reform is proven by his temperate sense of familial and sexual aspects of wine service. When Lady Davers belittles Pamela by trying to force her to serve wine, Mr B. re-establishes domestic harmony by serving wine to the women. With his daily two bottles of claret, the reformed Mr B. becomes a model of sobriety and genteel social construction.[102]

Austen's admiration of Richardson may be sensed in her attitudes to wine. A responsible housekeeper, she made it from oranges, currants and gooseberries, French wines beyond her family's means. She rejoiced when they came her way since she liked to be able to set "vulgar Economy" aside. Her brother's purchase of claret was noteworthy. Her interest in wine glasses and management of the wine closet reflects the pleasures she linked to French wine.[103] In *Mansfield Park*, beyond satirizing the abuse of wine, she employs it to define Fanny Price's scope for moral action. Dr Grant, the clergyman, rationalizes his epicurean lust for claret, thereby exposing his irresponsibility. However, Fanny needs to overcome her sexual and social passivity. She takes wine only if Edmund serves her. She will not relish it for herself. Yet she regards Edmund's mixing of her water and wine as a ritual binding her to him. Edmund, however, regards serving wine to Fanny as a matter of health rather than romance. When he learns that doing Mrs Norris's errands gives Fanny a headache, he makes her drink a glass of Madeira. She takes it; swallowing is easier than talking. Her need for rhetorical and symbolic agency permits no insignificant consumption or renunciation of wine.[104]

102 Richardson 1971, 161, 244, 251, 295, 354–5, 390, and 409.
103 Austen 1979, 209, 313, 79, and 23.
104 Austen 1966, 96 and 103.

Sterne's interest in physiology encompassed relations between drinking wine and heightened percipience. Scornful of Lockean psychology, he raises profound questions about how sensuous pleasures relate equally to perception and cognition. In *A Sentimental Journey* (1768), Yorick drinks the King of France's health in burgundy before claiming his praise of the French is infused by a warmth unrelated to the imbibed wine. Subjected to similar irony, he drinks a bottle of burgundy to translate the fragmentary newspaper story he stumbles on in Paris: his wish for enlightenment is materially and cognitively impossible; the pains he takes in the translation are huge yet trivial and ineffectual. His wine drinking is no less subject to irony in the final pages. Enjoying the Bourbonnais vintage, he is not moved by it since his sentimental attachment to Maria is prurient. Yet, at the farmhouse near Lyon where he joins in the "feast of love," his admiration of the graceful peasants among the vines seems genuine, as when he claims that the wine he drinks there is the best he has ever tasted and that its "delicious" taste remains on his "palate" at the time of writing. But the anticlimactic episode at the Savoyard inn where he shares a room with a lady counters the possibility that his wine drinking signifies spiritual insight. Spurning Savoyard wine as ungenerous, Yorick and the lady each drink a bottle of the burgundy she transports with her. Since the treaty by which they share the room owes much to the burgundy, his claims for their seeming propriety are unsettled by the closing prurient obliquity of his text. Throughout it, burgundy produces physiological reactions in Yorick which his sentimentality, Sterne delights to say, perversely rationalizes and avoids.[105]

In *Tristram Shandy* (1765), allusions to burgundy mock the travelogue's ideal narrative purposes and whimsically offer perceptual and cognitive discontinuities that invite readers to ponder how the senses and the brain interact. Menippean impulses lead Sterne to disrupt Tristram's journey through Burgundy with a tale of an Abbess of Andoüillets and a novice journeying to the "hot baths of *Bourbon*" to cure minor ailments. The Abbess's name is that of a small sausage made famously at Troyes from pork tripe. When the religieuses set off from their abbey situated between Burgundy and Savoy, they behave with normal decency. But their manners change because their muleteer, an

---

[105] Sterne 2003, 4, 85, 94, 99–100, and 102–4.

unthinking fellow, walks behind their carriage since he has there a "leathern cask" of "generous" wine grown on a "*Burgundian* hill." Once the cask is empty, this "son of Adam" stops at an inn, his mind full of burgundy and drinking companions. When his mistresses realize they have been abandoned, in their immediate fear of rape they urge the mules forward with foul oaths, articulating them by halves to save their consciences. Their sophistical rationalization underscores their spiritual fragility and questions the relation between travel and virtue.[106]

CODA

By probing dialectic in eighteenth-century British and French writing, *Imperial Paradoxes* shows that, in addressing imperial issues, authors are not single-minded, their variable stances deploying metaphors that qualify and transform their assertions. Thus, we know more about Mr Spectator than about Addison. Writers practised self-effacement by donning masks, also appreciating cultural media such as hallucinogens and intoxicants that heighten awareness and alter mental states. Turning again to Addison, we see how he upheld embodiment and synesthesia. A wine lover, he was proud of his cellar. Yet, in *The Spectator*, he castigates drunkards by elevating reason to a degree that prefigures nineteenth-century promotion of temperance and abstinence in favour of social control. He says there is no "greater monster" than a drunkard; no character is "more despicable and deformed, in the Eyes of all reasonable Persons." Wine, it seems, has "very fatal Effects on the Mind, the Body, and Fortune of the Person who is devoted to it." Its action is twofold in perception and cognition. It uncovers "every Flaw in the mind." If the "sober Man, by the Strength of Reason, may keep under and subdue every Vice or Folly to which he is most inclined," wine "makes every latent Seed sprout up in the Soul, and shew it self; it gives Fury to the Passions, and Force to those Objects which are apt to produce them." Altering our perceptions, wine changes moods and passions for the worse. It "heightens Indifference into Love, Love into Jealousie, and Jealousie into Madness. It often turns the Good-natured Man into an Ideot, and the Cholerick into an Assassin. It gives Bitterness to Resentment, it makes Vanity Insupportable, and displays every little

106 Sterne 1997, 453–9.

Spot of the Soul in its utmost Deformity." It "throws a Man out of himself, and infuses Qualities into the Mind, which she is a Stranger to in her sober Moments. The Person you converse with, after the third Bottle, is not the same who at first sat down at Table with you." Identity being unstable and corruptible, habitual imbibing undoes sociability and "insensibly weakens the Understanding, impairs the Memory, and makes those Faults habitual which are produced by frequent Excesses."[107]

The dialectic of passion and objectivity in Addison's didacticism explains why he appealed to many English classes and became a model for French commentators on public life.[108] He was not single-minded about alcohol. Like Defoe, he promoted port when advancing the trading benefits of the Methuen Treaty of 1703. Again, like Defoe, he not only promoted French wines by allowing advertisements for them into *The Guardian* but also like Walpole smuggled claret and burgundy from Dublin to stock his cellar.[109] Thus, he shunned the opposing political ideologies of claret and port drinkers. Like many authors, then, he embodies conflicts between imperial propaganda and personal taste. This reminds us that discursive writing, such as Sterne's Menippean whimsicality, is never simply confessional and that utopian prescriptions are not to be taken literally in an age that prized irony and paradox as well as sociability. The Blooms put this well:

Addison also acknowledged that conscientious toil, of the head or of the hands, was a responsibility owed to God and society. Conversely, he suspected solitude as a rejection of communal obligation and discipline. He either would not or could not concern himself with poets and artists, those lonely thinkers and gift bearers only able to work apart from the social group. A retreat from secular performance, no matter how austere or productive, in his judgment denoted civic failure and profanation.[110]

---

107 *The Spectator*, no. 569, Monday, 19 July 1714 (Addison 1966, 4:289–91).

108 See Nablow on Addison's "dispassionate observation of individuals and society" (1990, 15–16 and 44–74).

109 Bloom and Bloom 1971, 205–6; Stephens 1982, 524. Addison reprinted from newspapers the following advertisement: "a Parcel of *French* Wines, full of the Seeds of good Humour, Chearfulness, and Friendly Mirth."

110 Bloom and Bloom 1971, 30.

The Menippean writer, a contemporary of Addison, who most expressed social paradoxes is Bernard Mandeville (1670–1733). The 1724 edition of *The Fable of the Bees* rejects didacticism and the notion that morality is a unified code in order to exploit the mixed messages inherent in hedonism and consumerism. To Mandeville, trade is a social, not a moral, construct: a "dry shabby crooked Vine," it produces only when cultivated. Restrictions on consumption, like sumptuary laws, are not tools of cultivation or improvement. Were the rich prevented from buying burgundy and other luxury goods, neither social nor moral benefits would accrue: employment of the poor would not increase, nor would vice be diminished. To Mandeville, the drive for altered or heightened states of consciousness is common to all ranks: hedonism, the need for forgetfulness and escape from daily reality, affects all classes. Men intent on drunkenness yet unable to buy "*Hermitage* or *Pontack*" buy cheaper "ordinary *French* Claret." Whether or not lords get drunk on "*Burgundy, Champagne or Tockay*," foot soldiers will take stale beer to drink themselves to oblivion. As long as conspicuous consumption prevails, the rich will buy expensive wines less to display their social superiority than to gratify the need for pleasure. From an economic stance, decadence and luxury are not necessarily harmful, if "haughty Moralists" say so in their commitment to the "Dignity of their Species." Humans live by "boundless Pride" and excess of "stupid Vanity," ornamenting themselves in fashionable clothes made of wool and lace "robb'd from so innocent and defenceless an Animal as a Sheep" or "dying Worm." Fashion means "Good Manners have nothing to do with Virtue or Religion." In this "Comedy of Manners," the "Bond of Society exacts from every Member a certain Regard for others, which the Highest is not exempt from in the presence of the meanest even in an Empire." Sociability, deriving from natural principles, is never free from affectation and secrecy. He summarizes thus: "*I flatter my self to have demonstrated that, neither the friendly Qualities and kind Affections that are natural to Man, nor the real Vertues he is capable of acquiring by Reason and Self-Denial, are the Foundation of Society; but that what we call Evil in this World, Moral as well as Natural, is the grand Principle that makes us sociable Creatures, the solid Basis the Life and Support of all Trades and Employments without Exception.*"[111]

---

111 Mandeville 1970, 143–4, 150–2, 112, and 402.

Goldsmith challenges social mores more comparatively than Addison and Mandeville. In Letter 32 of *The Citizen of the World* (1762), his Chinese persona, Lien Chi Altangi, asserts that English nobles spend lavishly to display rank and that hangers-on surrender to the pleasure of being seen as retainers. The persona then compares the pitiable humiliations of hangers-on to servants of Tartar nobility. When those nobles get drunk on magic mushrooms, servants collect their urine to enjoy the mushroom broth at one remove. If Lien Chi Altangi does not find this custom in England, he finds analogous forms of self-degradation in the decline of aristocratic virtues; nobles dishonour their family history and blood lines, debasement of their lineage being sped by obsequious retainers who gratify themselves from living in the orbit of superiors. Goldsmith's ironic equation of the aristocracy with hedonistic consumerism, besides recalling Hurd, builds on the utopianism of ideal foreign cultures when he claims that in China there is no gap between appearance and reality; a lord's extensive retinue there simply signifies virtue. But a typical English lord has no blood line; it has been lost to cook maids and grooms, the lord himself a degenerate lacking taste, wit, wisdom, and all sense of generosity and charity. For centuries he has been known just for his good eating and fine horses, his retinue's function to flatter his taste and "descant upon his claret and cookery."[112]

That his persona appropriates Tartar customs fits Goldsmith's desire to counter ideas about the strange manners of the Chinese and to have those customs obliquely reflect English modes. Thus, when "the nobility and ladies are assembled, and the ceremonies usual between people of distinction over, the mushroom broth goes freely round; they laugh, talk double entendre, grow fuddled, and become excellent company." Lien Chi Altangi's English companion soon sees the applicability of urine drinking to the upper reaches of society. In this letter, Goldsmith comes close to imagining what anthropologists tell us about cultural practices related to communal need to transcend social identity and to desires to move beyond conventions of selfhood. But ritual aspects of festivity escape many eighteenth-century writers because they too simply associate wine with national and imperial politics. It is perhaps unfair to ask of a period that was so taken up with exploring taste why it did

---

[112] Goldsmith 1970, 87–90. Rudgley describes hallucinogenic mushrooms (*Amanita muscaria*) and the drinking of urine in Siberia, Mexico, the United States, and Canada (1994, 77–81 and 83–4).

not more than glimpse the aesthetic impulse to discover entoptic images, to perceive the structures of our perceptual organs and to experiment with the higher ordering that engages the brain in our organs. For it is only recently, according to Jamie Goode's essay on "Wine and the Brain," that neurological experiments have been able to measure interrelations between sensory modalities and to deduce how subjects can voluntarily effect synesthesia to heighten sensory awareness. As Goode says, we still "think that our sensory system" reveals "the world around us in an accurate and complete way." But what we actually "experience is an edited version of reality ... based on the information most relevant to our survival and functioning. For almost all purposes it does no harm for us to think of the world around us as revealed to us to be 'reality' – indeed, life would become quite complicated if we operated any other way – but for the purposes of [discussing wine and the brain] it's useful to realize that the version of reality we experience is an edited and partial one." How we experience flavours is complex. "The senses of taste and smell work together to perform two important tasks: identifying nutritious foods and drinks, and to protect us from eating things that are bad for us. The brain achieves this by linking food that we need with a reward stimulus – it smells or tastes 'good' – and making bad or unneeded foods aversive": flavour perceptions are necessarily connected to memories and emotions. Hence, hunger and appetite become powerful, "finely tuned" drives because nerve cells in the brain "respond to combinations of senses, such as taste and sight, or taste and touch, or smell and sight. This convergence of inputs, known as cross-modal processing, is acquired by learning, but it is one that occurs slowly, typically requiring many pairings of the different sensations before it is fixed." Experienced wine tasters strategically use several brain areas to analyze "sensory stimuli." Wine tasting evolves with experience and requires disciplined cognition. A wine tasted years apart is bound to be different given the brain's expanding awareness. The "learning component" of wine appreciation is reflected in that people "versed in one culture of wine may need to re-learn about wine when exploring another." Goode ends by describing how "a contrived sort of synaesthesia" based on senses more stable than taste can establish standards of aesthetic intensity that enable individuals to compare and contrast their appreciations of wine. He reports that "in one experiment, non-tasters matched the bitterness of black coffee to the brightness of low-beam headlights at night, while supertasters matched it slightly above high-beam headlights at night. A deliberate, voluntary synaesthesia such as this enables us to break free of the noise and confusion brought about through genetic differences in taste, making possible our recourse to descriptions from other senses from where it seems we live in closely similar worlds."[113]

By exploring synesthesia and dialectic, *Imperial Paradoxes* tests how literary history might evolve. The sociability of eighteenth-century literature may need revision given its conflicted views of consumerism. Cuisine, travel, fashion, and wine expose contraries in national identity and cultural exchange: cuisine invites us to ponder how travel does and does not entail being abroad; fashion shows how national boundaries are and are not traversed; wine reveals how the distant and foreign are implicated in the immediate and local, all consumerism ignoring and protecting the environment and natural history. In considering the relevance of cultural and interdisciplinary studies to English and French literature, *Imperial Paradoxes* asks how pedagogy might address tensions between literary delight and sensory pleasures and how much literary criticism should inform itself with aesthetic embodiment. Hence, having opened with David Hume, my text circles back to him:

To imagine, that the gratifying of any sense, or the indulging of any delicacy in meat, drink, or apparel, is of itself a vice, can never enter into a head, that is not disordered by the frenzies of enthusiasm ... Since luxury may be considered either as innocent or blamable, one may be surprised at those preposterous opinions which have been entertained concerning it; while men of libertine principles bestow praises even on vicious luxury, and represent it as highly advantageous to society; and, on the other hand, men of severe morals blame even the most innocent luxury, and represent it as the source of all the corruptions, disorders, and factions incident to civil government. We shall here endeavour to correct both these extremes.[114]

---

113 Jamie Goode, "Wine and the Brain," in Smith 2007, 82, 84–6, 89, and 94.
114 Hume, "Of Refinement in the Arts," 1965, 48–9.

Bibliography

Addison, Joseph. 1890. *The Works of the Right Honourable Joseph Addison*. Edited by Henry G. Bohn. 6 vols. London: George Bell and Sons.
– 1718. *Remarks on Several Parts of Italy, etc. In the Years 1701, 1702, 1703*. In Addison 1890, vol. 1.
Addison, Joseph, and Richard Steele. [1907] 1963–66. *The Spectator*. Edited by C. Gregory Smith. Introduction by Peter Smithers. 4 vols. London: Dent.
Akenside, Mark. 1857. *The Poetical Works of Mark Akenside*. Edited by Rev. George Gilfillan. Edinburgh: James Nichol.
Alkon, Paul K. 2006. *Winston Churchill's Imagination*. Lewisburg: Bucknell University Press.
Andrews, John. 1785. *A Comparative View of the French and English Nations in Their Manners, Politics, and Literature*. London: T. Longman and G.G.J. and J. Robinson.
Anon. 1740. *The Lady's Companion: Or, an Infallible Guide to the Fair Sex*. 2nd ed. London: T. Read.
Anon. [1817] 1970. *Statement Respecting the Earl of Selkirk's Settlement upon the Red River in North America; Its Destruction in 1815 and 1816; and the Massacre of Governor Semple and His Party*. Toronto: Coles Publishing.
Arbuthnot, John. 1892. *The Life and Works*. Edited by George A. Aitken. Oxford: Clarendon Press.
Aubert De Gaspé, Philippe-Joseph. [1863] 1974. *Canadians of Old*. Translated by Charles G.D. Roberts Toronto: McClelland and Stewart.
Austen, Jane. [1923] 1969. *Northanger Abbey* and *Persuasion*. Vol. 5 of *The Novels of Jane Austen*. Edited by R.W. Chapman. 6 vols. London: Oxford University Press.
– [1814] 1966. *Mansfield Park*. Edited by Tony Tanner. Harmondsworth: Penguin.

– [1816] 1971. *Emma*. Edited by David Lodge. London: Oxford University Press.
– [1932] 1979. *Jane Austen's Letters*. Edited by R.W. Chapman. Oxford: Oxford University Press.
Bacon, Francis. 1733. *The Philosophical Works of Francis Bacon, Baron of Verulam, Viscount St. Albans, and Lord High-Chancellor of England, Methodized, and Made English, from the Originals*. Edited by Peter Shaw. 3 vols. London: J.J. and P. Knapton, et al.
– [1905] 1962. *Essays*. Edited by Oliphant Smeaton. London: J.M. Dent.
Balleyguier, O. Delphin, ed. and trans. 1896. *Journal de Madame Cradock: Voyage en France (1783–1786)*. Paris: Perrin.
Barry, Edward. 1775. *Observations Historical, Critical, and Medical on the Wines of the Ancients and the Analogy between Them and Modern Wines*. London: T. Cadell.
Bate, Walter Jackson. [1946] 1961. *From Classic to Romantic: Premises of Taste in Eighteenth Century England*. New York: Harper and Row.
Batten, Charles L. Jr. 1978. *Pleasurable Instruction: Form and Convention in Eighteenth-Century Travel Literature*. Berkeley: University of California Press.
Beales, Derek. 2005. "Edmund Burke and the Monasteries of France." *Historical Journal* 48: 413–36.
Bell, John, ed. [1776–1781] 1977a. *Bell's British Theatre*. 21 vols. New York: AMS Press.
– [1784] 1977b. *Bell's British Theatre: Farces*. 4 vols. New York: AMS Press.
– [1792–1802] 1977c. *Bell's British Theatre: Selected Plays 1791–1802*. 16 vols. New York: AMS Press.
Benedict, Philip, ed. 1989. *Cities and Social Change in Early Modern France*. London: Routledge.
Berguer, Lionel Thomas, ed. 1823. *The British Essayists*. 45 vols. London: T. and J. Allman.
Black, Jeremy. 1985a. *The British and the Grand Tour*. London: Croom Helm.
– 1985b. "Dijon en 1725 par un touriste anglais." *Annales de Bourgogne* 57: 47–8.
Blair, Hugh. 1783. *Lectures on Rhetoric and Belles Lettres*. 3 vols. Dublin: Whitestone et al.
Blake, William. 1966. *Blake: Complete Writings*. Edited by Geoffrey Keynes. London: Oxford University Press.
Bloom, Edward A., and Lillian D. Bloom. 1971. *Joseph Addison's Sociable Animal in the Market Place on the Hustings in the Pulpit*. Providence: Brown University Press.
Boswell, James. 1769. *An Account of Corsica, The Journal of a Tour to That Island, and Memoirs of Pascal Paoli*. 3rd ed. London: Edward and Charles Dilly.
– [1791] 1953. *The Life of Samuel Johnson, LL.D*. Edited by R.W. Chapman. London: Oxford University Press.

Bourée, André. 1932. "La Société Dijonnaise vers le milieu du XVIIIe siècle." *Mémoires de L'Académie de Dijon* 100: 197–217.

Bourke, Richard. 2015. *Empire and Revolution: The Political Life of Edmund Burke*. Princeton: Princeton University Press.

Bradley, Martha. [1760?] *The British Housewife: Or, the Cook, Housekeeper's, and Gardiner's Companion*. London: S. Crowder and H. Woodgate.

Bradley, Richard. 1762. *The Country Housewife, and Lady's Director*. London: W. Bristow and York: C. Etherington.

Braudel, Fernand. 1984. *Civilization and Capitalism: 15th–18th Century*. Translated by Siân Reynolds. 3 vols. New York: Harper and Row.

Briggs, Peter M. 2005. "Joseph Addison and the Art of Listening: Birdsong, Italian Opera, and the Music of the English Tongue." *Age of Johnson* 16: 157–76.

Brillat-Savarin, Jean-Anthelme. [1825] 1994. *The Physiology of Taste*. Translated by Anne Drayton. London: Penguin Classics.

Broadus, Edmund Kemper. 1909. "Addison as a Literary Critic." *University of Alberta Magazine* February: 1–20.

Bromwich, David. 1992. *Politics by Other Means: Higher Education and Group Thinking*. New Haven: Yale University Press.

Brooke, Frances. [1769] 1985. *The History of Emily Montague*. Edited by Mary Jane Edwards. Ottawa: Carleton University Press.

Brown, James W. 1984. *Fictional Meals and Their Function in the French Novel 1789–1848*. Toronto: University of Toronto Press.

Brown, John Russell, ed. 1995. *The Oxford Illustrated History of Theatre*. Oxford: Oxford University Press.

Burke, Edmund. 1796. *Thoughts on the Prospect of a Regicide Peace, in a Series of Letters*. London: J. Owen

– 1968. *Edmund Burke on Revolution*. Edited by Robert A. Smith. New York: Harper and Row.

– 1968. *A Philosophical Enquiry into the Origin of Our Ideas of the Sublime and Beautiful*. Edited by J.T. Boulton. Notre Dame: University of Notre Dame Press.

– [1790] 2009. *Reflections on the Revolution in France*. Edited by L.G. Mitchell. Oxford: Oxford University Press.

Burney, Charles. 1771. *The Present State of Music in France and Italy: Or, The Journal of a Tour through Those Countries, Undertaken to Collect Materials for A General History of Music*. London: T. Becket.

Burney, Frances. [1788] 1982. *Evelina, Or, A Young Lady's Entrance into the World. In a Series of Letters*. Edited by Edward A. Bloom and Lillian D. Bloom. Oxford: Oxford University Press.

– [1788] 2000. *Evelina, Or, A Young Lady's Entrance into the World. In a Series of Letters*. Edited by Susan Kubica Howard. Peterborough, ON: Broadview.

Butel, Paul, and Jean-Pierre Poussou. 1980. *La Vie quotidienne à Bordeaux au xviiie siècle*. Paris: Hachette.

Carter, Charles. 1730. *The Complete Practical Cook: Or, A New System of the Whole Art and Mystery of Cookery*. London: W. Meadows, C. Rivington, and R. Hett.

Carver, Jonathan. [1778] 1974. *Travels through the Interior Parts of North-America in the Years 1766, 1767, and 1768*. Toronto: Coles Publishing.

Centlivre, Susanna. 1872. *The Works of the Celebrated Mrs. Centlivre*. 3 vols. London: John Pearson.

Chappell, Edward. [1817] 1970. *Narrative of a Voyage to Hudson's Bay in His Majesty's Ship Rosamond*. Toronto: Coles Publishing.

Churchill, Winston S. 1945. *Onwards to Victory: War Speeches by the Right Hon. Winston S. Churchill, 1943*. Compiled by Charles Eade. 2nd ed. London: Cassell.

Clarke, James. 2016. "A Most Cursed Hill: Painshill and the Beginnings of English Wine." *The World of Fine Wine: Email Newsletter*. Accessed 27 May 2020.

Colley, Linda. 1992. *Britons: Forging the Nation 1707–1837*. London: Pimlico.

Collingwood, R.G. [1938] 1963. *The Principles of Art*. Oxford: Clarendon.

Congreve, William. 1925. *Comedies*. Edited by Bonamy Dobrée. London: Oxford University Press, World's Classics.

Congreve, William. 1964. *Letters and Documents*. Edited by John C. Hodges. New York: Harcourt.

Cooper, Anthony Ashley, Earl of Shaftesbury. [1711] 1964. *Characteristics of Men, Manners, Opinions, Times*. Edited by John M. Robertson. 2 vols in one. Indianapolis: Bobbs-Merrill.

Corbett, Edward P.J. 1971. *Classical Rhetoric for the Modern Student*. New York: Oxford University Press.

Courtépée, Claude, and Edme Béguillet. [1775–1785] 1986. *Description général et particular du Duché de Bourgogne*. Edited by Pierre Gras et Jean Richard. 4 vols. Le Coteau: Édition Horvath.

Cowley, Hannah. 1979. *The Plays of Hannah Cowley*. Edited by Frederick M. Link. 2 vols. New York: Garland.

Crabbe, George. 1834. *The Poetical Works of the Rev. George Crabbe*. 8 vols. London: John Murray.

Crouzet, François. 1967. "England and France in the Eighteenth Century: A Comparative Analysis of Two Economic Growths." In *The Causes of the Industrial Revolution in England*, edited by R.M. Hartwell, 139–74. London: Methuen.

- 1996. *Britain, France and International Commerce: From Louis XIV to Victoria.* Aldershot: Variorum.
Curley, Thomas M. 1976. *Samuel Johnson and the Age of Travel.* Athens: University of Georgia Press.
Dampier, William. [1697] 2007. *Memoirs of a Buccaneer: Dampier's New Voyage round the World, 1697.* Mineola, NY: Dover.
Damrosch, Leo. 2019. *The Club: Johnson, Boswell, and the Friends Who Shaped an Age.* New Haven: Yale University Press.
Defoe, Daniel. 1955. *The Letters of Daniel Defoe.* Edited by G.H. Healey. Oxford: Clarendon.
- 1965. *A Review of the Affairs of France.* 9 vols. 19 February 1704 – 11 June 1713. Edited by Arthur Wellesley Secord. 22 vols. New York: Columbia University Press, 1938. Reprint. New York: AMS Press.
- [1928] 1974. *A Tour through the Whole Island of Great Britain.* Edited by G.D.H. Cole and D.C. Browning. London: J.M. Dent & Sons.
Desgraves, Louis. 1960. *Évocation du vieux Bordeaux.* Paris: Les Éditions de Minuit.
Digby, Kenelm. 1669. *The Closet of the Eminently Learned Sir Kenelme Digbie Kt. Opened.* London: H. Brome.
Dolan, Brian. 2001. *Ladies of the Grand Tour: British Women in Pursuit of Enlightenment and Adventure in Eighteenth-Century Europe.* New York: HarperCollins.
Doyle, William. 1974. *The Parlement of Bordeaux and the End of the Old Regime 1771–1790.* London: Benn.
- 1989. *The Oxford History of the French Revolution.* Oxford: Clarendon Press.
Dryden, John. 2001. *Selected Poems.* Edited by Steven N. Zwicker and David Bywaters. London: Penguin.
Du Bocage, Anne-Marie. 1770. *Letters concerning England, Holland and Italy.* 2 vols. London: E. and C. Dilly.
Dubos, Abbé Jean-Baptiste. [1719] 1748. *Critical Reflections on Poetry, Painting and Music. With an Inquiry into the Rise and Progress of Theatrical Entertainments of the Ancients.* 5th ed. Trans. Thomas Nugent. 3 vols. London: John Nourse.
Duncan, Sara Jeannette. [1904] 1961. *The Imperialist.* Edited by Claude Bissell. Toronto: McClelland and Stewart.
Eagleton, Terry. 1983. *Literary Theory: An Introduction.* Minneapolis: University of Minnesota Press.
Elias, Norbert. 1978. *The History of Manners: The Civilizing Process.* New York: Pantheon.
Ellis, John. 1974. *The Theory of Literary Criticism: A Logical Analysis.* Berkeley: University of California Press.

- 1997. *Literature Lost: Social Agendas and the Corruption of the Humanities.* New Haven: Yale University Press.

Erasmus, Desiderius. [1511–1521; 1668] 1958. *The Praise of Folly.* Translated by John Wilson. Ann Arbor: University of Michigan Press.

Evelyn, John. 1676. *A Philosophical Discourse of Earth, Relating to the Culture and Improvement of it for Vegetation, and the Propagation of Plants.* London: John Martyn.

- 1706. *Acetaria. A Discourse of Sallets.* 2nd ed. London: B. Tooke.
- 1959. *The Diary of John Evelyn.* Edited by E.S. De Beer. London: Oxford University Press.

Faber, Richard. 1975. *French and English.* London: Faber and Faber.

Farquhar, George. 1930. *The Complete Works of George Farquhar.* Edited by C. Stonehill. 2 vols. London: Nonesuch.

Ferguson, Niall. 2002. *Empire: The Rise and Demise of the British World Order and the Lessons for Global Power.* New York: Basic Books.

Ferry, Luc. [1990] 1993. *Homo Aestheticus: The Invention of Taste in the Democratic Age.* Translated by Robert De Loaiza. Chicago: University of Chicago Press.

Fielding, Henry. [1755] 1907. *The Journal of a Voyage to Lisbon.* Edited by Austin Dobson. London: Henry Frowde, Oxford University Press.

- [1742, 1741] 1961. *Joseph Andrews and Shamela.* Edited by Martin C. Battestin. Boston: Houghton Mifflin.
- [1743] 1972. "An Essay on Conversation." In *Miscellanies by Henry Fielding, Esq.* Edited by Henry Knight Miller. 3 vols. 1:119–52. Oxford: Clarendon Press.
- [1749] 1973. *Tom Jones.* Edited by Sheridan Baker. New York: W.W. Norton.
- [1742, 1741] 1999. *Joseph Andrews and Shamela.* Edited by Judith Hawley. London: Penguin.
- [1743] 2003. *The Life of Mr Jonathan Wild the Great.* Edited by Hugh Amory, Claude Rawson, and Linda Bree. Oxford: Oxford University Press.

Finberg, Melinda C., ed. 2001. *Eighteenth-Century Women Dramatists.* New York: Oxford University Press.

Fink, Beatrice. 1983. "L'Avénement de la pomme de terre." *Dix-huitième siècle* 15: 19–27.

- 1995. *Les Liaisons savoureuses: Réflexions et practiques culinaires au XVIIIe siècle.* Saint-Étienne: Publications de l'Université de Saint-Étienne.

Fish, Stanley. 1995. *Professional Correctness: Literary Studies and Political Change.* Oxford: Clarendon.

Fowler, Roger. 1981. *Literature as Social Discourse: The Practice of Linguistic Criticism.* Bloomington: Indiana University Press.

Francis, A.D. 1972. *The Wine Trade.* London: Black.

Fraser, Evan D.G., and Andrew Rimas. 2010. *Empires of Food: Feast, Famine, and the Rise and Fall of Civilizations.* New York: Free Press.

Fromm, Harold. 1991. *Academic Capitalism and Literary Value.* Athens: University of Georgia Press.

Frye, Northrop. [1947] 1969. *Fearful Symmetry: A Study of William Blake.* Princeton: Princeton University Press.

Fussell, Paul. 1965. *The Rhetorical World of Augustan Humanism: Ethics and Imagery from Swift to Burke.* London: Oxford University Press.

Garrick, David. 1980. *The Plays of David Garrick.* Edited by Harry William Pedicord and Frederick Louis Bergmann. 4 vols. Carbondale: Southern Illinois University Press.

Gatrel, Vic. 2006. *City of Laughter: Sex and Satire in Eighteenth-Century London.* New York: Walker.

Gay, John. 1926. *The Poetical Works of John Gay.* Edited by G.C. Faber. London: Oxford University Press, Humphrey Milford.

Gérin-Lajoie, Antoine. [1862–1864] 1977. *Jean Rivard.* Edited and translated by Veda Bruce. Toronto: McClelland and Stewart.

Gilfillan, George, ed. 1858. *The Poetical Works of Armstrong, Dyer, and Green.* Edinburgh: James Nichol, 1858.

Ginsberg, Benjamin. 2011. *The Fall of the Faculty: The Rise of the All-Administrative University and Why It Matters.* New York: Oxford University Press.

Giroux, Henri. 1981. "La Vie quotidienne aux XVIIe et XVIIIe siècles." In *Histoire de Dijon,* edited by Pierre Gras, 195–227. Toulouse: Éditions Privat.

Glasse, Hannah. 1747. *The Art of Cookery, Made Plain and Easy.* London: self-published.

Goldsmith, Oliver. [1934] 1970. *The Citizen of the World and the Bee.* Edited by Richard Church. London: J.M. Dent.

Graff, Gerald. 1979. *Literature against Itself: Literary Ideas in Modern Society.* Chicago: University of Chicago Press.

– 1992. *Beyond the Culture Wars: How Teaching the Conflicts Can Revitalize American Education.* New York: Norton.

Grant, George M. [1873] 1970. *Ocean to Ocean: Sanford Fleming's Expedition through Canada in 1872. Being a Diary Kept during a Journey from the Atlantic to the Pacific with the Expedition of the Engineer-in-Chief of the Canadian Pacific and Intercolonial Railways.* Toronto: Coles Publishing.

Grant, George. 1969. *Technology and Empire: Perspectives on North America.* Toronto: House of Anansi.

Gras, Pierre, ed. 1981. *Histoire de Dijon*. Toulouse: Éditions Privat.

Gravejat, Ambroise, with Marc Masson and Simone Martin. 1980. *La rente, le profit et la ville: Analyse de la constitution de la ville romaine antique et de la ville de Lyon du 6ᵉ au 19ᵉ siècle*. Paris: Éditions Anthropos.

Graves, Richard. [1773] 1967. *The Spiritual Quixote Or the Summer's Ramble of Mr. Geoffrey Wildgoose: A Comic Romance*. Edited by Clarence Tracy. London: Oxford University Press.

Gray, Hugh. [1809] 1971. *Letters from Canada, Written during a Residence There in the Years 1806, 1807, and 1808*. Toronto: Coles Publishing.

Gray, Thomas. [1912] 1955. *Poems, Letters and Essays*. Edited by John Drinkwater and Lewis Gibbs. London: J.M. Dent.

Grey, Francis William. [1899] 1970. *The Curé of St. Philippe*. Edited by Rupert Schieder. Toronto: McClelland and Stewart.

Grosley, M. 1772. *A Tour to London; or, New Observations on England, and Its Inhabitants*. Translated by Thomas Nugent. 2 vols. London: Lockyer Davis, Printer to the Royal Society.

Harrison, Sarah. 1735. *The House-Keeper's Pocket Book; and Compleat Family Cook*. 2nd ed. London: R. Ware.

Hartwell, R.M., ed. 1967. *The Causes of the Industrial Revolution in England*. London: Methuen.

Hawkes, Terence. 1977. *Structuralism and Semiotics*. Berkeley: University of California Press.

Hearne, Samuel. [1795] 1958. *A Journey from Prince of Wales's Fort in Hudson's Bay to the Northern Ocean 1769·1770·1771·1772*. Edited by Richard Glover. Toronto: Macmillan.

Hodges, Alison. 1974. "Further Notes on Painshill, Cobham, Surrey: Charles Hamilton's Vineyard." *Garden History* 3, no. 1: 77–80.

Holcroft, Thomas. 1980. *The Plays of Thomas Holcroft*. Edited by Joseph Rosenblum. 2 vols. New York: Garland.

Holland, Peter, and Michael Patterson. 1995. "Eighteenth-Century Theatre." In *The Oxford Illustrated History of Theatre*, edited by John Russell Brown, 255–98. Oxford: Oxford University Press.

Hollier, Denis, ed. 1989. *A New History of French Literature*. Cambridge: Harvard University Press.

Hume, David. 1953. *Political Essays*. Edited by Charles W. Hendel. Indianapolis: Bobbs-Merrill.

– 1965. *Of The Standard of Taste and Other Essays*. Edited by John W. Lenz. Indianapolis: Bobbs-Merrill.

- 1987. *Essays Moral, Political and Literary.* Edited by Eugene F. Miller. Revised ed. Indianapolis: Liberty Fund.
Hunt, Lynn. 1984. *Politics, Culture, and Class in the French Revolution.* Berkeley: University of California Press.
Hurd, Richard. 1764. *Dialogues on the Uses of Foreign Travel; Considered as a Part of an English Gentleman's Education: Between Lord Shaftesbury and Mr. Locke.* London: A. Millar and W. Thurlbourn; Cambridge: J. Woodyer.
Jacob, Margaret C. 2019. *The Secular Enlightenment.* Princeton: Princeton University Press.
James, Thomas. [1633] 1740. *The Dangerous Voyage of Capt. Thomas James in His Intended Discovery of a North West Passage into the South Sea.* London: O. Payne.
Jameson, Anna. [1838] 1970. *Winter Studies and Summer Rambles in Canada.* 3 vols. Toronto: Coles Publishing.
Jefferson, Thomas. 1903. *The Writings of Thomas Jefferson.* Edited by Andrew A. Lipscomb. 20 vols. Washington, DC: Thomas Jefferson Memorial Association.
Jenks, James. 1768. *The Complete Cook: Teaching the Art of Cookery in All Its Branches; and to Spread a Table, in a Useful, Substantial and Splendid Manner, at All Seasons in the Year. With Practical Instructions to Choose, Buy, Dress and Carve all Sorts of Provisions.* London: E. and C. Dilly.
Johnson, Hugh. 1989. *Vintage: The Story of Wine.* New York: Simon and Schuster.
[Johnson, Samuel]. 1744. *An Account of the Life of Mr Richard Savage, Son of the Earl Rivers.* London: J. Roberts.
- [1775] 1965. *Samuel Johnson's Journey to the Western Islands and James Boswell's Journal of a Tour to the Hebrides.* Edited by Allan Wendt. Boston: Houghton Mifflin.
- [1781] 1952. *Lives of The English Poets.* Edited by Arthur Waugh. 2 vols. London: Oxford University Press, World's Classics.
- 1824. *The Works of Samuel Johnson.* Edited by Arthur Murphy. 12 vols. London: Thomas Tegg et al.
- 1968. *The Political Writings of Dr Johnson.* Edited by J.P. Hardy. London: Routledge and Kegan Paul.
Kates, Gary. 1995. *Monsieur d'Éon Is a Woman: A Tale of Political Intrigue and Sexual Masquerade.* New York: Basic Books.
Kernan, Alvin, ed. 1997. *What's Happened to the Humanities?* Princeton: Princeton University Press.
Kingwell, Mark. [2000] 2001. *The World We Want: Virtue, Vice, and the Good Citizen.* Toronto: Penguin.
Kirby, William. [1877] 1969. *The Golden Dog.* Edited by Derek Crawley. Toronto: McClelland and Stewart.

Kölving, Ulla, and Christiane Mervaud, eds. 1997. *Voltaire et ses combats*. 2 vols. Oxford: Voltaire Foundation.

Korsmeyer, Carolyn. 1999. *Making Sense of Taste: Food and Philosophy*. Ithaca: Cornell University Press.

La Chapelle, Vincent. 1733. *The Modern Cook*. 3 vols. London: Self-published.

Lakoff, George. 1987. *Women, Fire, and Dangerous Things: What Categories Reveal about the Mind*. Chicago: University of Chicago Press.

Lakoff, George, and Mark Turner. 1989. *More Than Cool Reason: A Field Guide to Poetic Metaphor*. Chicago: University of Chicago Press.

Lakoff, George, and Mark Johnson. 1999. *Philosophy in the Flesh: The Embodied Mind and Its Challenge to Western Thought*. New York: Basic Books.

Lamb, Patrick. 1710. *Royal Cookery; Or, The Complete Court-Cook*. London: Abel Roper.

Laugier, Marc-Antoine. 1756. *An Essay on the Study and Practice of Architecture*. London: Stanley Crowder and Henry Woodgate.

La Varenne, François Pierre de. 1654. *The French Cook*. 2nd ed. Translated by I.D.G. London: Charles Adams.

Lehmann, Gilly. 2003. *The British Housewife: Cookery Books, Cooking and Society in Eighteenth-Century Britain*. Totnes, Devon: Prospect Books.

Levine, Lawrence W. 1996. *The Opening of the American Mind: Canons, Culture, and History*. Boston: Beacon.

Ligou, Daniel. 1981. "De Louis à la Révolution." In *Histoire de Dijon*, edited by Pierre Gras, 143–94. Toulouse: Éditions Privat.

Lipovetsky, Gilles. [1987] 1994. *The Empire of Fashion: Dressing Modern Democracy*. Translated by Catherine Porter. Princeton: Princeton University Press.

Locke, John. 1953. *Locke's Travels in France 1675–1679*. Edited by John Lough. Cambridge: Cambridge University Press.

— [1823] 1963. *The Works of John Locke*. 10 vols. London: Thomas Tegg et al. Reprinted in Aalen, Germany: Scientia Verlag.

Lough, John. 1987. *France on the Eve of Revolution: British Travellers' Observations 1763–1788*. London: Croom Helm.

MacMiadhacháin, Anna. 1976. *Spanish Regional Cooking*. Harmondsworth: Penguin.

MacPherson, Jay. 1994. "Swift's Very Knowing American." *Lumen* 13: 109–16.

Makaryk, Irena R., ed. 1993. *Encyclopedia of Contemporary Literary Theory: Approaches, Scholars, Terms*. Toronto: University of Toronto Press.

Mandeville, Bernard. 1970. *The Fable of the Bees*. Edited by Phillip Harth. Harmondsworth: Penguin.

Manguel, Alberto. 1998. *A History of Reading*. Toronto: Vintage.

Marc, Henri. 1898. *Recherches historiques sur le rempart Tivoli*. Dijon: Jobard.
Marnette, Monsieur. 1656. *The Perfect Cook*. London: Nathaniel Brooks.
Marshall, P.J., and Alaine Low, eds. 1998. *The Oxford History of the British Empire*, vol 2: *The Eighteenth Century*. Oxford: Oxford University Press.
Massialot, François. 1701. *The Court and Country Cook: Giving New and Plain Directions How to Order all Manner of Entertainments, and the Best Sort of the Most Exquisite a-la-mode Ragoo's*. Translated by J.K. London: W. Onley.
May, Robert. 1678. *The Accomplisht Cook, Or The Art and Mystery of Cookery*. 4th ed. London: Robert Hartford.
Mead, William Edward. 1914. *The Grand Tour in the Eighteenth Century*. Boston: Houghton.
Menon [1746] 1793. *The French Family Cook: Being a Complete System of French Cookery*. London: J. Bell.
Mennell, Stephen. [1985] 1996. *All Manners of Food: Eating and Taste in England and France from the Middle Ages to the Present*. Urbana: University of Illinois Press.
Mercier, Louis Sébastien. 1990. *Tableau de Paris (1782–88), Le nouveau Paris*. Edited by Michel Delon. In *Paris le jour, Paris la nuit*. Paris: Robert Lafont.
Merrett, Robert James. 1988a. "Bacchus in Restoration and Eighteenth-Century Comedy: Wine as an Index of Generic Decline." *Man and Nature / L'homme et la nature* 7: 179–93.
– 1988b. "The Idea of Burgundy in Eighteenth-Century Literature." In *Voyage et Tourisme en Bourgogne à l'époque de Jefferson*. Edited by Michel Baridon and Bernard Chevignard, 85–100. Dijon: Éditions universitaires.
– 1991. "Port and Claret: The Politics of Wine in Trollope's Barsetshire Novels." *Mosaic* 24: 107–25.
– 1992. "The Politics of Romance in *The History of Emily Montague*." *Canadian Literature* 133: 92–108.
– 1997. "Voltaire and Eighteenth-Century Britain's Sense of Europe." In *Voltaire et ses combats*, edited by Ulla Kölving and Christiane Mervaud, 2:1,095–105. Oxford: Voltaire Foundation.
– 2002a. "Problems of Self-Identity for the Literary Journeyman: The Case of Alexander Bicknell (d. 1796)," *English Studies in Canada* 28: 31–63.
– 2002b. "English Literature in the French Press: Testimony, Imitation, and Fictional Exchange." In *La Traduction des langues modernes au XVIIIe siècle*, edited by Annie Rivara, 171–89. Paris: Honoré Champion.
– 2012. "Liberal Arts Education in Canada," *Canadian Encyclopedia*. Toronto: McClelland & Stewart, 1998 and 1999 CD-ROM editions; 1999 print edition. Revised and updated 2012.

Micault, Claude. 1887. *Le Mercure Dijonnois 1742–1789*. Edited by Gabriel Dumay. Dijon: Darantière.

Miller, Stephen. 2014. "The Strange Career of Joseph Addison," *Sewanee Review* 122: 650–60.

Misson, Francis Maximilian. 1719. *M. Misson's Memoirs and Observations in His Travels over England with Some Account of Scotland and Ireland.* Translated by Mr Ozell. London: D. Browne et al.

Monk, Samuel Holt. 1962. *The Sublime: A Study of Critical Theories in XVIII-Century England*. Ann Arbor: University of Michigan Press.

Montagu, Mary Wortley. 1906. *Letters from the Right Honourable Lady Mary Wortley Montagu 1709 to 1762*. Edited by R.B. Johnson. London: Dent.

Moodie, Susanna. [1852] 1970. *Roughing It in the Bush*. Edited by Carl. F. Klinck. Toronto: McClelland and Stewart.

– [1853] 1976. *Life in the Clearings*. Edited by Robert L. McDougall. Toronto: Macmillan.

Moore, Cecil A., ed. 1933. *Twelve Famous Plays of the Restoration and Eighteenth Century*. New York: Modern Library.

Moore, John. 1781. *View of Society and Manners in France, Switzerland, and Germany: With Anecdotes relating to Some Eminent Characters*. 2 vols. 4th ed. London: W. Strahan and T. Cadell.

Muller, Jerry Z. 1993. *Adam Smith in His Time and Ours: Designing the Decent Society*. Princeton: Princeton University Press.

Munro, Thomas, ed. 1787. *The Olla Podrida*. Vol. 41 of *The British Essayists*, edited by Lionel Thomas Berguer (1823). London: T. and J. Allman.

Murray, James A.H., Henry Bradley, W.A. Craigie, and C.T. Onions, eds. 1970. *The Oxford English Dictionary Being a Corrected Re-Issue with an Introduction, Supplement, and Bibliography of A New English Dictionary on Historical Principles Founded Mainly on the Materials Collected by the Philological Society*. 13 vols. Oxford: Clarendon Press.

Nablow, Ralph A. 1990. *The Addisonian Tradition in France: Passion and Objectivity in Social Observation*. Rutherford: Fairleigh Dickinson University Press.

Nugent, Thomas. [1749] 1778. *The Grand Tour; Or, A Journey through the Netherlands, Germany, Italy and France*. 3rd ed. 4 vols. London: J. Rivington, B. Law, T. Caslon, G. Robinson, T. Cadell, W. Goldsmith, J. Bew, S. Hayes, W. Fox, and T. Evans.

Nussbaum, Martha C. 2006. *Hiding from Humanity: Disgust, Shame, and the Law*. Princeton: Princeton University Press.

– 2012. *Not for Sale: Why Democracy Needs the Humanities*. Princeton: Princeton University Press.

Otway, Thomas. 1932. *The Works of Thomas Otway*. Editd by J.C. Gosh. 2 vols. Oxford: Clarendon.

Palmer, Parker J., and Arthur Zajonc with Megan Scribner. 2010. *The Heart of Higher Education: A Call to Renewal: Transforming the Academy through Collegial Conversations*. San Francisco: Jossey-Bass.

Parker, John, ed. 1976. *The Journals of Jonathan Carver and Related Documents, 1766–1770*. Minnesota Historical Society Press.

Pepys, Samuel. 1983. *The Diary of Samuel Pepys*. Edited by Robert Latham and William Matthews. 11 vols. Berkeley: University of California Press.

Perkins, David. 1992. *Is Literary History Possible?* Baltimore: Johns Hopkins University Press.

Perrenet, Pierre. 1920. "Dijon au XVIIIe." *La Revue de Bourgogne* 8: 8–24.

Pinker, Steven. 2002. *The Blank Slate: The Modern Denial of Human Nature*. New York: Penguin.

— 2007. *The Stuff of Thought: Language as a Window into Human Nature*. New York: Viking.

Piozzi, Hester Lynch. 1786. *Anecdotes of the Late Samuel Johnson, LL.D. during the Last Twenty Years of His Life*. London: T. Cadell.

— 1789. *Observations and Reflections Made in the Course of a Journey through France, Italy, and Germany*. Dublin: H. Chamberlaine et al.

Playstowe, Philip. 1766. *The Gentleman's Guide, in His Tour through France*. Bristol: T. Cadell et al.

Pope, Alexander. 1963. *The Poems of Alexander Pope. A One-Volume Edition of the Twickenham Text with Selected Annotations*. Edited by John Butt. London: Methuen.

Porter, Roy. 1994. *London: A Social History*. Cambridge: Harvard University Press.

— [1997] 1999. *The Greatest Benefit to Mankind: A Medical History of Humanity*. New York: W.W. Norton.

— [2000] 2001. *Enlightenment: Britain and the Creation of the Modern World*. London: Penguin.

Postman, Neil. 2000. *Building a Bridge to the 18th Century: How the Past Can Improve Our Future*. New York: Vintage Books.

Proctor, Robert E. 1998. *Defining the Humanities: How Rediscovering a Tradition Can Improve Our Schools with a Curriculum for Today's Students*. 2nd ed. Bloomington: Indiana University Press.

Radcliffe, Ann. 1795. *A Journey Made in the Summer of 1794, through Holland and the Western Frontier of Germany with a Return down the Rhine*. 2nd ed. 2 vols. London: G.G. and J. Robinson.

Raffald, Elizabeth. 1769. *The Experienced English House-Keeper, for the Use and Ease of Ladies, House-Keepers, Cooks, &c*. Manchester: self-published.

Redding, Cyrus. *A History and Description of Modern Wines.* 3rd ed. London: Henry G. Bohn, 1851.

Rediker, Marcus. 1987. *Between the Devil and the Deep Blue Sea: Merchant Seamen, Pirates and the Anglo-American Maritime World, 1700–1750.* Cambridge: Cambridge University Press.

Reynolds, Joshua. [1797] 1965. *Discourses on Art.* Edited by Stephen O. Mitchell. Indianapolis: Bobbs-Merrill.

Richardson, John. [1842] 1974. *Richardson's War of 1812.* Edited by Alexander Clark Casselman. Toronto: Coles Publishing.

Richardson, Samuel. 1966. *The Correspondence of Samuel Richardson.* Edited by Anna Laetitia Barbauld. 6 vols. New York: AMS.

– [1740] 1971. *Pamela, or Virtue Rewarded.* Edited by T.C. Duncan Eaves and Ben D. Kimpel. Boston: Houghton Mifflin.

Rivara, Annie, ed. 2002. *La Traduction des langues modernes au XVIIIe siècle.* Paris: Honoré Champion.

Roston, Murray. 1992. *Changing Perspectives in Literature and the Visual Arts 1650–1820.* Princeton: Princeton University Press.

Rowan-Hamilton, Hariot Georgina, Marchioness of Dufferin and Ava. [1891] 1971. *My Canadian Journal 1872–78.* Toronto: Coles Publishing.

Rudé, George. 1971. *Hanoverian London 1714–1808.* London: Secker and Warburg.

Rudgley, Richard. 1994. *Essential Substances: A Cultural History of Intoxicants in Society.* New York: Kodansha International.

Sahlins, Peter. 2004. *Unnaturally French: Foreign Citizens in the Old Regime and After.* Ithaca, NY: Cornell University Press.

Salgado, Gamini. 1968. *Three Restoration Comedies.* London Penguin.

Sallengre, Albert-Henri de. [1722] 1743. *Ebrietatis Encomium: Or, The Praise of Drunkenness by Boniface Oinophilus.* Translated by Robert Samber. 2nd ed. London: E. Curll.

Sansom, Joseph. [1820] 1972. *Travels in Lower Canada, with the Author's Recollections of the Soil, and Aspect; The Morals, Habits, and Religious Institutions of that Country.* Toronto: Coles Publishing.

Saw, Ruth L. 1971. *Aesthetics: An Introduction.* Garden City, NY: Doubleday.

Scholes, Robert. 1982. *Semiotics and Interpretation.* New Haven: Yale University Press.

– 1998. *The Rise and Fall of English: Reconstructing English as a Discipline.* New Haven: Yale University Press.

Sgard, Jean, ed. 1991. *Dictionnaire des journaux.* Paris: Universitas.

Shadwell, Thomas. 1927. *The Complete Works of Thomas Shadwell*. Edited by Montague Summers. 5 vols. London: Fortune Press.

Shaw, Thomas. 1738. *Travels, Or Observations Relating to Several Parts of Barbary and the Levant*. Oxford: The Theatre.

Sherburn, George. [1956] 2002. *The Correspondence of Alexander Pope*. 5 vols. Electronic edition. Charlottesville, VA: Intelex.

Simon, André L. 1927. *Bottlescrew Days: Wine Drinking in England during the Eighteenth Century*. Boston: Small, Maynard.

Simpson, George. [1872] 1970. *Peace River. A Canoe Voyage from Hudson's Bay to Pacific, by the Late Sir George Simpson; (Governor, Hon. Hudson's Bay Company.) in 1828*. Toronto: Coles Publishing.

Smail, Daniel Lord. 2008. *On Deep History and the Brain*. Berkeley: University of California Press.

Smith, Adam. [1776] 1976. *An Inquiry into the Nature and Causes of the Wealth of Nations*. Edited by Edward Cannan. 2 vols in one. Chicago: University of Chicago Press.

Smith, Barry C., ed. 2007. *Questions of Taste: The Philosophy of Wine*. Oxford: Oxford University Press.

Smith, Robert. 1723. *Court Cookery: Or, The Compleat English Cook*. London: T. Wotton.

Smollett, Tobias, trans. 1755. *The History and Adventures of the Renowned Don Quixote*. 2 vols. London: A. Millar, et al.

– [1766] 1981. *Travels through France and Italy*. Edited by Frank Felsenstein. Oxford: Oxford University Press.

– [1771] 1984. *The Expedition of Humphrey Clinker*. Edited by Lewis M. Knapp. Revised by Paul-Gabriel Boucé. Oxford: Oxford University Press.

Spence, F.S. [1896] 1973. *The Facts of the Case: A Summary of the Most Important Evidence and Argument Presented in the Report of the Royal Commission on the Liquor Traffic Compiled under the Direction of the Dominion Alliance for the Total Suppression of the Liquor Traffic*. Toronto: Coles Publishing.

Spence, Joseph. 1975. *Letters from the Grand Tour*. Edited by Slava Klima. Montreal & Kingston: McGill-Queen's University Press.

Stanhope, Philip Dormer, Earl of Chesterfield. 1774. *Letters Written by the Late Right Honourable Philip Dormer Stanhope, Earl of Chesterfield to His Son, Philip Stanhope*. 2 vols. London: J. Dodsley.

– 1901. *Letters to His Son*. Edited by Oliver H.G. Leigh. Washington: H. Walter Dunne.

– 1929. *Lord Chesterfield's Letters to His Son*. Edited by E.K. Root. London: Dent.

Starr, G. Gabrielle. 2013. *Feeling Beauty: The Neuroscience of Aesthetic Experience.* Cambridge: MIT Press.

Steele, Richard. 1953. *The Tatler.* Edited by Lewis Gibbs. London: Dent

– 1959. *Richard Steele's Periodical Journalism 1714–16.* Edited by Rae Blanchard. Oxford: Clarendon.

Stephens, John Calhoun, ed. 1982. *The Guardian.* Lexington: University of Kentucky Press.

Sterne, Laurence. 1935. *Letters of Laurence Sterne.* Edited by Lewis Perry Curtis. Oxford: Clarendon.

– *A Sentimental Journey and Other Writings.* Edited by Ian Jack and Tim Parnell. Oxford: Oxford University Press.

– [1759–67] 1997. *The Life and Opinions of Tristram Shandy, Gentleman.* Edited by Melvyn New and Joan New. Introduction by Christopher Ricks. London: Penguin.

Stuart, James. [1771] 1978. *Critical Observations on the Buildings and Improvements of London.* Edited by Dianne Sigler Ames. Los Angeles: William Andrews Clark Memorial Library, The Augustan Reprint Society, nos. 189–90.

Stuart, Tristram. 2007. *The Bloodless Revolution: A Cultural History of Vegetarianism from 1600 to Modern Times.* New York: W.W. Norton.

Swift, Jonathan. 1912. *The Correspondence of Jonathan Swift, D.D.* Edited by F. Elrington Ball, 6 vols. London: G. Bell.

– 1960. *Gulliver's Travels and Other Writings.* Edited by Louis A. Landa. Boston: Houghton Mifflin.

– 1964a. *A Proposal for Correcting the English Tongue, Polite Conversation, Etc.* Edited by Herbert Davis with Louis Landa. Oxford: Basil Blackwell.

– 1964b. *Directions to Servants and Miscellaneous Pieces 1733–1742.* Edited by Herbert Davis Oxford: Basil Blackwell.

Szostak, Rick. 1991. *The Role of Transportation in the Industrial Revolution: A Comparison of England and France.* Montreal: McGill-Queen's University Press.

Tayler, Alistair, and Henrietta, eds. 1939. *The Stuart Papers at Windsor.* London: John Murray.

Temple, William. 1983. *Five Miscellaneous Essays by Sir William Temple.* Edited by Samuel Holt Monk. Ann Arbor: University of Michigan Press.

Thicknesse, Philip. 1766. *Observations on the Customs and Manners of the French Nation in a Series of Letters in which That Nation Is Vindicated from the Misrepresentations of Some Late Writers.* London: Robert Davis, G. Kearsley, and N. Young.

– 1777. *A Year's Journey through France and Part of Spain.* 2 vols. Bath: Self-published.

Thomson, Gladys Scott. 1937. *Life in a Noble Household, 1641–1700*. London: Jonathan Cape.

Thomson, James. 1908. *The Complete Works of James Thomson*. Edited by J. Logie Robertson London: Oxford University Press

Thomson, Peter. 1995. "English Renaissance and Restoration Theatre." In *The Oxford Illustrated History of Theatre*, edited by John Russell Brown, 173–219. Oxford: Oxford University Press.

Thrale, Hester Lynch. 1932. *The French Journals of Mrs Thrale and Doctor Johnson*. Edited by Moses Tyson and Henry Guppy. Manchester: Manchester University Press.

Tillotson, Geoffrey, Paul Fussell, Marshall Waingrow, and Brewster Rogerson, eds. 1969. *Eighteenth-Century English Literature*. Fort Worth: Harcourt Brace Jovanovich.

Tombs, Robert and Isabelle. 2007. *That Sweet Enemy: The French and the British from the Sun King to the Present*. New York: Alfred A. Knopf.

Traill, Catharine Parr. [1836] 1971. *The Backwoods of Canada*. Edited by Clara Thomas. Toronto: McClelland and Stewart.

Trotter, Thomas. [1804] 1988. *An Essay Medical, Philosophical, and Chemical on Drunkenness and Its Effects on the Human Body*. Edited by Roy Porter. London: Routledge.

Trusler, John. 1788. *The Honours of the Table, Or, Rules for Behaviour during Meals; with The Whole Art of Carving*. London: self-published.

Tryon, Thomas. 1691a. *A Dialogue between an East-Indian Brackmanny, Or Heather-Philosopher, and a French-Gentleman, Concerning the Present Affairs in Europe*. London: D. Newman and R. Baldwin.

– 1691b. *Pythagoras His Mystick Philosophy Reviv'd*. London: Tho. Salisbury.

– 1691c. *The Way to Health, Long Life and Happiness: Or, A Discourse of Temperance*. 2nd ed. London: D. Newman.

– 1701. *The Merchant, Citizen and Country-man's Instructor: Or, A Necessary Companion for All People*. London: E. Harris and G. Conyers.

Vanbrugh, John. 1989. *Four Comedies*. Edited by Michael Cordner. London: Penguin.

Verral, William. 1759. *A Complete System of Cookery*. London: self-published.

Wahl, Maurice. [1894] 1974. *Les Premières Années de la Révolution à Lyon 1788–1792*. Genève: Mégariotis Reprints.

Walpole, Horace. 1937–1983. *Horace Walpole's Correspondence*. Edited by W.S. Lewis et al. 48 vols. New Haven: Yale University Press.

Walter, Richard. 1748. *A Voyage round the World in the Years MDCCXL, I, II, III, IV. By George Anson*. London.

Walvin, James. 1997. *Fruits of Empire: Exotic Produce and British Taste 1660–1800*. New York: New York University Press.

Warton, Joseph. 1742. "Fashion: An Epistolary Satire to a Friend." London: R. Dodsley.

– 1782. "Verses Written at Montauban in France, 1750." In *A Collection of Poems in Six Volumes by Several Hands*, 4:217–18. London: J. Dodsley.

White, Gilbert. [1788-89] 1977. *The Natural History of Selbourne*. Edited by Richard Mabey. London: Penguin.

White, Jerry. 2013. *A Great and Monstrous Thing: London in the Eighteenth Century*. Cambridge: Harvard University Press.

White, Stephen K. 2002. *Edmund Burke: Modernity, Politics and Aesthetics*. London: Rowman & Littlefield.

Wood, Nigel (ed). 2007. *She Stoops to Conquer and Other Comedies*. Oxford: Oxford University Press.

Woodforde, James. [1935] 1978. *The Diary of a Country Parson 1758–1802*. Edited by John Beresford. Oxford: Oxford University Press.

Wraxall, Nathaniel William. 1784. *A Tour through the Western, Southern, and Interior Provinces of France*. London: Charles Dilly.

Wright, Edward. 1730. *Some Observations Made in Travelling through France, Italy, &c. in the Years 1720, 1721, and 1722*. 2 vols. London: Tho. Ward and E. Wicksteed.

Wright, John. 1795. *An Essay on Wines, Especially on Port Wine*. London: J, Barker.

Wycherley, William. 1996. *Love in a Wood, The Gentleman Dancing-Master, The Country Wife, The Plain Dealer*. Edited by Peter Dixon. Oxford: Oxford University Press.

Young, Arthur. [1794] 1970. *Travels during the Years 1787, 1788, & 1789; Undertaken More Particularly with a View of Ascertaining the Cultivation, Wealth, Resources, and National Prosperity of the Kingdom of France*. 2nd ed. 2 vols. London: W. Richardson. Reprint. New York: AMS.

Younger, William. 1966. *Gods, Men, and Wine*. London: Wine and Food Society in association with World Publishing Company.

Index

Aboriginal peoples: fur trade, 49–50, 117; myth of noble savage, 28, 99–100, 122; in South America, 232–3. *See also* Canada, Aboriginal peoples; Canada, Aboriginal peoples and alcohol

Absalom and Achitophel (Dryden), 46

The Accomplisht Cook (May), 190

An Account of Corsica (Boswell), 295–6

An Account of the Life of Mr Richard Savage (Johnson), 233–4

Acetaria (Evelyn), 192, 193–4

Addison, Joseph: about, 79–93, 336–7; on Bacon, 4–5; on biographies, 89–90; Broadus's "Addison," xiii, 79–83, 95; on classical knowledge, 54, 88–90, 92, 220–1; common readers, 81–5; cultural relativism, 44–5, 88; decline in reputation, 92–3; dialectic of passion and objectivity, 336–7; Dubos on, 44–5; on education, 92, 220–3; Ellis on, 99; on factionalism, 6; on fashion, 278–9; Fish on, 97–8; on government, 90–1, 221; on the Grand Tour, 220–3; imagination, 83–7; inclusive sensibility, 81, 85; irony and paradox, 337; Johnson on, 81–3, 92; on liberty, 90; literary historian and critic, 88–9; metaphors, 85–6, 91; on Milton, 80–2; perception, imagination, and cognition, 79–80, 85, 93, 336–7; on sensory experience, 83–9; synesthesia, 79, 84–7, 93, 336; on theatre, 52–3; on trade and commerce, 90–1, 221; on travel writers, 231n35; on wine and wine production, 295, 336–7

Addison, Joseph, works: *Remarks on Several Parts of Italy*, 220–3, 295; *The Spectator*, 6, 80–1, 84–92, 161n6, 279n197, 336–7; *The Tatler*, 81, 319

"Addison as a Literary Critic" (Broadus), xiii, 79–83, 95

The Advancement of Learning (Bacon), 3–4, 192

aesthetics: about, 15–17, 19, 22, 108–10, 340–1; in architecture, 67–9; cross-disciplinary principles, 110; dialectic in, 15–16; faculty of evaluation, 37–44; and government, 285–6; imagination, 80, 83;

imperial metaphors, 38; Kant on, 16; key questions, 69; lack of sensory and disciplinary boundaries, 15, 39, 109–10, 187; in liberal arts education, 21–2; mind-altering substances, 69; motive for literary analysis, 22; neuroscience of aesthetics, 109–12, 340–1; *OED* definition, 16; sixth sense, 15, 24, 40–4; suspended judgment, 37–45; taste as sense versus discrimination, 108–9. *See also* Dubos, Jean-Baptiste; literary history and literariness, 18th century; literary history and literariness, recent views; mind-altering substances, 18th century; mind-altering substances, recent views; mind-body relationship, 18th century; mind-body relationship, recent views; synesthesia; taste (aesthetic sensitivity)

aesthetics and sensory experience. *See* sensory experience, 18th century; sensory experience, recent views; sight; sixth sense; smell; sound; synesthesia; taste (gustatory); touch

Africa, travel writing, 214–15

agriculture. *See* Britain, agriculture; Britain, domestic life – food production; France, agriculture

agriculture, viticulture. *See* Britain, wine production; France, wine production; wine production

Akenside, Mark, 46–7

alcohol: about, 69–78; brain chemistry, 111–12; key questions, 69; secularization of, 70–1; Trotter's *Essay*, 75–8. *See also* drunkenness; health and alcohol; mind-altering substances, 18th century; mind-altering substances, recent views; wine and spirits

alcohol, countries. *See* Britain, wine and spirits; Canada, Aboriginal peoples and alcohol; Canada, wine and spirits; France, wine and spirits

altered consciousness, 69–71. *See also* mind-altering substances, 18th century; mind-altering substances, recent views

American colonies: British authority, 51–2; British traders, 49–50; Burke on, 11, 48–9; Johnson on, 49–52; Smith on, 235. *See also* United States

The Anatomy of Melancholy (Burton), 47–8

Andrews, John, 284–90

Anecdotes of the Late Samuel Johnson (Piozzi), 169–70, 301

Anne, Queen, 163n12

Annotations to Sir Joshua Reynolds's Discourses (Blake), 3, 7–8, 80

Anson, George, 50, 232–3

Arbuthnot, John, 166–8

architecture and public spaces: about, 65–9; aesthetics, 67–9; in Canadian fiction, 152–3; classical models, 67–9; estate management, 201–3, 240; imperial rivalries, 7, 65–9; landscapes, 68–9, 266–7, 303; Laugier's *Essay*, 67–9; rural towns, 237; Stuart's *Critical Observations*, 65–8. *See also* Britain, architecture and public spaces; France, architecture and public

spaces; London, architecture and public spaces
Aristotle, 4, 92
Armstrong, John, 333
Arnoux, Claude, 320
arthritis (gout), 72–3, 279–80, 320. *See also* health
The Art of Cookery (Glasse), 169, 171–2, 208n95, 208n97, 316
The Art of Preserving Health (Armstrong), 333
Aubert de Gaspé, Philippe-Joseph, 140–6, 151, 155–6
audible environments. *See* sound
Austen, Jane, 178–83, 334
Auxerre, France, 11, 273, 297, 307, 310, 325–6

The Backwoods of Canada (Traill), 127–8
Bacon, Francis, 3–6, 86, 192
Barry, Edward, 319–21
Bath, England, 238–9, 306
The Beaux' Stratagem (Farquhar), 59
Bedford, William Russell, Duke of, 55–6, 201–3
The Beggar's Opera (Gay), 60–1, 165
The Belle's Stratagem (Cowley), 331–2
Benedict, Philip, 248n74
Berlin, Isaiah, 11
beverages. *See* coffee; tea; wine and spirits
Bicknell, Alexander, 119–21
Blair, Hugh, 86n15
Blake, William, 3, 5–8, 79–80
Bloom, Edward A. and Lillian D., 168n21, 337
body-mind relationship. *See* mind-body relationship, 18th century;

mind-body relationship, recent views
A Bold Stroke for a Husband (Cowley), 331
Bon Ton (Garrick), 329–30
Bordeaux, France, and wine: about, 255–65, 298–9; architecture and public spaces, 256–7, 259–61, 298–9; British residents and visitors, 255–6, 258–61, 293–9, 307, 318; British technology, 274; Château-Trompette, 256–7, 259–60; claret as generic wine, 246; Defoe on, 255–6; demographics, 256, 258; economy, 260–4; inns and hotels, 259–63, 298; luxury items, 255, 259n105, 262–5, 272, 274–8; merchant community, 256–8, 260–5; Pontac family, 246–7, 303–4, 338; shipbuilding, 257–8; trade, 257–65, 272; transportation, 257–8, 260–1; travelogues, 293–5, 297, 298–9; vineyards, 298; wine trade, 256, 258–9, 307, 314, 318, 320–1. *See also* claret wine
Boswell, James, 170–1, 295–6
Boucher, Claude, 256–7
Boulton, J.T., 87
Bradley, Martha, 317, 324
Bradley, Richard, 247
brain science. *See* mind-body relationship, recent views
brandy: adulterated wines, 74, 78, 125, 322; in Canada, 117–19, 121–2, 125, 130–1, 133–6, 138–9, 142–4; drunkenness, 71; in food, 121, 135–6; frontier uses, 117, 119, 130, 131, 133, 136; wine codes,

119, 133, 135, 138–9, 142–4, 327; wine trade, 121–2, 258n99, 322
Briggs, Peter, 83–5, 103, 160n6
Brillat-Savarin, Jean-Anthelme, 18–21, 72, 78
Britain: dialectic in material and intellectual culture, 3, 7, 12–13, 155–6, 283–4, 341; hybrid culture, 10; literary history, 9–11, 13, 341; national identity, 10, 322–3, 341; period of Britishness, 10, 282. *See also* Britain, empire
Britain, agriculture: agrarian revolution, 235, 276–7; exports, 271–3; food markets, 235–7; gardens and orchards, 202–3, 238, 273–4; natural history, 186–8, 192–4; plant breeding, 273. *See also* Britain, domestic life—food production; Britain, wine production
Britain, architecture and public spaces, 65–9. *See also* London, architecture and public spaces
Britain, consumerism: about, 341; brain chemistry, 111–12; colonial trade, 235; conspicuous consumption, 183–4, 239–40, 338; Defoe on, 237–9; food markets, 236–7; imperial rivalries, 7, 112, 239–40, 282; irony and paradox, 282, 337–9; luxury items, 248–9; mind-altering substances, 69, 112–13; satire on, 54, 159–60, 183–4; Swift on, 159–60; wine codes, 328–30. *See also* Britain, economy and trade; Britain, fashion; Britain, wine trade; consumerism; mind-altering substances, 18th century

Britain, domestic life: art of conversation, 159–60, 165–6, 168–9, 175–6, 178, 180–4, 288–9; dining rooms, 179–80, 183, 201, 275; Fielding on, 175–6; food sharing, 178, 181–2, 188–90, 208, 212–13; gender roles, 175–7, 181; imperial rivalries, 223–4; kitchens, 179, 219; manners, 14–15, 171, 175–8, 181–4, 288–9, 334; tableware, 159–60, 176–80, 183–4, 188–91, 201, 204, 274–7; wine service, 334. *See also* Britain, fashion
Britain, domestic life – food production: annual cycles, 204; cattle enclosures, 186–7; ecclesiastical life, 186–90, 204; estate management, 187–8, 201–3, 240; fishing and hunting, 183–4, 189, 202, 204; food preservation, 189; gardens and orchards, 181–3, 187–9, 202–4, 238, 273–4, 318; homemade wine and beer, 178, 183, 306, 317, 318, 321; natural history, 186–8. *See also* Britain, agriculture; Britain, wine production
Britain, domestic life – servants: Austen's works, 178–81; Fielding's works, 174; French immigrants, 243–4; Graves's *Spiritual Quixote*, 210–11; Raffald's *Experienced English House-Keeper*, 204n89, 208n97, 210, 212n105, 213, 317–18; Swift's *Directions*, 159–60
Britain, ecclesiastical life: about, 184–91, 204; asceticism, 206, 210–11, 213; church calendar, 198, 207; Crabbe's poetry, 326–7; culinary discourse, 208–9, 212–13; food

production, 186–90, 204; food sharing, 188–90, 208, 212–13; gardens, 190, 204; Graves's *Spiritual Quixote*, 204–13; menus and items, 188, 190–1, 204, 209–13; table service, 188–91, 204; White's *Natural History*, 186–8; wine codes, 326–7; Woodforde's *Diary*, 186, 188–91

Britain, economy and trade: Addison on, 90–2, 221; animal breeding, 254; colonial trade, 234–5; Defoe's *Tour*, 54–6, 235–9; domestic knowledge, 227–8, 235; East India Co., 231, 235; Eden Treaty (1786), 262, 271–3, 275–6, 278, 280; food, 242–3, 271; free trade, 306–7, 323; imperial metaphors, 91; London as centre, 55–6; luxury items, 262–5, 274–82; mind-altering substances, 16; piracy and privateers, 231–3, 271; poverty, 284, 286, 287; Smith's *Wealth of Nations*, 225–6, 234–5, 237n52, 323; spice trade, 231; sumptuary laws, 277–8, 306–7, 338; technology, 274–5; trade balance with France, 271. *See also* Britain, agriculture; Britain, empire; Britain, wine trade; Canada, economy and trade; France, economy and trade

Britain, education: about, 24–33, 225–6; aesthetic training, 24–9, 31; ethical training, 28, 31–3; Hurd's Locke and Shaftesbury on, 29–33; imperial rivalries, 32; language learning, 225; nationalism, 32–3; reading and writing, 26–30; religious education, 29, 32–3; self-discourse, 24–6, 28–9, 31; Shaftesbury on, 24–33; Smith on, 225–6; social class, 225; university pedagogy, 226. *See also* Britain, travel; Britain, travel on the continent; education, 18th century; literary history and literariness, 18th century; natural history; Royal Society of London

Britain, empire: about, 45–52; anti-imperial satire, 45–8, 215–17; Blake on empires, 3, 5–6; colonial grants, 51–2; colonial trade, 234–5; crown authority, 51–2; democratic representation, 51–2; East India Co., 231, 235; economic exploitation, 49–52; Falkland Islands, 50–1; fur trade, 49–50, 121, 123–7, 134–5; humanizing of, 48; imperial metaphors, 7, 20–1, 38, 47, 91, 103; imperial rivalries, 45; key questions, 9–10, 13; literary history, 9–11, 13, 341; London as centre, 54; metaphors, 6, 48; nationalistic rhetoric, 46–7; paradoxes of travel, 231–5; piracy and privateers, 231–3, 271; political factionalism, 6, 23; psychological ideas of, 36; rationalism, 47; royal aspirations, 46; as unsatisfactory ideology, 69; war costs, 51. *See also* American colonies; Britain, economy and trade; Britain, government and politics; Canada, British Canada

Britain, empire – writing: Akenside's *Pleasures*, 46–7; Bacon on, 5–6; Burke's essays and speeches, 11, 48–9; Dryden's *Absalom and Achitophel*, 46; Dubos on, 36; Fielding's *Jonathan Wild*, 47, 228–9;

Goldsmith's *Deserted Village*, 234; Johnson's political writings, 49–52; Pope's *Dunciad*, 45–6, 215–16; Shaftesbury on, 23; Smith's *Wealth of Nations*, 234–5; Sterne's *Sentimental Journey*, 47–8, 228, 335; Swift's *Gulliver's Travels*, 216–20; Swift's *Modest Proposal*, 160–3; Thomson's *Britannia*, 46, 234. *See also* Canada, British and French Canada in literature – writing; Canada, travel writing

Britain, fashion: about, 277–82, 341; accessories, 281–2; aesthetics of, 15–17, 341; comparison with France, 288, 290–2; conformity, 288; decadent aristocrats, 45; Englishness, 282; French influences, 184, 239–40, 282; funeral pomp, 277–8; health benefits, 279–80; identity, status, and nationalism, 277–9; imperial rivalries, 7, 184, 239–40, 282; irony and paradox, 337–9; Johnson on, 13–15; in London plays, 54, 57, 61–2, 64–5; luxury items, 248–9, 255, 278–82; manners, 14–15; resorts, 238; semiotics of, 115–16; taste versus fashion, 290–1. *See also* Britain, consumerism; France, fashion

Britain, food: Andrews on, 287; asceticism, 195–7, 206, 210–11, 213; culinary analogies, 209; exports, 272–3; food preservation, 189; French influences, 184, 191–3, 197–201, 239–40; gastronomic codes, 212–13; Italian influences, 192; mockery of haute cuisine, 174–5; nationalism, 33–5, 195–6, 212–13; nutrition, 287; resort food, 238; spices and herbs, 196, 202, 231; synesthesia, 108–10; Tryon on, 194–7; vegetarianism, 177, 193–7; Woburn Abbey hospitality, 201–3. *See also* Britain, ecclesiastical life; Britain, wine and spirits; food; health and diet

Britain, food – fish: carp recipe, 247; exports, 271; fish ponds, 183–4, 189, 202, 204, 236–7; markets, 236–7, 242–3; seafood, 202, 236–7

Britain, food – French cultural exchange: about, 197–201; Graves's *Spiritual Quixote*, 212–13; imperial rivalries, 7, 33–5, 174–5, 223; La Varenne's *French Cook*, 197–9; Locke on, 33–5; Massialot's *Court and Country Cook*, 199–200; wine in recipes, 315–18

Britain, food – inns and eateries: cook-shops, 245; corruption, 305–6; Fielding's works, 174; French influences, 244–6; imperial rivalries, 244–5; menus and items, 159–60, 174–5, 191, 203, 205–6, 208–10, 245–6; Pepys on, 246–7, 322–3; Pontack's restaurant in London, 245–7; scorn for haute cuisine, 174

Britain, food – menus and items: comparison with France, 287, 314–15; country food, 184, 211, 239; court feasts, 184–5, 190–1, 193, 200–3; cultural pretensions, 184; French influences, 184, 190, 239–40, 244–6; Goldsmith's *She Stoops to Conquer*, 64, 184; Graves's *Spiritual Quixote*, 204–6, 209–13, 215; inns and eateries, 159–60, 174–5, 191, 203,

205–6, 208–10, 245–6; Swift's *Compleat Collection*, 159–60

Britain, food writing: about, 315–18; audiences, 199–200; encyclopedias, 200; etiquette, 175, 177; female writers of cookbooks, 172; Fielding on, 165–6, 175; Johnson on, 171–2; Pontack's restaurant's dishes, 247; Scriblerians, 164–8; Sterne on, 184–6; Tryon's works, 194–7; veal recipe, 164–5; wine in recipes, 315–18. *See also* food – recipes

Britain, food writing – cookbooks and other writing: Digby's *Closet*, 191–2; Evelyn's *Aceteria*, 192, 193–4; Glasse's *Art of Cookery*, 169, 171–2, 208n95, 208n97, 316; Jenks's *Complete Cook*, 172n32, 247; Lamb's *Royal Cookery*, 201; La Varenne's *French Cook*, 197–9; Locke's *Locke's Travels in France*, 33–5, 303–4; Marnette's *Perfect Cook*, 197–9; Massialot's *Court and Country Cook*, 199–200; May's *Accomplisht Cook*, 190, 191–2, 199; Miller's *Gardeners' Dictionary*, 273–4; Raffald's *Experienced English House-Keeper*, 204n89, 208n97, 210, 212n105, 213, 317–18; Woodforde's *Diary of a Country Parson*, 188–91; Wright's *Essay on Wine*, 73–5

Britain, food writing – literary: about, 172–84; Arbuthnot's *Martinus Scriblerus*, 166; Austen's works, 178–83; Burney's *Evelina*, 168–9, 177–8; Cervantes's *Don Quixote*, 173–5; Chesterfield's *Letters to His Son*, 169–70, 272n166, 288; Colman and Garrick's *Clandestine Marriage*, 183–4, 330; Fielding's works, 172–6; Goldsmith's *She Stoops to Conquer*, 184; Graves's *Spiritual Quixote*, 204–13, 215; Griffiths's *The Times*, 169; Locke's *Locke's Travels in France*, 33–5, 303–4; Richardson's *Pamela*, 176–7, 333–4; Sterne's *Tristram Shandy*, 166, 185, 335–6; Swift's *Gulliver's Travels*, 216–20. *See also* Britain, food writing – cookbooks and other writing; Britain, wine and spirits – writing

Britain, French cultural exchange and rivalry: about, 7, 102, 243–7, 283–92; architecture, 65–9; commercial rivalries, 248–9; dialectic, OED definition, 16; dialectic in material and intellectual culture, 3, 7, 12–13, 155–6, 283–4, 341; Dubos on, 35–45; fashion, 282, 288, 290–2; food, 284, 287, 314–15; French residents and visitors, 243–7, 284; government and politics, 284–9, 292; luxury items, 248–9, 274–82; manners, 288–9; Pontack's restaurant in London, 245–7; poverty, 284, 286, 287, 291–2; taverns and inns, 244–5; travel, 283–4, 289–92; wine and wine production, 284, 308–15. *See also* Britain, travel on the continent; France, British cultural exchange and rivalry

Britain, government and politics: Addison on, 90–1; comparison with France, 287–9, 292; democratic representation, 51–2; Dubos on, 36; electoral bribery, 327; factionalism, 6; fashion, 288–9; gradual political evolution, 50; Johnson's political writings, 49–52; wine and national politics, 339–40; wine codes, 309–11, 327. *See also* Britain, empire

Britain, London as centre. *See* London; London, architecture and public spaces; London, writing

Britain, theatre: about, 15–16, 52–65, 327–33; aesthetic pretensions, 62–3; aristocratic decadence, 15, 329–32; classical plays, 52–3; comedies, 53–4, 56–65; commerce, 60–3; consumerism, 330; criminal underworld, 60–1; cuckolds, 52, 53, 58; fashion, 54, 57, 61–2, 64–5, 178; imperial rivalries, 177; London's topography in plays, 54–65; lower-class characters, 54, 56–7; margins of empire, 54; mercantile wealth, 16, 60–3, 65; nationalism, 330–1; opera houses, 177–8; patriarchy, 57, 65; satire, 54, 63–4; sentimentality, 63–4, 330–2; sexualized sites, 57–8; social fantasy, 332–3; stereotypes, 15–16, 54, 56–7, 59–60; urbanity and rusticity, 59, 64; wine codes, 327–33; women characters, 57–63. *See also* London; London, architecture and public spaces

Britain, theatre – plays and other writing: Addison's essays, 52–3; Burney's *Evelina*, 177–8; Centlivre's plays, 327, 332; Colman and Garrick's *Clandestine Marriage*, 62, 183–4, 330; Colman's *Musical Lady*, 62–3; Congreve's plays, 58–9; Cowley's plays, 331–2; Cumberland's *Fashionable Lover*, 53–4, 63–4; Etherege's *Man of Mode*, 58; Farquhar's plays, 59, 327–8; Foote's plays, 61–2, 330; Garrick's plays, 62, 183–4, 327, 329–30; Gay's *Beggar's Opera*, 60–1, 165; Goldsmith's *She Stoops to Conquer*, 64, 184, 330–1; Holcroft's plays, 332–3; Hume on, 53; Murphy's *Citizen* and *Old Maid*, 63; Otway's *Friendship in Fashion*, 327–8; Shadwell's plays, 327–9; Sheridan's *School for Scandal*, 64–5, 331; Steele's *Tender Husband* and *Conscious Lovers*, 59–60; Vanbrugh's *Relapse*, 59; Wycherley's plays, 56–8, 178

Britain, travel: about, 214–40; Bacon on, 5; British insularity, 31; consumerism, 11n29, 235–40; dialectic of imperialism and nationalism, 214–20; domestic knowledge, 31, 227–8, 235–8; domestic travel, 54–6, 235–9; exotic food customs, 214–15; food markets, 235–6; London as centre, 236; piracy and privateers, 231–3, 271; resorts, 238; Scotland, 239–40; South America, 232–3; turnpikes, 237n52; waterways, 236–7. *See also* Britain, travel on the continent; Britain, travel writing

Britain, travel in Canada. *See* Canada, travel; Canada, travel writing

Britain, travel on the continent: about, 283–4; aesthetic training, 27–9; benefits and harms, 215–16, 220, 226–9, 289–90; classical knowledge, 11, 220–1, 293; comparison with French travel, 283–4, 289–90; demographics, 292;

dialectic in, 284–5; dining customs, 223–4; Germany, 229–31, 301–2; Grand Tour, 27–33, 220–4, 226–9, 293–5, 303, 310; Holland, 229–30; imperial rivalries, 7, 32–3, 223, 226–7, 289–92; Italy, 220–3; language learning, 225; monasteries, 11; moral duty, 31; nationalism, 223, 226–7, 308; negative influences, 215–16, 220; reputations, 289–90; satires of travel writing, 228–9, 289–90; travelogues, 5, 27, 54–6, 226–31, 235, 293–5. *See also* Britain, French cultural exchange and rivalry

Britain, travel writing: Addison's *Remarks*, 220–3, 295; Andrews's *Comparative View*, 284–90; Boswell's *Account of Corsica*, 295–6; Burney's *Present State of Music*, 295–6; Cradock's *Journal*, 258–9; Dampier's *New Voyage*, 232–3; Defoe's *Tour*, 54–6, 235–9; Digby's *Closet*, 191–2; empirical, 229–31; Fielding's *Jonathan Wild* and *Journal of a Voyage*, 47, 165–6, 228–9, 242–3; Hurd's *Dialogues*, 31–3; Johnson's *Richard Savage*, 233–4; Locke's *Locke's Travels in France*, 33–5, 303–4; Nugent's *Grand Tour*, 293–5; *Olla Podrida* essays, 226–8; Piozzi's *Observations and Reflections*, 299–301; Playstowe's *Gentleman's Guide*, 297–8; Pope's *Dunciad*, 45–6, 215–16; Radcliffe's *Journey*, 229–31, 301–2; Shaftesbury's *Characteristics of Men*, 23–30, 72; Shaw's *Travels*, 214–15; Smith's *Wealth of Nations*, 225–6; Spence's *Letters*, 220, 223–4, 266, 310; Sterne's *Tristram Shandy* and *Sentimental Journey*, 47–8, 166, 184–6, 228, 305, 335–6; Swift's *Gulliver's Travels*, 216–20; Thicknesse's *Observations* and *Year's Journey*, 311–13; Thrale's *French Journals*, 308; Walpole's letters, 292–3; Walter's *Voyage*, 232–3; Warton's "Fashion" and "Verses," 290–2; Wraxall's *Tour*, 297, 298–9; Young's *Travels*, 9, 259–60, 313–15, 324

Britain, wine and spirits: about, 75–8, 115, 292–302, 322–3, 341; aesthetic experience, 76–8; French restaurants, 245–7; French views on, 284; homemade wine and beer, 178, 183, 306, 317, 318, 321; imperial rivalries, 7, 223, 313–15; irony and paradox, 337–9; as medical remedy, 77–8; motives for drinking, 75–6; national identity, 322–3; in novels, 333–6; in plays, 327–33; political ideologies of claret and port, 115, 319, 337; sensory experience, 71; synesthesia, 108–10, 340–1; wine codes, 326–36. *See also* drunkenness; health and alcohol; mind-altering substances, 18th century; mind-altering substances, recent views

Britain, wine and spirits – writing: Armstrong's *Art of Preserving Health*, 333; Austen's *Mansfield Park*, 334; Barry's *Observations*, 319–21; Centlivre's plays, 327, 332; Chesterfield's *Letters*, 310–11; Colman and Garrick's *Clandestine Marriage*, 330; Cowley's plays,

331–2; Crabbe's poetry, 326–7; Defoe on wine and wine trade, 318, 337; Farquhar's plays, 59, 327–8; Fielding's *Joseph Andrews*, 305–6; Foote's plays, 61–2, 330; Garrick's plays, 327, 329–30; Goldsmith's *She Stoops to Conquer*, 330–1; Holcroft's plays, 332–3; Hughes's *Compleat Vineyard*, 323; Locke's *Locke's Travels in France*, 303–4; Mandeville's *Fable of the Bees*, 338; Moore's *View of Society*, 313; Otway's *Friendship in Fashion*, 327–8; Pepys's *Diary*, 322–3; Redding's *History*, 322; Richardson's *Pamela*, 176–7, 333–4; Rose's *English Vineyard Vindicated*, 323; Sallengre's *Ebrietatis Encomium*, 71–2; Shadwell's plays, 327–9; Smollett's *Humphrey Clinker* and *Travels*, 306–8, 311–12; Steele on, 319; Sterne on, 166, 185–6, 305; Sterne's novels, 335–6; Swift's *Directions* and *Gulliver*, 159–60, 220; Thicknesse's *Observations* and *Year's Journey*, 311–13; Trotter's *Essay*, 75–8; Wright's *Essay on Wines*, 321–2; Young's *Travels*, 313–15

Britain, wine production: about, 303–6; fermentation processes, 74–5, 295, 304, 308, 320, 323; French influences, 284, 295, 303–4; landscape design, 303; nationalism, 308, 323; ownership of vineyards, 284, 321, 323; publications on, 73–5, 323. *See also* Britain, agriculture; Britain, domestic life – food production

Britain, wine trade: about, 16, 306–12; adulterated wine, 73–4, 305–8, 312, 318–22; Burgundy wines, 309–12; corruption, 305–6, 310, 312, 318–22; imperial rivalries, 309–10; Methuen Treaty (1703), 306, 318, 337; reliance on French fashion, 310; rural sufficiency versus corrupt urbanity, 305–6; sumptuary laws, 306–7, 338; tariffs, 153–4; wine codes, 309–12, 327; wine prices, 245–6, 309–10. *See also* wine trade

Britain, writing. *See* Britain, food writing – cookbooks and other writing; Britain, food writing – literary; Britain, theatre – plays and other writing; Britain, travel writing; Britain, wine and spirits – writing

Britannia (Thomson), 46, 234

The British Housewife (M. Bradley), 317, 324

Broadus, Edmund Kemper: "Addison as a Literary Critic," xiii, 79–83, 95; career, 92; on imagination, 79–80, 83; literariness, 95, 103–4; on Milton, 79–80

Bromwich, David, 113

Brooke, Frances, 122n11, 137–40, 155, 157–8

Burgundy, France, and wine: adulterated wine, 319; Barry on, 319–20; in British novels, 333–6; burgundy, 223–4, 309–13, 333–6; Chambertin vineyard, 309, 313, 320; imperial rivalries, 309–14; Playstowe on, 297; travelogues, 297, 307, 310–14; vineyards, 313; wine codes, 309–12, 326, 328–36; wine tourism, 309–14; wine trade, 309–11, 313. *See also* France, wine and spirits

Burke, Edmund, 7, 11–13, 38n28, 48–9, 87
Burney, Charles, 295–6
Burney, Fanny, 168–9, 177–8
Burton, Robert, 47–8
Bury St Edmund's, 239

Canada: American relations, 114, 125–6, 138; bilingualism, 122; dialectic in signifiers, 7, 16, 139, 141–6, 149–51, 155–8; immigrants, 127–30; imperial rivalries, 7, 114–16, 125–6, 138–40, 146; legal pluralism, 121–2; literary history, 9–11, 13, 341; missionaries, 119–21; national identity, 10, 113–14, 140–5, 341

Canada, Aboriginal peoples: cultural exchange, 117–18, 135, 163n12; economic exploitation, 49–50, 124–7; food, 117–18, 120, 135; fur trade, 49–50, 117, 121, 123–7, 134–5; Inuit, 118, 123–4; mistreatment of, 114, 126–7, 129–30; myth of noble savage, 28, 122; self-induced visions, 120, 124; stereotypes, 124–5; warfare and slavery, 117, 120–1, 134; women, 139, 157–8

Canada, Aboriginal peoples and alcohol: adulterated "rum," 124, 127, 134, 144; alcohol free-traders, 134; alcohol use, 138, 152, 155; cultural exchange, 118–20; drinking codes, 119, 138, 139, 144; drunkenness, 119, 124–5, 129–30, 138, 152; electoral bribery, 154; fur trade rivalries, 124–5; regional differences, 119; reward for work, 119, 126–7; social order, 126–7, 152; stereotypes, 120; temperance, 121, 126–7. *See also* Canada, wine and spirits

Canada, British Canada: about, 114, 121–2, 125–33; architectural codes, 152–3; bilingualism, 122; British culture, 114–16, 122, 137–8, 141–2, 151–6; Conquest, 137, 139, 142, 148; cultural pluralism, 152–3, 155–8; factionalism, 115; festivities, 117, 134–6, 152–3; gender and power, 157–8; gentility and sensibility, 137–40; immigrants, 152–3; imperial rivalries, 7, 114–16, 138–40, 146; London publishers, 115, 119–20, 137; national identity, 113–14, 123–5, 140–2, 155–8; Quebec Act (1774), 121–2; sensibility, 157–8; social hierarchies, 122–3, 126–8, 130–3, 152; taste, 157–8; triangular relations with British and French, 145–6; wine codes, 127–33, 136–58; women settlers, 127–33. *See also* Canada, British and French Canada in literature – writing; Canada, travel

Canada, British and French Canada in literature – writing: Aubert de Gaspé's *Canadians of Old*, 140–6, 151, 155–6; Brooke's *Emily Montague*, 122n11, 137–40, 155, 157–8; Dufferin's *My Canadian Journal*, 132–3; Duncan's *Imperialist*, 140, 149, 151–6; Gérin-Lajoie's *Jean Rivard*, 140, 146–8; Grey's *Curé of St Philippe*, 140, 149–51; Jameson's *Winter Studies*, 127, 128–30; Kirby's *Golden Dog*, 140, 148–9;

Moodie's *Roughing It* and *Life in the Clearings*, 127, 130–3; Traill's *Backwoods*, 127–8. See also Canada, travel writing

Canada, economy and trade: consumerism, 136; free trade, 123–4, 151; fur trade, 49–50, 117–19, 121, 123–7, 134–5; Hudson's Bay Co., 118–19, 123–7, 134; mining industry, 136; Quebec Act (1774), 121–2; settlers, 124–5. See also Canada, wine trade

Canada, food: Aboriginal peoples, 117–18, 120, 135; disgust, 118; food codes, 132–3, 144; French Canada, 125, 144; as imperial project, 135–6; menus and items, 125, 144; mining towns, 136; plum pudding, 135–6; social hierarchies, 132–3; travel, 117–18, 135–6. See also Canada, wine and spirits; food

Canada, French Canada: about, 114–26; Conquest, 137, 139, 142, 148; factionalism, 115; food, 125; French travel writers, 119–20; habitants, 121–2, 125–6, 137–9; imperial rivalries, 7, 114–16, 125–6, 138–40, 146; legal pluralism, 122; missionaries, 119–20; Quebec Act (1774), 121–2; triangular relations with British and French, 145–6; US relations, 125–6; wine codes, 115, 125, 136–40. See also Canada, British and French Canada in literature – writing; Canada, French Canada in literature

Canada, French Canada in literature: about, 136–56; Aboriginal people, 138, 143–4; American culture, 138–9; assimilation, 142, 144, 150–1, 155; British culture, 137–8, 141–4; dialectic in signifiers, 16, 139–40, 141–2, 144–6, 149–51, 155–8; festivities, 142–3, 145, 147, 152–3, 156; food, 137–8, 144, 147; French culture, 138–9, 142–4, 148–9; gothic romance, 148–9; habitants, 137–9, 141–4, 146–8; literary allusions, 141; mythical idealism, 146–7; nationalism, 141–5, 148–51; religion, 141–2, 147, 149–51; seigneurs, 138, 142–6; settlement and reconstruction, 146–8; social hierarchies, 137–8, 144, 147, 152; supernatural, 145; temperance, 146–51; triangular relations, 145–6; wine codes, 136–40, 142–58. See also Canada, British and French Canada in literature – writing

Canada, travel: about, 116–27, 133–6; classical allusions, 122–3; disgust, 118; festivities, 117, 118, 127, 134–6; Fleming's travels, 133–6; food, 117–18, 135–6; French travel writers, 119–20; frontier drinking codes, 133–4; fur trade, 117, 121, 123–7, 134–5; habitant culture, 122–3, 125–6; hardships, 117–18; Red River Settlement, 123–5; social hierarchies, 126–7; wine and spirits, 117, 119, 122, 126–7. See also Canada, Aboriginal peoples; Canada, Aboriginal peoples and alcohol

Canada, travel writing: Carver's *Travels*, 119–21; Chappell's *Narrative*, 123–5; Grant's *Ocean to*

Ocean, 133–6; H. Gray's *Letters*, 121–3; Hearne's *Journey*, 117–19, 121; T. James's *Dangerous Voyage*, 116–17, 133; Sansom's *Travels*, 125–6; Simpson's *Peace River*, 126–7. *See also* Canada, British and French Canada in literature – writing

Canada, wine and spirits: about, 114–16, 155–6; in cold climates, 139; communal solidarity, 128; domestic versus public drinking, 132–3; drunkenness, 116, 127–9, 131–2, 136, 138; electoral bribery, 147–8, 154; festivities, 117, 129, 132–5, 152–3, 156; French Canada, 126, 136–40; French wines, 115, 125, 143–4; frontier drinking, 133–6; fur trade rivalries, 124–5; health remedy, 117, 119, 128; hygienic beverage, 115, 117, 133–4, 293; immigrants, 127–30; imperial rivalries, 7, 114–16, 137, 138–40; irony and paradox, 137n28, 140; mind-altering substances, 114; nation building, 137; reward for work, 119, 126–8, 130–1, 133–4; Royal Commission (1896), 116, 118–19, 137; semiotics, 115–16, 136–40, 155–6; social hierarchies, 126–8, 130–3, 138; temperance, 116, 126–7, 129, 131, 146–51, 153, 157; travel, 117, 118, 119, 122, 126–7; wine codes, 115–16, 125, 127–40, 143–4, 149–58. *See also* Britain, wine and spirits; Canada, Aboriginal peoples and alcohol

Canada, wine and spirits – types: adulterated drinks, 125–7, 134, 143–4; almond liqueur, 135; cognac, 125; homemade wine and beer, 115, 128, 147–8, 152; Madeira, 125, 126–8, 137; rum, 130; sherry, 148; whisky, 128–31, 134, 154. *See also* brandy; champagne and sparkling wines; claret wine; port wines

Canada, wine trade: about, 115, 149; with Aboriginal peoples, 126–7; adulterated wines, 125; barrel making, 121; cultural dialectic, 142–5, 149; H. Gray's data on, 121; nation building, 123; semiotics, 155–6; taxes, 129. *See also* Canada, Aboriginal peoples and alcohol; wine trade

Canada, writing. *See* Canada, British and French Canada in literature – writing; Canada, travel writing

Canadians of Old (Aubert de Gaspé), 140–6, 151, 155–6

Caribbean, 16, 231, 257

Carter, Charles, 315–16

Carver, Jonathan, 119–21

Centlivre, Susanna, 327, 332

Cervantes, Miguel de, 173–5, 204

Chambertin vineyard, France, 309, 313, 320

champagne and sparkling wines: adulterated wine, 312; in Canada, 133, 136, 154; as court wine, 326; in recipes, 316; sparkling wines, 319–20; wine codes, 326, 328–32, 334, 338. *See also* wine and spirits

Chappell, Edward, 123–5

Characteristics of Men (Shaftesbury), 23–30. *See also* Shaftesbury, 1st Earl of

Charles I, 117, 286

Charles II, 46, 193, 201–2, 304

Chesleden, William, 280
Chesterfield, Philip Dormer Stanhope, Earl of, 169–70, 224n23, 272n166, 288, 310–11
chocolate, 112
Churchill, Winston, 1, 3
Cicero, 42, 43
The Citizen (Murphy), 63
The Citizen of the World (Goldsmith), 339
The Clandestine Marriage (Colman and Garrick), 62, 183–4, 330
claret wine: adulterated wine, 319–22; in British novels, 333–6; in Canada, 115, 133, 135–6, 138, 143, 153; French exports, 304; generic Bordeaux wine, 246; in Holland, 230; political ideologies, 115, 319, 327, 337; prices in France, 304; in recipes, 315–18; wine codes, 115, 309, 319, 327–33, 337; wine trade, 115. *See also* Bordeaux, France, and wine; wine and spirits
class. *See* social class and hierarchies
classical arts: Addison on, 52, 54, 88–90, 92, 220–1; architecture, 67–8, 197; British travel on the continent, 11, 25–7, 29–30, 220–1, 293; sixth sense, 24, 42–4; theatre, 52
The Closet of [Kenelme Digbie] (Digby), 191–2
clothing. *See* Britain, fashion; France, fashion
coffee, 19, 112, 340–1
cognition. *See* literary history and literariness, recent views; mind-body relationship, 18th century; mind-body relationship, recent views

Colbert, Jean-Baptiste, 285
Colley, Linda, 10
Collins, Anthony, 32, 167
Colman, George, 62–3, 183–4, 330
colonization. *See* Britain, empire; empires and imperialism
commerce. *See* Britain, economy and trade; consumerism; economy and trade; France, economy and trade
The Commissary (Foote), 61
A Comparative View (Andrews), 284–90
A Compleat Collection [of Conversation] (Swift), 159–60
The Compleat Vineyard (Hughes), 323
The Complete Cook (Jenks), 172n32, 247
The Complete Practical Cook (Carter), 315–16
A Complete System of Cookery (Verrall), 200–1, 316–17
Congreve, William, 58–9, 310
The Conscious Lovers (Steele), 60
consciousness. *See* mind-altering substances, 18th century; mind-altering substances, recent views; mind-body relationship, 18th century; mind-body relationship, recent views
consumerism: about, 7, 112, 341; brain chemistry, 111–12; colonial trade, 235; conspicuous consumption, 338; global trade rivalries, 112; identity, 7, 282; illicit trade, 282; and imperialism, 7, 112; imperial rivalries, 282; irony and paradox, 282, 337–9; mind-altering substances, 16, 69, 112–13; national typologies, 282; and synesthesia, 9; wine codes, 328–30.

See also Britain, consumerism; fashion; food; France, consumerism
continental travel. *See* Britain, travel on the continent; Britain, travel writing
cookbooks and recipes. *See* Britain, food writing – cookbooks and other writing; food – recipes; France, food – cookbooks and other writing
Cooper, Anthony Ashley. *See* Shaftesbury, Anthony Ashley Cooper, 3rd Earl of
Corsica, 295, 296
The Country Housewife (R. Bradley), 247
The Country Wife (Wycherley), 57–8
The Court and Country Cook (Massialot), 199–200
Court Cookery (Smith), 315
Courtépée, Claude, 266
Covent Garden, London, 55, 56, 57, 58, 59, 61, 202, 245n66
Cowley, Hannah, 331–2
Crabbe, George, 326–7
Cradock, Mrs, *Journal*, 258–9
Critical Reflections on Poetry, Painting and Music (Dubos). *See* Dubos, Jean-Baptiste
Cromwell, Oliver, 36, 235–6
Crouzet, François, 258n99, 259n106
Le Cuisinier royal et bourgeois (Massialot), 199–200
La Cuisinière bourgeoise (Menon), 224, 315
Cumberland, Richard, 53–4, 63–4
The Curé of St Philippe (Grey), 140, 149–51
Curley, Thomas, 214

Damasio, Antonio, 111
Dampier, William, 232–3
The Dangerous Voyage of Capt. Thomas James (James), 116–17, 133
deep history, 110–13, 293
Defoe, Daniel, 54–6, 235–9, 255–6, 318, 337
The Deserted Village (Goldsmith), 234–5
dialectic: about, 15–16; cultural knowledge, 21–2; empire as dialectic of art and science, 3; in literariness, 96–7; in material and intellectual culture, 3, 7, 12–13, 155–6, 283–4, 341; *OED* definition, 16
A Dialogue between an East-Indian Brackmanny (Tryon), 194–5
Dialogues on the Uses of Foreign Travel (Hurd), 29–33
Diary (Evelyn), 193
The Diary of a Country Parson (Woodforde), 186, 188–91
The Diary of Samuel Pepys (Pepys), 246–7, 322–3
Digby, Kenelm, 191–2
Dijon, France: about, 265–70, 297; architecture and public spaces, 265–70; British residents and visitors, 186, 265–70, 293–5, 307, 310, 312; Burgundy's capital, 265; Cîteaux Abbey, 297; cost of living, 297; demographics, 265–6; educational institutions, 265; monastery of Cîteaux, 297; Playstowe on, 297; Spence on, 310; Sterne on, 186; transportation, 265; travelogues, 293–5, 297, 312; Vauxhall Gardens, 267–70; wine, 186, 307, 310. *See also* Burgundy, France, and wine

Dilly, Edward and Charles, 171–2
dining rooms. *See* Britain, domestic life
Directions to Servants (Swift), 159–60
Discourses on Art (Reynolds), 7–8, 12n34
diseases. *See* health; health and alcohol; health and diet; science and medicine
disgust. *See* taste and disgust
Dissertation sur la situation de bourgogne (Arnoux), 320
Dollond, John, 263n119
domestic servants. *See* Britain, domestic life – servants
Don Quixote (Cervantes), 173–5, 204
The Double Dealer (Congreve), 58
Dowson, Thomas, 70
Drake, Francis, 233
drinking. *See* alcohol; drunkenness; mind-altering substances, 18th century; mind-altering substances, recent views; wine and spirits
drugs, 69. *See also* mind-altering substances, 18th century; mind-altering substances, recent views
drunkenness: about, 71–8; Addison on, 336–7; in Britain, 312–13; in Canada, 119, 124–5, 127–9, 131–2, 136; Canada's Royal Commission (1896), 116; cultural contexts, 75–8, 338; in France, 312–13; health effects, 71, 75–8; motives for, 16, 69, 75, 77–8; Sallengre's *Ebrietatis Encomium*, 71–2; sensory experiences, 76–7; and social class, 338; Trotter's *Essay*, 75–8; wine codes, 327, 330–1. *See also* alcohol; health and alcohol; mind-altering substances, 18th century; mind-altering substances, recent views; wine and spirits

Dryden, John, 46, 247
Du Bocage, Anne-Marie, 283–4
Dubos, Jean-Baptiste: on Addison, 44–5; aesthetic theory, 35–6; *Critical Reflections*, 35–45; cultural exchange, 35, 44–5; faculty of evaluation, 37–44; metaphors, 38, 41–2, 44; mind-body relationship, 39–44; national identity and taste, 39–41, 44–5; psychological ideas of empire, 36; sixth sense, 40–4; suspended judgment, 37–45; on taste, 39–41, 44–5
Dufferin, Hariot, 132–3
Duhamel du Monceau, Henri Louis, 274
Duncan, Sara Jeannette, 140, 149, 151–6
Dunciad (Pope), 45–6, 72, 215–16
Du Plessis, Armand Jean, 285
Dupré de Saint-Maur, Nicolas, 256–7

ears. *See* sound
East India Co., 231, 235
eating. *See* food; smell; taste (gustatory)
Ebrietatis Encomium (Sallengre), 71–2
economy and trade: Addison on, 90–1; global imperial trade, 234–5; imperial metaphors, 7, 91; market control, 243; mind-altering substances, 16. *See also* Britain, economy and trade; France, economy and trade; wine trade
Eden Treaty (1786), 262, 271–3, 275–6, 278, 280

education, 18th century: about, 15–16; Addison on, 92, 95; classical arts, 92, 96, 220–1; Enlightenment ideals, 96; immanent impulses, 92, 95; lack of disciplinary boundaries, 15, 39, 109–10, 187; sister arts, 15; travel writing and debates on, 227–8. *See also* aesthetics; Britain, education; Britain, travel on the continent; literary history and literariness, 18th century; mind-body relationship, 18th century; natural history; Royal Society of London

education, recent views: about, 15–16, 21–2, 93–113; administration, 95, 97; aesthetic experience, 22; citizenship ideals, 22n6; cognitive science, 103; corporatism, 22n6, 93, 95, 103, 105; cultural knowledge in, 21–2; decline of humanities, 105; dialectics, 21–2, 96–7, 104–5; diversity versus homogeneity, 94–5, 97, 99–100, 104; English studies, 92–3, 95; interdisciplinary learning, 21–2, 97, 102; irony and paradox, 104; key questions, 9–10, 13; literariness, 93–9; local versus universal interest, 93, 97; pedagogy, 103–5; presentism, 103–4; senses in, 21–2; truth and language, 95–7, 106–7. *See also* literary history and literariness, recent views; mind-body relationship, recent views

education, recent views – writers: Bromwich, 113; Fish, 21, 85n13, 97–8, 101; Fromm, 22; Kermode, 104–5; Kernan, 104; Kingwell, 21–2, 83; Levine, 94–6; Nussbaum, 21–2, 158; Perkins, xiii–xiv, 101–2; Postman, 9n21, 10n24, 97, 105, 106–7

The Elements of Agriculture (Miller, trans.), 274n174

Elizabeth I, 286

Ellis, John, 98–100

embodiment. *See* mind-body relationship, 18th century; mind-body relationship, recent views

Emma (Austen), 179–83

empires and imperialism: Bacon on, 5–6; Burke on, 12, 48–9; Dubos on, 36; as image of interior world of learning, 6–7; key questions, 9–10, 13; limits on democratic participation, 23; literary history, 9–11, 13, 341; metaphors for, 6; political factionalism, 6, 23; psychological ideas of, 36; Shaftesbury on, 23; as unsatisfactory ideology, 69. *See also* Britain, economy and trade; Britain, empire; Britain, empire – writing

The Englishman Returned from Paris (Foote), 330

The English Vineyard Vindicated (Rose), 323

entoptic images, 16, 70, 340. *See also* mind-altering substances, 18th century; mind-altering substances, recent views

Epsom-Wells (Shadwell), 328–9

An Essay [on Architecture] (Laugier), 67–9

An Essay [on drunkenness] (Trotter), 75–8

"An Essay on Conversation" (Fielding), 175–6, 178

"Essay on Health" (Bacon), 86
An Essay on Wines (J. Wright), 73–5, 321–2
Essential Substances (Rudgley), 69–71, 110, 339
Etherege, George, 58
Europe. *See* France; Germany; Holland; Italy; Portugal; Spain
Evelina (F. Burney), 168–9, 177–8
Evelyn, John, 192–4, 246–7, 303, 323
The Expedition of Humphrey Clinker (Smollett), 239–40, 274n174, 306–8
The Experienced English House-Keeper (Raffald), 204n89, 208n97, 210, 212n105, 213, 317–18
eyes. *See* painting aesthetics; sensory experience, 18th century; sensory experience, recent views; sight

The Fable of the Bees (Mandeville), 338
The Facts of the Case (Spence), 116, 118–19, 137
Falkland Islands, 50–1
The False Alarm (Johnson), 50
Farquhar, George, 59, 327–8
fashion: aesthetics of, 15–17, 341; conformity, 288; fashion versus taste, 290–1; irony and paradox, 337–9; semiotics of, 115–16; status, 277. *See also* Britain, fashion; France, fashion
The Fashionable Lover (Cumberland), 53–4, 63–4
"Fashion: An Epistolary Satire" (Warton), 290–1
Ferguson, Niall, 231–2
Ferry, Luc, 35–6

Fielding, Henry: art of conversation, 165–6, 175–6, 178; Cervantes's influence, 173–5; corrupt urbanity versus rural sufficiency, 305–6; dining and reading analogy, 172; food and table manners, 165, 174–6; satire of travel writing, 47, 228–9; as a Scriblerian, 165–6; subordination of reason to theology, 47; wine trade, 305–6
Fielding, Henry, works: "An Essay on Conversation," 175–6, 178; *Joseph Andrews*, 174, 305–6; *The Journal of a Voyage*, 174, 242–3, 306; *The Life of Mr Jonathan Wild*, 47, 165–6, 228–9; *Tom Jones*, 172–3, 174–5, 306
Fish, Stanley, 21, 85n13, 97–8, 101
five senses. *See* sight; sixth sense; smell; sound; taste (gustatory); touch
Fleming, Sandford, 133–6
food: aesthetics of, 15–16, 18–21, 108–10, 341; Brillat-Savarin on, 18–21, 72, 78; dining and reading analogy, 172; gastronomic codes, 212–13; imperial imagery, 21; imperial rivalries, 7, 33–5, 174–5, 223; semiotics of, 115–16; South American, 232–3; synesthesia, 108–10, 340–1. *See also* Britain, food; Britain, food writing – cookbooks and other writing; Britain, food writing – literary; Canada, food; France, food; France, food – cookbooks and other writing; health and diet; smell; taste (gustatory)
food – recipes: carp, 247; crepes, 34–5; fricassee, 34; frogs and snails,

224; hasty pudding, 205; herb potage, 33–4; peach fritters, 317; pudding, 34; soup, 33–4; veal, 164–5; wine in recipes, 315–18. *See also* Britain, food writing – cookbooks and other writing; France, food – cookbooks and other writing

food production. *See* Britain, agriculture; Britain, domestic life – food production

food writing. *See* Britain, food writing – cookbooks and other writing; Britain, food writing – literary; France, food – cookbooks and other writing

Foote, Samuel, 61–2, 330

France: dialectic in material and intellectual culture, 3, 7, 12–13, 155–6, 283–4, 341; hybrid culture, 10; literary history, 9–11, 13, 341; national identity, 10, 44–5, 324–6, 341. *See also* Bordeaux, France, and wine; Burgundy, France, and wine; Dijon, France; Lyon, France; Paris

France, agriculture: British influences, 273–4, 276; fish markets, 242–3; gardens and orchards, 273–4; poverty of peasants, 291–2, 307, 313. *See also* France, wine production

France, architecture and public spaces: in Bordeaux, 256–7, 259–61, 298–9; classical models, 67–8; in Dijon, 265–70; imperial rivalries, 7, 65–9; Laugier's *Essay*, 67–9; Louis XIV as patron, 65–6, 68–9, 197; in Lyon, 249–50; in Paris, 16, 65–9; Versailles, 68–9, 197

France, British cultural exchange and rivalry: about, 7, 247–70, 283–92; animal breeding, 254; architecture, 65–9; in Bordeaux, 255–65; British demographics, 256, 258, 265–6, 292; British residents and visitors, 30–5, 185–6, 226–9, 243–7, 265, 284–92, 298; dialectic, *OED* definition, 16; dialectic in material and intellectual culture, 3, 7, 12–13, 155–6, 283–4, 341; in Dijon, 265–70; Dubos on aesthetics, 35–45; fashion, 277–8, 282, 288, 290–2; food, 192–4, 197–9, 223–4, 284, 287, 314–15; government and politics, 284–9; imperial rivalries, 7, 102; luxury items, 248–9, 253–4, 262–5, 274–82; in Lyon, 249–55, 280; manners, 288–9; manufacturing, 248, 251–3, 259n105, 278; medicine, 280–1; poverty, 284, 286, 287, 291–2, 313; technology, 274, 280; trade, 248–9; travel, 283–4, 289–90; wine and wine production, 284, 308–15. *See also* Britain, travel on the continent; France, economy and trade

France, Canada's relationship. *See* Canada, British and French Canada in literature – writing; Canada, French Canada; Canada, French Canada in literature

France, consumerism: brain chemistry, 111–12; and British exports, 255, 271–7; imperial rivalries, 7, 282; irony and paradox, 282; sumptuary laws, 277–8; and urban growth, 248n74, 249, 252, 262–5. *See also* consumerism; France, economy and trade; France, fashion

France, domestic life: art of conversation, 288–9, 311; British trade goods, 274–6; cooks, 241; cultural exchanges, 317; dining tables, 317; ecclesiastical life, 11, 198, 297; food markets, 240–3; imperial rivalries, 244–5; inns (*auberges*), 244–5, 294, 311–12; manners, 288–9; menus and items, 223–4, 294–5, 314–15; servants, 241, 275; social class, 240–3; tableware, 223–4, 241, 263, 274–6, 311, 314, 315; travelogues, 294–5, 311–12; wall hangings, 264–5. *See also* France, consumerism

France, economy and trade: about, 248–9; in Bordeaux, 255–65; British imports, 271–7; British technology, 274, 276, 278; consumerism and urban growth, 248n74, 249, 252, 262–5; Corsican exports, 296; Eden Treaty (1786), 262, 271–3, 275–6, 278, 280; food markets, 241–3; free trade, 276–7; imperial rivalries, 7, 248–9; luxury items, 248–9, 254–5, 262–5, 274–82; in Lyon, 249–55; manufacturing, 251–4, 259n105, 260, 262, 278–80; mind-altering substances, 16, 111–12; poverty, 284, 286, 287, 291–2, 297, 307, 313; shipbuilding, 257–8; silk industry, 251–4; sumptuary laws, 277–8; trade, 257–8; transportation, 242, 257–8, 293–4. *See also* France, consumerism; France, wine trade

France, fashion: about, 277–82, 341; aesthetics of, 15–17, 341; British influences, 248–9, 274–82; comparison with Britain, 288, 290–2; conformity, 288; court culture, 277–8, 282; health benefits, 279–80; identity, status, and nationalism, 277–9; imperial rivalries, 7, 277–82; influence on markets, 240–1; irony and paradox, 337–9; luxury items, 262–5, 277–82; semiotics of, 115–16; sumptuary laws, 277–8; versus taste, 290–1; travelogues, 297–9; wine codes, 309–10; women's bodies and ideological conflict, 278–9. *See also* Britain, fashion; France, consumerism; France, domestic life

France, food: aesthetics, 18–21, 341; comparison with British food, 287; ecclesiastical influences, 198; fasting, 120; food markets, 240–1; French and English terms, 315; influence on British cooking, 192–4, 197–201, 239–40, 243–7; inns and restaurants, 244–5, 293–8, 307, 311–12; Locke on, 33–5; menus and items, 33, 311; metaphors of embodied taste, 78; nutrition, 287; recipe for frogs and snails, 224; scientific experimentation, 19–20; spices and herbs, 197–8; Sterne on, 185–6; synesthesia, 17, 19–21, 108–10; wine in recipes, 315–18. *See also* food; food – recipes; France, domestic life; France, wine and spirits

France, food – cookbooks and other writing: Brillat-Savarin's

Physiology of Taste, 18–21, 72, 78; La Chappelle's *Modern Cook*, 200; La Varenne's *Le Cuisinier français*, 197–9; Massialot's *Le Cuisinier royal et bourgeois*, 199–200; Menon's cookbooks, 200, 224, 315; Pontack's dishes, 247; travelogues, 293–8, 311–12; Verrall's *Complete System*, 200–1. *See also* food – recipes

France, government and politics: absolutism, 15, 32, 289; comparison with Britain, 284–9, 292; Dubos on, 36; fashion, 288–9, 292; French Revolution, 11–13, 49; wine codes, 309–11. *See also* Louis XIV

France, travel to Britain: imperial rivalries, 7, 283–4, 289–90. *See also* France, British cultural exchange and rivalry

France, wine and spirits: about, 324–6, 341; burgundy, 223–4, 309–13, 333–6; Corsican wine, 296; court favourites, 309; estate wines, 245–7; imperial rivalries, 7, 223; motives for drinking, 75–6; national identity, 324–6; Sallengre's *Ebrietatis Encomium*, 71–2; travelogues, 293–9; wine codes in British literature, 326–36. *See also* Bordeaux, France, and wine; brandy; Burgundy, France, and wine; champagne and sparkling wines; claret wine; port wine

France, wine production: about, 324–6; Addison on, 295; adulterated wines, 73–4, 306–8, 312, 318–22, 324; British ownership of vineyards, 321; Chambertin vineyard, 313, 320; on Corsica, 296; experiments, 324–5; fermentation processes, 295, 304, 308, 320, 324–5; T. Gray on, 308; landscaping, 303–4; Locke on, 303–4, 307–8; national identity, 324–6; poverty, 291–2, 307, 313; regional orientation, 324; Thrale on, 308; vine exports to Britain, 303–4; vineyards, 292, 303–4, 313–14; vineyard scenery, 302, 303, 310; Warton on, 291–2

France, wine trade: about, 16, 305–14; adulterated wine, 306–8, 312, 318–22, 324; British ban on, 246–7; class hierarchy, 309–10; corruption, 305–7, 310, 312, 318–22; economics of, 313–14, 325–6; Johnson on, 309; national identity, 324–6; regulatory controls, 324; secretive trade, 326. *See also* Bordeaux, France, and wine; Burgundy, France, and wine; wine trade

France, writing: Arnoux's *Dissertation*, 320; Brillat-Savarin's *Physiology of Taste*, 18–21, 72, 78; Du Bocage's *Letters concerning England*, 283–4; Dubos's *Critical Reflections*, 35–45; Duhamel du Monceau's *Gentilhomme Cultivateur* and *Traité de la Culture des Terres*, 274; Maupin's *Théorie*, 324–6; Mercier's *Tableau de Paris*, 240–2; Micault's *Le Mercure Dijonnois*, 268–9; Misson's *M. Misson's Memoirs*, 243–5; Sallengre's *Ebrietatis Encomium*, 71–2; travel writers, 214n2. *See also* France, food – cookbooks and other writing

The French Cook (La Varenne), 197–9

The French Family Cook (Menon), 200, 224n23, 315
The French Gardiner (Evelyn), 193, 323
The French Journals of Mrs Thrale (Thrale), 308–9
Friendship in Fashion (Otway), 327–8
Fromm, Harold, 22
Frye, Northrop, 3n4, 83
Fumifugium (Evelyn), 193
Further Thoughts on Agriculture (Johnson), 309
Fussell, Paul, 105–6

The Gardeners' Dictionary (Miller), 273–4
Garrick, David, 62, 183–4, 327, 329–30
gastronomy. *See* food
Gay, John, 54n57, 60–1, 164–5
gender: censuring of female readers, 82; educational diversity versus homogeneity, 94–5, 97, 99–100, 104; female writers of cookbooks, 172, 315–16; hierarchy of senses and gender, 109; images of empire, 48; misogyny in plays, 327, 329; prostitution, 327–30; romantic tales by travellers, 289–90; sexualization of London sites, 57–8; unfaithful spouses, 47, 58; wine codes, 327–36
Geneste, David, 284
Le Gentilhomme Cultivateur (Duhamel), 274
The Gentleman Dancing Master (Wycherley), 57
The Gentleman's Guide (Playstowe), 297–8
Gérin-Lajoie, Antoine, 140, 146–8

Germany: Radcliffe's *Journey*, 229–31, 301–2
Ginsberg, Benjamin, 9n22, 95
Glasse, Hannah, 169, 171–2, 208n95, 208n97, 316
The Golden Dog (Kirby), 140, 148–9
Goldsmith, Oliver, 64, 184, 234–5, 330–2, 339
Goode, Jamie, 340–1
A Gotham Election (Centlivre), 327
gothic literature, 148–9, 179
gout (arthritis), 72–3, 279–80, 320
government and politics. *See* Britain, empire; Britain, government and politics; empires and imperialism; France, government and politics
Graff, Gerald, 94, 95–7, 100
Grand Tour. *See* Britain, travel on the continent
The Grand Tour (Nugent), 293–5
Grant, George, 114
Grant, George Munro, *Ocean*, 133–6
Graves, Richard: about, 204–13; asceticism, 206, 210–11, 213; community formation, 212–13; culinary discourse, 208–13; food, 204–6, 208–13; gentility and consumerism, 210–11, 213; nationalism, 212–13; *The Spiritual Quixote*, 204–13, 215
Gray, Hugh, 121–3
Gray, Thomas, 308, 310n44
Grey, Francis, 140, 149–51
Griffiths, Elizabeth, 169
Grosley, Jean-Pierre, 284
Gulliver's Travels (Swift), 216–20
gustatory taste. *See* taste (gustatory)

hallucinogenic mushrooms, 339. *See also* mind-altering substances,

18th century; mind-altering substances, recent views
Hamilton, Charles, 284, 321
Handel, George Frederick, 45
Harley, Robert, 318
Harrison, Sarah, 247
Hawkes, Terence, 115–16
health: gout (arthritis), 72–4, 279–80, 320; medical texts, 281. *See also* science and medicine
health and alcohol: about, 72–8; adulterated wine, 71, 73–4, 322, 329–30; Armstrong's *Art of Preserving Health*, 333; Barry's *Observations*, 319–21; brain chemistry, 111–12; gout (arthritis), 72–4, 320; hygienic beverage, 117; palliative care, 117; port's harms, 333; as remedy, 74, 77–8, 316n58, 319–21, 328; Sallengre's *Ebrietatis Encomium*, 71–2; Smollett on harms, 308; Trotter's *Essay*, 75–8; as water purifier, 115, 117, 293; Wright's *Essay on Wines*, 73–4. *See also* drunkenness
health and diet: Arbuthnot's *Martinus Scriblerus*, 166–7; brain chemistry, 111–12; French food, 185–6, 198, 240–2; Graves's *Spiritual Quixote*, 211; Italian influences on British food, 186; leprosy, 186; meal times and ill health, 197; medicinal plants, 274; mixing of foods and ill health, 196–7, 211; potatoes, 272–3; remedies for weak lungs, 185–6, 272n166; skin disorders, 187; tea as remedy, 210; Tryon on, 194–6; vegetarianism, 177, 193–7
Health's Grand Preservative (*The Way to Health*) (Tryon), 195–7

hearing. *See* sound
Hearne, Samuel, 117–19
heart and sixth sense, 42. *See also* sixth sense
Hegel, Wilhelm Friedrich, 16
Hill, Aaron, 323
Hinduism and vegetarianism, 194–5
History and Description of Modern Wines (Redding), 322
The History of Emily Montague (Brooke), 122n11, 137–40, 155, 157–8
Hogarth, William, 76, 263
Holcroft, Thomas, 332–3
Holland, 229–31, 301–2
The Honours of the Table (Trusler), 177
housekeepers. *See* Britain, domestic life – servants
The House-keeper's Pocket Book (Harrison), 247
Hughes, William, 323
Hume, David, 3, 33n20, 53, 87–8, 174n34, 341
The Humorists (Shadwell), 328
Hurd, Richard, 29–33

illnesses. *See* health; health and alcohol; health and diet; science and medicine
imperialism. *See* Britain, empire; Britain, empire – writing; empires and imperialism
The Imperialist (Duncan), 140, 149, 151–6
Imperial Paradoxes: about, 6–7, 112–13, 336–41; consumerism, 112; cross-cultural methods, 6–7, 10, 104; dialectic in culture, 7, 12–13, 15–16,

341; interdisciplinary focus, 19, 21, 97, 102, 104; irony and paradox, 93, 104, 137n28, 140, 337–9; key questions, 9–10, 13, 69; limitations of private contemplation, 14–15; literary history, xiii–xiv, 9–11, 13, 101–2, 106–7, 110–13, 293, 341; material culture, 5–6; nationalism, 10; OED definitions of *aesthetic, dialectic,* and *synesthesia,* 16–17; synesthesia, 17, 108–10, 340–1; teaching of 18th c. literature, 93

The Inconstant (Farquhar), 327–8

India, 16, 62, 235

Indigenous peoples. *See* Aboriginal peoples; Canada, Aboriginal peoples; Canada, Aboriginal peoples and alcohol

Indonesia, 193, 235

"Inebriety" (Crabbe), 326

inns. *See* Britain, food – inns and eateries; France, food

intoxicants, 69. *See also* alcohol; drunkenness; mind-altering substances, 18th century; mind-altering substances, recent views; wine and spirits

An Introduction to the Political State of Great-Britain (Johnson), 49–50

Ireland: Irish in Bordeaux, 256, 258n99; Swift's *Modest Proposal,* 159, 160–3

Islam: travel literature, 214–15

Italy: British exports to, 236; consumerism, 223; Corsica, 296; court feasts, 193; food and wine, 300–1, 314–15; Grand Tours, 220–3, 229, 303; influence on British food, 186, 192; music, 44–5, 63, 295–6; national identity and taste, 44; political systems, 221–3; trade, 222–3; travelogues, 300–1, 314–15; wine production, 296, 303; wine trade, 296

Jamaica, 231–2

James, Thomas, 116–17, 133

James II, 193, 201

Jameson, Anna, 127, 128–30

Jean Rivard (Gérin-Lajoie), 140, 146–8

Jefferson, Thomas, 259

Jenks, James, 172n32, 247

Johnson, Hugh, 325n83

Johnson, Mark, 80, 107–8

Johnson, Samuel: on Addison, 81–3, 92, 221; aesthetics, 13–14; on American colonies, 48–52; Boswell on, 170–1; Burke's friendship, 13; on cookbooks, 171–2; crown's authority, 48; on economic exploitation, 49–50; enjoyment of food, 169–71; on fashion, 13–15; guests for meals, 171; on imperialism, 309; Kingwell on, 83; on Magellan's use of wine, 117n5; political writings, 49–52; on private contemplation, 14–15; strict monarchist, 48; textual criticism and cultural history, 82–3; on Thomson's naivety, 46n42; on travelogues, 309; on vineyards, 308–9; on war, 51–2

Johnson, Samuel, works: *The False Alarm,* 50; *Further Thoughts,* 309; *An Introduction to the Political State,* 49–50; *Lives of the English Poets,* 81, 221, 233; "Meditation on a

Pudding," 135n26; *Observations*, 50; *Richard Savage*, 233–4; *Taxation No Tyranny*, 51–2; *Thoughts on the Late Transactions*, 50–1
Joseph Andrews (Fielding), 174, 305–6
Journal of a Tour (Boswell), 135n26, 170–1
The Journal of a Voyage (Fielding), 174, 242–3, 306
Journal of Madame Cradock (Cradock), 258–9
A Journey from Prince of Wales's Fort (Hearne), 117–19
A Journey Made in the Summer (Radcliffe), 229–31, 301–2

Kant, Immanuel, 16, 35
Kermode, Frank, 104–5
Kernan, Alvin, 104
Kett, Reverend, Trinity College, 226–7
Kingwell, Mark, 21–2, 83
Kirby, William, 140, 148–9
The Knights (Foote), 330
Korsmeyer, Carolyn, 108–9, 213

Lacan, Jacques, 140n32
La Chapelle, Vincent, 169, 200, 224
The Lady's Companion (anon.), 316
Lakoff, George, 80, 107–8
Lamb, Patrick, 201
Lancaster, James, 231
Lascaux cave art, 69–70
Laugier, Marc-Antoine, 67–9
La Varenne, Francois Pierre de, 197–9
Law, John, 287
Lethe (Garrick), 329
Letters (Austen), 178–9
Letters (Defoe), 318, 337

Letters (Sterne), 184–6, 305
Letters concerning England (Du Bocage), 283–4
Letters from Canada (H. Gray), 121–3
Letters from the Grand Tour (J. Spence), 220, 223–4, 266, 310
Letters to His Son (Chesterfield), 169–70, 272n166, 288, 310–11
Levine, Lawrence, 93–5
Lewis-Williams, David, 70
liberal arts education. *See* education, 18th century; education, recent views
The Life and Opinions of Tristram Shandy (Sterne), 166, 185, 335–6
Life in the Clearings (Moodie), 127, 131–3
The Life of Mr Jonathan Wild (Fielding), 47, 165–6, 228–9
The Life of Samuel Johnson (Boswell), 170–1
lifestyle and fashion. *See* Britain, fashion; France, fashion
Lipovetsky, Gilles, 277
liquor and spirits. *See* alcohol; drunkenness; wine and spirits
literary history and literariness, 18th century: about, 105–7, 112–13, 341; dialectical knowledge, 21, 113; enlightenment as contested term, 113; image-systems, 106; imagination, 80, 83; imperialism as contested term, 113; interdisciplinary, 21; literary history, xiii–xiv, 9–11, 13, 101–2, 110–13, 341; logic and rhetoric, 112–13; synesthesia, 84–7; truth and language, 106–7. *See also* Addison, Joseph; education, 18th century

literary history and literariness, recent views: about, 92–113, 341; Addison's pedagogical appeal, 92–3; definition of literature, 98–101; dialectics in, 96–7, 100–4; diversity versus homogeneity, 94–5, 97, 99–100, 104; interdisciplinary learning, 19, 21, 97, 102; limitation of philosophizing on theory, 105; literary history, xiii–xiv, 9–11, 13, 93, 101–2, 106–7, 110–13, 293, 341; logic and rhetoric, 112–13; metaphor and cognition, 19, 80, 103, 105–8; motivation for, 22; paradox and analysis, 93, 104; pedagogy, 102–5; social contexts, 98–102; synesthesia, 93, 108–10, 340–1; textual performance, 98–101; truth and language, 95–7, 106–7; Western canon, 93, 99–100. *See also* education, recent views; mind-body relationship, recent views

literary history and literariness, recent views – writers: Briggs, 83–5, 103, 106n6; Broadus, 79, 83; Bromwich, 113; Ellis, 98–100; Fish, 21, 85n13, 97–8, 101; Graff, 94, 95–7, 100; Kingwell, 21–2, 83; Lakoff, Johnson, and Turner, 80, 107–8; Nussbaum, 21–2, 158; Perkins, xiii–xiv, 101–2; Ricks, 105; Scholes, 93, 137n28

Lives of the English Poets (Johnson), 81, 221, 233

Locke, John: empiricism, 80, 83, 168; ethical training, 31–3; on food, 33–5; in France, 30–5, 303–4; on the Grand Tour, 32–3; Hurd's Locke in *Dialogues*, 29–33; imagination, 80, 86; *Locke's Travels in France*, 33–5, 303–4; *Observations* [*on Vines*], 303–4; Shaftesbury's mentor, 30; wine production, 303–4, 307–8

London: about, 16, 54–6, 65–9; book publishers, 115, 119–20, 137; in comedies, 53–4, 56–62; commercial images, 54–6, 61–2, 66; criminals, 60–1; fashion, 54, 57, 61, 64–5; French residents, 243–7; imperial centre, 54–6, 91; imperial rivalries, 7, 65–9; pollution, 193; poverty, 286, 287; resorts, 238; sexualization of, 57–8; social hierarchies, 54; as symbol of the nation, 54; theatrical allusions to topography, 54; travel guides, 54–6; urban sprawl, 54–6; wine codes, 310. *See also* Britain, theatre; Britain, theatre – plays and other writing; Royal Society of London

London, architecture and public spaces: about, 54–68; classical architecture, 16, 67–8; Covent Garden, 55, 56, 57, 58, 59, 61, 202, 245n66; estate management, 201–3; fish markets, 242–3; Grosvenor Square, 61–2, 65–6; Hyde Park, 54, 56, 58–9; Pontack's French restaurant, 245–7; public spaces and squares, 16, 55–6, 61, 66–7; restaurants, 245–6; size limits, 286; St James's Park, 57–60, 64, 66–7; street noises, 58, 84; urban renewal, 55–6, 64, 245–6; Vauxhall Gardens, 267–70; Westminster, 55; Woburn Abbey, 201–3

London, writing: Andrews on, 286; Defoe's *Tour*, 54–6, 235–9; Evelyn's

Fumifugium and *Diary*, 193; Gay's *Trivia*, 54n57; Pepys on, 246–7, 322–3; Stuart's *Critical Observations*, 65–8. *See also* Britain, theatre – plays and other writing
London Exchange, Lyon, France, 249–55
Louis XIII, 286
Louis XIV: absolutism, 10, 285; architecture and public spaces, 65–6, 68–9, 197; arts patron, 65–6, 285–6; Château-Trompette, 256–7, 259; fashion influences, 277, 282; feasts, 197, 199; food markets, 240–1; preferred wine, 309; regional divisions, 10; taste, 285–6; Versailles, 68–9, 197; wine trade, 304
Louis XVI, 278
Love in a Wood (Wycherley), 56–7
Lower Canada. *See* Canada; Canada, French Canada
The Lyar (Foote), 61
Lyon, France: about, 249–55; British residents and visitors, 293–5, 297, 299–300; industrial centre, 249–55, 274, 300; London Exchange, 249–55; luxury items, 280; Tolozan family, 254–5; travelogues, 293–5, 297–301; vineyards, 299–300

Madeira wine, 121, 125–8, 137, 316–17
The Male-Coquette (Garrick), 329
Mandeville, Bernard, 338
manners. *See* Britain, domestic life; France, domestic life
The Man of Mode (Etherege), 58
The Man of Ten Thousand (Holcroft), 332–3

Mansfield Park (Austen), 334
Marnette, Monsieur, 197–9
The Marriage of Heaven and Hell (Blake), 79n1, 83
Martinus Scriblerus (Arbuthnot), 166–8
Massialot, François, 199–200
Maupin, Monsieur, 324–6
May, Robert, 190, 191–2, 199
The Mayor of Garratt (Foote), 62
Mazarin, Jules Raymond, 285
medicine. *See* health; health and alcohol; health and diet; science and medicine
"Meditation on a Pudding" (Johnson), 135n26
Memoirs and Observations (Misson), 243–5
Memoirs of Martinus Scriblerus (Arbuthnot), 166–8
men. *See* gender
Mennell, Stephen, 191
Menon, 200, 224, 315
The Merchant, Citizen and Country-man's Instructor (Tryon), 197
Mercier, Louis-Sébastien, 227, 240–2
Le Mercure Dijonnois (Micault), 268–9
metaphor: Aristotle on, 4; imperial metaphors, 7, 20–1, 38, 47, 91, 103; as mode of cognition, 19, 80, 103, 105–8; recent views, 80, 107–8; Shaftesbury on, 23
Methuen Treaty (1703), 306, 318, 337
Micault, Claude, 268–9
Miller, Philip, 273–4
Milton, John, 80–2, 87
mind-altering substances, 18th century: about, 16, 69–78; aesthetic

experience, 76–8; as "century of addiction," 112; climate's influence, 77; communal experiences, 70–1; consumerism, 69, 112; cultural shaping, 69, 75–8; entoptic imagery, 16, 70; hallucinogenic mushrooms, 339; key questions, 69; Menippean texts, 16, 71, 335, 337–8; motives for use, 16, 75–6, 339; sacred settings, 69–71; Sallengre's *Ebrietatis Encomium*, 71–2; secularization of, 70–1; social hierarchies, 70, 112, 126–7, 339. *See also* alcohol; drunkenness; wine and spirits

mind-altering substances, recent views: about, 69–71, 112–13, 339–41; altered versus normal consciousness, 69–71; brain chemistry, 111–13; communal experiences, 70–1; consumerism, 112; cultural shaping, 69–71; culture as biological phenomenon, 111–13; deep history, 110–13, 293; entoptic imagery, 16, 70, 340; Hawkes on, 115–16; intoxicants, defined, 69; key questions, 69; legality and legitimacy, 70–1; motives for use, 16, 69, 339; physiology of sight, 70; Rudgley's *Esssential Substances*, 69–71, 110, 339n112; sacred settings, 69–70; secularization of, 70–1; semiotics, 115–16; social hierarchies, 70, 112, 144, 339. *See also* alcohol; drunkenness; wine and spirits

mind-body relationship, 18th century: about, 9, 15–17, 19, 112–13; Blake on, 8, 79–80, 83; Brillat-Savarin on, 18–21, 72, 78; deep history, 110–13, 293; desire to extend perception into mind, 16; dualism versus unity, 8–9, 19, 69, 79–80, 83, 167–8; Dubos on, 35–6, 39–41, 44–5; embodiment, 9; faculty psychology, 103; food, 166, 194–7, 287; Fussell on, 105–6; key questions, 69; mapping of interior mind, 103; metaphors and symbols, 103, 105–8; moral philosophy, 103, 106; national identities and taste, 39–41, 44–5, 341; national types, 287; reason and imagination, 19, 80; Scriblerians on, 166–8; sixth sense, 40–4; spirit over body, 83; synesthesia, 19–21; taste, 83; Tryon on, 194–7. *See also* aesthetics; mind-altering substances, 18th century; national identities and taste; sensory experience, 18th century; synesthesia

mind-body relationship, recent views: about, 102–13; aesthetics and embodied taste, 108–12, 213; brain chemistry, 111–13; categories and senses, 103, 107; cognitive science, 8on5, 102–3, 107–8, 110–13; culture as biological phenomenon, 110–13; deep history, 110–13, 293; dualism versus unity, 19, 69, 83, 107, 111; key questions, 13, 69; Korsmeyer on, 108–9, 213; metaphor and cognition, 19, 80, 103, 105–8; neuroscience of aesthetics, 109–12, 340–1; Pinker on, 8on5; Rudgley on, 69–71, 110, 339n112; Smail on, 110–13, 293; Starr on, 109–10; synesthesia, 103, 108–10, 340–1; unconscious cognition, 103. *See also* mind-altering substances,

recent views; sensory experience, recent views
The Minor (Foote), 61–2, 330
The Miser (Shadwell), 327–8
Misson, Francis Maximilian, 243–5
The Modern Cook (La Chapelle), 169, 200, 224
A Modest Proposal (Swift), 159, 160–3
Montagu, Mary Wortley, 310
Montpellier, France, 304
Moodie, Susannah, 127, 130–3
Moore, John, 313
Morgan, Henry, 231–2
Morocco, 215
Munro, Thomas, 227–8
Murphy, Arthur, 63
music. *See* sound
The Musical Lady (Colman), 62–3
My Canadian Journal (Dufferin), 132–3
"My Own Life" (Hume), 53n56

Narrative of a Voyage to Hudson's Bay (Chappell), 123–5
national identities and taste: about, 341; Arbuthnot's *Martinus Scriblerus*, 166–7; architecture, 65–9; Dubos on, 39–41, 44–5; Hume on, 88; mind-body relationship, 39–42, 166–7, 287; plural identities, 103; semiotics of, 115–16; sixth sense, 40–4; taste differences, 39–41, 44; training of taste, 39–40, 88; viticulture metaphor, 41
nationalism: about, 7, 9; in architecture, 65–9; Boswell on Corsica, 296; comparison of Britain and France, 290–2; and consumerism, 7, 112; in cookbooks, 317; and fashion, status, 277–8; Hurd on, 32–3; imperial rivalries, 309–11; in literary history, 9–11, 13, 341; travelogues, 308; vineyard landscapes, 308; wine codes, 309–11, 330–1. *See also* Britain, French cultural exchange and rivalry; France, British cultural exchange and rivalry
natural history: about, 192–3, 231–5; agriculture, 186–7, 192–4; botany, 186, 247n72; Evelyn on, 192–4; food, 232; lack of disciplinary boundaries, 15, 187; ornithology, 186; South American travel, 231–3; White's *Natural History*, 186–8. *See also* Royal Society of London
The Natural History of Selborne (White), 186–8
neuroscience, 109–13. *See also* mind-body relationship, recent views
New Atlantis (Bacon), 3–4
New France. *See* Canada, French Canada
Newton, Isaac, 287
New Voyage round the World (Dampier), 232–3
Nice, France, 266n138
Night Thoughts (Young), 117–18
Northanger Abbey (Austen), 179
nose. *See* smell
Novum Organum (Bacon), 3–4
Nugent, Thomas, 293–5
Nussbaum, Martha, 21–2, 158–9

Observations on the Customs (Thicknesse), 311
Observations on the Present State (Johnson), 50
Observations [on Vines] (Locke), 303–4

Observations [on the Wines] (Barry), 319–21
Observations and Reflections Made in the Course of a Journey (Piozzi), 299–301
Ocean to Ocean (Grant), 133–6
"Of Civil Liberty" (Hume), 33n20, 53
"Of Empire" (Bacon), 5–6
"Of Refinement in the Arts" (Hume), 341
"Of Simplicity and Refinement in Writing" (Hume), 53n55
"Of Studies" (Bacon), 4
"Of the Original Contract" (Hume), 3
"Of the Standard of Taste" (Hume), 88, 174n34
The Old Batchelor (Congreve), 58
The Old Maid (Murphy), 63
Olla Podrida (periodical), 226–8
opium, 70–1
Otway, Thomas, 327–8
Ozell, John, 245n66

painting aesthetics: Dubos on, 36–8, 41–4; hierarchy of senses, 38–9, 108–9; lack of sensory and disciplinary boundaries, 15, 39, 109–10, 187; Lascaux caves, 69–70; neuroscience of aesthetics, 109–12, 340–1; *OED* definition of *aesthetic*, 16; sensory experience, 37–8; sister arts, 15, 37, 39, 109–10; sixth sense, 40–4; Starr on, 109–10; suspended judgment, 37–45; synesthesia, 15, 108–10, 340–1. *See also* sight; synesthesia
Pamela (Richardson), 176–7, 333–4
Paradise Lost (Milton), 80–2
Paris: about, 16; architecture and public spaces, 16, 65–9, 286; British residents and visitors, 186, 247–8, 265, 293–5; demographics, 265; fashion, 240–1; food, 240–3, 294, 311; imperial rivalries, 7, 16, 65–9; inns and hotels, 311; music, 295; poverty, 286, 287; social class, 240–3; travelogues, 293–5; Vauxhall Gardens, 267; Versailles, 68–9, 197; wine, 294–5, 307. *See also* France
Paris, writing: Andrews's *Comparative View*, 286; Laugier's *Essay*, 67–9; Mercier's *Tableau de Paris*, 240–2; Nugent's *Grand Tour*, 293–5. *See also* France, writing
The Parish Register (Crabbe), 327
"The Patron" (Crabbe), 326–7
Peace River (Simpson), 126–7
A Peep behind the Curtain (Garrick), 327
Pepys, Samuel, 246–7, 322–3
perception. *See* sensory experience, 18th century; sensory experience, recent views
The Perfect Cook (Marnette), 197–9
Peri Bathous (Pope), 165–6
Perkins, David, xiii–xiv, 101–2
A Philosophical Discourse of Earth (Evelyn), 192
A Philosophical Enquiry (Burke), 7, 49
The Physiology of Taste (Brillat-Savarin), 18–21, 72, 78
Pinker, Steven, 80n5
Piozzi, Hester Lynch (formerly Thrale), 169–70, 299–301, 308–9
Plato, 24, 36, 42
The Platonick Lady (Centlivre), 332
plays. *See* Britain, theatre; Britain, theatre – plays and other writing; theatre aesthetics

Playstowe, Philip, 297–8
The Pleasures of the Imagination (Akenside), 46–7
poetry aesthetics: Dubos on, 37–9, 42–4; imperial metaphors, 15; lack of sensory and disciplinary boundaries, 15, 39, 109–10, 187; neuroscience of aesthetics, 109–12, 340–1; *OED* definition of *aesthetic*, 16; Plato on, 36; reading processes, 37; sensory experience, 37–9; sister arts, 15, 37–9, 109–10; sixth sense, 40–4; Starr on, 109–10; suspended judgment, 37–45; synesthesia, 15, 108–10, 340–1; taste, 38–9. See also reading processes; synesthesia
Poitiers, France, 275–6
Pontac family, London and Bordeaux, 246–7, 303–4, 338
Pontack's restaurant, London, 245–7, 303–4, 315
Pope, Alexander, 45–6, 72, 165–6, 215–16
port wine: about, 73–5; adulterated wine, 73–4, 306–7, 319–22; British political ideologies, 115, 319; British wine codes, 115, 322, 326–7, 330–1, 333; in Canada, 115, 123, 125, 126–7, 148, 153; in Holland, 230; Methuen Treaty (1703), 306, 318, 337; political ideologies, 337; in recipes, 315–18; wine production, 74–5; wine trade, 115; Wright's *Essay on Wines*, 73–5. See also wine and spirits
Porter, Roy, 6n12, 55n61, 72–3
Portugal: adulterated wine, 73–4, 321–2; Duoro Co., 322; Methuen Treaty (1703), 306, 318, 337; Portuguese in France, 256; semiotics of wine, 322; wine trade with Britain, 306, 318, 322, 337; wine trade with Canada, 115. See also port wine
Postman, Neil, 9n21, 10n24, 97, 105, 106–7
Present State of Music in France and Italy (C. Burney), 295–6
The Professed Cook (Menon), 200
psychotropic mechanisms. See mind-altering substances, 18th century; mind-altering substances, recent views
public spaces. See architecture and public spaces

Quintilian, 42, 43

racialized people in education: diversity versus homogeneity, 94–5, 97, 99–100, 104. See also education, recent views; literary history and literariness, recent views
Radcliffe, Ann, 229–31, 301–2
Raffald, Elizabeth, 204n89, 208n97, 210, 212n105, 213, 317–18
Ramsden, Jesse, 262n115
Ray, John, 186
readers: aesthetic training, 26–9, 88; of classical literature, 88–9; common readers, 6, 21, 23, 81–5, 99; conversation as supplement, 227; development of taste, 26–8, 88; Johnson on, 81–2; London publishers' influences on, 115, 119–20, 137; Shaftesbury on, 26–9; speech communities, 84; women readers, 82; young readers, 26–7. See also

literary history and literariness, 18th century; literary history and literariness, recent views
reading processes: about, 37–9; Addison on, 88; Bacon on, 4; dining and reading analogy, 172; Dubos on, 37–9; eating metaphors, 4; Hume on taste, 88; key questions, 13; natural ideals, 28; neuroscience of aesthetics, 109–12, 340–1; oral and print culture, 38; poetry aesthetics, 37; sensory experience, 38–9; Shaftesbury on, 26–7; silent reading versus recitation, 38–9; as solitary, 38; suspended judgment, 37–45; training of taste, 88; visual aesthetics, 38–9. *See also* poetry aesthetics
recipes. *See* food – recipes
The Recruiting Officer (Farquhar), 327
Redding, Cyrus, 322
Reflections on the Revolution in France (Burke), 11–13
The Relapse (Vanbrugh), 59
religion and spirituality: Aboriginal visions, 120, 124; educational role of church, 29–33; Hurd on, 29–33; mind-altering substances, 69–71; missionaries in Canada, 119–21; Shaftesbury on, 23, 25, 29. *See also* Britain, ecclesiastical life; France, domestic life
Remarks on Several Parts of Italy (Addison), 220–3, 295
restaurants. *See* Britain, food – inns and eateries; France, food
"A Review of the Affairs of France" (Defoe), 255–6, 318
Reynolds, Joshua, 7–8, 12n34

Rheims, France, 53, 308, 312
Richardson, Samuel, 176–7, 323, 333–4
Richardson's War of 1812 (J. Richardson), 123
Richelieu, Cardinal, 285–6
Ricks, Christopher, 105
rivalries, 7. *See also* Britain, French cultural exchange and rivalry; France, British cultural exchange and rivalry
The Road to Ruin (Holcroft), 332
Rose, John, 323
Roughing It in the Bush (Moodie), 127, 130–1
Rousseau, Jean-Jacques, 12, 100, 141, 171, 308
Royal Commission on the Liquor Traffic (1896, Canada), 116, 118–19, 137
Royal Cookery (Lamb), 201
Royal Society Club, 247
Royal Society of London: about, 192–3; R. Bradley as member, 247; Digby as member, 192; Evelyn as member, 192–4, 246; London dinners, 246–7; medical research, 280–1; Miller as member, 273–4; optical instruments, 262n115, 263n119; Shaw as member, 214; Swift's satire on science and music, 219. *See also* education, 18th century; natural history; science and medicine
Rudgley, Richard, 69–71, 110, 339n112
Russell, William. *See* Bedford, William Russell, Duke of

Sahlins, Peter, 10

Sallengre, Albert-Henri de, 71–2
salmagundi, 203
Sansom, Joseph, 125–6
satura (medley), 160
Scholes, Robert, 93, 137n28
The School for Scandal (Sheridan), 64–5, 331
science and medicine: adoption of classical languages, 10; dialectic in, 16; experimental psychology, 19–20; French influences, 191–7; lack of disciplinary boundaries, 15, 109–10, 187; medicine, 280–1; optical instruments, 262n115, 280; Swift on, 219. *See also* health; health and alcohol; health and diet; natural history; Royal Society of London
Scotland: Act of Union (1707), 141; cattle, 235–6; domestic tourism, 239–40; Enlightenment, 225; food, 235–6, 239–40; nationalism, 141; whisky, 154
Scriblerians: about, 163–8; Arbuthnot's *Martinus Scriblerus*, 166–8; epic poem recipe, 165; Fielding's *Jonathan Wild*, 165–6; Martin Scriblerus, 163–8; mind-body dualism, 167–8; Pope's *Peri Bathous*, 165–6; scholarly redundancy and cultural decadence, 163–4; veal recipe, 164–5
Seduction (Holcroft), 332
Selkirk, Thomas Douglas, 5th Earl of, 123–5
semiotics, 115–16, 136–40, 155–6
sensory experience, 18th century: about, 15–17; Brillat-Savarin on, 18–21, 72, 78; Dubos on, 35–45; education of, 5, 15; gendered hierarchy, 109; hierarchy of senses, 38–9, 108–9, 115–16; imagination, 80, 83; imperial metaphors, 38, 103; OED definition of *aesthetic*, 16; oral and print culture, 38–9; physiology of, 20–1, 39–41; scientific experimentation, 19–21; synesthesia, 17, 20–1, 84–7; taste as sense versus discrimination, 108–9. *See also* aesthetics; mind-altering substances, 18th century; mind-body relationship, 18th century; synesthesia
sensory experience, recent views: about, 16–17, 69–72, 102–3, 340–1; entoptic imagery, 16, 70, 340; Hawke on, 115–16; hierarchy of senses, 108–9, 115–16; mind-altering substances, 69–72; neuroscience of aesthetics, 109–12, 340–1; as reality, 340–1; research on, 340–1; Rudgley on, 69–71, 110, 339n112; semiotics of, 115–16; Starr on, 109–10; synesthesia, 17, 19–21, 108–10, 340–1; taste as sense versus discrimination, 108–9. *See also* mind-body relationship, recent views; synesthesia
Sensus Communis (Shaftesbury), 23n7, 29
A Sentimental Journey (Sterne), 47–8, 228, 335
servants. *See* Britain, domestic life – servants
Seven Years War (1756–1763): migration to France, 258, 292; propaganda during, 50–1; Royal Navy, 232; trade during, 271
sexuality: cuckolds, 58; prostitution, 327–30; sexualization of London

sites, 57–8; wine as virility enhancement, 328; wine codes, 327–8. *See also* gender

Shadwell, Thomas, 328–9

Shaftesbury, 1st Earl of, 46

Shaftesbury, Anthony Ashley Cooper, 3rd Earl of: about, 23–31; aesthetic training, 26–31; on artistic vanity and imperialism, 23–4; on British insularity, 31; *Characteristics of Men*, 23–30; classical arts, 25–7, 29–30; on drunkenness, 72; formation of taste, 26–9; Grand Tour, 27–8, 30–1; Hurd's Shaftesbury in *Dialogues*, 29–33; on imperialism, 24–5; Locke as mentor, 30; noble savage myth, 28, 99–100; for pan-European sensibility, 25–6; on reading and writing, 26–30; on religion, 23, 25, 29–30; on secularism, 23, 25, 29–30; on self-discourse, 24–6, 28–9, 31n18; *Sensus Communis*, 23n7, 29; sixth sense, 24

Shaw, Peter, 4

Shaw, Thomas, 214–15

Sheridan, Richard Brinsley, 64–5, 331

She Stoops to Conquer (Goldsmith), 64, 184, 330–1

sight: Addison on, 85–7; book arts, 38–9; Dubos on, 38–9; entoptic imagery, 16, 70, 340; hierarchy of senses, 38–9, 108–9; metaphors, 38, 85; neuroscience of aesthetics, 109–12, 340–1; physiology of, 70; semiotics of, 115–16; silent reading versus recitation, 38–9; synesthesia, 86–7, 108–10, 340–1. *See also* painting aesthetics; sensory experience, 18th century; sensory experience, recent views; synesthesia

Simpson, George, 126–7

Sir Harry Wildair (Farquhar), 327

sister arts: Dubos's aesthetics, 36–44; lack of sensory and disciplinary boundaries, 15, 39, 109–10, 187; motivation, 41; neuroscience of aesthetics, 109–12, 340–1; Starr on, 109–10; suspended judgment, 37–45. *See also* painting aesthetics; poetry aesthetics; synesthesia

sixth sense, 15, 24, 40–4

skin. *See* touch

Smail, Daniel Lord, 110–13, 293

smell: hierarchy of senses, 108–9; recent research, 340; scientific experimentation, 20; semiotics of, 115–16; synesthesia, 86–7, 108–10; and taste, 20, 340. *See also* sensory experience, 18th century; sensory experience, recent views; synesthesia

Smith, Adam, 225–6, 234–5, 237n52, 323

Smith, Robert, 315

Smollett, Tobias: *Humphrey Clinker*, 239–40, 274n174, 306–8; *Travels*, 307–8, 311–12

social class and hierarchies: Aboriginal people, 126–7; aristocratic degeneracy, 338–9; conspicuous consumption, 338; consumerism and brain chemistry, 111–12; disgust and servants, 159; drunkenness, 338–9; educational diversity versus homogeneity, 94–5, 97, 99–100, 104; food markets, 240–3; sharing of mind-altering

substances, 70, 112, 126–7; wine codes, 328–36
Some Observations Made in Travelling (E. Wright), 310
sound: Addison on, 83–4; Dubos on, 38, 42–5; harmony, 19; hierarchy of senses, 108–9; imperial rivalries, 177; lack of sensory and disciplinary boundaries, 15, 39, 109–10, 187; London street cries, 58, 84; music, 44–5, 63, 72, 84, 147, 295–6; national identity and taste, 44–5; neuroscience of aesthetics, 109–12, 340–1; *OED* definition of *aesthetic*, 16; poetry aesthetics, 38; semiotics of, 115–16; silent reading versus recitation, 38–9; sixth sense, 40–4; speech communities, 84; Swift's satire on music, 219; synesthesia, 17, 19–21, 84, 86–7, 108–10, 340–1. *See also* sensory experience, 18th century; sensory experience, recent views; synesthesia
Les Soupers de la Cour (Menon), 200
South America, 50–1, 231–3
Southwell, Edward, 266
Spain: Cervantes's *Don Quixote*, 173–5; Digby's *Closet*, 191–2; food, 173–5, 193; imperial rivalries, 233, 309; Madeira wine, 121, 125–8, 137, 316–17; olla podrido (national dish), 173, 226n26; wine codes, 128, 137, 309, 319; wine trade, 121, 125–8, 236
The Spectator, 6, 58n68, 80–1, 84–92, 161n6, 336–7
"Speech on Conciliation with America" (Burke), 48–9
Spence, F.S., 116, 118–19, 137

Spence, Joseph, 220, 223–4, 266, 310
spirits. *See* Britain, wine and spirits; Canada, wine and spirits; France, wine and spirits; wine and spirits
The Spiritual Quixote (Graves), 204–13, 215
Sprat, Thomas, 192
Stanhope, Philip. *See* Chesterfield, Philip Dormer Stanhope, Earl of
Starr, Gabrielle, 109–10
Steele, Richard, 58n68, 59–60, 319
Sterne, Laurence: in France, 184–6, 305; *Letters*, 184–6, 305; perception, imagination, and cognition, 228, 335–6; *A Sentimental Journey*, 47–8, 228, 335; *Tristram Shandy*, 166, 185, 335–6
Stuart, James, 65–8
The Sullen Lovers (Shadwell), 328
Swift, Jonathan: about, 159–63, 216–20; art of conversation, 159–60; *Compleat Collection*, 159–60; consumerism, 159–60; *Directions to Servants*, 159–60; *Gulliver's Travels*, 216–20; gustatory taste, 217–18; *A Modest Proposal*, 159, 160–3; Scriblerian, 163–8; shift from distaste to disgust, 159, 161–3; veal recipe, 164–5; wine production, 303
Sylva (Evelyn), 193
synesthesia: about, 17, 107–12, 340–1; Addison on, 79, 84–7, 93, 336; artistic evolution, 19–21; Brillat-Savarin on, 19–21; Burke on, 87; cognitive unconscious, 107; complementary senses, 19–21; and consumerism, 9, 112; hierarchy of senses, 108–9; key questions, 69; Korsmeyer on, 108–9; lack of

sensory boundaries, 15, 39, 109–10, 187; metaphors and categories, 107–8; mind-altering substances, 69; neuroscience of aesthetics, 109–12, 340–1; *OED* definition, 17; recent views, 103, 340–1; Starr on, 109–10; Sterne on, 228; voluntary synesthesia for awareness, 340–1. *See also* mind-body relationship, 18th century; mind-body relationship, recent views

Tableau de Paris (Mercier), 227, 240–2
tableware. *See* Britain, domestic life; France, domestic life
Talleyrand, Charles-Maurice de, 246
Target, Guy Jean Baptiste, 247–8
taste (aesthetic sensitivity): about, 15–17, 83, 108–9, 339–40; Addison on, 87–8; Andrews on, 285–6; Blake on, 8; Brillat-Savarin on, 18–21, 72, 78; Defoe on, 237; development of, 44; disembodied taste, 83; Dubos on, 37–44, 83; embodiment of, 39–41, 108–9; faculty of evaluation, 37–44; faculty of mind versus sensory taste, 83, 87–8, 108, 109; fashion versus taste, 290–1; French *goût*, 72–3; government, aesthetic theory, and taste, 285–6; Hume on metaphor for, 87–8; imperial imagery, 21; Korsmeyer on, 108–9; metaphors, 42; mind-body relationship, 39–44; national identity, 39–41, 44, 88, 341; neuroscience of aesthetics, 109–12, 340–1; Reynolds on, 7–8, 12n34; Shaftesbury on, 83; sixth sense, 40–4; Starr on, 109–10; training of taste, 39–40, 44, 88. *See also* aesthetics; national identities and taste

Taste (Foote), 61
taste (gustatory): about, 18, 20, 108–9; Addison on, 87–8; aesthetics of, 18–20, 108–10; Brillat-Savarin on, 18–21, 72, 78, 158; disgust, 118, 159, 161–3; Dubos on, 44; faculty of mind versus sensory taste, 83, 87–8, 108–9; gastronomy, defined, 18; hierarchy of senses, 108–9; as metaphor for aesthetic sensitivity, 87–8, 108–9; physiology of, 20–1; recent research, 340; satire on, 159–60; scientific experimentation, 20; semiotics of, 19, 115–16; and smell, 20, 340; Swift's *Gulliver's Travels*, 159–60, 217–19; synesthesia, 17, 19–21, 108–9, 228, 340–1; training of taste, 158–9, 340–1. *See also* sensory experience, 18th century; sensory experience, recent views; synesthesia

taste and disgust: Addison on, 86; dehumanization, 159, 162–3; gustatory taste, 118, 158–9, 163; physiological distaste to ideational disgust, 159, 161–3; projective disgust, 159; Swift's *Modest Proposal*, 160–3

The Tatler, 81–5
Taxation No Tyranny (Johnson), 51–2
tea, 78, 210
Temple, William, 303
The Tender Husband (Steele), 59
theatre aesthetics: about, 37–9; Dubos on, 37–9, 42–4; *OED* definition of *aesthetic*, 16; sensory experience, 37–8; sixth sense, 40–4; suspended

judgment, 37–45. *See also* Britain, theatre; Britain, theatre – plays and other writing
Théorie (Maupin), 324–6
Thicknesse, Philip, 311–13
Thomson, Gladys, 203n87
Thomson, James, 46, 234
Thomson, Peter, 54n59
Thoughts on [the Falkland's Islands] (Johnson), 50–1
Thoughts on the Prospect of a Regicide Peace (Burke), 49
Thrale, Hester (later Piozzi), 169–70, 299–301, 308–9
The Times (Griffiths), 169
tobacco, 70–1, 112, 127, 257. *See also* mind-altering substances, 18th century; mind-altering substances, recent views
Toland, John, 32
Tolozan family, France, 254–5
Tom Jones (Fielding), 172–3, 174–5, 306
touch: Brillat-Savarin on, 19; hierarchy of senses, 108–9; semiotics of, 115–16; synesthesia, 17, 19–21, 340–1. *See also* sensory experience, 18th century; sensory experience, recent views; synesthesia
Tourny, Louis-Urbain-Aubert de, 256–7
A Tour [through France] (Wraxall), 297, 298–9
A Tour [through Great Britain] (Defoe), 54–6, 235–9
The Town before You (Cowley), 332
Traill, Catharine Parr, 127–8
Traité de la Culture des Terres (Duhamel), 274

travel: aesthetics of, 15–16, 341; dialectic in culture, 283–4; paradoxes of imperial travel, 231–5; South America, 232–3. *See also* Britain, travel; Britain, travel on the continent; Britain, travel writing; Canada, travel; Canada, travel writing; France, travel to Britain
Travels (Shaw), 214–15
Travels during the Years (Young), 9, 259–60, 313–15, 324
Travels in France (Locke), 33–5, 303–4
Travels in Lower Canada (Sansom), 125–6
Travels through France and Italy (Smollett), 307–8, 311–12
Travels through the Interior Parts of North-America (Carver), 119–21
Treatise of Human Nature (Hume), 53n56
Tristram Shandy (Sterne), 166, 185, 335–6
Trivia (Gay), 54n57
Trotter, Thomas, 75–8
Troyes, France, 278, 280, 325, 335–6
Trusler, John, 177
Tryon, Thomas, 194–7
Turkey, 214–15, 235
Turner, Mark, 80, 107–8

United States: recent educational trends, 94–7; travel writing on Canada, 125–6. *See also* American colonies
Upper Canada. *See* Canada; Canada, British Canada
urban life. *See* London; Paris

Vanbrugh, John, 59

Index

Vauxhall Gardens, 267–70
Verrall, William, 200–1, 316–17
Versailles, 68–9, 197
"Verses Written at Montauban" (Warton), 291–2
A View of Society and Manners (Moore), 313
visual experiences. *See* painting aesthetics; sight; synesthesia
viticulture. *See* Britain, wine production; France, wine production; wine production
A Voyage round the World (Walter), 50, 232–3

Walpole, Horace, letters, 11n29, 266n138, 292–3, 337
Walter, Richard, 232–3
War of 1812, 123
War of the Spanish Succession, 256, 318–19
Warton, Joseph, 290–2
Warton, Thomas, 308n40, 309n41
The Way of the World (Congreve), 58–9
The Way to Health (Tryon), 195–6
The Wealth of Nations (Smith), 225–6, 234–5, 237n52, 323
Wedgewood, Josiah, 264
West Indies, 231–2, 236, 257
White, Gilbert, 186–8
The Whole Duty of a Woman (anon.), 316
The Whole Duty of Man (anon.), 207
Wilkes, John, 50, 171, 333
wine and spirits: about, 71–2, 76–8, 114–15, 340–1; aesthetics of, 15–17, 76–8, 341; brain chemistry, 111–12; in cookbook recipes, 315–18; dregs as metaphor, 140; imperial rivalries, 7, 309; motives for drinking, 16, 69, 75–6, 339; neuroscience of aesthetics, 109–12, 340–1; ritual aspects of festivity, 339–40; semiotics, 115–16, 136–40, 155–6; sensory experience, 71, 73–4, 76; synesthesia, 108–10, 340–1; wine tasting, 340–1. *See also* drunkenness; health and alcohol; mind-altering substances, 18th century; mind-altering substances, recent views; synesthesia
wine and spirits, countries. *See* Britain, wine and spirits; Canada, Aboriginal peoples and alcohol; Canada, wine and spirits; France, wine and spirits
wine and spirits, types. *See* Bordeaux, France, and wine; brandy; Burgundy, France, and wine; champagne and sparkling wines; claret wine; Madeira wine; port wine
wine production: British homemade drinks, 178, 183, 306, 317, 318, 321; Canadian homemade drinks, 115, 128, 147–8, 152; cultural exchanges, 303–4; economics of, 302, 313–14, 325–6; fermentation processes, 304, 308, 320, 323–5; Germany, 301–2; Italy, 296, 303; landscaping, 303–4; as metaphor for taste, 41; Radcliffe on, 229–31, 301–2; travelogues, 293–5, 301–2; vineyard scenery, 302, 303, 310. *See also* Britain, wine production; France, wine production
wine trade: about, 16; adulterated wine, 16, 73–4, 305–8, 312, 318–22; casks and barrels, 121, 312–13;

consumerism, 112; corruption, 305–7, 310, 312, 318–22; economics of, 309, 313–14; Mandeville on, 338; Methuen Treaty (1703), 306, 318, 337; mind-altering substances, 16; Portugal wine trade, 318; secretiveness, 326; semiotics of, 115–16, 149, 319. *See also* Britain, wine trade; Canada, wine trade; France, wine trade

Winter Studies and Summer Rambles (Jameson), 127, 128–30

Woburn Abbey, London, 201–3

The Woman-Captain (Shadwell), 329

women. *See* gender

Woodforde, James, 186, 188–91

Woollett, William, 263

Wraxall, Nathaniel William, 297, 298–9

Wright, Edward, 310

Wright, John, 73–5, 321–2

Wycherley, William, 56–8

A Year's Journey (Thicknesse), 311–13

Young, Arthur, 9, 259–60, 313–15, 324

Young, Edward, 117–18

Younger, William, 72, 117n5